T0345134

Conquering JavaScript

Conquering JavaScript: The Practical Handbook helps the reader master the JavaScript (JS) programming language for faster and more robust development. JS is a highly popular language and is often termed as the 'language of the web.' In addition to the internet, JS is also being used actively in game development, mobile apps, progressive applications, and now even desktop apps. As such, it is safe to say that JS is probably the most cross-platform language currently in use, and it rises in popularity with each passing day.

This book covers the basics and moves on to advanced concepts using a hands-on approach with practical lessons and tutorials. JS programming, JS frameworks and various use-case scenarios are discussed in detail. Bridging the gap between beginner and intermediate-level JS literature, this book is a valuable resource to build robust knowledge.

About the Series

The *Conquering JavaScript* series covers a wide range of topics, pertaining specifically to the JavaScript programming ecosystem, such as frameworks and libraries. Each book of this series is focused on a singular topic, and covers said topic at length, focusing especially on real-world usage and a code-oriented approach, adhering to an industry-standard coding paradigm, so as to help the learners gain practical expertise that can be useful for real-world projects.

Some of the key aspects of books in this series are:

- Crystal-clear text, spanning various JavaScript-related topics sorted by relevance.

- Special focus on practical exercises with numerous code samples and programs.

- A guided approach to JS coding with step-by-step tutorials and walkthroughs.

- Keen emphasis on the real-world utility of skills, thereby cutting the redundant and seldom-used concepts and bloatware.

- A wide range of references and resources to help the readers gain the most out of the books.

The *Conquering JavaScript* series of books assume a basic understanding of coding fundamentals.

The *Conquering JavaScript* series is edited by Sufyan bin Uzayr, a writer and educator having over a decade of experience in the computing field. Sufyan holds multiple degrees, and has taught at universities and institutions worldwide. Having authored and edited over 50 books thusfar, Sufyan brings a wide array of experience to the series. Learn more about his works at sufyanism.com.

https://www.routledge.com/Conquering-JavaScript/book-series/CRCCONJAV

Conquering JavaScript
The Practical Handbook

Edited by
Sufyan bin Uzayr

CRC Press
Taylor & Francis Group
Boca Raton London New York

CRC Press is an imprint of the
Taylor & Francis Group, an **informa** business

First edition published 2024
by CRC Press
6000 Broken Sound Parkway NW, Suite 300, Boca Raton, FL 33487-2742

and by CRC Press
4 Park Square, Milton Park, Abingdon, Oxon, OX14 4RN

CRC Press is an imprint of Taylor & Francis Group, LLC

ISBN: 9781032411675 (hbk)
ISBN: 9781032411668 (pbk)
ISBN: 9781003356578 (ebk)

DOI: 10.1201/9781003356578

Typeset in Minion
by codeMantra

For Dad
_____

Contents

About the Editor

Sufyan bin Uzayr is a writer, coder, and entrepreneur with over a decade of experience in the industry. He has authored several books in the past, pertaining to a diverse range of topics, ranging from History to Computers/IT.

He is the Director of Parakozm, a multinational IT company specializing in EdTech solutions. He also runs Zeba Academy, an online learning and teaching vertical with a focus on STEM fields.

He specializes in a wide variety of technologies, such as JavaScript, Dart, WordPress, Drupal, Linux, and Python. He holds multiple degrees, including ones in management, IT, literature, and political science.

He is a digital nomad, dividing his time between four countries. He has lived and taught in numerous universities and educational institutions around the globe. He takes a keen interest in technology, politics, literature, history, and sports, and in his spare time, he enjoys teaching coding and English to young students.

Learn more at sufyanism.com.

Acknowledgments

There are many people who deserve to be on this page, for this book would not have come into existence without their support. That said, some names deserve a special mention, and I am genuinely grateful to

- My parents, for everything they have done for me.

- The Parakozm team, especially Divya Sachdeva, Jaskiran Kaur, and Simran Rao, for offering great amounts of help and assistance during the book-writing process.

- The CRC team, especially Sean Connelly and Danielle Zarfati, for ensuring that the book's content, layout, formatting, and everything else remain perfect throughout.

- Reviewers of this book, for going through the manuscript and providing their insight and feedback.

- Typesetters, cover designers, printers, and everyone else, for their part in the development of this book.

- All the folks associated with Zeba Academy, either directly or indirectly, for their help and support.

- The programming community in general, and the web development community in particular, for all their hard work and efforts.

– Sufyan bin Uzayr

Zeba Academy – Conquering JavaScript

The "Conquering JavaScript" series of books are authored by the Zeba Academy team members, led by Sufyan bin Uzayr, consisting of:

- Divya Sachdeva

- Jaskiran Kaur

- Simran Rao

- Aruqqa Khateib

- Suleymen Fez

- Ibbi Yasmin

- Alexander Izbassar

Zeba Academy is an EdTech venture that develops courses and content for learners primarily in STEM fields, and offers educational consulting and mentorship to learners and educators worldwide.

Additionally, Zeba Academy is actively engaged in running IT Schools in the CIS countries, and is currently working in partnership with numerous universities and institutions.

For more info, please visit https://zeba.academy.

CHAPTER 1

Introduction to JavaScript

IN THIS CHAPTER

➤ What is JS?

➤ Advantages and Disadvantages

➤ Evolution of JS

➤ What are frameworks?

➤ Comparison with Vanilla JS

JavaScript is a dynamic language of programming for computers.

Its implementations allow client-side script to interact with users and build dynamic sites, and it is most frequently used as a component of web pages.

It is an object-oriented computer program that may be interpreted.

LiveScript was the original name of JavaScript, but Netscape changed it to JavaScript owing to the buzz that Java was creating.[1]

JavaScript was first released in Netscape 2.0 in 1995; however, it was called LiveScript back then. The language's general-purpose core is integrated in Netscape, Internet Explorer, and other web browsers.

DOI: 10.1201/9781003356578-1

The ECMA-262 Specification established a standard version of JavaScript's core language.

- JavaScript is an interpreted language for programming that is lightweight.
- Designed for the development of network-centric applications.
- Java complements and integrates it.
- HTML-complementary and HTML-integrated.
- Open and platform-independent.

JavaScript is quick, extremely quick. It easily outperforms earlier languages such as PHP.

For example, if our company delivers email newsletters to consumers, node.js (a JavaScript platform) is unquestionably our best choice. We can send 600 emails in about 3 seconds, while PHP would take around a half-minute.

Node.js is a JS-based framework that has rapidly become a developer favorite. The developers at our Toronto-based web development firm swear by it. Node.js debuted in January 2012 and has witnessed a 180% increase in use since then. It is also the most popular language on the open-source code repository GitHub. JavaScript is used in some manner in 21% of all code on GitHub. Ruby, the second most popular programming language, appears in just 13% of projects on the site.

Free code may be found anywhere. Because JavaScript is so widespread, libraries of JavaScript code may be found all over the place. jQuery is one of the most well-known. Because it contains a large number of pre-written events and objects, this library enables developers to write much more in much less time. Google's search engine, Dell's home page, and the Bank of America all employ jQuery (to name a few). If our existing website does not utilize JavaScript, we are losing out. It's the future language, and it's becoming more popular by the day. Working with JavaScript is now required for a pleasant user experience. Every day, web development firms in Toronto migrate from PHP and other older languages to JavaScript. We remained ahead of the curve here since we've been utilizing JS to develop our webpages for quite some time. From the speedy load times of JS sites to their simplicity and the wonderful experience they deliver, there is just no excuse not to contact us now and usher in a new era for our website.

CLIENT-SIDE JAVASCRIPT

The most frequent version of the language is client-side JavaScript. For the HTML code to be understood by the browser, the script must be integrated into or utilized as a reference by an HTML page. It suggests that a web page need not be static HTML, but rather might incorporate programs that communicate with users, manage browsers, and dynamically create HTML content.

The JavaScript client-side technique outperforms classic CGI server-side scripts in many ways. JavaScript might be used to validate user input in a form field, such as an email address. The JavaScript code is called when the user submits the form, and only if all of the inputs are accurate are they transmitted to the web server.

JavaScript may be used to record explicitly or implicitly performed actions by users, such as button clicks, link navigation, and other actions.

WHAT IS THE PURPOSE OF JAVASCRIPT?

The scripting language's early versions were restricted for internal usage.

The path was opened for ECMAScript to be published when Netscape submitted JavaScript to ECMA International as a standard specification for internet browsers.

It was a general-purpose high-level programming language used to guarantee the interoperability of online pages across various browsers and devices.[2]

Since then, JavaScript has grown with new browsers such as Mozilla Firefox and Google Chrome.

The latter even began creating V8, the first contemporary JavaScript engine that translates bytecode into native machine code.

AngularJS, jQuery, and ReactJS are just a few of the frameworks and tools available for JavaScript today.

Initially executed on the client side, the JavaScript implementation has expanded to the server side after the introduction of Node.js, a cross-platform server environment based on the Google Chrome JavaScript V8 engine.

While it primarily caters to web-based applications, JavaScript programming capabilities have numerous uses in many fields.

The following are some simple JavaScript applications.

1. **Web and Mobile Applications**

   The creation of JavaScript frameworks, comprising JavaScript code libraries, enables developers to leverage pre-written JavaScript code in their applications.

   It saves them effort and time from having to write programming features from start.

   Each JavaScript framework contains features that try to ease the creation and testing procedure. For instance, frontend JavaScript frameworks like jQuery and ReactJS boost design efficiency.

   They let developers reuse and alter code components without influencing each other, function or value-wise. However, mobile app development frameworks like Cordova and Titanium make it feasible to construct native or hybrid apps.

   The execution of JavaScript code in Node.js also plays a significant part in web development.

   Node.js may minimize server response time owing to its single-threaded nature and non-blocking design and remove latency. Node.js is also light enough just to act as a scalable tool for microservices, enabling us to construct a single program combining small services with independent processes.

2. **Development of Web Servers and Server Applications**

   JavaScript allows developers to construct web servers and back-end infrastructure using Node.js, saving time and effort in web server development.

   When visitors browse a web page, the built-in HTTP module allows us to create a simple HTTP server that displays plain text. To handle HTTP requests, we may use Node.js's native web server, Node-OS, or third-party ones such as Microsoft Internet Information Services (IIS) and Apache.

   Remember that Node-OS works best on Linux-based operating systems since it is built on top of the Linux kernel.

3. **Interactive Website Behavior**

   Adding dynamicity to web pages is one of JavaScript's primary roles.

This includes showing animations, changing the visibility of text, and constructing dropdown menus. While we may create a website using just HTML and CSS code, it will only have a static appearance. A user may interact with web pages and have a better surfing experience by using JavaScript.

Furthermore, JavaScript allows us to update HTML content and attribute values without having to refresh the web page. The reason for this is that JavaScript has the following data types:

- String: Textual data enclosed in quote marks. "Hello Everyone," "Hello Everyone," and "Display 'Hello Everyone' text" are some examples.

- Number: Includes integer and floating-point values ranging from $(2^{53} - 1)$ to $-(2^{53} - 1)$.

- Boolean: A Boolean data type has true and false values.

- BigInt: Represents arbitrary length integer data.

- Null: A value that is not present.

- Undefined: Undefined variables are those that have been declared but have not yet been assigned.

- Symbol: Gives items unique identifiers.

- Object: Used to write sophisticated data structures using curly brackets. For instance, {item:"Book," information:"biography"}.

Primitive data types, which include all data types except object, may only hold a single piece of data. Meanwhile, the object data type may hold a set of values.

Cookies can also be used with JavaScript to improve the online browsing experience of users. The document is required for creating, reading, and removing cookies in JavaScript. cookie attribute, which serves as a getter and setter of cookie values.

4. **Game Creation**

When used with HTML5 and an Application Programming Interface (API) such as WebGL, JavaScript may assist us in creating a game. There are several JavaScript-based game engines available, including Phaser, GDevelop, and Kiwi. JavaScript is accessible for visual rendering, code recycling, and cross-platform applications.

Angry Birds, The Wizard, and 2048 are examples of games created utilizing JavaScript game engines.

WHAT MAKES JAVASCRIPT SO SPECIAL?

JavaScript has some benefits that set it apart from its competitors. Some benefits of using JavaScript include the following:

- JavaScript's basic structure makes it easier to understand and implement, and it runs quicker than certain other languages. Errors are also simple to identify and repair.

- Scripts written in JavaScript may be run in a web browser without a server or a compiler. Furthermore, most major browsers allow JavaScript to build code while the application is running.

- JavaScript is interoperable with other languages such as PHP, Perl, and Java. It also opens up data science and machine learning to developers.

- There are several tools and forums accessible to assist newcomers with limited technical abilities and JavaScript understanding.

- Another advantage of acting on the client side is that JavaScript minimizes the number of queries sent to the server. Data validation is possible through the web browser, and updates only apply to specific web page areas.

- Updates the JavaScript development team and ECMA International are constantly updating and creating new frameworks and libraries to ensure the industry's relevancy.

WHAT ARE JAVASCRIPT'S FLAWS?

JavaScript, like any other programming language, has limitations that must be considered. Some of the drawbacks of utilizing JavaScript are as follows:

- Different web browsers read JavaScript code differently, resulting in inconsistencies. To avoid degrading the user experience, we should test our JavaScript script in all prevalent web browsers, including older versions.

- JavaScript code that runs on the client side is subject to abuse by careless users.

- Debugging is supported by several HTML editors; however, it is less efficient than in other editors. Because browsers do not display error messages, locating the problem may be difficult.

How Does JavaScript Work on Our Website?

JavaScript is either incorporated in a web page or referenced via a separate. js file.

When a user views that web page, their browser will execute the script as well as the HTML and CSS code, resulting in a working page shown in the browser tab.

The script is downloaded and executed on the workstations of the visitors.

This is distinct from a server-side language, in which the script is processed by the server before being sent to the browser.

When a web browser encounters a block of JavaScript code, it will analyze it from top to bottom.

Because it is order-sensitive, remember to reference the objects or variables inside the block before altering them.

Variables with no values will produce an undefined error.

WHAT MAKES JAVASCRIPT UNIQUE AMONG PROGRAMMING LANGUAGES?

JavaScript is widely used because of its flexibility, making it a top programming language. Many developers see it as their first option until they need a function that JavaScript does not offer.

Let's have a look at a couple of the most popular programming languages:

C#: C# is an object-oriented programming language used to create programs that operate inside the .NET framework. It is statically typed, which means that its variables may be identified at build time. Unlike

JavaScript, C# offers operator and conversion overloading, enabling us to manipulate data types.

Java: Java, being an object-oriented programming language, is capable of running complex, multi-part applications. Unlike JavaScript, Java is tightly typed, meaning that its variables must be tied to particular data types. Java needs a just-in-time (JIT) compiler to execute its script.

PHP: PHP is a server-side language typically used in PHP-based content management systems like WordPress. Its major aim is to transport data to and from a database, construct HTML pages, and monitor sessions. Unlike JavaScript, PHP can access databases explicitly and supports both lowercase and uppercase variables.

Ruby: Ruby is a general-purpose language for programming that allows for metaprogramming, which means it may examine and alter other programs as well as itself.

Its most popular framework, Ruby on Rails, allows us to construct massive web applications cheaply and time efficiently. JavaScript's implementation on Node.js draws influence from the Ruby on Rails framework.

TOOLS FOR JAVASCRIPT DEVELOPMENT

One of JavaScript's primary advantages is that it does not need the use of costly development tools. We may begin with a basic text editor like Notepad. We don't even need to acquire a compiler since it's an interpreted language in the context of a web browser.

Various manufacturers have created extremely great JavaScript editing tools to make our lives easier. Several of them are mentioned below.

Microsoft FrontPage: Microsoft FrontPage is a popular HTML editor created by Microsoft.

FrontPage also includes a variety of JavaScript features to help web developers create dynamic webpages.

Macromedia Dreamweaver MX: Macromedia Dreamweaver MX is a popular HTML and JavaScript editor among professional web developers.

It comes with a number of useful prebuilt JavaScript components, connects effectively with databases, and adheres to emerging standards such as XHTML and XML.

Macromedia HomeSite 5: Macromedia's HomeSite 5 is a well-liked HTML and JavaScript editor that can be used to effectively manage individual webpages.

What Is the Current State of JavaScript?

The ECMAScript Edition 5 standard will be issued as the first upgrade in over 4 years.

The difference between JavaScript 2.0 and Edition 5 of the ECMAScript standard is quite minimal. The specification for JavaScript 2.0 may be found at www.ecmascript.org/.

Today, both Netscape's JavaScript and Microsoft's JScript adhere to the ECMAScript standard; however, both languages continue to offer capabilities that are not included in the standard.

JAVASCRIPT'S EVOLUTION

JavaScript continues its reign as the most popular programming language, with 67.8% of developers using it in 2019.

Its rise to the world's most popular programming language is inextricably linked to the rise of the internet itself.

It was developed out of necessity and is now used to build 95.2% (1.52 billion) of websites, including some of the world's largest, such as Facebook and YouTube.

We wouldn't have popular and useful web apps like Google Maps and eBay without it.

What Is Modern JavaScript and How Can It Be Used?

JavaScript is used to bring web pages to life and make them interactive. Scripts are programs written in JavaScript. Because scripts are directly linked to HTML, they are performed as soon as the page loads in our browser.[3]

To be honest, scripts are simple text. That is, they do not require any further or preparatory development. And, it is this property that distinguishes JavaScript from the Java programming language. We may wonder why it's called JavaScript. It had a different name in the beginning: LiveScript.

However, at the time, Java was a popular programming language, and marketers opted to adopt a similar name to attract additional users.

JS, which was originally intended to be part of Java, grew swiftly, and eventually became a separate programming language with its own ECMAScript definition.

In terms of frontend development, GBKSOFT employs the JavaScript Programming Language, the Node.js environment, and the AngularJS framework.

The final two are frameworks created in the JavaScript Programming Language.

What JavaScript Can Do for Us

Modern JavaScript is a risk-free programming language.

Because it lacks low-level tools, it does not have access to low-level resources such as memory or CPU. In reality, JS was first focused solely on browsers and browser interaction. Because the browser area is independent of the operating system, JavaScript is playing it safe. However, as time passed, developers began to apply JavaScript outside of the browser area. As a result, the capabilities of JavaScript now depend solely on the context in which it is run. JavaScript can do everything relating to web page manipulations, user interactions, and server interactions when it is executing in the browser (to some extent).

Create new HTML tags, delete existing ones, modify the style of elements, display or hide components, and so on.

React to user activities such as mouse movements and clicks, keyboard typing, and so on.

Put in a request to the server and get results without having to reload the page (AJAX technology).

Receive and configure cookies, request data, show messages, and so forth.

There are plenty of additional features and options.

Because JavaScript lacks access to the operating system, it cannot read, record, or copy arbitrary files or run applications.

Modern browsers can deal with files, but only with restricted access and only if the user actively drops files into the browser window or selects them using an <input> element.

JavaScript cannot communicate with other tabs while functioning in a certain tab unless the user specifically permits it.

Nonetheless, it is only feasible if they share a single domain, protocol, and port.

What Distinguishes JavaScript?

JavaScript has at least three major advantages, which are as follows:

- JavaScript is completely compatible with HTML and CSS.

- JavaScript makes it simple to accomplish simple tasks.

- All current browsers support this language and include it by default.

- By the way, JavaScript is the only language that supports all three functionalities at the same time, making it the most widely utilized technology for developing browser interfaces.

JavaScript Tendencies

HTML5: HTML5 is a new version of HTML that supports new tags and browser capabilities such as

- Reading and writing files to disc.

- Built-in browser database that allows data to be stored directly on the user's machine.

- Multitasking and the utilization of many CPU cores at the same time.

- Video and audio are being played without the use of Flash.

- Drawing in 2D and 3D with hardware support (for example in modern games).

Though many HTML5 capabilities are still under development, current browsers are beginning to support them. In other words, JavaScript grows in strength, and everything shifts to desktop apps.

ECMAScript 5: To remain creative and current, JavaScript and ECMAScript are always improving by introducing new features and capabilities.

For example, the upcoming ECMAScript 6 will take the language syntax one step farther.

However, while adopting new standards, it is critical to maintain maximum compatibility with earlier versions in order to avoid problems with the current ones.

Here are some more prominent JavaScript trends for 2020:

- Through GraphQL, everything is more focused on solution-driven APIs.

- Web components should be framework agnostic.

- Modular and reusable components are preferred.

- With its intriguing features, Angular 7 is becoming increasingly popular.

- React is 'getting back on track' after being outperformed by Vue.JS.

- TypeScript is gaining popularity like never before.

Standardizing JavaScript

JavaScript adheres to two standards:

- ECMA International is hosting ECMA-262. It is the fundamental criterion.

- The International Organization for Standardization (ISO) and the International Electrotechnical Commission (IEC) host ISO/IEC 16262. (IEC). This is a supplementary need.

These standards specify a language named ECMAScript, not JavaScript.

Sun (now Oracle) held a trademark for the latter term, thus a different name was adopted.

The prefix 'ECMA' refers to the organization that hosts the major standard.

The organization's initial name was ECMA, which stood for European Computer Manufacturers Association.[4]

Because the organization's operations had grown outside Europe, the name was eventually changed to ECMA International (with 'Ecma' being a proper name, not an abbreviation).

The first all-caps acronym shows how to spell ECMAScript.

In theory, JavaScript and ECMAScript are interchangeable. The following difference is sometimes made:

- JavaScript refers to both the language and its implementations.

- The language standard and language versions are referred to as ECMAScript.

As a result, ECMAScript 6 is a language version (its 6th edition).

ECMAScript Version History

This is a summary of ECMAScript versions:

- ECMAScript 1 (June 1997): The standard's first version.

- ECMAScript 2 (June 1998): Minor upgrade to bring ECMA-262 up to date with the ISO standard.

- ECMAScript 3 (December 1999): Adds "[…] regular expressions, improved string handling, new control statements [do-while, switch], try/catch exception handling, […]."

- ECMAScript 4 (deprecated in July 2008): Would have been a huge improvement (including static typing, modules, namespaces, and other features), but proved too ambitious, separating the language's stewards.

- ECMAScript 5 (December 2009): Added a few standard library features as well as strict mode.

- ECMAScript 5.1 (June 2011): Another minor upgrade to align Ecma and ISO standards.

- ECMAScript 6 (June 2015): A major upgrade that fulfilled many of ECMAScript 4's promises. This is the first version with a formal designation based on the year of publication, ECMAScript 2015.

- ECMAScript 2016: First annual release (June 2016). When compared to the huge ES6, the shorter release life cycle resulted in fewer new features.

- ECMAScript 2017 (June 2017). The second annual release.

- Following ECMAScript versions (ES2018, for example) are always confirmed in June.

JavaScript vs. Java

Although there is some overlap, JavaScript and Java (another powerful computer language for data scientists after Python) have essentially nothing in common.

JavaScript got its moniker from Netscape's support for Java applets in its browser.

Many believe it was also a marketing ploy to take attention away from Java, which was the most talked-about language at the time.[5]

Java applications must first be compiled into executable code before they can be executed.

However, JavaScript is far more dynamic since it is meant to be interpreted at runtime.

To put it mildly, JavaScript didn't have the best beginnings. Java developers considered JavaScript as more of a 'UI glue,' something that designers and non-engineers would utilize because of its poor performance. However, having a 'glue' language enabled the internet to really blossom.

Programmers might respond more quickly to inputs and construct interactive components.

As a result, JavaScript spread like wildfire and swiftly became the web's language franca.

WHO CONTROLS JAVASCRIPT?

JavaScript is a common programming language, yet attribution and locating the owner of JavaScript may be difficult.

The initial version had two owners, Oracle and Netscape, but newer versions need a third owner. Brendan Eich created the JavaScript Programming Language while working for Netscape.[6]

Brendan Eich also founded the Mozilla Foundation. Oracle owns the trademark 'JavaScript.'

This had nothing to do with the JavaScript Programming Language, yet it was related to it. So it's not incorrect to assert that Brendan Eich, Mozilla, Netscape, Oracle, or Sun Microsystem own JavaScript. JavaScript is owned by at least two people. In short:

- Because of the legal name, Oracle.

- Depending on the JavaScript engine we use, certain companies such as Google, Microsoft, Mozilla, and others may be used.

- The first version of JavaScript was created by Netscape.

Oracle's Trademark Is JavaScript

Oracle owns the trademark 'JavaScript.' This had nothing to do with the JavaScript Programming Language, yet it was related to it. Sun Microsystems, the company that created Java, first trademarked the term 'JavaScript.'

Oracle later acquired Sun Microsystems, and all of their trademarks were transferred to Oracle.

As a result, Oracle presently holds the JavaScript trademark. Some argue that Sun Microsystem's trademarking of 'JavaScript' is based on the same logic as

```
Java is equivalent to JavaScript
as a car is to carpet.
```

Various Variations

The original JavaScript has been changed to conform to ECMA-262 Edition 5 and subsequent versions. Many engines support the JavaScript Computer Language. This includes the following:

- SpiderMonkey (the original engine)

- Rhino (made by Norris Boyd, also an employee of Netscape)

- SquirrelFish or Nitro (by Apple for Safari)

- V8 (by Google as a part of Chrome browser)

- Carakan (by Opera)

- Chakra (by Microsoft for Internet Explorer)

JAVASCRIPT FRAMEWORK

Consider constructing websites and web apps like building a house—we could produce all of our own construction materials from scratch and start building without any plans, but that method would be extremely time-consuming and inefficient.[7]

It's more likely that we'd buy pre-fabricated building components (wood, bricks, countertops, etc.) and then assemble them to our specifications using a plan.

Coding is really similar. Though it is possible to create a website from scratch, it is often more efficient to use an already design as a starting point and then modify it to meet our needs. This is where JavaScript frameworks come in.

JS frameworks, at their most basic, are sets of JavaScript code libraries that give coders with pre-written JS code to utilize for routine programming functions and tasks—literally, a framework around which to create websites or web apps.

For example, if we require a standard JavaScript picture carousel on a website, we may leverage code from a framework to offer the functionality (while we spend more time creating the unique features of our site that don't have a simple, plugin solution).

This may seem familiar if we've heard of the unique JavaScript library jQuery, but there's a subtle (but significant) differential between singular JavaScript libraries and JavaScript frameworks.

The jQuery and JavaScript Libraries

When necessary, JS libraries such as jQuery are utilized by inserting library code into the rest of our site's code. If we wish to utilize a jQuery template for an autocomplete feature, for example, we would put the relevant jQuery code, which then fetches the feature from the jQuery library and shows it in the web browser of our user. In other words, when a frontend developer employs a library such as jQuery, the developer employs jQuery code to 'call' the jQuery library, which subsequently gives the desired content.

What Distinguishes JavaScript Frameworks from Libraries?

While contrasting a library with a framework, the following should be kept in mind when trying to define the term 'framework.' Using JS frameworks is a more holistic procedure since it gives a structure (like a skeleton or scaffolding… or a framework) that organizes the areas of our site where the framework is installed. Page templates offer this structure by making room for snippets of code from the framework's libraries (which the JavaScript framework 'calls' on its own).

The advantage of adopting JavaScript frameworks is the general efficiency and organization they offer to a project—our code will be cleanly formatted, and the framework will give ready-made solutions to common coding challenges. On the other hand, all of that structure might be a disadvantage of working with a framework—any JavaScript code that create on top of JS frameworks must adhere to the framework's rules and conventions, restricting the flexibility we have when writing totally by hand.

Frontend Frameworks

There are varied types of Frontend Frameworks, which we will discuss below:

REACT

Facebook built React.js, an efficient and versatile JavaScript toolkit for designing user interfaces.[8]

For all intents and purposes, React is a JS library; however, it is often referred to as a web framework and compared to other open-source JavaScript frameworks. Because it uses predictable JavaScript code that is simple to debug, React makes it simple to construct interactive user interfaces.

It also has a REACT component system, which allows blocks of JavaScript code to be created once and reused in other portions of the program or even other apps.

ANGULAR

AngularJS is a famous enterprise-level JavaScript framework used for constructing big and complicated corporate applications.

It is an open-source web framework designed by Google and backed by both Google and Microsoft.

VUE

Vue.js is a modern framework for designing user interfaces.

It is an up-and-coming framework that aids developers in interacting with other libraries and current applications.

It contains an ecosystem of libraries that enable developers to construct complicated and solid single-page apps.

Backend Frameworks

There are varied types of Backend Frameworks, which we will discuss below:

EXPRESS

Express.js is a versatile, simple, lightweight, and very well platform for Node.js applications.

It is unquestionably the most widely used framework for server-side Node.js applications.

Express delivers a large variety of HTTP functions, as well as maximum speed.

It is perfect for constructing a basic, single-page application that can manage several requests at the same time.

NEXT.JS

Next.js is a basic framework that enables a JavaScript developer to use React.js to construct server-side rendering and static web apps.

It is one of the most recent and popular frameworks, and it takes pleasure in its simplicity.

Next.js solves many of the issues that developers have while designing apps using React.js.

It includes several crucial features 'out of the box,' making JavaScript programming a breeze. React.js is the most popular JavaScript framework/library in the present employment market. Because JavaScript has so many frameworks, it might be difficult to determine which one to learn first. We could start with any framework, but if our objective is to acquire a job, learning React first will give us a higher chance.

The same can be said about Express.js, the most frequently used and sought-after backend framework. JavaScript frameworks make it easy to create online apps and deal with JavaScript.

This is why they are so popular among programmers. There are several frameworks because they may be used to tackle various challenges.

Before opting to adopt any specific JavaScript framework, thoroughly analyze our project needs. Aside from the distinct technological capabilities of JavaScript frameworks, each framework has its own learning curve, community engagement/support, documentation, and compatibility.

WHAT ARE THE BENEFITS AND DRAWBACKS OF JAVASCRIPT FRAMEWORKS?

JavaScript Frameworks: Frameworks offer the foundation for developers to build JavaScript programs. This saves developers the time and effort of starting from scratch with a working foundation. This foundation comprises a collection of JavaScript code libraries.[9]

The libraries are compiling code for the particular application type that we may work on. The framework will effectively define the program's structure on its own. Each JavaScript framework uses a distinct function. JavaScript is a solid choice for web development, and many of its structures are built around it.

The following are the most popular JavaScript frameworks these days:

- Vue JS

- Angular

- React Native

- Ember JS

- Mithril

- Meteor

- Node JS

- Polymer

- Next JS

- Aurelia

Let's compare the best JavaScript frameworks and see what makes each one special.

1. **AngularJS:** AngularJS is a client-side JavaScript MVC framework for developing dynamic websites. AngularJS originated as a Google project but has now evolved into an open-source framework. Because AngularJS is fully based on HTML and JavaScript, there is no need to learn another grammar or language.

   Pros:

   - Data synchronization between the model and the display.

   - Model updates are immediately visible in the display.

   - The application of guidelines: This enables developers to utilize features and create change instructions.

- Dependency injection: A method that is dependent on software components.

- It makes it easy to manage and use. It features an MVVM-based architecture: This Model-View-Model Architecture enables us to separate data from view.

- Help with application management.

Cons:

- It does not support JavaScript in many choices.

- A developer must be familiar with MVC in order to utilize angular.

2. **React Native:** Using a JavaScript framework they are already acquainted with, web developers can now construct mobile apps that feel and look fully "native."

    Because much of the code we write can be shared between platforms, React makes it straightforward to create for both Android and iOS at the same time.

Pros:

- It converts the physical DOM into a virtual DOM.

- It helps developers write better code and generate better user interfaces.

- It contains unidirectional data.

- Child elements have no effect on parent components.

- Use JSX to increase code reusability.

Cons:

- It is tough to learn and understand.

- It is a framework with inadequate documentation.

3. **Vue.js:** Because it is a progressive JavaScript framework, we can use it to construct UIs (User Interfaces) and SPAs (Single-Page Applications).

It's a simple framework that allows us to create online apps with minimum understanding of HTML, CSS, and JavaScript.

Pros:

- Vue JS makes use of HTML templates.

- The DOM is used to collect data.

- Data is sent in both directions.

- Vue JS is more reactive than previous frameworks.

- It is straightforward to interface with different frameworks.

Cons:

- Its versatility overburdens the developer.

- It is the most recent library, and there are fewer developers.

4. **Ember JS**: Ember Js is a JavaScript development platform.

It is a single framework used to build a single web application.

It will construct a superb one-page web application coupled with others using idioms, best practices, and patterns.

It is also scalable, using ecosystem patterns provided by the framework.

Advantages:

- Powerful add-ons

- Ember CLI

- Convention over configuration

- Community

- Stability sans stagnation

- Ember Octane

Cons:

- Difficult to learn

- Sluggish Popularity Due to Strong Opinions

5. **Mithril**: Mithril is another JS framework that is speedy and utilized to get tasks done efficiently.

   Another advantage of this framework is its small size, which is less than 10 KB.

   It also has routing and XHR functionality.

Pros:

- Lightweight

- React is faster

- It is compatible with ES6

- Development that is quite active

- Flux-compatible intelligent auto-redrawing system

- A Short Learning Curve

Cons:

- Virtual Dom

6. **Meteor:** Meteor is another isomorphic JavaScript framework that is largely used for websites. We may finish our project fast by using NODE JS for prototyping.

   Node JS also aids in the development of cross-platform applications for Android, iOS, and Web. Another great feature is that data is immediately updated when we connect to MongoDB.

Pros:

- It is simple to get started and rapidly distribute a prototype to end consumers

- Hot code deployment

- Full-stack responsiveness

- This is useful for real-time applications

- Allows us to create an MVP

Cons:

- Auto-bundling

- Build system that optimizes itself

- There is a speed issue

- Development is unpredictable

7. **Node JS**: Node JS is a well-known Java Framework.

It will make Node JS lightweight and practical by using an event-driven, non-blocking I/O mechanism.

The ecosystem package, nmp, is the world's most comprehensive open-source ecosystem library.

Pros:

- Asynchronous event-driven IO facilitates concurrent request processing

- It is simple to learn

- The identical piece of code should be used on both the server and client sides

- NPM, or Node packaged modules, is massive and still expanding

- A vibrant and busy community

- Stream large files

Cons:

- There is no scalability

- A relational database is a must-have

- Callback that is nested

- CPU-intensive activities are not supported

8. **Polymer:** Polymer is an open-source JavaScript toolkit that is used to create online applications using web components. The language is created by Google engineers and GitHub contributors. Furthermore, Google is integrating the modern design idea via its material design framework.

Benefits:

- Web components
- Design of materials
- Backed by Google
- Data Binding
- Open-source
- Designer friendly. HTML concepts

Cons:

- We need to work harder to build components that work in all browsers.
- Shadow DOM is used by several browsers.
- Mobile Performance is slow.

9. **Next,** JS is a JavaScript framework designed to develop very fast and user-friendly static webpages.

Then, with the assistance of React, we create a web application.

As a consequence of automated static optimization, static and dynamic have now combined.

Its primary purpose is to construct a hybrid application.

Pros:

- Automatic server rendering and code separation
- Setup is simple
- Generator of static websites
- Simple to set up

- Development that is frictionless

- Static regeneration that is incremental

- The filesystem as an API

- React apps that are isomorphic

- Testing

- Very well documented

- Built-in file-based routing and hooks

Cons:

- The price of flexibility

- Management and development

- It has an opinion

- There is no built-in state manager

- There aren't enough plugins

10. **Aurelia:** Aurelia creates sophisticated browsers, web apps, and desktop applications using a library of JavaScript components.
    It, too, is open source and incorporates web standards.

Pros:

- Conventions made simple

- Extensible modern architecture

- Combines nicely with other components

- Simple to use

- Dependency

- Injection

- Excellent modular router

- Data Binding that is Adaptive

- Full Stack, IoC, Modularity, Simplicity

- Based on the ES7 standard

- Rapid development

- Excellent documentation

- Compliance with changing standards

- A gentle learning curve

- Outstanding Assistance (paid)

Cons:

- Limited documentation

- Small community

Library vs. Framework

The distinction between a framework and a library is a frequent issue of debate in the software world.

In reality, experts have recommended that the boundary between them might be hazy, but it is necessary to distinguish between them. A JS framework is a comprehensive toolset that helps shape and organize our web-based application, while a JS library is a collection of pre-written code snippets that are less concerned with shaping our application and more concerned with offering a use-as-needed library of functionality.

Model View Controller (MVC)

Model View Controller is a software design paradigm used by modern JavaScript frameworks. It is often utilized in the creation of user interfaces that separate related computer logic into three interrelated pieces. The model is the pattern's fundamental web component since it is the application's dynamic data structure. It is in charge of the application's data. The view contains all of the code associated with expressing the application's data the user interface code. The interpreter is the controller. It receives input and transforms it into model or view instructions. To give structure and flexibility in software development, frameworks are designed around the MVC design pattern.

VANILLA JS VS. REACT JS: WHICH SHOULD WE USE FOR OUR DEVELOPMENT?

Vanilla JS vs. React JS has long been a source of contention, since both may be used to create JavaScript apps. This session will provide a full comparison of Vanilla versus React JS, including performance, UI, and other factors.

Web application utilization is expanding every day, and the apps are getting more complicated and dynamic.[10]

People often wish to discover sites where they can compare vanilla vs react, and here we can find all points, including a performance comparison of reacting versus Vanilla JS.

As a result, developers choose to utilize diverse libraries when designing web apps in order to boost development pace.

Web applications may be complicated and need a lot of dynamic functionality, which is why developers choose to utilize frameworks such as React JS, Angular, Vanilla JS, and others.

We may simply locate React JS professionals that provide a variety of React JS development services.

Vanilla JS vs React JS Functionality

Before we begin the full comparison of React JS vs Vanilla JS, we'd like to clarify the primary difference between these two JavaScript and how React JS and Vanilla JS operate.

If we want to learn more about the advantages of utilizing React over vanilla JS, this article will provide us with all the information we need.

Both are used to create JavaScript apps.

React JS: What Is Its Role in the Application's View Layer?

To build interfaces that make use of UI components, many developers have turned to React JS, a free and open-source JavaScript framework. React JS is a frontend JavaScript library that will allow us to build user-friendly apps.

We'll learn how React JS may be used to create a variety of user interfaces tailored to single-page apps. Developers may sometimes utilize React JS to manage the viewing layer for various sorts of mobile and online apps.

Why Is Vanilla JS Used?

Vanilla JS is known as vanilla JavaScript, and developers use it to build JavaScript code that does not need the usage of libraries.

Vanilla JS is a scripting language that does not impose any restrictions on how developers construct data in their applications.

Vanilla JS apps may not always deliver the greatest outcomes for the application.

Vanilla JS is well-known among developers since it is one of the simplest frameworks that anybody can learn fast.

Stack Data Structure Comparison between React JS vs Vanilla JS

We'll see that communication across JavaScript components requires a lot of interaction through bridges so that we can communicate with both sides.

As we may know, React JS and Vanilla JS are both JavaScript frameworks used to create various online apps.

If we're curious, the stack data structure of React JS and Vanilla JS will vary.

We are erroneous since the concepts in both JavaScript frameworks are the same.

We will see that a stack may be defined as an ordered collection of elements that adhere to the Last In First Out (LIFO) principle.

If we remove any items from the stack, the one at the top is eliminated first.

As a result, the stack data structure of React JS and Vanilla JS is extremely similar.

Performance Comparison between Vanilla JS with React JS

When comparing the performance of Vanilla JS versus React, we will notice several areas of difference. Consider that React JS, unlike Vanilla JS, is a free and open-source frontend JavaScript framework for building UIs using reusable UI components.

Vanilla JS is a cross-platform framework for developing sophisticated JavaScript applications. Vanilla JS versus React performance-based comparison might be difficult, but we've got us covered. Because of the virtual DOM capability, React JS is efficient in handling diverse UI modifications.

React JS converts every UI change to DOM and then compares it to the Regular DOM on a regular basis. As a result, this method aids in determining the adjustments required for the normal DOM. This whole process may be so rapid that developers may believe there would be performance difficulties with UI rendering.

However, React JS offers a set of workarounds that will overcome any performance problem. We may be shocked to learn that Vanilla JS is much quicker than other JavaScript frameworks. As a result, we may argue that it outperforms leading frontend frameworks.

We will see that Vanilla JS initially produces the UI over 30 times quicker than React JS, which is one of the key reasons why Vanilla Js outperforms React JS.

Handling UI state changes in Vanilla Js is simpler and quicker than in React JS.

Vanilla JS outperforms React JS in terms of performance.

Future Prospects

Future comparison of React vs Vanilla Js is crucial because it will show us which JavaScript is best.

ReactJs is an important library that developers may use to create JavaScript apps.

We will see that ReactJs is a framework for developing fast and scalable online apps.

New plugins for future elements are continually being developed in this framework.

Because the technology is utilized in a variety of industries, ReactJs developers and ReactJs Development Companies that provide varied React js development services have a promising future.

The ReactJs community will also expand over time, and the framework will be updated.

Vanilla Js is also known as pure JavaScript since it does not include any other libraries, such as jQuery.

Some developers may use it as a joke to educate younger devs that many things can be done without the usage of extra JavaScript libraries.

It is possible to build web applications using JavaScript.

That is why we must grasp the fundamental concepts of JavaScript and study Vanilla Js.

New JavaScript frameworks will be launched in the future.

However, before utilizing such frameworks, we must be familiar with Vanilla Js.

Winner: Both ReactJs and Vanilla js are promising since they are both needed by all JavaScript frameworks, although ReactJs has a somewhat better future.

Testing

It will be difficult to determine the victor of a comparison of Vanilla JS vs React JS for testing.

We may test ReactJs code just as we would any other simple JavaScript code.

ReactJs has many testing libraries that may be used for testing.

The ReactJs testing library is a collection of helper libraries that allow us to test ReactJs components without depending on their implementation details.

We might claim that this way of evaluating ReactJs assures that it is the best practice for ensuring code accessibility.

We must also set up the ideal testing environment for all ReactJs components when testing the ReactJs code.

Many people are unaware that Vanilla js code may be readily tested.

Jest, a JavaScript testing framework that focuses on simplicity, must be installed by the developers.

This Jest JavaScript testing framework is also compatible with AngularJS and ReactJS.

With the aid of Jest, testing with Vanilla js is a breeze.

Installing npm or yarn on the device is necessary for developers who want to test Vanilla js code in Jest.

Winner: Because testing in ReactJs and Vanilla JS is straightforward, both are winners.

Security

We'll see that ReactJs is a JavaScript framework for creating web apps.

ReactJs has fewer attacking points than other frameworks that are used to construct various web apps. Because few security concerns have been disclosed, ReactJs is not completely safe.

Because ReactJs is compatible with a variety of open-source components, it lacks robust default security settings. As a result, ReactJs is exposed to several security vulnerabilities. Because of weaknesses in the security mechanism, ReactJs online apps are not completely safe. Vanilla js may demand multiple credentials for APIs at times; however, this framework does not provide short-term tokens.

If developers wish to ensure the security of online applications, they may employ the method of intermediary APIs.

Vanilla JS is a simple framework for creating amazing and powerful JavaScript apps. We may be shocked to learn that Vanilla js is also popular among developers since there are no known security vulnerabilities as of now.

Winner: If we compare Vanilla versus React js for security considerations, Vanilla js is the obvious winner.

ReactJs and Vanilla js UI/UX Performance

ReactJs is a free and open-source JavaScript toolkit used to create various UI components.

Some of the top React UI frameworks for our project can be found here.

Ant Design is the second most used UI framework in the world, and it is utilized in ReactJs.

We'll see that it combines an enterprise-class UI design language with a collection of high-quality ReactJs UI components. Ant Design's documentation is thorough, and thanks to a plethora of examples and frameworks, Ant Design is always up to date.

Material UI is a user interface component built using ReactJs that may streamline the creation of websites. Many developers use this UI since it is the most popular ReactJs UI framework that gives different material design concepts provided by Google.

There are several UI libraries available in Vanilla js that may be used to improve online apps.

Vanilla js's JavaScript 3D library, Three, is well-liked by programmers because of its thorough documentation.

This 3D library is simple to use and provides superior performance.

Cheerio is a UI framework for Vanilla js that may be regarded as a faster, more versatile, and better server-side version of core jQuery.

Winner: For UI/UX speed, ReactJs outperforms Vanilla JS since developers don't have to input DOM because it occurs automatically in ReactJs.

Convenience for the Developer

Vanilla js versus Reacts js will be a pretty close comparison in terms of developer ease.

ReactJs is one of the most widely used JavaScript libraries nowadays, as we can see.

ReactJs was released in 2013; however, it is still widely used by web developers since it is incredibly user-friendly.

It is one of the greatest JavaScript UI frameworks for creating viewing pages.

ReactJs is more handy for developers since it is more than simply a library because it includes JSX and several virtual DOMs.

ReactJs is used by developers because it gives them entire flexibility to construct high-quality interfaces for any application. Some developers may be wondering whether Vanilla js is still utilized, and we can assure that it is. If developers are creating basic code to modify the DOM in the browser, why require a large framework when Vanilla js would satisfy.

ReactJs or another framework may be used by developers to construct complicated frontend web apps. Both ReactJs and Vanilla are handy for developers, but ReactJs has more features, thus many developers choose it.

Maintenance

ReactJs maintenance regularly analyses and monitors the online application. It will ensure that the web applications' security, speed, output, and overall performance are satisfactory. If developers want to maintain their applications up to date, quicker, and fresh, they should remember that ReactJs offers a solid maintenance solution.

ReactJs offers three kinds of maintenance services: ReactJs startup maintenance, ReactJs professional maintenance, and ReactJs business maintenance.

We will notice that developers dislike using the Vanilla js framework due to the expense of upkeep. If the developers code an eCommerce website with Vanilla js, the maintenance and development time will be higher.

We will notice that it is one of the primary reasons why developers choose to utilize numerous JavaScript frameworks available on the market, such as AngularJS, ReactJS, Vue.js, and so on.

Winner: ReactJs is much superior to Vanilla js in terms of maintenance since developers can easily maintain web apps.

Development Cost

Both are efficient JavaScript frameworks for creating web applications.

We will see that ReactJs developers may charge between $20 and $40 per hour to create ReactJs web apps. Vanilla js developers may charge over $1,000 to create vanilla js web apps.

However, due to the popularity of ReactJs web apps, many in the market choose to engage ReactJs developers for web app development.

Winner: While developing a Vanilla JS application may be less expensive, many prefer to employ a ReactJs developer, which may be pricey at times.

5 REASONS WHY OUR WEBSITE NEEDS JAVASCRIPT

This website was written with JavaScript, the language of the internet. JavaScript, or 'Js' for short, is widely used throughout the web.

HTML (Hypertext Markup Language), CSS (Cascading Style Sheets), and JavaScript are the 'big three' languages that all Toronto web development companies want their programmers to know.[11]

HTML is the language used to instruct a web browser on what to display on a website.

The Cascading Style Sheets (CSS) language instructs the browser on how to arrange and style the material for optimal visual presentation.

The page's functionality is determined by JavaScript. JavaScript is used to create all the fancy effects seen on contemporary websites, such as pop-ups, transitions, and scrolling animations. Ten years ago, while seeking information, most consumers searched for simple text. We would most likely abandon a page that included nothing but text and no other visuals in the modern day. Today's development norms evolve in conjunction with the ever-shifting web ecosystem.

Explain How Using JavaScript Will Enhance Our Website

- **Developing applications for end users:** It's unusual since it's not executed on the web server itself. As web designers, we understand how crucial it is for our readers to have a quick website load time. The longer something takes to load, the less enjoyable it is for the user. When a JavaScript animation loads, it executes in the background on the viewer's device CPU. This drastically lessens the demand on the web server and shortens the time it takes for pages to load.

- **Small learning curve:** JavaScript isn't the sole online programming language, and learning it isn't particularly difficult. Some more are

Python, C++, and a few others. This makes it the most widely used language, and it also makes it the simplest to master. JavaScript syntax is quite close to the English language. It doesn't take weeks for developers to create a new site since they don't have to spend time figuring out the purpose of each line of code. A single second may make or break a project in the frantic world of Toronto web development. Our website will be live to the public quicker if the developer employs JavaScript.

- **Compatible with other languages:** Web servers utilize a wide variety of languages, and it's important that they all work together smoothly. The list of popular programming languages includes Python, PHP, Ruby, Rails, ASP.NET, and Java, just to name a few. JavaScript's compatibility with a wide variety of server languages ensures that our audience will always enjoy a dynamic and engaging experience.

- **Uses the DOM model:** The DOM model is a way of organizing a website's structure so that its components may be styled as "objects" with their own attributes. This makes it simple for JavaScript to apply animations and transitions to any element. There is no specific programming language for working with the DOM (Document Object Model). Using JavaScript, a developer may create a DOM for a website.

- **Compiler-free programming:** Traditional programming makes use of a compiler; compiler-free programming avoids this step. For a browser to function, raw code must be compiled into understandable syntax by a compiler. The page takes longer to load as a result of this. As a result, it will take longer for our site to be ready for launch. On the other side, browsers have built-in support for JavaScript. In the same manner that they can translate HTML, they can do so with this. In other words, we can read it without a compiler.

AJAX Uses to Load Sections of Pages Independently

JavaScript has been more popular since it was first released in 1995. JavaScript is used to improve the user experience on an astonishing 92% of websites on the internet today. With AJAX, we may update certain parts of a website without having to refresh the whole page. This is accomplished via the use of JavaScript. We've probably seen this on many social media and video sharing websites as well as the likes of Google.com and YouTube. Consider what occurs when we play a video on YouTube. After the website loaded, we may begin playing the video. If we leave a comment while the video is playing, it will appear in the comments box once we scroll down and post.

We covered what is JS, advantages and disadvantages, and the evolution of JS in this chapter. Furthermore, we discussed what frameworks are and how they differ from Vanilla JS.

NOTES

1 JavaScript – Overview: www.tutorialspoint.com/javascript/javascript_ overview.htm Accessed on: 20 September 2022.
2 What Is JavaScript? A Basic Introduction to JS for Beginners: www. hostinger.in/tutorials/what-is-javascript Accessed on: 20 September 2022.
3 What Is Modern JavaScript and How to Use It?: www.altamira.ai/blog/what-is-modern-javascript-and-how-to-use-it/#:~:text=Since%20JavaScript%20does%20not%20have,via%20an%20tag. Accessed on: 21 September 2022.
4 History and Evolution of JavaScript: https://exploringjs.com/impatient-js/ ch_history.html Accessed on: 22 September 2022.
5 The History of JavaScript: Everything You Need to Know: www.springboard.com/blog/data-science/history-of-javascript/ Accessed on: 20 September 2022.
6 Who Owns JavaScript?: https://iq.opengenus.org/who-owns-javascript/ Accessed on: 20 September 2022.
7 Tech 101: What Is a JavaScript Framework? Here's Everything You Need to Know: https://skillcrush.com/blog/what-is-a-javascript-framework/ Accessed on: 20 September 2022.
8 What Is a JavaScript Framework?: https://generalassemb.ly/blog/what-is-a-javascript-framework/ Accessed on: 20 September 2022.
9 What Are the Pros and Cons of JavaScript Frameworks?: www.geeksforgeeks.org/what-are-the-pros-and-cons-of-javascript-frameworks/ Accessed on: 21 September 2022.
10 Vanilla JS vs React JS: What to Choose for Your Development?: https://taglineinfotech.com/react-js-vs-vanilla-js/ Accessed on: 21 September 2022.
11 5 Reasons Why You Need JavaScript in Your Website: https://vestrainet. com/5-reasons-why-you-need-javascript-in-your-website.html Accessed on: 22 September 2022.

CHAPTER 2

Getting Started with JavaScript I

IN THIS CHAPTER

- ➤ Data Types and Operators
- ➤ Functions
- ➤ Objects and Arrays
- ➤ Error Handling
- ➤ Events

In the previous chapter, we covered Introduction to JavaScript, and in this chapter, we will discuss Getting started with JavaScript and some core concepts.

SELECTING THE BEST JAVASCRIPT EDITOR FROM SEVEN OPTIONS

Our page is nothing more than a dead static document without JavaScript.

We can develop user interfaces using JavaScript. Our page is nothing more than a dead static document without JavaScript. We may use JavaScript to design user interfaces that respond to user activities, adding movement and interactivity to the user experience.

DOI: 10.1201/9781003356578-2

As a result, we may consider JavaScript to be the heart of a website.

If JavaScript is so vital, we should think about the tools we use to deal with it.

While there is nothing stopping us from working just in Notepad, using a decent JavaScript editor will undoubtedly enhance our experience and increase our productivity.

We'll go through our selection of seven JavaScript editors. We'll offer a short summary of each item and discuss its benefits and drawbacks.

What Is the Difference between a JavaScript Editor and an IDE?

But, before we get into the editors, let's take a step back and discuss how editors vary from a comparable tool: IDEs.[1]

What Exactly Is an Editor?

Let us begin with editors. Text editors are tools that enable you to create and edit plain-text files, as the name implies. That's all. An editor, in the traditional sense, isn't always a programming tool; it may be used to modify text files for any purpose. Of course, one of these reasons is to write code.

IDE Definition

IDE is an abbreviation for Integrated Development Environment. An IDE is just an editor with a variety of handy programming tools. An IDE is a specialist tool for software development as opposed to a simple text editor.

What exactly is the package that comes with an IDE? This may vary, but some common additions are as follows:

- A debugger, compiler, and source code analyzer are all included.

- Highlighting syntax.

- Project scaffolding functionality based on pre-defined templates.

- Connection to the compiler and build tools.

- Auto-complete features that are advanced.

- Database connection wizards and assistance.

- GUI development functionality / Rapid Application Development.

- Integration with terminals and version control software.

- Management and execution of automated tests, particularly unit testing.

- Advanced find/replace capabilities and even refactoring are available.

When Conflicts Arise

But here's the catch: The once-wide gap between editors and full-fledged IDEs is closing with each passing year.

The distinctions between the two instruments are not as obvious as they formerly were.

For decades, programmers have used editors to code, augmenting their capabilities via the use of plugins. See also Vim and Emacs.

Modern editors, on the other hand, use a different approach. For example, Visual Studio Code is often regarded as a text editor, but many would argue that it may also be regarded as an IDE owing to its many integrations. In contrast to editors, which may be used to modify any kind of text file, programming-related or not, IDEs are often tailored to a particular programming language or framework.

However, we're sure there are several exceptions to this rule. At the end of the day, the categorization that assign to a tool is unimportant as long as one understand its strengths and shortcomings and can make an educated selection.

The Top 7 JavaScript Editors

It's really tough to move from one code editor to another later on. After all, how often can you really expect to find new ways to speed up the development process? As a result, it is preferable to set aside some time in advance to choose among the finest JavaScript (JS) editors. Let us explore.

1. **Atom**

   Before delving into Atom's features, it's important to first grasp what Electron is. Electron is a JavaScript-based framework for creating cross-platform desktop programs. In a word, the electron is the foundation of the atom.

   Atom is one of the most popular JavaScript source code editors. Atom is completely free. The editor is available for a variety of operating systems, including Mac, Windows, and Linux. This open-source editor is also quite simple to set up. Other features include intelligent code completion and an intuitive file system viewer.

Atom makes it simple to integrate GitHub and Git control. Plugins created in Node.js are also supported by the editor. The interface supports HTML, CSS, and JS, among other languages.

Atom also features a function called fuzzy finder. The fuzzy finder speeds up your work by allowing for rapid file switching. Do we want more? Atom's capabilities may be expanded by installing packages such as Minimap, auto-close HTML elements, and a linter.

Pros:

- Git integration.

- Cross-platform compatibility.

- Support for multiple cursors.

Cons:

- It is sometimes unstable.

- Code execution failure.

- Slower than other top editors.

2. **Visual Studio Code**

Many individuals consider of Visual Studio (VS) Code when they think of the greatest integrated development environments (IDEs) for JS programming. This free and open-source editor is compatible with Linux, Windows, and macOS. IntelliSense support allows for automated completions when writing in HTML, CSS, JS, or PHP.

Another function that this editor has is code refactoring. Furthermore, the editor creates native and managed code. This code editor has built-in support for JS. Debugging tools for TypeScript, Node.js, and JavaScript are also included.

VS Code also features a peek capability. This feature enables us to expand a function in-line and inspect the code rather than traveling straight to the line where the function is declared.

Another useful tool provided by VS Code is Task Runner. It supports the usage of Gulp, Grunt, or MSBuild for setup tasks.

We can use the built-in Git functionality to conduct operations like publish, commit, push, pull, and rebase. We may also tweak and enhance Visual Studio Code by adding new features and plugins.

Pros:

- Memory use is minimal.

- Integration with the console.

- Task organization.

- Marketplace provides a large selection of extensions for extending functionality.

- WSL incorporation (Windows Subsystem for Linux).

Cons:

- Lag at times.

- Some widely used programming languages are not supported.

- Inadequate source control.

3. **The eclipse**

Eclipse is a well-known Java IDE. However, full-stack engineers often utilize Eclipse for JavaScript development. However, for JS, we must install certain more plugins. Of course, the flexible plugin system facilitates use. A unified development environment promotes peak performance. Along with speed, developers may expect reliability and resilience. When we set up the Oomph Project, we can also automate and replicate similar workspaces.

Eclipse's highlight is the precise performance of JavaScript Development Tools.

A new Docker UI aids in the creation of Docker images and containers using the Docker CLI.

Almost all packages integrate with Git. Another notable aspect is the automatic error reporting. The IDE may use this functionality to communicate issues identified in the IDE to eclipse.org.

Pros:

- Effective project management.

- Advanced troubleshooting.

- Excellent auto-complete.

Cons:

- To take effect, most modifications need a reboot.

- For beginners, it is difficult.

- Poor customer service.

4. **Sublime Text**

Sublime Text is another free and open-source JS editor. It's cross-platform, which means there's plenty of space for customization. There is no clutter on the UI.

As a result, the editor is more user-friendly. Some of its outstanding features include a significant performance gain and enhanced pane management. Other functions include Go to Symbol and Go to Definition. We may also get packages like SideBar Enhancements for copying, pasting, moving, and renaming. Getting things set up might take some time at first. However, once installed, Sublime Text will give a seamless experience. Also, if we want to use Sublime Text, here are some plugins that need to install: DocBlockr, SideBar Enhancements, JsFormat, and SublimeLinter, which are all available.

The greatest thing is that you may check out all of the features for free.

This JS editor also provides a trial version so that developers may see how it works.

After the trial time expires, we must pay $80 for three years of use to have access to all features.

Pros:

- Editing mode with no distractions.

- Working on many projects is simple.

- Help with automation.

Cons:

- Awful library stack.

- Debugging is lacking.

- There is no default printing.

5. **Brackets**

   Adobe developed the open-source coding editor Brackets. This lightweight and quick JS editor includes JavaScript functionality. Brackets are compatible with Mac, Windows, and Linux. Some important capabilities are function searching and rapid project switching. Users may utilize these tools to search for various project files while typing in real time.

   The Extract functionality turns PSD data into CSS. Live Preview is one of the finest features of Brackets. We can observe how any changes to the code are affecting the code in real time. The functionality is similar to Adobe Dreamweaver. We may additionally improve the editor's capabilities by adding plugins. Some of these features include an autoprefixer, code folding, a Markdown preview, smart highlighting, and snippets.

Pros:

- A straightforward user interface.

- Minimization of code.

- Browser preview in real time.

Cons:

- Long launch time.

- Project management is difficult.

- When dealing with huge files, performance suffers.

6. **NetBeans**

NetBeans is a multiplatform IDE for developing JavaScript applications.

The nicest thing is that the time between installing NetBeans and using it is less than with other editors. NetBeans has features like as syntactic and semantic code highlighting, smart code completion, and Subversion. Mercurial and built-in Git support is also available.

Here's another useful feature for us!

NetBeans' workspace may be easily customized.

Aside from that, we may simply drag and rearrange tabs in the app frame.

And, as we all know, each developer has a unique development style.

We may edit the toolbar buttons in NetBeans to suit our needs and preferences.

And do we know what else is useful?

Users may develop their own keyboard shortcuts!

Pros:

- Effective for automation.

- Excellent refactoring.

- Excellent service management.

Cons:

- More system resources are used.

- Support for integration is inadequate.

- Pop-ups are annoying.

7. **Vim**

We couldn't say goodbye without acknowledging the legendary Vim. Vim stands for VI Upgraded, and it is an improved version of an older free text editor called vi, which was first designed for the Unix system. Even though vim has long been associated with Linux and the Unix community, it is now available for Windows.

Vim is perhaps the most basic of the editors on our list. Though a graphical interface is available with vim, it is often a text-based editor. This editor has a somewhat high learning curve. However, if we've overcome the first learning curve and become skilled with it, vim may help us attain great levels of productivity, especially when we consider its extensive ecosystem of plugins.

Pros:

- Lightweight and efficient.

- Cross-platform.

- Very adaptable.

- Plugin ecosystem to increase functionality.

Cons:

- The learning curve is steep.

Time to Select the Best JavaScript Editor

In the preceding part, we examined the seven greatest JavaScript editors.

Now comes the hard part choosing the best one. This is simply like picking the greatest operating system. One who uses Windows would undoubtedly defend it, saying that it is superior and that they would never switch to any other OS. Conversely, those that use Linux or Mac are likely to think their system is much better to everything else out there. When it refers to JavaScript editors we have to evaluate a few criteria before picking one:

- Flexibility.

- Help with integration.

- Excellent project management.

- Performance.

- Advanced troubleshooting.

However, when it comes to JS editors, Visual Studio Code is the clear winner, regardless of our individual preferences.

Experienced programmers like ourselves have no other choice than to use Visual Studio Code. The editor allows for quick and simple code and file management and searching. Furthermore, we have shortcuts to quickly access any icon or operation. We can type codes and navigate between folders without putting down the keyboard.

If we're just starting out in the world of computer programming, VS Code's capabilities will be a huge help. We had no trouble picking up the keyboard shortcuts or any of the other features. Plus, the integrated command line interface is a great help to those who work with Angular or Node. If you have Node.js installed, you can also use VS Code to debug our code. Plus, we needn't fret about getting help with VS Code since it's built by Microsoft. All of the features and how to's are well documented and shown in a plethora of written and video materials.

With a JavaScript Editor, You May Improve the
Efficiency of Your Work Environment

A website may be built using a variety of technologies, but three are always present: HTML, CSS, and JavaScript. Each of these technologies is concerned with a single issue. HTML organizes and defines our page.

CSS helps it seem fantastic. It comes to life thanks to JavaScript. If we're a developer, we're probably excited about making your workplace more enjoyable and efficient. A superb JavaScript editor is the way to go in this scenario.

Personally, we can't always absolutely assess and compare text editors to determine which one is the finest. The opinion differs according on the demands of each user. Spending some time with each of the top options is a fantastic method to determine which the finest JavaScript editor is. This will assist us in comprehending the many characteristics and, ultimately, making the best decision.

HOW TO INSTALL JAVASCRIPT IN VISUAL STUDIO CODE

JavaScript is a web object-oriented computer program used in web browsers to create interactive effects by having our website behaves and thinks. An IDE, or integrated development environment, helps programmers to merge the numerous components of creating a computer program into a single handy area. It includes a debugger, a source code editor, and local build automation. Visual Studio Code is a great IDE that practically every JavaScript developer uses.[2]

Visual Studio Code is a free cross-platform text editor that supports over 40 programming languages and is mostly used for frontend development.

It is a Microsoft product that can be used in practically all major operating systems, including Linux, Windows, and macOS. Visual Studio Work is frequently used for JavaScript development since it is lightweight while yet having sophisticated built-in capabilities like as IntelliSense (which allows us to code faster by displaying intelligent code completion), formatting, refactorings, code navigation, debugging, and much more.

In this session, we'll look at how to configure Visual Studio Code for JavaScript.

Let's begin by installing Visual Studio Code on our Windows system.

Installation of Visual Studio Code in Windows

To begin installing Visual Studio Code, we must first download it from the following link:

https://code.visualstudio.com/

When we go to the aforementioned URL, we'll see a blue button labeled Download for Windows. Select this button.

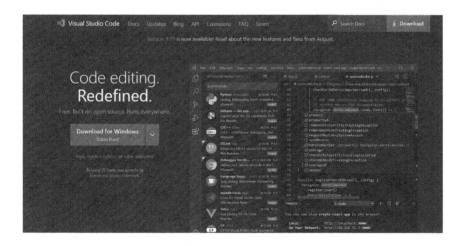

Installation of VScode

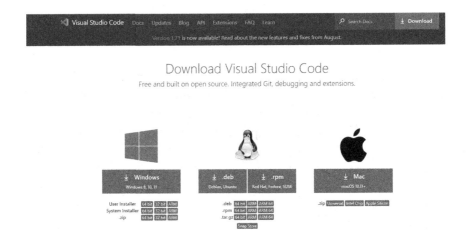

Download page of VScode

When we press the blue button, the following will happen:

Setup start of VScode

When our download is complete, double-click the downloaded file seen in the preceding picture.

When we're finished, a window will appear with a license agreement for Visual Studio Code.

Choose "I accept the agreement" and then click the Next button:

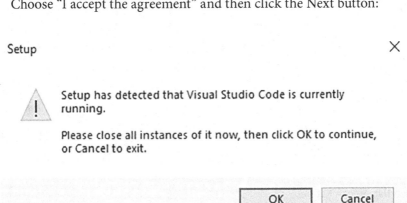

Process start of Setup

Accept Agreement

The following box that appears will allow us to pick more tasks. Select all of the settings we need and then press the Next button:

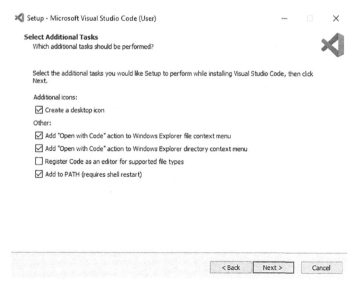

Task Selections

When we click the Next button, the Ready to Install box appears, and we must click the Install button:

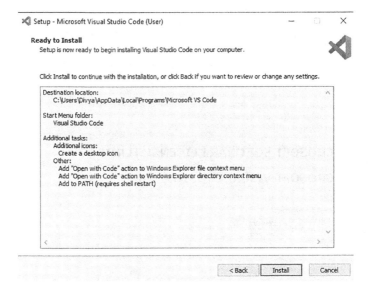

Installation Box

The installation process will now begin:

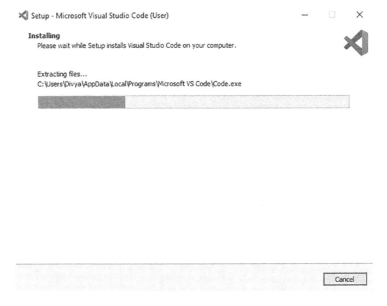

Begin of Installation

Once the setup is finished, click the Finish button to start Visual Studio Code.

Setup Done

Setup Visual Studio Code

Now that we've finished downloading and installing Visual Studio Code, let's configure our JavaScript editor. The first step in configuring Visual Studio Code is to install the necessary extensions that will allow us to code more effectively and fast. The extension symbol is visible on the left, as illustrated in the picture below:

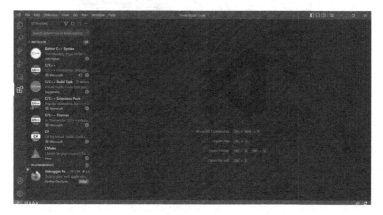

Setup of Editor

Search for the extension we wish to install after clicking the extension's icon.

Search of Extensions

Install the LiveServer addon, which is quite handy due to its automated live-reload capability.

We don't need to save our file since it will save and display the result on our browser every time we alter our code.

Search for the Live Server in the extension tab and click on the button shown below:

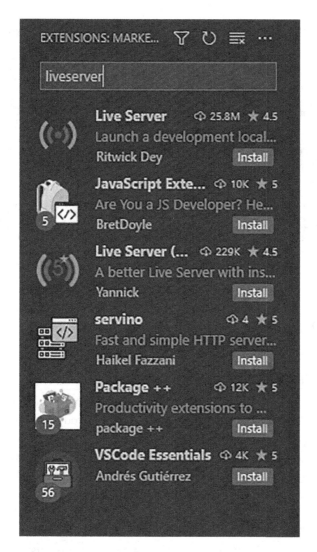

LiveServer Extensions

When we click on the Live Server, the install option will appear on the right-hand side.

To install Live Server, click the install button.

Our Live Server will be installed when we click the install button:

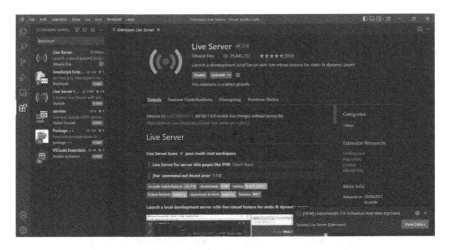

LiveServer Extensions installed

The JavaScript (ES6) code snippet, which has a ton of built-in code snippets, is another useful item we may install in Visual Studio Code.

Installing ES6 code snippets is similar to installing the Live Server extension.

INSTALLING VISUAL STUDIO CODE ON LINUX

Microsoft developed Visual Studio Code, a free and open-source, cross-platform integrated development environment (IDE) or code editor that enables programmers to create apps and write code in a number of languages, including C, C++, Python, Go, and Java, to name a few.[3] This guide will lead us through installing Visual Studio Code on Linux. More specifically, we will learn how to install Visual Studio Code on both Debian and RedHat-based Linux variants.

Installing Visual Studio Code on Debian, Ubuntu, or Linux Mint

On Debian-based computers, the most popular way of installing Visual Code Studio is to enable the VS Code repository and install the Visual Studio Code package that use the apt package manager.

```
$ sudo apt update
```

Once updated, execute to install any needed dependencies.

```
$ sudo apt install software-properties-common
apt-transport-https
```

Next, import Microsoft's GPG key using the wget command to obtain the repository:

```
$ wget -qO- https://packages.microsoft.com/keys/
microsoft.asc | gpg --dearmor > packages.microsoft.gpg
$ sudo install -o root -g root -m 644 packages.
microsoft.gpg /etc/apt/trusted.gpg.d/
$ sudo sh -c 'echo "deb [arch=amd64 signed-by=/etc/
apt/trusted.gpg.d/packages.microsoft.gpg] https://
packages.microsoft.com/repos/vscode stable main" > /
etc/apt/sources.list.d/vscode.list'
```

Use the next command to install Visual Studio Code and update the system after we've enabled the repository:

```
$ sudo apt update
$ sudo apt install code
```

Because of its size, installation takes around 5 minutes. Once installed, utilize the project coordinator to find and open Visual Code Studio.

NODE.JS INSTALLATION ON WINDOWS

We will install Node.js with following steps:

Configuring the Node Development Environment

The Node may be installed on a computer in a variety of methods. Our approach is determined by the system's current development environment. There are many package installers for various contexts. Node may be installed by downloading the source code and building the program. Another method is to clone the GIT repository in all three environments and then install Node on the machine.[4]

Node Installation on Windows (WINDOWS 10):
To install Node.js on Windows, we must first do the following steps:

Step 1: Get the Node.js '.msi' installer.

Downloading the installer is the first step in installing Node.js on Windows.

Go to the official Node.js website, https://nodejs.org/en/download/, and download the.msi file that corresponds to our system environment (32-bit & 64-bit).

On our machine, an MSI installer will be downloaded.

Downloading NodeJs

Step 2: Start the Node.js installation.

We must now install the node.js installer on our computer. To install Node.js, we must first complete the following steps:

- Double-click the.msi installer to launch it.

The Node.js Setup Wizard will be launched.

- Welcome to the Node.js Installation Wizard.

"Next" should be selected.

Caption: Node.js wizard screen

- The End-User License Agreement (EULA) will be shown after selecting "Next."

Choose "I accept the terms of the License Agreement" by checking the box next to it.
"Next" should be selected.

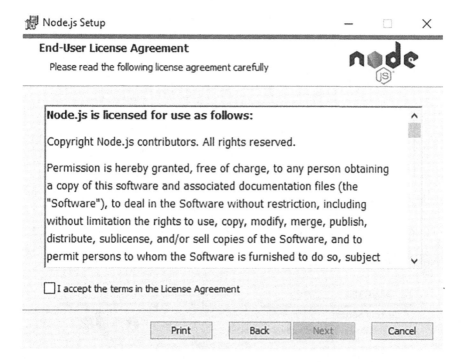

Node.js agree screen

- Choose Destination Folder

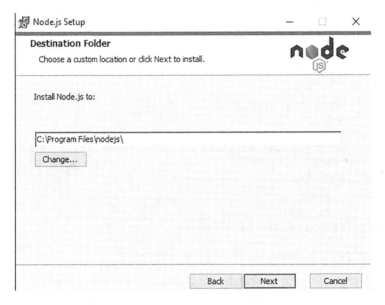

Node.js choose folder

- Custom Configuration

"Next" should be selected.

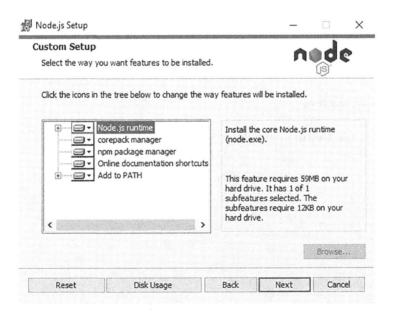

Node.js custom setup

- Node.js is now ready for installation.

Choose "Install."

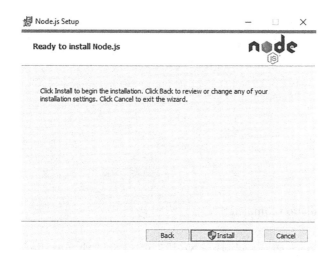

Node.js installation start

NOTE:

"This step needs administrator rights," a prompt will appear. Authenticate as a "Administrator" to the prompt.

- Node.js installation

Do not close or cancel the installer until it has finished installing.

- Finish the Node.js Setup Wizard.

Click the "Finish" button.

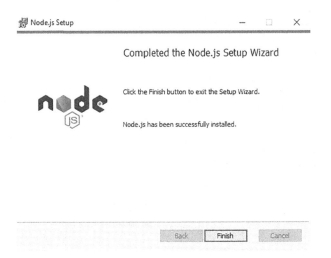

Node.js installation complete

Step 3: Check to see whether Node.js was correctly installed.

To verify whether node.js is fully installed on our machine, use the following line at our command prompt or Windows Powershell:

```
C:\Users\Admin> node -v
```

If node.js was fully installed on our machine, the command prompt will display the version of node.js that was installed.

Step 4: Update the Local npm version.

The last step in installing Node.js is to update our local npm version (if necessary)—the package manager that comes with Node.js.

To fast update the npm, use the following command.

```
npm install npm -global // Updates 'CLI' client
```

NOTE:

We do not need to modify the system variables since the Windows installer handles them automatically when installing using the.msi installer.

If we use another format to install node.js on our PC, the system variable path for node.js should be as follows:

```
PATH : C:\Users\[user-name]\AppData\Roaming\npm
C:\Program Files\nodejs (Path to nodejs folder)
```

NODE.JS INSTALLATION ON LINUX

Node.js is a JavaScript runtime based on the V8 JavaScript engine in Chrome. Node.js may be installed on your Ubuntu Linux laptop in a variety of methods.[5] We may install Node.js using either Ubuntu's official repository or the NodeSource repository. The NodeSource repository allows us to install the most recent version of Node.js.

Installing Node On Ubuntu 18.04 and 16.04: Ubuntu has two repositories, the official one and the NodeSouce one, from which you may download and install Node.js.

Install Node.js from the official Ubuntu repository: In a few keystrokes, you can install Node.js from the Ubuntu repository. To install Node.js on our Ubuntu operating system, follow the instructions below.

Step 1: Launch a terminal or press Ctrl+Alt+T.

Step 2: Run the following command to install node.js:

```
sudo apt install nodejs
```

Step 3: Once installed, use the following command to check the installed version:

```
node -v or node -version
```

It is strongly advised to install Node Package Manager (NPM) with Node.js. NPM is an open-source Node.js package library.

Use the following code to install NPM:

```
sudo apt install npm
npm -v or npm -version
```

Node and NPM will be installed successfully on our Ubuntu computer.

Using the NodeSouce repository, install Node.js

The most recent version of Node.js may be downloaded from the NodeSource repository.

To install Node.js on Ubuntu, follow the instructions below.

Step 1: To update and upgrade the package management, open your terminal or press Ctrl + Alt + T and enter the following commands:

```
sudo apt-get update
sudo apt-get upgrade
```

Step 2: Run the following command to install Python software libraries:

```
sudo apt-get install python-software-properties
```

Step 3: Install the Node.js PPA on the machine.

```
curl -sL https://deb.nodesource.com/setup_10.x | sudo
-E bash -
```

Note: We are installing version 10 of node.js; if we wish to install version 11, replace setup 10.x with setup 11.x.

Step 4: Run the following command to install Node.js and NPM on our Ubuntu machine:

```
sudo apt-get install nodejs
```

Step 5: Once installed, use the following command to check the installed version:

```
node -v or node –version
npm -v or npm –version
```

Finally, on our Ubuntu system, we have successfully installed Node.js and NPM.

HOW DO WE START AND EXECUTE A NODE.JS PROJECT IN VISUAL STUDIO CODE?

The instructions below will walk us through the process of creating a basic NodeJS project and executing it in the VS Code editor.[6]

Step 1: In our VS Code editor, create an empty folder and transfer it there using the following command.

```
mkdir demo
cd demo
code .
```

Step 2: In our folder, create a file called app.js.

Step 3: Install Modules: Install the modules by running the following command.

```
npm install express
npm install nodemon
```

Step 4: In the package.json file, add these two instructions that are required for launching and dynamically executing the code once changes are made in our Node.js app.

```
"start": "node app.js",
"dev": "nodemon app.js"
```

package.json File Configuration:

```
{
    "name": "demo",
    "version": "1.0.0",
    "description": "",
    "main": "app.js",
    "scripts": {
      "test": "echo \"Error: no test specified\" &&
      exit 1",
      "start": "node app.js",
      "dev": "nodemon app.js"
    },
    "author": "",
    "license": "ISC",
    "dependencies": {
      "express": "^4.17.1",
      "nodemon": "^2.0.12"
    }
}
```

Step 5: The following is the structure of our project:

- app.js

- package-lock.json

- package.json

Step 6: Add the following code to the app.js file.

```
// Require module
const express = require('express');
```

```
// Create express object
const app = express();

// Handling the GET request
app.get('/', (req, res) => {
 res.send('Simple Node App is '
  + 'running on this server')
 res.end()
})

// Port-Number
const PORT = process.env.PORT ||5000;

// Server-Setup
app.listen(PORT,console.log(
`Server started on the port ${PORT}`));
```

Step 7: Use the following command to launch the application:

```
npm run dev
```

Step 8: In our browser, go to http://localhost:5000/ and we will get the output:

TOP VISUAL STUDIO CODE EXTENSIONS FOR JAVASCRIPT DEVELOPERS

Today, we'll show the plugins that are a game changer for JavaScript developers and elevate VS Code to new heights.[7]

JavaScript (ES6) Code Snippets

Working with a predetermined snippet collection helps us to boost our efficiency.

We may tailor the snippets to our needs by adding more packages or creating our own.

The customization possibilities for creating our own snippets are where its value resides; we haven't done much of it on our own, but we have installed other plugins to obtain tools for React, React Native, Redux, and other frameworks.

Simply search for "VS Code code snippets" + our framework to locate a collection that works for us.

Download from: https://marketplace.visualstudio.com/items?item Name=xabikos.JavaScriptSnippets

Download Page of JavaScript (ES6) code snippets

ESLint

There is no doubt that ESList is one of the most widely used and beloved add-ons in the JS community. The extension applies ESLint rules to our code and displays the results in the editor. It enables us to find and rapidly correct rule inconsistencies. It's a must-have for all JS developers since it boosts productivity and code quality.

Download from: https://marketplace.visualstudio.com/items?item Name=dbaeumer.vscode-eslint

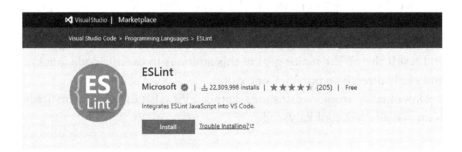

Download Page of ESList

Prettier

With VS Code, Visual Studio, Atom, Vim, Sublime Text, and a number of other programs, Prettier is an opinionated code formatter.

This useful little addon ensures that our scripts are uniformly structured and indented, and it displays colored keywords for more readable code.

It decreases formatting time and hence enhances productivity. It contributes to great code readability.

Download from: https://marketplace.visualstudio.com/items?item Name=esbenp.prettier-vscode

Download Page of Prettier

Quokka.js

Quokka.js allows us to quickly prototype JavaScript in our VS Code editor. It is a live JavaScript and TypeScript playground.

It is often referred to be the modern-day scratchpad for JS developers. Have we ever wanted to test something quickly and found yourself in our browser's console, running some JS? Or do we launch the node process and test it there? The major goal of this addon is to execute code quickly and easily directly in our VS Code editor.

Download from: https://marketplace.visualstudio.com/items?item Name=WallabyJs.quokka-vscode

Download Page of Quokka

REST Client

REST Client is a Visual Studio Code addon that lets us submit an HTTP request and examine the result right in the editor. It's Postman for VS Code, with the added benefit of being incorporated inside the code editor.

REST Client is compatible with both REST and GraphQL APIs. It is one of the greatest vscode extensions for API developers in terms of productivity.

Download from: https://marketplace.visualstudio.com/items?item Name=humao.rest-client

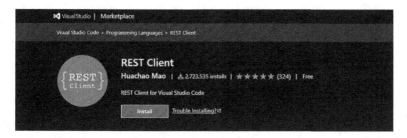

Download Page of REST Client

Debugger for Chrome

JavaScript debugging may be a nuisance. Chrome and other browsers provide fantastic features to assist us with our work. Nonetheless, they are sometimes difficult to work with or do not deliver a good overall experience, particularly when dealing with frameworks and several libraries.

Microsoft Debugger for Chrome is a Chrome extension that lets us debug our code for any little change. The Chrome console debugger is very strong when it comes to determining which lines and functions caused the issue, as well as seeing its data processing. Run our code via Chrome and debug it in our code editor.

Download from: https://marketplace.visualstudio.com/items?item Name=msjsdiag.debugger-for-chrome

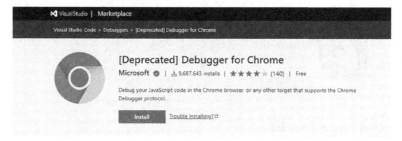

Download Page of Debugger for Chrome

Live Server

We may use Live Server to launch a local development server with a live-reload option for static and dynamic sites. This may not be very useful for individuals working with frameworks that already have live-reload enabled, such as React, but it is a lifesaver if we are working with other web pages or static material.

Download from: https://marketplace.visualstudio.com/items?item Name=ritwickdey.LiveServer

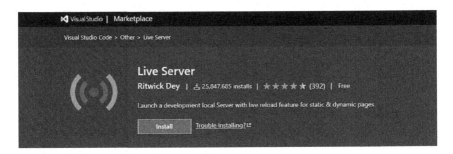

Download Page of Live Server

Live Share

This one is fantastic, and we're not sure whether anything similar exists for WebStorm, but it enables us to share our code editor with others.

It's ideal for pair programming, particularly as working from home becomes more popular.

Download from: https://marketplace.visualstudio.com/items?item Name=MS-vsliveshare.vsliveshare

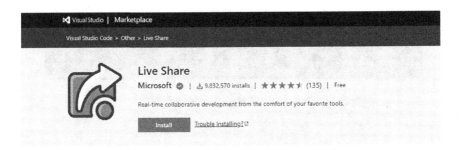

Download Page of Live Share

Babel JavaScript VSCode

JavaScript has advanced dramatically in recent years, and with the development of frameworks and libraries like as React, Flow, and GraphQL, many new forms of 'syntaxes' are now possible. Babel JavaScript offers syntax highlighting for new JavaScript syntax and these specific 'languages,' keeping our JavaScript editor up to date and looking good.

Download from: https://marketplace.visualstudio.com/items?item Name=mgmcdermott.vscode-language-babel

Download Page of Babel JavaScript

JavaScript Booster

One of our preferred WebStorm features is now accessible in VS Code.

By evaluating our code and its context, JavaScript booster automatically proposes short methods to restructure or improve our code.

It supports a wide range of code activities, including refactoring conditions, declarations, functions, typescript, promises, JSX, and many more.

Download from: https://marketplace.visualstudio.com/items?item Name=sburg.vscode-javascript-booster

Download Page of JavaScript Booster

Tabnine

Another issue that arises while switching from Webstorm to VS Code is the quality of auto-completions.

Code completion works great in VS Code, but it lags well below what Webstorm or PyCharm can offer.

However, owing to the Tabnine, VS Code receives a significant increase.

Tabnine use artificial intelligence to provide cutting-edge recommendations and it has far surpassed my expectations.

It is such a great tool that we use it for VS Code as well as the whole JetBrains product suite.

Let us look at some of their characteristics:

- Code completion is insane.

- Capability to learn from one's own and one's team's projects.

- Users have the option of running models locally or receiving cloud completions, in which case the developer's code is encrypted and instantly removed.

- The models are built using open-source programming.

- There are no licensing difficulties.

- There are free and premium versions.

Download from: https://tabnine.com/

Download Page of Tabnine

WHAT EXACTLY IS 'VANILLA JAVASCRIPT'?

The phrase vanilla script refers to pure JavaScript (or simple JavaScript) that does not include any other libraries.

It was often used as a joke that 'nowadays various things may also be done without the usage of any extra JavaScript libraries.'

One of its lightest frameworks ever made is the vanilla script. It's quite easy to use and comprehend, and it's also very straightforward.[8]

Using the vanilla script, you may construct big and influential apps as well as websites. The individuals who developed vanilla JavaScript are always striving to enhance it and make it more helpful for web developers.

Let's look at some of the most prominent websites using simple JavaScript right now:

The websites listed below are presently utilizing vanilla JavaScript, and they are also mentioned on the vanilla JavaScript home page.

- Google
- Facebook
- Yahoo
- Wikipedia
- YouTube
- Twitter
- Apple
- Amazon
- LinkedIn
- MSN
- Windows Live
- eBay
- Microsoft
- Tumblr
- Pinterest
- Netflix

- PayPal

- Reddit

- Stack Overflow

Most people may also find it difficult to accept that the number of websites that use vanilla JavaScript is much more than the number of websites that utilize JQuery.

Why Should We Learn Pure JS?

This is a typical issue among beginners: why should they learn and utilize vanilla Js when there are so many other sophisticated frameworks and packages available?

We intend to study and use vanilla js for our projects for a variety of reasons.

The three biggest and most essential of them are discussed below.

Website Performance

Because it is the most costly and critical portion of the frontend stack, this is far better for web performance than many other frameworks and tools. Unlike HTML and CSS files, which are only accessible when downloaded, vanilla js code must be built and processed. A 50kb js file has a considerably greater influence on web speed than the same size HTML and CSS files.

User Interface

It offers a simple yet user-friendly development experience. A developer may begin building an application or website using JavaScript by simply opening a text editor. There is no need for the developer to undertake time-consuming tasks such as npm install, compilation processes, and no build, among others.

It also Makes Working with Frameworks Simpler

If a developer still wants to utilize one of the other frameworks, this makes working with them more pleasant. As we are all aware, getting started with a framework is difficult. The documentation has a lot of assumed knowledge, and knowing how all accessible tools function makes it much simpler to learn.

Many newcomers with minimal understanding attempt to study a framework; no surprise, they get stopped someplace and eventually stop concentrating on the basics of Vanilla js.

When they are comfortable, they begin studying frameworks again, and this time they learn considerably faster. Other significant benefits of the vanilla script include:

- **Interoperability:** We can inject JavaScript into any of the web pages, but not in another programming language. Consider PHP. We may also use it in a variety of applications because it supports other languages such as PHP and Pearl, among others.

- **Server Load:** Load on the server. Because we all know that JavaScript is executed on the client side, it minimizes the total need for server utilization. Furthermore, the basic program does not require any interaction from the server.

- **Rich user interfaces:** We can use JavaScript to construct high-quality features like drag-and-drop and components like a slider. This can have a good influence on the user experience on the website.

- **Speed:** Because it is executed on the client side and does not require any external resources, its speed is great. Calls to a backend server have no effect on the performance of JavaScript.

Vanilla Script's Disadvantages

- One of the most fundamental downsides of vanilla script is client-side security, since we all know that JavaScript code is readable on the client. As a result, anybody with the ability to change it may use it as a weapon or tool for nefarious reasons.

- Another significant drawback of JavaScript is the absence of a Debugging Facility.

- We can't utilize it for network-based apps since there isn't any such support.

- The vanilla script also lacks certain features, such as multiprocessors and multithreading.

- It also prohibits reading and writing data for security reasons.

HELLO WORLD PROGRAM IN JAVASCRIPT

In this example, we will learn three alternative methods to print 'Hello World' in JavaScript.

A 'Hello, World!' program is a basic program that prints the phrase "Hello, World!" on the screen.[9]

Because it is a fairly basic program, it is often used to teach newbies a new programming language.

We'll print 'Hello, World!' in three different ways.

- console.log()

- alert()

- document.write()

1. **Using console.log()**
   The console.log() function is used to debug the code.
   Code:

```
// program of hello world
console.log('Hello World!');
```

2. **Using alert()**
   The alert() function displays an alert box with the supplied message over the current window.
   Code:

```
// program of hello world
alert("Hello, World!");
```

3. **Using document.write()**
   When we wish to print information to an HTML document, we use document.write().

```
// program of hello world
document.write('Hello, World!');
```

SYNTAX OF JAVASCRIPT

JavaScript may be applied by placing JavaScript statements inside <script>... </script> HTML tags on a web page.

We may insert the <script> tags containing our JavaScript wherever on our web page, although it is usually best to keep it inside the <head> tags.

The <script> tag instructs the browser to begin reading any content between these tags as a script.

The following is a basic syntax for our JavaScript.

```
<script ...>
 code
</script>
```

The script tag requires two critical attributes.

- **Language:** This element defines the scripting language that is being used. Its value is often JavaScript. Despite the fact that subsequent versions of HTML (and its successor, XHTML) have phased out the usage of this feature.

- **Type:** The value of type is now recommended to be "text/javascript" to indicate the scripting language being used.

As a result, our JavaScript portion will look like this:

```
<script language = "javascript" type = "text/
javascript">
    JavaScript-code
 </script>
```

OUR FIRST JAVASCRIPT CODE

Let's try printing "Hello Everyone" as an example. We included an optional HTML comment around our JavaScript code. This is done to protect our code from browsers that do not support JavaScript.[10]

The remark concludes with "//-->" Because "//" represents a comment in JavaScript, we include it here to prevent a browser from seeing the end of the HTML comment as JavaScript code. Then we'll call a function document. This inserts a string into our HTML document

This function can create text, HTML, or both. Take a look at the code below.

```
<html>
   <body>
```

```
    <script language = "javascript" type = "text/
    javascript">
       <!--
          document.write("Hello Everyone")
       //-->
    </script>
  </body>
</html>
```

Line Breaks and Whitespace

JavaScript disregards spaces, tabs, and newlines in JavaScript scripts. We may freely utilize spaces, tabs, and newlines in our program, and we can style and indent it in a clean and uniform manner that makes the code simple to read and comprehend.

Semicolons Are Not Required

Simple statements in JavaScript, like those in C, C++, and Java, are usually followed by a semicolon character. JavaScript, on the other hand, permits us to eliminate this semicolon if each of our statements is on a distinct line. The following code, for example, might be written without semicolons.

```
<script language = "javascript" type = "text/
javascript">
    <!--
       var1 = 30
       var2 = 10
    //-->
  </script>
```

However, semicolons must be used when formatting in a single line, as seen below.

```
<script language = "javascript" type = "text/
javascript">
    <!--
       var1 = 30; var2 = 10;
    //-->
  </script>
```

Case Sensitivity

JavaScript is a case-sensitive programming language. This implies that all language keywords, variables, function names, and other identifiers must be entered with consistent letter capitalization.

In JavaScript, the identifiers Time and TIME will have distinct meanings. NOTE: When naming variables and functions in JavaScript, use caution.

COMMENT IN JAVASCRIPT

JavaScript comments are an effective technique to convey information. It is used to include code information, cautions, or recommendations so that the end user can easily read the code.[11] The browser's built-in JavaScript engine disregards the JavaScript comment.

Benefits of JavaScript Comments

JavaScript comments have primarily two benefits.

- To make coding more understandable, it may be used to develop the code so that the end user understands it easily.

- To prevent the needless code, it can also use to prevent the code from running. Sometimes, we add code to do a certain activity. However, the code may need to be disabled after a while. In this instance, it is preferable to utilize comments.

JavaScript Comment Types

In JavaScript, there are two kinds of comments.

- Single-line comment

- Multiline comment

Single-Line Comment in JavaScript

It is denoted by two forward slashes (//). It can be used both before and after the sentence.

Let's look at an example of a single-line comment, which is put before the statement.

```
<script>
    // It is the singleline comment
```

```
document.write("hello everyone");
</script>
```

Let's look at an example of a single-line comment, which is placed after the statement.

```
<script>
    var c=30;
    var d=10;
    var e=c+d;//It adds values of c and d variable
    document.write(e);//prints sum of 30 and 10
</script>
```

Multiline Comment in JavaScript

It may be used to add single or multiple line comments. As a result, it is more convenient.

It is symbolized as a forward slash followed by an asterisk, followed by another forward slash. As an example:

```
/* code here  */
```

It can be used before, after, or in the midst of a sentence.

```
<script>
    /* It is the multiline comment.
    It will not display */
    document.write("instance of javascript multiline
comment");
    </script>
```

VARIABLE IN JAVASCRIPT

A JavaScript variable is nothing more than the name of a storage place.[12]

Variables in JavaScript are classified into two types: local variables and global variables.

There are several guidelines to follow when declaring a JavaScript variable (also known as identifiers).

- The name begins with the letter (a-z or A-Z), underscore (_), or dollar ($) symbol.

- We can put numbers (0–9) after the initial letter, for example value1.

- Variables in JavaScript are case sensitive; therefore, x and X are different.

JavaScript Variables That Are Correct

```
var d = 20;
var _value="sonoo";
```

JavaScript Variables That Are Not Correct

```
var  321=20;
var *bb=310;
```

Variable in JavaScript Example

Let's look at a basic JavaScript variable example.

```
<script>
var c = 30;
var d = 10;
var e=c+d;
document.write(e);
</script>
```

Local Variable in JavaScript

A local variable in JavaScript is declared within a block or function. It is only available within the function or block. As an example:

```
<script>
    function cde(){
    var k=10;//local variable
    }
    </script>
```

OR

```
<script>
    If(20<15){
    var y=40;// local variable
```

```
    }
    </script>
```

The Global Variable in JavaScript

A global variable in JavaScript may be accessed from any function.

A global variable is one that is defined outside of the function or declared with the window object. As an example:

```
<script>
    var data=250;//gloabal variable
    function d(){
    document.writeln(data);
    }
    function e(){
    document.writeln(data);
    }
    d();//call JavaScript function
    e();
    </script>
```

Declaring a Global Variable in JavaScript within a Function

We must utilize the window object to define JavaScript global variables within a function. As an example:

```
window.value=70;
```

It may now be defined within any function and accessed from any function. As an example:

```
function m(){
    window.value=120;//declaring the global variable
by window object
    }
    function n(){
    alert(window.value);//accessing the global
variable from the other function
    }
```

Internals of Global Variable

When we declare a variable outside of a function, it is automatically added to the window object. We may also get to it via the window object. As an example:

```
var value=60;
function a(){
alert(window.value);//access global variable
}
```

DATA TYPES IN JAVASCRIPT

JavaScript supports many data types for storing various sorts of values. In JavaScript, there are two kinds of data types:[13]

- Primitive data type

- Non-primitive data type

JavaScript is a dynamic type language; therefore, there's no need to specify the variable's type before using it in code. To indicate the data type, we must use var here.

It may store any sort of value, such as integers, strings, and so on. As an example:

```
var a=60;//hold number
var b="Raman";//hold string
```

Primitive Data Types in JavaScript

In JavaScript, there are five basic data types. These are their names:

Data Type	Description
String	Indicates a string of characters, such as "hi."
Number	Depicts a set of numbers, e.g., 100.
Boolean	Indicates a Boolean value that can be either false or true.
Undefined	Signifies an undefined value.
Null	Represents null, that is, no value at all.

NON-PRIMITIVE DATA TYPES IN JAVASCRIPT

The following are the non-primitive data types:

Data Type	Description
Object	Represents an instance that allows us to access members.
Array	Indicates a set of values that are comparable.
RegExp	Stands for regular expression.

OPERATORS IN JAVASCRIPT

Operators in JavaScript are symbols that are employed to perform actions on operands. As an example[14]:

```
var sum=30+10;
```

The arithmetic operator + is used here, while the assignment operator = is used. In JavaScript, there are several sorts of operators.

- Arithmetic operators

- Comparison (relational) operators

- Bitwise operators

- Logical operators

- Assignment operators

- Special operators

Arithmetic Operators

To conduct arithmetic operations on the operands, arithmetic operators are employed.[15]

JavaScript arithmetic operators are the operators listed below.

Operator	Description	Example
+	Addition	20+20=40
−	Subtraction	30−10=20
*	Multiplication	20*20=400
/	Division	40/10=4
%	Modulus (remainder)	40%10=0
++	Increment	var a=20; a++; Now a=21
--	Decrement	var a=20; a--; Now a=19

Comparison Operators

The comparison operator in JavaScript compares the two operands. The following are the comparison operators:

Operator	Description	Example
==	Is equal to	20==10 = false
===	Identical (equal and of same type)	20==10 = false
!=	Not equal to	20!=10 = true
!==	Not Identical	10!==10 = false
>	Greater than	30>20 = true
>=	Greater than or equal to	30>=20 = true
<	Less than	30<20 = false
<=	Less than or equal to	30<=20 = false

Bitwise Operators

Bitwise operators apply bitwise operations to operands. The following are the bitwise operators:

Operator	Description	Example
&	Bitwise AND	(20==10 & 10==33) = false
|	Bitwise OR	(20==10 | 10==33) = false
^	Bitwise XOR	(20==10 ^ 10==33) = false
~	Bitwise NOT	(~20) = −20
@	Bitwise Left Shift	(10≪2) = 40
@	Bitwise Right Shift	(10≫2) = 2
@>	Bitwise Right Shift with Zero	(10≪>2) = 2

Logical Operators

JavaScript logical operators include the basic operators.

Operator	Description	Example
&&	Logical AND	(20==10 && 10==33) = false
||	Logical OR	(20==10 || 10==33) = false
!	Logical Not	!(20==10) = true

Assignment Operators

JavaScript assignment operators include the following operators.

Operator	Description	Example
=	Assign	20+20 = 40
+=	Add and assign	var a=20; a+=10; Now a = 30
-=	Subtract and assign	var a=10; a-=20; Now a = 10
*=	Multiply and assign	var a=20; a*=10; Now a = 200
/=	Divide and assign	var a=20; a/=2; Now a = 10
%=	Modulus and assign	var a=20; a%=2; Now a = 0

Special Operators

JavaScript special operators include the following operators.

Operator	Description
(?:)	Based on the condition, the Conditional Operator returns a value. It's similar to if-else.
,	Multiple expressions can be evaluated as a single statement using the Comma Operator.
delete	The Delete Operator removes a property from an object.
in	Operator determines if an object has the specified attribute.
instanceof	Tests to see whether the object is an instance of the provided type makes an instance (object) checks the object's type.
new	It ignores the return value of the expression.
typeof	Validates what the generator's iterator returns in a generator.
void	Based on the condition, the Conditional Operator returns a value. It's similar to if-else.
yield	Multiple expressions can be evaluated as a single statement using the Comma Operator.

IF-ELSE STATEMENTS IN JAVASCRIPT

The if-else statement in JavaScript is used to run code whether the condition is true or false.

In JavaScript, there are three types of if statements:[16]

- If Statement
- If else statement
- If else if statement

If Statement

It only analyses the content if the expression is true. The JavaScript if statement's signature is shown below.

```
if(expression){
//content to evaluate
}
```

Flowchart:

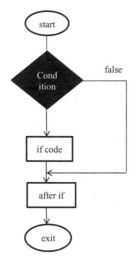

Statement of if

Let's look at a basic if statement in JavaScript.

```
<script>
var a=40;
if(a>20){
document.write("The value of a is greater than 20");
}
</script>
```

If...else Statement

It determines if the condition is true or false. The syntax of the if-else statement in JavaScript is shown below.[17]

```
if(expression){
    //content to evaluate if the condition is true
    }
    else{
    //content to evaluate if the condition is false
    }
```

Flowchart:

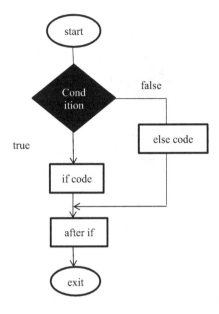

Statement of if-else

Let's look at an example of an if-else statement in JavaScript to determine if a number is even or odd.

```
<script>
var d=40;
if(d%2==0){
document.write("d is even number");
}
else{
document.write("d is odd number");
}
</script>
```

If...else if Statement

It only analyses the content if one of multiple expressions is true. The JavaScript if else if statement's signature is shown below.

```
if(expression1){
```

```
//content to evaluate if the expression1 is true
}
else if(expression2){
//content to evaluate if the expression2 is true
}
else if(expression3){
//content to evaluate if the expression3 is true
}
else{
//content to evaluate if no expression is true
}
```

Flowchart:

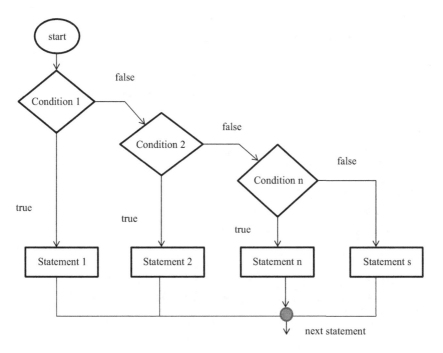

Statement of if-else-if

Let's look at a basic if-else-if expression in JavaScript.

```
<script>
var d=40;
if(d==20){
```

```
document.write("d is equal to 10");
}
else if(a==25){
document.write("d is equal to 15");
}
else if(a==40){
document.write("d is equal to 20");
}
else{
document.write("d is not equal to 20, 25 or 40");
}
</script>
```

SWITCH IN JAVASCRIPT

The JavaScript switch statement is used to perform a single piece of code from a collection of expressions. It is the same as the else if statement that we studied on the previous page. However, it is more handy than if...else... if since it may be used with integers, characters, and so on.[18]

The JavaScript switch statement's signature is shown below.

```
switch(expression){
    case value1:
     code to execute;
     break;
    case value2:
     code to execute;
     break;
    ......

    default:
     code to execute if the above values are not
matched;
    }
```

Let's look at a basic switch statement in JavaScript.[19]

```
<script>
var grade='B';
var result;
switch(grade){
```

```
case 'A':
result="Grade A";
break;
case 'B':
result="Grade B";
break;
case 'C':
result="Grade C";
break;
default:
result="No Grade";
}
document.write(result);
</script>
```

Let's look at how the switch statement works in JavaScript.

```
<script>
var grade='B';
var result;
switch(grade){
case 'A':
result+="Grade A";
case 'B':
result+="Grade B";
case 'C':
result+="Grade C";
default:
result+=" No Grade";
}
document.write(result);
</script>
```

LOOPS IN JAVASCRIPT

JavaScript loops are used to repeat code using for, while, do-while, and for-in loops.

It makes the code smaller. It is most often used in arrays.[20]

In JavaScript, there are four kinds of loops:

- for loop
- while loop

- do-while loop

- for-in loop

for loop

The JavaScript for loop loops over the components a certain number of times.

If the number of iterations is known, it should be utilized. The syntax for the for loop is shown below.

```
for (initialization; condition; increment)
{
    code to execute
}
```

Let's look at a simple for loop in JavaScript.

```
<script>
for (x=1; x<=5; x++)
{
document.write(6 + "<br/>")
}
</script>
```

while loop

The JavaScript while loop iterates over the components indefinitely.

When the expected number of iterations is uncertain, this method should be used. The while loop syntax is seen below.

```
while (condition)
{
    code to execute
}
```

Let's look at a simple while loop in JavaScript.

```
<script>
    var x=12;
    while (x<=16)
    {
    document.write(x + "<br/>");
```

```
x++;
}
</script>
```

do-while loop

The JavaScript do-while loop, like the while loop, iterates the items indefinitely.

Regardless of whether the condition is true or not, the code is performed at least once. The following code demonstrates the do-while loop syntax.

```
do{
    code to execute
}while (condition);
```

Let's look at a basic do-while loop in JavaScript example.

```
<script>
var x=22;
do{
document.write(x + "<br/>");
x++;
}while (x<=26);
</script>
```

for-in loop

The JavaScript for-in loop is used to iterate through an object's attributes. It consists of three crucial components:

- The loop initialization, in which we set our counter to a beginning value. Before the loop starts, the initialization statement is performed.[21]

- The test statement determines whether or not a particular condition is true. If the condition is met, the code contained inside the loop will be performed; otherwise, the control will exit the loop.

- The iteration statement, which allows us to raise or decrease the counter.

- All three components may be presented on a single line, separated by semicolons.

```
for (initialization; test condition; iteration
statement) {
    Statement(s) to execute if the test condition is true
}
```

To discover how a for loop works in JavaScript, try a simple example.

```
<html>
    <body>
        <script type = "text/javascript">
            <!--
                var count;
                document.write("Start Loop" + "<br />");

                for(count = 0; count < 10; count++) {
                    document.write("The Current Count : " +
                    count );
                    document.write("<br />");
                }
                document.write("Loop stop!");
            //-->
        </script>
        <p>Set variable to a different value and then
try</p>
    </body>
</html>
```

FUNCTIONS IN JAVASCRIPT

JavaScript functions are used to do out tasks. To reuse the code, we may call the JavaScript method many times.

The Benefit of the JavaScript Function

JavaScript functions have primarily two benefits:

- Code reusability: We may invoke a function several times to save coding time.

- Less coding: This reduces the size of our software. We don't need to write a lot of code every time we do the same thing.

Syntax of JavaScript Functions

The syntax for defining a function is as follows.

```
function function_Name([arg1, arg2, ...argN]){
    //code to execute
    }
```

JavaScript functions may take zero or more parameters.

Let's look at a basic JavaScript function that doesn't take any parameters.

```
<script>
    function msg(){
    alert("hey this is my message");
    }
    </script>
    <input type="button" onclick="msg()" value="call
    function"/>
```

Function Arguments

Functions may be called by giving parameters. Let's look at an example of a function with just one parameter.

```
<script>
    function getcube(numb){
    alert(number*numb*numb);
    }
    </script>
    <form>
    <input type="button" value="click"
onclick="getcube(4)"/>
    </form>
```

Function with Return Value

We may utilize a function that returns a value in our application. Let us look at an example of a function that returns a value.

```
<script>
```

```
function getInfo(){
return "hey everyone How are you?";
}
</script>
<script>
document.write(getInfo());
</script>
```

Function Object

The function constructor's purpose in JavaScript is to build a new Function object.

It runs the code on a global scale.

However, if we directly use the constructor, a function is built dynamically but in an insecure manner.

Syntax:

```
new Function ([arg_1[, arg_2[, ....arg_n]],]
functionBody)
```

Parameter

- **arg_1, arg_2,..., arg_n:** It represents the function parameter.

- **functionBody:** This is the definition of the function.

Function Methods

Method	Description
apply()	It is used to invoke a function that takes this value as well as a single array of arguments.
bind()	It is used to implement a new function.
call()	It is used to invoke a function that takes this value and a list of arguments.
toString()	It gives us the result as a string.

Let's look at function methods and their descriptions.

Examples of JavaScript Function Objects

Example 1

Let's look at an example of displaying the total of two integers.

```
<script>
```

```
var add=new Function("numb1","numb2","return
numb1+numb2");
document.writeln(add(12,7));
</script>
```

Example 2

Let's look at an example to demonstrate the strength of offered value.

```
<script>
var pow=new Function("numb1","numb2","return Math.
pow(numb1,numb2)");
document.writeln(pow(21,4));
</script>
```

OBJECTS IN JAVASCRIPT

A JavaScript object is a stateful entity with behavior (properties and method), for example, a vehicle, a pen, a bicycle, a chair, a glass, a keyboard, and a monitor.

JavaScript is an object-oriented programming language. In JavaScript, everything is an object. JavaScript is template-based rather than class-based.[22] We don't construct a class to retrieve the object here. However, we guide the creation of things.

Object Creation in JavaScript

Objects may be created in three ways.

- By object literal.

- By generating instance of Object directly (using the new keyword).

- By making use of an Object constructor (using the new keyword).

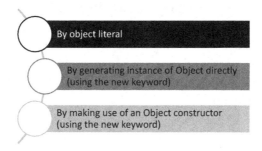

Object Creation in JavaScript

1. **Object by object literal**

    The syntax for constructing an object using an object literal is as follows:

    ```
    object={property1:value_1,property2:value_2.....
    propertyN:value_N}
    ```

    As we can see, property and value are distinguished by : (colon). Let's look at a basic example of object creation in JavaScript.

    ```
    <script>
    emp={id:113,name:"Shiva Kishan",salary:45000}
    document.write(emp.id+" "+emp.name+" "+emp.salary);
    </script>
    ```

2. **By generating an Object instance**

    The syntax for generating an object directly is as follows:

    ```
    var object_name=new Object();
    ```

    The new keyword is used to construct the object in this case. Let's look at an example of directly constructing an object.

    ```
    <script>
    var emp=new Object();
    emp.id=107;
    emp.name="Rita Kaur";
    emp.salary=52000;
    document.write(emp.id+" "+emp.name+" "+emp.salary);
    </script>
    ```

3. **By making use of an Object constructor**

    We must construct a function with parameters here. This keyword may be used to assign each parameter value to the current object.

    The keyword this relates to the current object.

    The following example shows how to create an object using an object constructor.

    ```
    <script>
    function emp(id,name,salary){
    this.id=id;
    ```

```
this.name=name;
this.salary=salary;
}
e=new emp(105,"Vinay Sharma",33000);

document.write(e.id+" "+e.name+" "+e.salary);
</script>
```

Creating a Method in a JavaScript Object

In a JavaScript object, we may specify methods. However, before we define method, we must add a property in the function with the same name as method. The following is an example of defining a method in an object.

```
<script>
function emp(id,name,salary){
this.id=id;
this.name=name;
this.salary=salary;

this.change_Salary=change_Salary;
function change_Salary(other_Salary){
this.salary=other_Salary;
}
}
e=new emp(102,"Suraj Garewal",39000);
document.write(e.id+" "+e.name+" "+e.salary);
e.changeSalary(41000);
document.write("<br>"+e.id+" "+e.name+" "+e.salary);
</script>
```

Object Methods in JavaScript

Object's numerous methods are as follows:

S.No	Methods	Description
1	Object.assign()	Enumerable and own properties are transferred from a source object to a destination object using this method.
2	Object.create()	This function is used to generate a new object using the prototype object and properties given.
3	Object.defineProperty()	This approach is used to characterize some of the property's behavioral characteristics.

(Continued)

S.No	Methods	Description
4	Object.defineProperties()	Multiple object attributes can be created or configured using this technique.
5	Object.entries()	This function returns an array containing arrays of key-value pairs.
6	Object.freeze()	This strategy avoids the removal of existing properties.
7	Object.getOwnPropertyDescriptor()	This function returns a property descriptor for the given object's property.
8	Object.getOwnPropertyDescriptors()	This function retrieves all of an object's own property descriptors.
9	Object.getOwnPropertyNames()	This function produces an array of all properties discovered (enumerable or not).
10	Object.getOwnPropertySymbols()	This function produces an array containing all of our own symbol key attributes.
11	Object.getPrototypeOf()	The prototype of the given object is returned by this method.
12	Object.is()	This function compares two values to see if they are the same.
13	Object.isExtensible()	This method detects whether or not an object is extendable.
14	Object.isFrozen()	This method detects whether or not an item was frozen.
15	Object.isSealed()	This method detects whether or not an item is sealed.
16	Object.keys()	This function returns an array containing the names of the properties of the supplied object.
17	Object.preventExtensions()	This technique is used to prohibit an object from extending.
18	Object.seal()	This approach disables the addition of new properties and labels all current properties as non-configurable.
19	Object.setPrototypeOf()	This function assigns the prototype of one object to another.
20	Object.values()	This method returns a value array.

ARRAY IN JAVASCRIPT

An object that represents a group of identical objects in JavaScript is called an array.

In JavaScript, there are three methods to create an array.[23]

• By array literal.

- By explicitly generating an Array instance (using new keyword).

- By making use of an Array constructor (using new keyword).

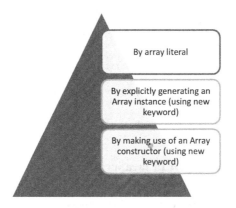

Array in JavaScript

1. Array literal in JavaScript

The syntax for building an array using an array literal is as follows:

```
var arrayname=[value_1,value_2.....value_N];
```

As we can see, values are enclosed by [] and separated by, (comma).

Let's look at a basic example of constructing and utilizing an array in JavaScript.

```
<script>
var emp=["Simran","Vijay","Rajat"];
for (x=0;x<emp.length;x++){
document.write(emp[x] + "<br/>");
}
</script>
```

The .length attribute returns the array's length.

2. Array directly in JavaScript (new keyword)

The syntax for constructing an array directly is as follows:

```
var array_name=new Array();
```

In this case, the new keyword is used to construct an array object. Let's look at an example of directly generating an array.

```
<script>
var x;
var emp = new Array();
emp[0] = "Ajay";
emp[1] = "Vinay";
emp[2] = "Johny";

for (x=0;x<emp.length;x++){
document.write(emp[x] + "<br>");
}
</script>
```

3. The array constructor in JavaScript (new keyword)

We must build an array instance by providing parameters to the constructor so that we do not have to specify a value manually.

The following is an example of object creation using an array constructor.

```
<script>
var emp=new Array("Jaya","Vinay","Simran");
for (x=0;x<emp.length;x++){
document.write(emp[x] + "<br>");
}
</script>
```

Array Methods in JavaScript

Let's go through the JavaScript array methods and their descriptions.

Methods	Description
concat()	It creates a new array object from two or more merged arrays.
copywithin()	It replaces the provided array's elements with its own and returns the transformed array.
entries()	It generates an iterator object and a loop that loops through each key/value pair.
every()	It checks if all of the items of an array fulfill the function criteria.
flat()	It generates a new array with sub-array entries concatenated recursively until the desired depth is reached.
flatMap()	It uses a mapping function to map all array items, then flattens the result into a new array.
fill()	It populates an array with static values.

(Continued)

Methods	Description
from()	It generates a new array containing an identical duplicate of another array element.
filter()	It returns a new array containing the entries that satisfy the function's requirements.
find()	It returns the value of the first array element that meets the provided criterion.
findIndex()	It returns the index of the first member in the provided array that meets the criterion.
forEach()	It calls the specified method once for each array element.
includes()	It determines whether the provided element is present in the provided array.
indexOf()	It searches the provided array for the specified element and provides the index of the first match.
isArray()	It determines whether the provided value is an array.
join()	It creates a string by joining the members in an array.
keys()	It constructs an iterator object that just includes the array keys, then loops through these keys.
lastIndexOf()	It returns the value of the first array element that meets the provided criterion.
map()	It executes the supplied function on each array element and returns the new array.
of()	It generates a new array from a configurable number of parameters, which can be of any type.
pop()	It removes and returns the array's final element.
push()	It appends one or more array elements to the end.
reverse()	It flips the items of the provided array.
reduce(function, initial)	It runs the specified function for each value in the array from left to right, reducing the array to a single value.
reduceRight()	It runs the specified function for each value in the array from right to left, reducing the array to a single value.
some()	It determines if any member of the array satisfies the implemented function's test.
shift()	It removes and returns the array's first member.
slice()	It returns a new array containing a duplicate of the specified array's portion.
sort()	It returns the sorted elements of the provided array.
splice()	It adds and removes elements from the specified array.
toLocaleString()	It returns a string containing all of the members in the array supplied.
toString()	It translates the items of a given array into string form while leaving the original array alone.
unshift()	It inserts one or more elements at the start of the provided array.
values()	It generates a new iterator object with values for each array index.

STRING IN JAVASCRIPT

A string in JavaScript is an object that represents a series of characters.[24] In JavaScript, there are two methods for creating strings.

- Using a string literal

- Using a string object (using new keyword)

1. **Using a string literal**

    Double quotes are used to construct the string literal. The syntax for constructing a string using a string literal is as follows:

```
var string_name="string_value";
<script>
var str="This is the string literal";
document.write(str);
</script>
```

2. **Using a string object (using new keyword)**

    The new keyword's syntax for creating a string object is as follows:

```
var string_name=new String("string_literal");
```

    In this case, the new keyword is used to construct a string instance. Let's take a look at a JavaScript string that was formed using the new keyword.

```
<script>
var stringname=new String("hey everyone");
document.write(stringname);
</script>
```

String Methods in JavaScript

Let's go over the examples for the JavaScript string methods.

Methods	Description
charAt()	The char value located at the specified index is returned.
charCodeAt()	It provides the character's Unicode value at the specified index.
concat()	It allows us to combine two or more strings.
indexOf()	It gives the position of a char value inside the given string as a response.
lastIndexOf()	It provides the location of a char value inside the given string by returning the results of its search starting from the last position.
search()	It searches a provided text for a specified regular expression and, if a match is discovered, returns its location.
match()	If a match is discovered, it checks a given text for a specified regular expression and returns that regular expression.
replace()	It substitutes the provided string with the given string.
substr()	Based on the specified beginning position and length.
, i	It is used to obtain a portion of the given string. substring() Based on the specified index
, i	It is used to get a section of the given text. slice() We may use it to get a section of the given string. We can provide both positive and negative indices thanks to it.
toLowerCase()	It lowercases the string that is sent to it.
toLocaleLowerCase()	It transforms the provided string to lowercase letters based on the current locale of the host.
toUpperCase()	It changes the string to uppercase letters.
toLocaleUpperCase()	It turns the provided text to an uppercase letter based on the host's current locale.
toString()	A string that represents the particular object is returned.
valueOf()	It returns the string object's primitive value.
split()	It creates substring arrays from a string and then returns the resultant array.
trim()	It removes the white space from the string's left and right sides.

1. String charAt(index) Method in JavaScript

The charAt() function of the JavaScript String returns the character at the specified index.

```
<script>
var str="heyeveryone";
```

```
document.write(str.charAt(2));
</script>
```

2. **JavaScript String concat(str) (Method)**

The String concat(str) method in JavaScript concatenates or unites two strings.

```
<script>
var st1="heyeveryone ";
var st2="concat example";
var st3=st1.concat(st2);
document.write(st3);
</script>
```

3. **String indexOf(str) Method in JavaScript**

The JavaScript String indexOf(str) function returns the string's index position.

```
<script>
var st1="hey from eveyrone indexof";
var n=st1.indexOf("from");
document.write(n);
</script>
```

4. **Method JavaScript String lastIndexOf(str)**

The JavaScript String lastIndexOf(str) function returns the string's last index point.

```
<script>
var st1="everybody from eveyrone indexof";
var n=st1.lastIndexOf("every");
document.write(n);
</script>
```

5. **The toLowerCase() method in JavaScript**

The String toLowerCase() function in JavaScript returns the provided string in lowercase characters.

```
<script>
var st1="JavaScript toLowerCase Instance";
var st2=st1.toLowerCase();
```

```
document.write(st2);
</script>
```

6. The toUpperCase() method in JavaScript

The String toUpperCase() function in JavaScript returns the provided string in uppercase characters.

```
<script>
var st1="JavaScript toUpperCase Inatnce";
var st2=st1.toUpperCase();
document.write(st2);
</script>
```

7. String slice(beginIndex, endIndex) Method in JavaScript

The String slice(beginIndex, endIndex) function in JavaScript returns the sections of a string from beginIndex to endIndex. The beginIndex is inclusive and endIndex is exclusive in the slice() function.

```
<script>
var st1="abcdefgh";
var st2=st1.slice(3,6);
document.write(st2);
</script>
```

8. String trim() Method in JavaScript

The JavaScript String trim() function eliminates whitespace from the beginning and end of a string.

```
<script>
var st1="    javascript trim    ";
var st2=st1.trim();
document.write(st2);
</script>
```

9. String split() method in JavaScript

```
<script>
var str="This is the JavaScript website";
document.write(str.split(" ")); //splits given
string.
</script>
```

DATE OBJECT IN JAVASCRIPT

We may use the JavaScript date object to retrieve the year, month, and day. The JavaScript date object may be used to show a timer on a website.

To generate a date object, we may utilize several Date[25] constructors. It includes methods for retrieving and setting the day, month, year, hour, minute, and seconds.

Constructor

To build a date object, we may use one of four Date constructor variants.

- Date()

- Date(milliseconds)

- Date(dateString)

- Date (year, month, day, hours, minutes, milliseconds, seconds)

Date Methods in JavaScript

Let's go through the JavaScript date methods and their descriptions.

Methods	Description
getDate()	It generates an integer number, ranging from 1 to 31, which represents the day for the specified date and time in local time.
getDay()	It produces an integer number between 0 and 6 that reflects the weekday based on local time.
getFullYears()	It returns the integer number representing the year in local time.
getHours()	It produces an integer number between 0 and 23 representing the hours in local time.
getMilliseconds()	It returns an integer number between 0 and 999 representing milliseconds in local time.
getMinutes()	It produces an integer number between 0 and 59 representing the minutes in local time.
getMonth()	It actually gives an integer value between 0 and 11 that, based on local time, reflects the month.
getSeconds()	It produces an integer number between 0 and 60 representing the seconds in local time.
getUTCDate()	It produces an integer number between 1 and 31 representing the day for the given date in universal time.
getUTCDay()	It generates an integer number, ranging from 0 to 6, which corresponds to the day of the week in universal time.

(Continued)

Methods	Description
getUTCFullYears()	It returns the integer number representing the year in universal time.
getUTCHours()	It returns an integer number between 0 and 23 representing the hours based on universal time.
getUTCMinutes()	It produces an integer number between 0 and 59 representing the minutes in universal time.
getUTCMonth()	It produces an integer number between 0 and 11 representing the month in universal time.
getUTCSeconds()	It returns an integer number between 0 and 60 representing the seconds in universal time.
setDate()	It determines the day value for the given date using local time.
setDay()	It determines the specific day of the week based on local time.
setFullYears()	It determines the year value for the given date using local time.
setHours()	It determines the hour value for the given date using local time.
setMilliseconds()	It determines the millisecond value for the given date using local time.
setMinutes()	It determines the minute value for the given date using local time.
setMonth()	It determines the month value for the given date using local time.
setSeconds()	It determines the second value for the given date based on local time.
setUTCDate()	It determines the day value for the given date using universal time.
setUTCDay()	It establishes the specific day of the week based on universal time.
setUTCFullYears()	It determines the year value for the given date using universal time.
setUTCHours()	It determines the hour value for the given date using universal time.
setUTCMilliseconds()	It computes the millisecond value for the given date using universal time.
setUTCMinutes()	Minute values for the given date are calculated using UTC.
setUTCMonth()	It determines the month value for the given date using universal time.
setUTCSeconds()	It determines the second value for the given date using universal time.
toDateString()	It returns a Date object's date component.
toISOString()	It returns the date in ISO standard string form.
toJSON()	It returns a string containing the Date object's representation. During JSON serialization, it also serializes the Date object.
toString()	It returns a string representation of the date.
toTimeString()	It gives us the time component of a Date object.
toUTCString()	The input date is converted to a string representing UTC time.
valueOf()	It returns a Date object's basic value.

Date Example in JavaScript

Let's look at a simple example of printing a date object. It publishes both the date and the time.

```
Current Date and Time: <span id="text"></span>
<script>
var today=new Date();
document.getElementById('text').innerHTML=today;
</script>
```

Let's look at another code to print the date, month, and year.

```
<script>
    var date=new Date();
    var day=date.getDate();
    var month=date.getMonth()+1;
    var year=date.getFullYear();
    document.write("<br>The Date is:
"+day+"/"+month+"/"+year);
    </script>
```

Example of JavaScript Current Time

Let's look at a basic example of printing the system's current time.

```
Current Time: <span id="text"></span>
<script>
var today=new Date();
var h=today.getHours();
var m=today.getMinutes();
var s=today.getSeconds();
document.getElementById('text').
innerHTML=h+":"+m+":"+s;
</script>
```

Example of a JavaScript Digital Clock

Let's look at a basic example of displaying a digital clock using a JavaScript date object.

In JavaScript, we may specify intervals using either the setTimeout() or setInterval() methods.

```
Current Time: <span id="text"></span>
<script>
window.onload=function(){getTime();}
```

```
function getTime(){
var today=new Date();
var h=today.getHours();
var m=today.getMinutes();
var s=today.getSeconds();
// add zero in the front of numbers<10
m=checkTime(m);
s=checkTime(s);
document.getElementById('text').
innerHTML=h+":"+m+":"+s;
setTimeout(function(){getTime()},1200);
}
//setInterval("getTime()",1000);//another way
function checkTime(i){
if (x<10){
  x="0" + x;
  }
return x;
}
</script>
```

MATH IN JAVASCRIPT

The JavaScript math object has a number of constants and methods for performing mathematical operations.[26] It does not have constructors, unlike the date object.

Math Methods

Let's go through the JavaScript math methods and their descriptions.[27]

Methods	Description
abs()	It gives the absolute value of the number provided.
acos()	The arccosine of the provided integer in radians is returned.
asin()	It computes the arcsine of the provided number in radians and returns it.
atan()	It returns the arc-tangent in radians of the provided integer.
cbrt()	It returns the cube root of the integer supplied.
ceil()	The function returns the smallest integer greater than or equal to the given parameter.
cos()	It returns the cosine of the number provided.
cosh()	The hyperbolic cosine of the provided integer is returned.

(Continued)

Methods	Description
exp()	It returns the provided number's exponential form.
floor()	The largest integer that is less than or equal to the given value is returned.
hypot()	It gives back the cube root of the sum of the squares of the given numbers.
log()	It computes the natural logarithm of a number.
max()	It returns the greatest possible value of the provided numbers.
min()	It returns the smallest of the provided numbers.
pow()	It returns the value of the base multiplied by the power of the exponent.
random()	It returns a random number between 0 (inclusive) and 1 (exclusive) (exclusive).
round()	It returns the integer value that is closest to the specified number.
sign()	It returns the sign of the number provided.
sin()	It returns the sine of the number provided.
sinh()	The hyperbolic sine of the provided integer is returned.
sqrt()	It computes the square root of the input number.
tan()	It returns the tangent of the integer provided.
tanh()	The hyperbolic tangent of the supplied integer is returned.
trunc()	It gives back an integer portion of the provided number.

Math.sqrt(n)

The math.sqrt(n) function in JavaScript returns the square root of the provided integer.

```
The Square Root of 14 is: <span id="p1"></span>
<script>
document.getElementById('p1').innerHTML=Math.sqrt(14);

</script>
```

Math.random()

The math.random() function in JavaScript provides a random integer between 0 and 1.

```
The Random Number is: <span id="p2"></span>
<script>
document.getElementById('p2').innerHTML=Math.random();
</script>
```

Math.pow(m, n)

The JavaScript math.pow(m, n) function returns m^n, which is m to the power of n.

```
5 to the power of 2 is: <span id="p3"></span>
<script>
document.getElementById('p3').innerHTML=Math.pow(5,2);
</script>
```

Math.floor(n)

The math.floor(n) function in JavaScript delivers the lowest integer for the supplied value.

For example, 3 for 3.7, 5 for 5.9, and so on.

```
The Floor of 5.2 is: <span id="p4"></span>
<script>
document.getElementById('p4').innerHTML=Math.
floor(5.2);
</script>
```

Math.ceil(n)

The math.ceil(n) function in JavaScript gives the biggest integer for the supplied number.

For example, 4 for 3.7, 6 for 5.9, and so on.

```
The Ceil of 5.2 is: <span id="p5"></span>
<script>
document.getElementById('p5').innerHTML=Math.
ceil(5.2);
</script>
```

Math.round(n)

The JavaScript calculation. The round(n) function returns the rounded integer that is closest to the provided number.

If the fractional component is equal to or larger than 0.5, the upper value 1 is used; otherwise, the lower value 0 is used. For instance, 4 for 3.7, 3 for 3.3, 6 for 5.9, and so on.

```
The Round of 5.2 is: <span id="p6"></span><br>
The Round of 5.6 is: <span id="p7"></span>
<script>
```

```
document.getElementById('p6').innerHTML=Math.
round(5.2);
document.getElementById('p7').innerHTML=Math.
round(5.6);
</script>
```

Math.abs(n)

The math.abs(n) function in JavaScript returns the absolute value of the provided integer.

For example, 4 for --4, 6.6 for -6.6, and so on.

```
The Absolute value of -6 is: <span id="p8"></span>
<script>
document.getElementById('p8').innerHTML=Math.abs(-6);
</script>
```

NUMBER OBJECT IN JAVASCRIPT

We may express a numeric value using the JavaScript number object.

It may be either integer or floating point. To represent floating-point numbers, the JavaScript number object adheres to the IEEE standard.[28]

In JavaScript, we may build a number object with the Number() constructor. As an example:

```
var nm=new Number(value);
```

If the value cannot be converted to a number, it returns NaN (Not a Number), which may be tested using the isNaN() function.

We may also directly assign a number to a variable. As an example:

```
var x=110;//integer value
var y=132.7;//floating point value
var z=14e6;//exponent value, output: 140000
var n=new Number(15);//integer value by number object
```

Number Constants in JavaScript

Check out the defined JavaScript constants for numbers.

Constant	Description
MIN_VALUE	The biggest minimum value is returned.
MAX_VALUE	The biggest maximum value is returned.
POSITIVE_INFINITY	overflow value, yields positive infinity.
NEGATIVE_INFINITY	overflow value, yields negative infinity.
NaN	reflects the value "Not a Number."

Number Methods in JavaScript

Let's go through the JavaScript number methods and their descriptions.

Methods	Description
isFinite()	It checks to see if the provided value is a finite number.
isInteger()	It checks to see if the provided number is an integer.
parseFloat()	It translates a string into a floating-point number.
parseInt()	It turns the string provided into an integer number.
toExponential()	It returns the string that represents the provided number in exponential notation.
toFixed()	It returns a string with the exact digits following a decimal point.
toPrecision()	It returns a string representing a number with the precision requested.
toString()	It returns the specified number as a string.

JAVASCRIPT BOOLEAN

A JavaScript Boolean object represents a value in one of two states: true or false.[29]

The JavaScript Boolean object may be created with the Boolean() constructor, as seen below.

```
Boolean bn=new Boolean(value);
```

The JavaScript Boolean object's default value is false.

Example of a JavaScript Boolean

```
<script>
document.write(30<40);//true
document.write(12<8);//false
</script>
```

Boolean Properties

Property	Description
constructor	The reference to the Boolean function that produced the Boolean object is returned.
prototype	allows us to include attributes and methods in a Boolean prototype.

Boolean Methods

Method	Description
toSource()	The source of the Boolean object is returned as a string.
toString()	converts a Boolean to a String.
valueOf()	converts another type to a Boolean value.

ERRORS AND EXCEPTIONS IN JAVASCRIPT

An exception denotes the occurrence of an abnormal circumstance that necessitates the use of unique operational approaches. An exception in programming is a piece of code that deviates from the regular flow of the code. Such exceptions need the use of particular programming structures in order to be executed.

What Exactly Is Exception Handling?

Exception handling is a procedure or method in programming that is used to handle and execute anomalous statements in code. It also allows you to regulate the flow of the code/program.

Various handlers that process the exception and execute the code are utilized to handle the code. For instance, dividing a non-zero number by zero always results in infinity, and this is an exception. Thus, it may be performed and managed with the aid of exception handling.

To raise an exception in exception handling, a throw statement is utilized. When an abnormal state arises, throw is used to throw an exception.

Wrapping the function in a try...catch block handles the thrown exception.

If an error occurs, the catch block is performed; otherwise, just the try block instructions are executed.

Thus, numerous forms of mistakes may occur in a programming language, interfering with the correct execution of the program.

In programming, there are three categories of errors:

a. Syntax errors.

b. Runtime errors.

c. Logical errors.

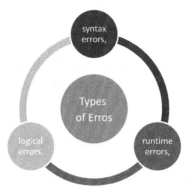

Types of errors

Errors in Syntax

Syntax mistakes, also known as parsing errors, occur during the compile process in conventional programming languages and during the interpret process in JavaScript.[30]

The following line, for instance, gives a syntax error because it lacks a closing parenthesis.

```
<script type = "text/javascript">
    <!--
        window.print(;
    //-->
 </script>
```

When a syntax error occurs in JavaScript, just the code contained inside the same thread as the syntax mistake is impacted, and the remainder of the code in other threads is run as long as it does not rely on the code containing the problem.

Runtime Errors

During execution (after compilation/interpretation), runtime errors, also known as exceptions, occur. For example, the following line results in a runtime error because, although the syntax is valid, it attempts to invoke a method that does not exist.

```
<script type = "text/javascript">
    <!--
        window.printme();
```

```
//-->
</script>
```

Exceptions also have an effect on the thread in which they occur, enabling other JavaScript threads to proceed normally.

Logical Errors

The most difficult form of mistake to locate is a logic error. These problems are not caused by syntactic or runtime issues.

They arise instead when we make a mistake in the logic that drives our script and do not obtain the desired outcome. We cannot notice such issues since the sort of logic we want to include in our software is determined by our business requirements.

Statement of try...catch...finally

The most recent JavaScript versions introduced exception handling features.

JavaScript has the try...catch...finally structure and the throw operator for handling exceptions. JavaScript syntax mistakes can be caught, but not programmer-generated or runtime exceptions. The try...catch...finally block syntax is as follows:

```
<script type = "text/javascript">
    <!--
        try {
            // Code run
            [break;]
        }

        catch ( e ) {
            // Code run if an exception occurs
            [break;]
        }

        [ finally {
            // Code that is always run regardless of
// whether or not an exception occurs
        }]
    //-->
</script>
```

Either the catch block or the finally block must come before the try block (or one of both). The catch block is executed if an exception is thrown inside the try block and is reported in the e variable. After try/catch, the optional finally block runs unconditionally.

Examples

Here's an example of attempting to call a non-existent function, which results in an exception.

Let's see how it acts without try...catch–

```
<html>
    <head>
        <script type = "text/javascript">
            <!--
                function myFunc() {
                    var k = 120;
                    alert("The Value of variable k is : " +
k );
                }
            //-->
        </script>
    </head>

    <body>
        <p>Click following to see the result:</p>

        <form>
            <input type = "button" value = "Click Here"
onclick = "myFunc();" />
        </form>
    </body>
</html>
```

Let us now utilize try...catch to capture this error and provide a user-friendly message.

If we wish to conceal this problem from a user, we may also suppress this message.

```
<html>
   <head>

      <script type = "text/javascript">
         <!--
            function myFunc() {
               var k = 120;
               try {
                  alert("Value of variable k is : " + k );
               }
               catch ( e ) {
                  alert("Error: " + e.description );
               }
            }
         //-->
      </script>

   </head>
   <body>
      <p>Click following to see the result:</p>

      <form>
         <input type = "button" value = "Click Here"
onclick = "myFunc();" />
      </form>

   </body>
</html>
```

Finally, we may use a block that will always run unconditionally after the try/catch.

Here's an illustration.

```
<html>
   <head>

      <script type = "text/javascript">
         <!--
            function myFunc() {
               var k = 120;
```

```
            try {
                alert("The Value of variable k is :
" + k );
            }
            catch ( e ) {
                alert(«Error: " + e.description );
            }
            finally {
                alert("Finally block will execute
always!" );
            }
        }
        //-->
    </script>

  </head>
  <body>
    <p>Click following to see the result:</p>

    <form>
        <input type = "button" value = "Click Here"
onclick = "myFunc();" />
    </form>

  </body>
</html>
```

The throw Statement

We may use the toss statement to raise either built-in or custom exceptions. These exceptions may later be recorded and appropriate action taken.

Example

The example below shows how to utilize a throw statement.

```
<html>
  <head>

    <script type = "text/javascript">
        <!--
```

```
            function myFunc() {
                var j = 120;
                var k = 0;

                try {
                    if ( k == 0 ) {
                        throw( "Divide by zero error." );
                    } else {
                        var m = j / k;
                    }
                }
                catch ( e ) {
                    alert("Error: " + e );
                }
            }
        //-->
    </script>

</head>
<body>
    <p>Click following to see the result:</p>

    <form>
        <input type = "button" value = "Click Here"
onclick = "myFunc();" />
    </form>

</body>
</html>
```

An exception may be thrown in one code using a string, an integer, a Boolean, or an object, and then caught in another function using a try... catch block, as we saw above.

The onerror() function

To begin handling errors, JavaScript introduced the onerror event handler. When an exception occurs on the page, the error event is dispatched on the window object.

```
<html>
    <head>
```

```
<script type = "text/javascript">
  <!--
    window.onerror = function () {
      alert("Error occurred.");
    }
  //-->
</script>

</head>
<body>
  <p>Click following to see the result:</p>

  <form>
    <input type = "button" value = "Click Here"
onclick = "myFunc();" />
  </form>

</body>
</html>
```

The onerror event handler returns three pieces of information that may be used to determine the specific nature of the error.

- **Error message:** The same message that the browser would show for the specified issue.

- **URL:** The URL of the file where the problem occurred.

- **Line number:** The line number in the provided URL that resulted in the error.

Here's an example of how to get this information.

Example

```
<html>
  <head>

    <script type = "text/javascript">
      <!--
```

```
              window.onerror = function (msg, url, line)
{
          alert("The Message : " + msg );
          alert("The url : " + url );
          alert("The Line number : " + line );
      }
    //-->
  </script>

</head>
<body>
  <p>Click following to see the result:</p>

  <form>
      <input type = "button" value = "Click Here"
onclick = "myFunc();" />
  </form>

</body>
</html>
```

We may present extracted data in whichever manner we believe is best.

We may use the onerror method to display an error message if there is a difficulty loading an image, as demonstrated below.

We may use onerror with a variety of HTML elements to show suitable error messages.

EVENTS IN JAVASCRIPT

We will discuss events in JavaScript below:

What Exactly Is an Event?

JavaScript communicates with HTML through events, which are generated in response to changes made to a page by the user or the browser. After the website loads, something happens. When the user triggers an action, also known as an event.[31]

Any keypress, window close, window resize, etc., are also considered events.

Developers may utilize these events to perform JavaScript programmed replies, such as closing buttons, displaying messages to users, validating data, and nearly any other sort of response conceivable. Events are a component of the Document Object Model (DOM) Level 3, and each HTML element has a collection of events that may be used to execute JavaScript code.

onclick Event Type

This is the most common event kind, which happens when a user hits the left mouse button.

We may apply validation, warnings, and so on to this event type.

Example

Consider the following example.

```
<html>
   <head>
      <script type = "text/javascript">
         <!--
            function sayHey() {
               alert("Hey Everyone")
            }
         //-->
      </script>
   </head>

   <body>
      <p>Click following button and see result</p>
      <form>
         <input type = "button" onclick = "sayHey()"
value = "Say Hey" />
      </form>
   </body>
</html>
```

onsubmit Event Type

When we attempt to submit a form, an event called onsubmit happens. We may use this event type for form validation.

Example

The following code demonstrates how to utilize onsubmit. Before sending form input to the website, we use the validate() method. If the validate() method returns true, the form is submitted; otherwise, the data is not submitted.

Consider the following example.

```
<html>
   <head>
      <script type = "text/javascript">
         <!--
            function validation() {
               here all validation goes
               . . . . . . . .
               return either true or false
            }
         //-->
      </script>
   </head>

   <body>
      <form method = "POST" action = "t.cgi" onsubmit
= "return validate()">
         . . . . . . .
            <input type = "submit" value = "Submit" />
      </form>
   </body>
</html>
```

onmouseover and onmouseout

These two event types will assist us in creating great effects with images or even text. When we move our mouse over an element, the onmouseover event is triggered, and when we move our mouse away from that element, the onmouseout event is triggered.

Consider the following example.

```
<html>
   <head>
      <script type = "text/javascript">
         <!--
```

```
            function over() {
                document.write ("Mouse-Over");
            }
            function out() {
                document.write ("Mouse-Out");
            }
        //-->
    </script>
</head>

<body>
    <p>Bring our mouse inside division to see the
outcome:</p>
    <div onmouseover = "over()" onmouseout =
"out()">
            <h2> This is inside division </h2>
    </div>
</body>
</html>
```

Standard HTML 5 Events

For our convenience, the standard HTML 5 events are given below. Script denotes a JavaScript function that will be performed against the event.

Attribute	Value	Description
Offline	script	When the document is offline, this event occurs.
Onabort	script	An abort event is triggered.
onafterprint	script	This event occurs after the document has been printed.
onbeforeonload	script	This event occurs before the document is loaded.
onbeforeprint	script	This event occurs before the document is printed.
onblur	script	When the window loses focus, this event occurs.
oncanplay	script	Triggers when media can begin playing but must pause for buffering.
oncanplaythrough	script	When media can be played all the way through without pausing for buffering, this event is triggered.
onchange	script	When an element changes, this triggers.
onclick	script	Triggers when the mouse is clicked.
oncontextmenu	script	When a context menu is invoked, this event is triggered.
ondblclick	script	Triggers when the mouse is double-clicked.
ondrag	script	When an element is dragged, this event occurs.

(*Continued*)

Attribute	Value	Description
ondragend	script	At the end of a drag operation, this triggers.
ondragenter	script	When an element is dragged to a proper drop target, this event is triggered.
ondragleave	script	When an element is moved over a valid drop target, this event occurs.
ondragover	script	Triggers when a drag operation begins.
ondragstart	script	Triggers when a drag operation begins.
ondrop	script	When a dragged element is dropped, this event occurs.
ondurationchange	script	When the length of the media is modified, this event occurs.
onemptied	script	When a media resource element becomes unexpectedly empty, this event is triggered.
onended	script	When the medium has reached its finish, this triggers.
onerror	script	When an error occurs, this function is triggered.
onfocus	script	When the window is focused, this event occurs.
onformchange	script	When a form changes, this event is triggered.
onforminput	script	When a form receives user input, this event is triggered.
onhaschange	script	When the document changes, this event is triggered.
oninput	script	When an element receives user input, this event is triggered.
oninvalid	script	When an element is invalid, this event is triggered.
onkeydown	script	When a key is pressed, this event occurs.
onkeypress	script	When a key is pressed and released, this event occurs.
onkeyup	script	When a key is released, this event occurs.
onload	script	When the document is loaded, this event occurs.
onloadeddata	script	When media data is loaded, this event occurs.
onloadedmetadata	script	When a media element's duration and other media data are loaded, this event occurs.
onloadstart	script	When the browser begins to load the media data, this event occurs.
onmessage	script	When the message is triggered, this function is called.
onmousedown	script	When a mouse button is pushed, this event occurs.
onmousemove	script	When the mouse cursor moves, this event is triggered.
onmouseout	script	When the mouse cursor leaves an element, this event is triggered.
onmouseover	script	When the mouse cursor passes over an element, this event is triggered.
onmouseup	script	When a mouse button is released, this event occurs.
onmousewheel	script	When the mouse wheel is turned, this event occurs.
onoffline	script	When the document is offline, this event occurs.

(Continued)

Attribute	Value	Description
onoine	script	When the document becomes online, this event occurs.
ononline	script	When the document becomes online, this event occurs.
onpagehide	script	When the window is hidden, this event occurs.
onpageshow	script	When the window becomes visible, this event occurs.
onpause	script	When media data is halted, this event occurs.
onplay	script	Triggers when media data is about to begin playing Triggers when media data has begun playing Triggers when the history of the window changes.
onplaying	script	When the browser retrieves media data, this event occurs.
onpopstate	script	Triggers when the playing rate of the media data changes. Triggers when the ready-state changes.
onprogress	script	When the document is redone, this event occurs.
onratechange	script	When the window is resized, this event occurs.
onreadystatechange	script	When an element's scrollbar is scrolled, this event is triggered.
onredo	script	When a media element's seeking property is no longer true and the seeking has stopped, this event is triggered.
onresize	script	When media data is halted, this event occurs.
onscroll	script	Triggers when media data is about to begin playing Triggers when media data has begun playing Triggers when the history of the window changes.
onseeked	script	This event happens when the browser retrieves media data.
onseeking	script	When the seeking attribute of a media element is true and the searching has begun, this event is triggered.
onselect	script	When an element is chosen, this function is triggered.
onstalled	script	When there is a mistake in retrieving media data, this event is triggered.
onstorage	script	When a document is loaded, this event is triggered.
onsubmit	script	When a form is submitted, this event occurs.
onsuspend	script	When the browser has been downloading media data but has stopped before the whole media file has been retrieved, this event is triggered.
ontimeupdate	script	When the media's playing position changes, this event occurs.
onundo	script	When a document executes an undo, this event is triggered.
onunload	script	When the user exits the document, this event occurs.
onvolumechange	script	Triggers when the volume of media is changed, as well as when the volume is set to "mute."
onwaiting	script	When media has stopped playing but is expected to restart, this event is triggered.

In this chapter, we discussed about the installation of Visual Studio Code and node js. We went through Vanilla JavaScript, Data Types and Operators, Functions, and Objects and Arrays. We also discussed Error Handling and Events.

NOTES

1 Choosing the Best JavaScript Editor From 7 Options: www.testim.io/blog/best-javascript-editor-6-options/ Accessed on: 22 September 2022.

2 How to Setup Visual Studio Code for JavaScript: https://linuxhint.com/set-up-visual-studio-code-for-javascript/#:~:text=Select%20all%20the%20options%20you,Visual%20Studio%20Code%20will%20launch Accessed on: 22 September 2022.

3 How to Install Visual Studio Code on Linux: www.tecmint.com/install-visual-studio-code-on-linux/ Accessed on: 23 September 2022.

4 Installation of Node.js on Windows: www.geeksforgeeks.org/installation-of-node-js-on-windows/ Accessed on: 22 September 2022.

5 Installation of Node.js on Linux: www.geeksforgeeks.org/installation-of-node-js-on-linux/?ref=lbp Accessed on: 22 September 2022.

6 How to Create and Run Node.js Project in VS code editor?: www.geeksforgeeks.org/how-to-create-and-run-node-js-project-in-vs-code-editor/ Accessed on: 22 September 2022.

7 The Best VS Code Extensions for JavaScript Developers: https://livecodestream.dev/post/best-vscode-extensions-for-javascript/ Accessed on: 22 September 2022.

8 What Is "Vanilla JavaScript"?: www.javatpoint.com/what-is-vanilla-javascript Accessed on: 22 September 2022.

9 JavaScript Program to Print Hello World: www.programiz.com/javascript/examples/hello-world Accessed on: 24 September 2022.

10 JavaScript—Syntax: www.tutorialspoint.com/javascript/javascript_syntax.htm Accessed on: 24 September 2022.

11 JavaScript Comment: www.javatpoint.com/javascript-comment Accessed on: 24 September 2022.

12 JavaScript Variable: www.javatpoint.com/javascript-variable Accessed on: 24 September 2022.

13 Javascript Data Types: www.javatpoint.com/javascript-data-types Accessed on: 24 September 2022.

14 JavaScript Operators: www.javatpoint.com/javascript-operators Accessed on: 24 September 2022.

15 JavaScript Operators: www.geeksforgeeks.org/javascript-operators/ Accessed on: 24 September 2022.

16 JavaScript If-else: www.javatpoint.com/javascript-if Accessed on: 24 September 2022.

17 JavaScript—if...else Statement: www.tutorialspoint.com/javascript/javascript_ifelse.htm Accessed on: 24 September 2022.

18 JavaScript Switch: www.javatpoint.com/javascript-switch Accessed on: 24 September 2022.

19 JavaScript Switch Case—JS Switch Statement Example: www.freecodecamp.org/news/javascript-switch-case-js-switch-statement-example/ Accessed on: 24 September 2022.

20 JavaScript Loops: www.javatpoint.com/javascript-loop Accessed on: 24 September 2022.

21 JavaScript—For Loop: www.tutorialspoint.com/javascript/javascript_for_loop.htm Accessed on: 24 September 2022.

22 JavaScript Objects: www.javatpoint.com/javascript-objects Accessed on: 26 September 2022.

23 JavaScript Array: www.javatpoint.com/javascript-array Accessed on: 26 September 2022.

24 JavaScript String: www.javatpoint.com/javascript-string Accessed on: 26 September 2022.

25 JavaScript Date Object: www.javatpoint.com/javascript-date Accessed on: 26 September 2022.

26 JavaScript Math: www.javatpoint.com/javascript-math Accessed on: 26 September 2022.

27 JavaScript—The Math Object: www.tutorialspoint.com/javascript/javascript_math_object.htm Accessed on: 27 September 2022.

28 JavaScript Number Object: www.javatpoint.com/javascript-number Accessed on: 27 September 2022.

29 JavaScript Boolean: www.javatpoint.com/javascript-boolean Accessed on: 27 September 2022.

30 JavaScript —Errors & Exceptions Handling: www.tutorialspoint.com/javascript/javascript_error_handling.htm Accessed on: 27 September 2022.

31 JavaScript—Events: www.tutorialspoint.com/javascript/javascript_events.htm Accessed on: 27 September 2022.

CHAPTER 3

Getting Started with JavaScript II

IN THIS CHAPTER

- ➤ Asynchronous Development

- ➤ DOM Manipulation

- ➤ HTTP and Forms

- ➤ Working with APIs

In the previous chapter, we covered Data Types and Operators, Functions, Objects and Arrays, Error Handling, Events, and in this chapter, we will discuss APIs and DOM.

HOW CAN WE BUILD AN ASYNCHRONOUS NODE.JS FUNCTION?

In Node.js, write the asynchronous function with 'async' before the function name.

As a consequence, the asynchronous method returns an implicit Promise.

The async function aids in the asynchronous execution of promise-based code through the event-loop. A value is always returned by async functions. To wait for the promise, use the await function within the asynchronous function. The function is forced to wait until the promise produces a result.[1]

Install async from npm in Node.js using the command:

```
npm i async
```

Using the require() function in our Node.js app, use async.

Example 1

Write an asynchronous function in Node.js to compute the square of an integer.

- Make a folder for our project.
- To initialize the package.json file within the project folder, run the following command.

```
npm init -y
```

- Use the following command to install async:

```
npm i async
```

- Make a server.js file and add the following code to it.
- Use npm start to execute the code.

```
var async = require("async");

function square(k) {
    return new Promise((resolve) => {
        setTimeout(() => {
            resolve(Math.pow(k, 2));
        }, 2000);
    });
}

async function output(k) {
    const ans = square(k);
    console.log(ans);
```

```
}

output(10);
var async = require("async");

function square(k) {
    return new Promise((resolve) => {
        setTimeout(() => {
            resolve(Math.pow(k, 2));
        }, 2000);
    });
}

async function output(k) {
    const ans = await square(k);
    console.log(ans);
}

output(10);
```

Example 2

Using await, write an asynchronous function to compute the sum of two integers within Node.js. To start a Node.js project, follow the steps outlined above.

```
var async = require("async");

function square(j, k) {
    return new Promise(resolve => {
        setTimeout(() => {
            resolve(j + k);
        }, 2000);
    });
}

async function output(j, k) {
    const ans = await square(j, k);
    console.log(ans);
}

output(10, 20);
```

HOW DO WE WRITE AN ASYNCHRONOUS FUNCTION IN JAVASCRIPT?

JavaScript is a synchronous, single-threaded language. The code is run one step at a time. However, in certain cases, JavaScript may seem to be asynchronous.[2]

Example

```
<!DOCTYPE html>
<html lang="en">
<head>
    <meta charset="utf-8" />
    <title></title>
</head>
<body>
    <div id="message"></div>
    <script>
        var msg = document.getElementById("message");

        function fd1() {
            setTimeout(function () {
            msg.innerHTML += "
<p>fd1 is start</p>
";
            msg.innerHTML += "
<p>fd1 is end</p>
";
            }, 100);
        }
        function fd2() {
            msg.innerHTML += "
<p>fd2 is start</p>
";
            fd1();
            msg.innerHTML += "
<p>fd2 is end</p>
";
        }

        fd2();

    </script>
```

```
</body>
</html>
```

Now, we can observe that after calling setTimeout(fd1, 100), our program does not wait for the timer to complete before proceeding to the next line.

This happens because JavaScript adds the event to the event queue and continues running the program as usual if we wish to conduct an event. The engine checks the event queue on a regular basis to determine whether an event needs to be called or not. However, we may want our code to wait until a certain event or task is done before processing more instructions.

Async, await, and promises are used to implement asynchronous functions.

- **async:** The term "async" specifies an asynchronous function.

```
Syntax
async function Function_Name(){
    ...
}
```

- **await:** The "async" function includes "await," which stops the "async" function's execution. "await" can only use inside the "async" function.

- **Promise:** A Promise is a value that acts as a proxy. It informs us about the asynchronous event's success or failure. A Promise must include a resolve() or reject() call, or otherwise the Promise's consumer would never know whether the Promise is fulfilled or not. If this occurs, the program will continue to wait for await and that code block will never be run again. There's a lot more to Promise, but we can make Asynchronous work without knowing anything about it.

Example

Let's recreate the same example using the Asynchronous function.

```
<!DOCTYPE html>
<html lang="en">
<head>
    <meta charset="utf-8" />
```

```html
    <title></title>
</head>
<body>
    <div id="message"></div>
    <script>
        var msg = document.getElementById("message");

        function fd1() {
            return new Promise(function (resolve,
reject) {
                setTimeout(function () {
                msg.innerHTML += "
<p>fd1 is start</p>
";
                    msg.innerHTML += "
<p>fd1 is end</p>
";
                    resolve();
                }, 100);
            })
        }

        async function fd2() {
            msg.innerHTML += "
<p>fd2 is start</p>
";

            // Engine waits for the fd1() to finish it's
            // execution before executing next line
            await fd1();
            msg.innerHTML += "
<p>fd2 is end</p>
";
        }

        fd2();

    </script>
</body>
</html>
```

In the preceding example, the program waits for fd1() to finish before continuing.

Until a Promise is obtained, the "await" command halts the execution of that code segment. Use resolve to fulfill the Promise (). It denotes that the Promise has been fulfilled. Similarly to resolve, we can use reject() to determine whether or not a Promise has been rejected.

We don't need to go into the reject() method right now since it's mostly used for debugging and error purposes.

Example

We can include a value in resolve if we want the Promise to return one (variable).

```
<!DOCTYPE html>
<html lang="en">
<head>
    <meta charset="utf-8" />
    <title></title>
</head>
<body>
    <div id="message"></div>
    <script>
        var msg = document.getElementById("message");

        function fd1() {
            return new Promise(function (resolve,
reject) {
                setTimeout(function () {
                msg.innerHTML += "
<p>fd1 is start</p>
";
                    msg.innerHTML += "
<p>fd1 is end</p>
";
                    resolve(1);
                }, 100);
            })
        }
```

```
        async function fd2() {
            msg.innerHTML += "
<p>fd2 is start</p>
";
                var p = await fd1();
                if (p == 1) msg.innerHTML += "
<p>Promise Received</p>
"
                msg.innerHTML += "
<p>fd2 is ending</p>
";
        }

        fd2();

    </script>
</body>
</html>
```

Waiting for Multiple Promises

What if we had to wait while a number of processes ran simultaneously? There are two methods that we can do this.

Example

We may write numerous await statements in a row.

```
<!DOCTYPE html>
<html lang="en">
<head>
    <meta charset="utf-8" />
    <title></title>
</head>
<body>
    <div id="message"></div>
    <script>
        var msg = document.getElementById("message");

        function fd1() {
            return new Promise(function (resolve, reject) {
                setTimeout(function () {
```

```
                    msg.innerHTML += "
<p>fd1 is start</p>
";
                    msg.innerHTML += "
<p>fd1 is end</p>
";
                    resolve();
                }, 1000);
            })
        }

        function fd3() {
            return new Promise(function (resolve,
reject) {
                setTimeout(function () {
                    msg.innerHTML += "
<p>fd3 is start</p>
";
                    msg.innerHTML += "
<p>fd3 is end</p>
";
                    resolve();
                }, 1000);
            })
        }

        async function fd2() {
            msg.innerHTML += "
<p>fd2 is start</p>
";
            await fd1();
            await fd3();
            msg.innerHTML += "
<p>fd2 is end</p>
";
        }

        fd2();

    </script>
</body>
</html>
```

Example

The second option to wait for several Promises is to use Promise.all to execute the Promises in parallel (iterable object).

Syntax:

```
await Promise.all(iterable object);
```

```html
<!DOCTYPE html>
<html lang="en">
<head>
    <meta charset="utf-8" />
    <title></title>
</head>
<body>
    <div id="message"></div>
    <script>
        var msg = document.getElementById("message");

        function fd1() {
            return new Promise(function (resolve,
reject) {
                setTimeout(function () {
                msg.innerHTML += "
<p>fd1 is start</p>
";
                msg.innerHTML += "
<p>fd1 is end</p>
";
                resolve();
                }, 1000);
            })
        }

        function fd3() {
            return new Promise(function (resolve,
reject) {
                setTimeout(function () {
                msg.innerHTML += "
<p>fd3 is start</p>
";
                msg.innerHTML += "
<p>fd3 is end</p>
```

```
";
                resolve();
            }, 1000);
        })
    }

    async function fd2() {
        msg.innerHTML += "
<p>fd2 is start</p>
";
        await Promise.all([fd1(), fd3()]);
        msg.innerHTML += "
<p>fd2 is end</p>
";
    }

    fd2();

    </script>
</body>
</html>
```

Synchronous and Asynchronous in JavaScript

Synchronous JavaScript

As the name implies, synchronous means in a sequence, which means that each statement of the code is performed one by one.

So, effectively, a statement must wait for the previous statement to be performed before proceeding.[3]

Let us look at an instance to better grasp this.

Example

```
<script>
    document.write("Hey"); // First
    document.write("<br>");

    document.write("Mayank") ;// Second
    document.write("<br>");

    document.write("How are you doing"); // Third
</script>
```

In the preceding code snippet, the first line of code, Hey, will be recorded first, followed by the second line, Mayank, and finally, the third line, after its completion How are you doing.

As we can see, the codes operate sequentially. Every line of code waits for the one before it to be executed before it is run.

Asynchronous JavaScript

Asynchronous code enables the program to be run instantly, but synchronous code prevents continued execution of remaining code until the current one is completed. This may not seem to be a major issue, but when seen in context, it might result in the User Interface being delayed.

Let's look at an example of how Asynchronous JavaScript works.

```
<script>
    document.write("Hey"); // First
    document.write("<br>");

    document.write("Mayank") ;// Second
    document.write("<br>");

    document.write("How are you doing"); // Third
</script>
```

In the preceding code snippet, the first line of code Hey will be logged first, followed by the second line Mayank, and finally, the third line will be recorded after its completion.

How are you doing. As we can see, the codes operate sequentially. Every line of code waits for the one before it to be executed before it is run.

Asynchronous JavaScript: Asynchronous code enables the program to be run instantly, but synchronous code prevents continued execution of remaining code until the current one is completed. This may not seem to be a major issue, but when seen in context, it might result in the User Interface being delayed.

Let's look at an example of how Asynchronous JavaScript works.

```
<script>
    document.write("Hey");
    document.write("<br>");
```

```
setTimeout(() => {
    document.write("Let's wait and see what
occurs");
    }, 1000);

    document.write("<br>");
    document.write("End");
    document.write("<br>");
</script>
```

So, instead of performing the setTimeout function, the code first logs in Hey, then End, and then executes the setTimeout function. As usual, the Hey statement was logged in first.

Because we execute JavaScript in browsers, there exist web APIs that manage these things for users. So, what JavaScript does is call the setTimeout method in such a web API, and then we continue to execute our code as normal. As a result, it does not obstruct the execution of any other code. Instead, it is pushed to the call stack and executed once all other code has finished. This is how asynchronous JavaScript works.

Explain the Difference between Asynchronous and Deferred JavaScript

In general, when we use a script element to load any JavaScript code, the browser pauses HTML processing and begins downloading the JavaScript file first.[4]

Until the browser has completely downloaded and processed the script, the HTML element's script tag will not be activated. The browser waits for the script to be downloaded and run before continuing to analyze the remainder of the page.

In current browsers, the script is often bigger than the HTML file, resulting in a greater download size and a longer processing time. This increases the page's load time and limits the user's ability to browse the website. Async and defer characteristics are used to fix this issue.

Syntax: A standard script is supplied on the page as follows.

```
<script src = "script.js"></script>
```

Asynchronous

When the HTML parser discovers this element, it sends a request to the server to get the script. If the script has to be downloaded while the page is being parsed and displayed, the async functionality will do it in the background. When the script is downloaded, the HTML parsing is halted and the script is executed. When the operation is complete, HTML parsing will restart.

The page and other scripts do not wait for async scripts, and they do not wait for them. It is ideal for both independent and externally located scripts.

Syntax:

```
<script async src = "script.js"></script>
```

Deferred

The defer property instructs the browser not to interfere with HTML processing and to only run the script file once the HTML page has been completely processed.

When a script with this attribute is discovered, the downloading of the script begins asynchronously in the background, and the scripts are only run once the HTML parsing is completed.

Syntax:

```
<script defer src = "script.js"></script>
```

Asynchronous vs Deferred

Asynchronous	Deferred
Asynchronous prevents the page from being parsed.	Deferred never obstructs the page.
Asynchronous scripts do not rely on one another. As a result, if a smaller script comes second in the list, it will be loaded before the prior lengthier script.	Deferred scripts keep their relative order, which implies that the first script will be loaded first, followed by the others.
Script execution begins with pause parsing.	However, script execution begins only after parsing is complete but before the document's DOMContentLoaded event.

DOCUMENT OBJECT MODEL

The document object is used to represent the whole HTML document.

A document object is created when an HTML file is loaded into a browser.

The html document is represented by the root element.

It has characteristics as well as methods.[5]

We may add dynamic material to our web page using the document object.

It is, as previously said, the object of window. So

```
window.document
```

is the same as

```
document
```

Across all platforms and languages, the W3C Document Object Model (DOM) provides an interface for dynamic access to and modification of a document's content, structure, and style.

Document Object Properties

Let's look at the document object's properties that may be viewed and updated.

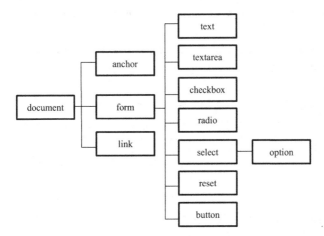

Document object properties

Document Object Methods

We may use its methods to access and modify the contents of the document. The following are the most significant document object methods:

Method	Description
write("string")	The specified string is written to the document.
writeln("string")	The specified string is written to the document, with a newline character at the conclusion.
getElementById()	The element with the specified id value is returned.
getElementsByName()	retrieves all entries with the specified name value.
getElementsByTagName()	retrieves all items with the specified tag name.
getElementsByClassName()	retrieves all entries with the specified class name.

Document Object Accessing Field Value

In this instance, we will get the value of the user's supplied text. To access the value of the name field, we use document.form1.name.value. The root element here is document, which represents the HTML document.

- form's name is form11.

- name is the name of the input text's attribute.

- the value property returns the value of the supplied text.

Let's look at a basic example of a document object that displays the user's name along with a welcome message.

```
<script type="text/javascript">
    function printvalue(){
    var name=document.form11.name.value;
    alert("Welcome here: "+name);
    }
    </script>

    <form name="form11">
    Enter Name:<input type="text" name="name"/>
    <input type="button" onclick="printvalue()"
value="print name"/>
    </form>
```

METHOD DOCUMENT.GETELEMENTBYID() IN JAVASCRIPT

The function document.getElementById() retrieves the element with the supplied id.

We used document.form1.name.value on the previous page to acquire the value of the input value. To access the value of the input text, we may use the document.getElementById() function instead. However, we must specify an id for the input field.

Let's look at a small document example.[6]

The getElementById() function returns the cube of the provided integer.

```
<script type="text/javascript">
    function getcube(){
    var numb=document.getElementById("numb").value;
    alert(numb*numb*numb);
    }
    </script>
    <form>
    Enter No:<input type="text" id="numb"
name="numb" /><br/>
    <input type="button" value="cube"
onclick="getcube()" />
    </form>
```

GETELEMENTSBYCLASSNAME()

The getElementsByClassName() function is used to select or get items based on the value of their class name. This DOM function produces an array-like object containing all members of the supplied classname. When we use the getElementsByClassName() function on any element, it searches the whole document and returns just those elements that match the requested or provided class name.[7]

Syntax:

```
var ele=document.getELementsByClassName('name');
```

The necessary parameter to be given here is name. It is the string that defines whether to match a single classname or many class names.

Method getElementsByClassName() Example

Let's look at some instances to learn about and comprehend the method's actual use.

Example

It is a basic class implementation that, when the variable k is invoked, produces an array-like object.

```
<html>
<head> <h5>The DOM Methods </h5> </head>
<body>
<div class="Class">
This is a basic class implementation
</div>
<script type="text/javascript">
var k=document.getElementsByClassName('Class');
document.write("On calling k, it will return arrsy-
like object: <br>"+k);
</script>
</body>
</html>
```

Similarly, we can use the getElementsByClassName() function to get element collections for various classes.

Distinction between the Methods getElementsByClassName(), querySelector(), and querySelectorAll()

- getElementsByClassName(): This method searches for items that match the supplied class name and provides a list of the elements that match. The items returned are a live HTML collection of elements. If the Document Object Model is changed, these live components will be updated.

- querySelector(): This function returns a single element that matches the supplied classname. If no matching element is found, it returns null.

The essential aspect to remember is that all of the methods mentioned above return either one element or a list, but the getELementsByClassName() function handles dynamic updates, while the other two handle static updates.

METHOD DOCUMENT.GETELEMENTSBYNAME() IN JAVASCRIPT

The function document.getElementsByName() retrieves all elements with the given name.[8] The following is the syntax for the getElements-ByName() method:

```
document.getElementsByName("name")
```

Example

In this example, we'll count the total number of genders. To retrieve all of the genders, we use the getElementsByName() function.

```
<script type="text/javascript">
    function totalelements()
    {
    var allgenders=document.getElementsByName("gender");
    alert("Total Genders is:"+allgenders.length);
    }
    </script>
    <form>
    Male:<input type="radio" name="gender"
value="male">
    Female:<input type="radio" name="gender"
value="female">

    <input type="button" onclick="totalelements()"
value="The Total Genders">
    </form>
```

METHOD DOCUMENT.GETELEMENTSBYTAGNAME() IN JAVASCRIPT

The function document.getElementsByTagName() retrieves all elements with the supplied tag name.[9]

The following is the syntax for the getElementsByTagName() method:

```
document.getElementsByTagName("name")
```

Example

In this example, we'll count the total number of paragraphs in the document.

To do this, we used the document.getElementsByTagName("p") function, which returns the total number of paragraphs.

```
<script type="text/javascript">
    function countpara(){
    var totalpara=document.getElementsByTagName("p");
    alert("The total p tags are: "+totalpara.length);

    }
    </script>
    <p>This is the pragraph</p>
    <p>We are going to count the total number of
paragraphs by getElementByTagName() method.</p>
    <p> Let's look at a basic example</p>
    <button onclick="countpara()">count paragraph</
    button>
```

Another Example

In this instance, we'll count the total number of h2 and h3 tags in the document.

```
<script type="text/javascript">
    function counth2(){
    var totalh2=document.getElementsByTagName("h2");
    alert("The total h2 tags are: "+totalh2.length);
    }
    function counth3(){
    var totalh3=document.getElementsByTagName("h3");
    alert("The total h3 tags are: "+totalh3.length);
    }
    </script>
    <h2>This is the h2 tag</h2>
    <h2>This is the h2 tag</h2>
    <h3>This is the h3 tag</h3>
    <h3>This is the h3 tag</h3>
```

```
<h3>This is the h3 tag</h3>
<button onclick="counth2()">count h2</button>
<button onclick="counth3()">count h3</button>
```

THE INNERHTML IN JAVASCRIPT

The innerHTML property is used to write dynamic html on an HTML document. It is typically used in web sites to produce dynamic html, such as registration forms, comment forms, and links.[10]

InnerHTML Property Example

When the user activates the button, an HTML form will be generated. In this example, we're dynamically creating the html form within the div with the id mylocation. This location is identified by using the document.getElementById() function.

```
<script type="text/javascript" >
function showcommentform() {
var data="Name:<input type='text' name='name'><br>Comm
ent:<br><textarea rows='5' cols='90'></textarea>
<br><input type='submit' value='Post Comment'>";
document.getElementById('mylocation').innerHTML=data;
}
</script>
<form name="my_Form">
<input type="button" value="comment"
onclick="showcommentform()">
<div id="mylocation"></div>
</form>
```

Example of a Comment Form Using innerHTML

```
<!DOCTYPE html>
<html>
<head>
<title>First JS</title>
<script>
var flag=true;
function commentform(){
var cform="<form action='Comment'>Enter Name
is:<br><input type='text' name='name' /><br/>
```

```
Enter Email:<br><input type='email'
name='email'/><br>Enter Comment is:<br/>
<textarea rows='5' cols='75'></textarea><br><input
type='submit' value='Post Comment'/></form>";
if(flag){
document.getElementById("mylocation").innerHTML=cform;
flag=false;
}else{
document.getElementById("mylocation").innerHTML="";
flag=true;
}
}
</script>
</head>
<body>
<button onclick="commentform()">Comment</button>
<div id="mylocation"></div>
</body>
</html>
```

THE INNERTEXT IN JAVASCRIPT

The innerText property may be used to display dynamic text on an HTML page. Text will be read as conventional text rather than html text in this case. It is usually used in web sites to produce dynamic content such as writing the validation message, password strength, and so on.[11]

Example of JavaScript innerText

In this example, we'll show the password strength when the key is released after being pressed.

```
<script type="text/javascript" >
    function validate() {
    var msg;
    if(document.my_Form.userPass.value.length>6){
    msg="good";
    }
    else{
    msg="poor";
    }
    document.getElementById('mylocation').
innerText=msg;
    }
```

```
</script>
<form name="my_Form">
<input type="password" value="" name="userPass"
onkeyup="validate()">
    Strength:<span id="mylocation">no strength</span>
    </form>
```

5 METHODS FOR MAKING HTTP REQUESTS IN JAVASCRIPT

Modern Javascript supports several methods for sending HTTP requests to distant services. Having so many alternatives for requesting and dynamically loading information in web applications, from the built-in XMLHttpRequest object to third-party libraries like Axios, has made it simpler than ever before.[12]

So, we'll go through several methods for delivering HTTP requests in Javascript. Starting with the language's native choices, we'll look at the following five modules and send various forms of HTTP requests using them.

- XMLHttpRequest

- Fetch

- Axios

- SuperAgent

- Ky

XMLHttpRequest

XMLHttpRequest is a Javascript native API that contains the mechanism of sending HTTP requests without the need to refresh a previously loaded web page (AJAX requests). Despite the fact that developers seldom use the XMLHttpRequest directly anymore, it is nevertheless the building component that functions behind many popular HTTP request modules.

Understanding how to submit requests using the XMLHttpRequest method, for example, might assist us in dealing with unusual use scenarios if a third-party library does not support it.

Here's how we can use the XMLHttpRequest API to send GET queries and asynchronously receive data from a remote API:

```
//creation of XMLHttpRequest object
const xhr = new XMLHttpRequest()
//open the remote server URL for the get request
xhr.open("GET", "https://world.openfoodfacts.org/
category/pastas/1.json")
//send the Http request
xhr.send()

//the Event Handlers

//triggered when response is completed
xhr.onload = function() {
  if (xhr.status === 210) {
    //parse JSON datax`x
    data = JSON.parse(xhr.responseText)
    console.log(data.count)
    console.log(data.products)
  } else if (xhr.status === 404) {
    console.log("No records found")
  }
}

//triggered when network-level error occurs with
request
xhr.onerror = function() {
  console.log("The Network error occurred")
}

// triggered on regular basis when client receives
data
//used to track the status of the request
xhr.onprogress = function(e) {
  if (e.lengthComputable) {
    console.log(`${e.loaded} B of ${e.total} B
loaded!`)
  } else {
    console.log(`${e.loaded} B loaded!`)
  }
}
```

As seen in this example, sending a GET request with XMLHttpRequest includes three steps:

- Make an XMLHttpRequest.

- Opening the indented type HTTP request.

- Sending the request.

Once the request is sent, we can handle its response using the event handlers supplied by the XMLHttpObject. We've utilized two event handlers in this case: onload, onerror, and onprogress. It is vital to remember that the onerror function only handles network-level requests problems. To discover HTTP problems, we must specifically examine the HTTP status code within the onload method.

We may use XMLHttpRequest to send POST requests in a similar manner.

```javascript
// creation of XMLHttpRequest object
const xhr = new XMLHttpRequest()
// open the POST request
xhr.open("POST", "/food")
// set the content-type header to JSON
xhr.setRequestHeader("Content-Type", "application/
json");
// send the JSON data to remote server
xhr.send(JSON.stringify(food))

// the Event Handlers

// track the data upload progress
xhr.upload.onprogress = function(e) {
   console.log(`${e.loaded}B of ${e.total}B uploaded!`)
}

// trigger when data upload is finished
xhr.upload.onload = function(e) {
   console.log("The Upload completed")
}

// trigger when response is fully received
xhr.onload = function() {
   console.log(xhr.status)
}

// trigger due to the network-level error
```

```
xhr.onerror = function() {
  console.log("The Network error occurred")
}
```

The primary difference between the previous GET and the present POST request is that when submitting JSON data, the content-type headers are explicitly specified. In addition, a POST request can generate an additional event type when compared to a GET request. They are upload events that may be accessed using the xhr.upload field. When the request body must convey a large quantity of data, these event handlers assist us in tracking the data upload process (e.g., images and files)

Advantages of XMLHttpRequest

- All recent browser versions are compatible with the approach because it is natively supported.

- This eliminates the requirement for external dependencies.

- At the most basic level, it is possible to view and manipulate asynchronous HTTP requests.

Disadvantages of XMLHttpRequest

- The code is rather verbose and lengthy.

- There is no async/await or promise-based syntax support.

- The majority of recent HTTP request packages give straightforward abstractions over the difficult XMLHttpRequest API.

Fetch

Fetch is a contemporary and streamlined native JavaScript API for making HTTP requests. It includes promise functionality and improves on the verbose syntax of the previously described XMLHttpRequest. Fetch has become one of the most common ways to send HTTP requests in JavaScript nowadays as an API designed with current application and developer needs in mind.

As seen in this example, we can use Fetch to send HTTP requests from the client side by using a promise-based syntax.

```
fetch("https://world.openfoodfacts.org/category/
pastas/1.json")
    .then(response => {
    // indicates whether response is successful
(status code 200-299) or not
    if (!response.ok) {
        throw new Error('Request failed with the
status ${reponse.status}')
    }
    return response.json()
    })
    .then(data => {
        console.log(data.count)
        console.log(data.products)
    })
    .catch(error => console.log(error))
```

Fetch greatly decreases code complexity and verbosity by using simplified syntax and promises. Because the problems captured in the catch function belong to the network level, not the application level, we must utilize the 'response.ok' field in this implementation to determine if the response contains an HTTP error or not.

The fetch function accepts a configuration object as the second parameter, allowing for easy customization of HTTP data like as headers, content-types, request method, and so on. The whole set of configuration options supported by Fetch may be seen in its official manual.

Making POST requests using Fetch follows the same technique as in the previous example. In this case, we utilize the config object to indicate the request method and the data to be submitted.

Let's see how this works with async/await:

```
async function postData () {
    const food = {
        name: "Rice",
        weight: 410,
        quantity: 4
    }

    const response = await fetch("/food", {
        method: "POST",
```

```
    body: JSON.stringify(food),
    headers: {
      "Content-Type": "application/json"
    }
  })

  if (!response.ok) {
    throw new Error(`Request failed with the status
${reponse.status}`)
  }
  console.log("Request is successful!")
}
```

Advantages of Fetch

- Provides a streamlined, native method for making HTTP requests in JavaScript.

- Simple to understand and apply to any level of difficulty.

- Allows us to create clearer, more succinct code by supporting promise-based implementation.

- It improves upon XMLHttpRequest in many ways, including the ability to do no-cors requests and combine Request and Response objects with the built-in Cache API.

Disadvantages of Fetch

- Some key XMLHttpRequest functionality, such as request abort and request progress monitoring, are missing. (However, a separate AbortController object may be used to govern request aborts and timeouts.)

- Accepts a response even if there is an HTTP error. We must manually check for and handle HTTP problems.

- Not compatible with Internet Explorer, but hopefully this is no longer an issue.

Axios

Axios is a well-known third-party program for performing HTTP requests in JavaScript. Under the hood, it collaborates with the native XMLHttpRequest API to provide a straightforward and comprehensive collection of functionality for handling specific challenges such as intercepting HTTP requests and delivering simultaneous requests. It, like Fetch, enables promises for dealing with asynchronous requests.

When performing GET requests using Axios, we may compile the request using the specialized axios.get() function. We've presented an example of implementation here:

```
axios.get("https://world.openfoodfacts.org/category/
pastas/1.json")
  .then(response => {
    // access the parsed JSON response data using the
response.data field
    data = response.data
    console.log(data.count)
    console.log(data.products)
  })
  .catch(error => {
    if (error.response) {
      //get the HTTP error code
      console.log(error.reponse.status)
    } else {
      console.log(error.message)
    }
  })
```

Axios reduces the amount of effort required on our end to perform HTTP requests when compared to Fetch. The response.data property contains the interpreted JSON data. There is no need to explicitly check for status code before processing the response when using Axios since the catch method covers HTTP failures as well. Error.response checks, which remember the specific HTTP error code, allow us to classify incoming failures in the catch function.

We utilize the specialized axios.post() function to send POST requests with Axios, as seen in the following example, which is built using async/await:

```
async function postData () {
    const food = {
      name: "Rice",
      weight: 410,
      quantity: 4
    }

    try {
      const response = await axios.post("/food", food)
      console.log("Request issuccessful!")
    } catch (error) {
      if (error.response) {
        console.log(error.reponse.status)
      } else {
        console.log(error.message)
      }
    }
}
```

Axios simplifies this implementation once again by transforming Javascript objects to JSON without our intervention. These Axios methods use a last argument that specifies HTTP settings.

Advantages Axios

- It has a basic, succinct, and simple-to-learn syntax.

- Supports a diverse range of functionality not seen in many other accessible HTTP packages. These include intercepting HTTP requests, sending multiple requests at the same time, canceling sent requests, automated JSON data translation, monitoring request progress, and so on.

- All major browser versions, including Internet Explorer, are supported.

- Client-side XSRF protection is provided.

Disadvantages Axios

- Because the module is not native, it adds an external dependence to the program.

SuperAgent

SuperAgent was one of the first third-party tools for performing HTTP requests in JavaScript. It, like Axios, implements the XMLHttpRequest API behind the hood and includes a complete set of functionality useful in a variety of request processing jobs. Both promise-based and callback-based solutions are supported by the package.

When sending HTTP requests using SuperAgent, we may use its specialized methods to launch a certain sort of request. As seen in this example, we can utilize the superagent.get() function to send GET queries.

```
superagent
  .get("https://world.openfoodfacts.org/category/
pastas/1.json")
  .then(response => {
    // get the parsed JSON response data
    data = response.body
    console.log(data.count)
    console.log(data.products)
  })
  .catch(error => {
    if (error.response) {
      console.log(error.status)
    } else {
      console.log(error.message)
    }
  })
```

With the promise-based syntax, SuperAgent follows a similar approach to Axios for delivering GET requests. It automatically parses the response body into a JavaScript object without developer interaction. It also collects HTTP failures within the catch method, which are identified using the error.response field. In the event of a network issue, the columns labeled "error.response" and "error.status" will be blank.

Similarly, we may send POST requests using SuperAgent.

```
superagent
  .post("/food")
  .send(food)
  .then(response => console.log("Request is
successful!"))
```

```
.catch(error => {
  if (error.response) {
    console.log(error.status)
  } else {
    console.log(error.message)
  } .
})
```

SuperAgent thinks the given data is in JSON by default and handles data transformation and content-type headers on its own. We utilize SuperAgent's transmit() function to pass the data given with the POST request.

Advantages of SuperAgent

- Offers a simple, promise-based approach for delivering HTTP requests.

- It's a robust and well-supported Javascript module.

- Retries requests if a network or other transitory error occurs while making a request.

- Allows for the extension of the package's functionality through the use of a continually increasing list of plugins. These plugins provide functionality to SuperAgent such as mimicking fake HTTP calls, caching request and response data, queueing and throttling requests, and so on.

- All major browser versions are supported. However, prior versions of Internet Explorer require the deployment of a polyfill to allow capabilities such as promise support. What does it matter at this point?

Disadvantages of SuperAgent

- Adds an external requirement as the module is not native.

- Monitoring request progress is not supported.

Ky

Ky is a new Javascript module that may be used to make asynchronous HTTP requests from a web application's frontend. The native Fetch API is used as the foundation, but it has been enhanced with a clearer syntax and more functionality.

Ky's specialized HTTP methods have a straightforward syntax for making requests. Here's an instance of a GET request sent using Ky and async/await.

```
async function getData () {
    try {
        const data = await ky.get("https://world.
openfoodfacts.org/category/pastas/2.json").json()
        console.log(data.count)
        console.log(data.products)
    } catch (error) {
        if (error.response) {
            console.log(error.response.status)
        } else {
            console.log(error.message)
        }
    }
}
```

POST requests can be sent in a similar manner:

```
async function postData () {
    try {
        const response = await ky.post("/food", { json:
food })
        console.log("The Request is successful")
    } catch (error) {
        if (error.response) {
            console.log(error.reponse.status)
        } else {
            console.log(error.message)
        }
    }
}
```

Advantages of Ky

- Provides a straightforward, lightweight, promise-based API for performing HTTP requests.

- Supports request timeout, retry, and progress monitoring to address several restrictions in the native Fetch API.

- Hooks are provided for altering requests throughout their lifecycle: beforeRequest, afterResponse, beforeRetry, and so on.

- All current browsers, including Chrome, Firefox, and Safari, are supported. Ky offers an alternate package, Ky-Universal, for Internet Explorer support; I'm not sure why they bother.

Disadvantages of Ky

- In comparison to the other mature, diverse solutions covered in this essay, this is a very new package. This function adds an external dependence.

HTTP COOKIES

A web cookie, also known as an HTTP cookie, is a little piece of data sent by the server to the online browser. The cookies may be stored by the browser and sent back to the server along with subsequent requests.[13] Cookies are commonly used to detect repeated requests from the same site (browser). It assists the user in remaining logged in and tracking his data, such as user name and session. It's also a good idea to keep track of the stateful information for the stateless HTTP protocol.

If we are a developer, we cannot avoid cookies because they are necessary for session management and monitoring other user information. A cookie is as crucial nowadays as any other app functionality. Cookies facilitate various tasks for both the user and the programmer.

Cookies have been around for a while and are still changing now. A cookie is just textual data about a web app. When a user visits a website, certain information is stored to the system's local storage so that the app may recognize the user and display appropriate results if they visit again.

When the user visits a website, the server requests the application's home page, and when he performs a specific action, the server requests any other page of the application. So, if the user visits the 100th time, the request will be unique each time. Because server queries are so intense, saving data directly to the server is unfeasible; moreover, it may cause a server overload. Furthermore, if the user does not return, the information gathered will be outdated.

As a result, in order to remember the user's identity, the server transmits cookies with the response, which are saved to the system's local storage. When the same client performs the same request again, the server will identify its identity and display the appropriate response.

Cookies are unique to the server, thus even if the user has numerous cookies on their system, the server can identify its cookie.

In this part, we shall cover the following cookie-related topics:

- Cookies are used.

- How Do Cookies Work?

- Cookies generated by JavaScript.

- Cookie Specifications.

- Cookie Varieties.

Utilization of Cookies

The cookie is commonly used in the following ways:

- **Session Management:**

  The cookie's principal function is to handle user logins, shopping cart data, gaming scores, and anything else the server should remember the next time the user comes in.

  In general, session management enables the user to interact securely with the server via the application. Because the user continues to engage with the web application, each time they visit the website, they generate a new request. As a result, it makes it simple to follow their status and activities during the session.

- **Tracking**

  Tracking is capturing user activity and evaluating their behaviors in order to tailor material for them. It tracks and analyzes their behaviors and interests, as well as the pages they visit. The time spent on a page or throughout the website during a session may be included in the tracking information. Because the user tracking contains sensitive information, the user should be aware of the hazards of accessing unsecured websites and, if feasible, avoid visiting such websites.

- **Personalization**

  Cookies aid in the customization of user preferences, themes, and other settings. Most of the time, these settings are synced with a central database to personalize things for users the first time they log in. When the user signs in or restarts the program, the user customization saves information about the user's preferences and settings for future use.

- **Authentication**

  Cookies are also essential for user authentication. When a user checks in, the server responds with the Set-Cookie HTTP header, which sets a cookie with a unique "session identifier."

  The cookie is sent across the internet via the Cookie HTTP header the next time the same user requests the same website.

  As a result, the server can determine who made the request.

How Do Cookies Work?

Each time a user interacts with a website, a new request is made to the server, and each time he does any action within the program, a new request is sent to the server. Every new request submitted by a separate user was taken into account by the server.

To identify requests from the same user, developers must include the cookie in the server's response, which is kept in the system's local memory. If the same user submits a request to the server, the server recognizes the user using cookies.

The web browser is the client-side communication channel that sends requests from the client to the server.

Once the cookie is added by the developers, the requests submitted by users are detected, and the server provides the answer based on the customization.

Cookies are critical from the standpoints of both users and developers. It aids both parties in responding appropriately.

Let's look at how to make cookies with JavaScript.

Cookies in JavaScript

Let's look at how to make cookies with JavaScript:

Create Cookies

When a request is received, the server may respond with one or more Set-Cookie headers. It will be saved in the system's local storage. So, the next time when the browser sends a request to the server, it will also send the cookie along with the request.

We may optionally set an expiration date or time period after which the cookie will be invalid and will not be transmitted. We may also apply some extra constraints to a specified domain and path to limit when the cookie is transmitted.

To create, read, update, and remove cookies, JavaScript offers the document.cookie property.

The syntax for creating a cookie is as follows:

```
document.cookie="cookiename=value";
```

An HTTP cookie can be generated in two ways. Cookies can be created on the client using the browser interface or added from the server in the file's script section. To add from the client side, we may open the console and type the JavaScript code into the browser. Set-cookie headers can be included from the server side to generate one or more cookies.

Let's look at how cookies are created on both the client and server sides.

Client Side

To access the cookie from the client side, open the console in our browser and enter the following code:

```
document.cookie="mycookie=1"
```

Using the web browser's dev tool, we can also examine the cookies saved on the local system. To see if the cookie has been added, go to the dev tool's application tab and pick the Cookies tab.

Web Server Side

To add the server cookie, we must create the cookie on an activity when the user visits the page.

Consider the following scenario:

```
<!DOCTYPE html>
<html lang="en">
<head>
    <meta charset="UTF-8">
    <meta name="viewport" content="width=device-width,
initial-scale=2.0">
    <meta http-equiv="X-UA-compatible" content
="ie=edge">
    <title>Document</title>
</head>
<body>
    <button id ='setcookie'>Set Cookie</button>
    <script>
```

```
    const my_Cookie = document.
getElementbyID("setcookie")
    myCookie.addEventLister("click", e=> document.
cookie = "mycookie=2")
    </script>
</body>
</html>
```

It will display a button component on our website page based on the pre-ceding example. When we press the button, the requested cookie is cre-ated for our system storage.

Similarly, we may construct the cookie with any other event listener. To set the cookie, we can alternatively add an onload event.

Let's look at few cookie properties:

Properties of Cookies

The cookie attributes are consistent across all sorts of cookies; the follow-ing are some of the typical cookie properties:

Scope of Cookies

The scope of a cookie specifies which URLs are transmitted with the cookie. Cookie scope is separated into two distinct attributes:

- **Path**

    The path is one of the properties that define a cookie's scope. It defines a specified URL route in the HTTP header to transmit the cookie. To set the cookie to various routes, use the following code:

```
document.cookie="cookiefirst=1; path=/path1"
document.cookie=" cookiesecond=2; path=/path2"
```

When we visit a website with the provided URL, such as exam-ple.com/path1, we will now submit a cookie header with the value "cookiefirst=1."

If we navigate to another URL, such as example.com/path2, we will submit a cookie header with the value "cookiesecond=2."

Except for the defined URLs, other requested routes will not transmit any cookie headers.

- **Domain**

  The domain is the cookie's second property. Domains function as a container for cookies. The cookie provides a unique domain name to itself, which assists the administrator in keeping the cookies particular and organized for each http request for web pages. An example of a domain-specific cookie is shown below:

  Domain=google.com will enable cookies for the domain google.com and its subdomains, including pasta.google.com.

- **Expires and Max-age**

  A cookie's "Expires" and "Max-Age" parameters define its lifetime or expiration date. They are classified as persistent cookies. With the exception of the term "permanent cookie," the "Expires" property can remove a cookie on a certain date. Furthermore, the "Max-Age" characteristic deletes cookies after a given time.

  Session cookies, on the other hand, are destroyed when the current session expires. Some browsers allow us to choose when the current session will finish, which can be any length of time, including indefinitely.

- **SameSite**

  The SameSite property enables us to set the cookie when a link within a page is clicked. We've spoken about how to establish http cookies for a certain URL, but what if we want to put the cookie on a link inside that direct URL? Using the SameSite, we may transmit cookies by clicking on a link from a redirected new page. We can instruct SameSite to transmit cookies in response to cross-site requests or if a user clicks on a link on a web page.

  Let's have a look at an actual scenario where the SameSite property enables cross-site cookies. The flow chart below explains how cookies are transmitted and received while moving from one page to another.

  The user navigates to a URL (for example, google.com)

  They'll get a first-party cookie.

  The user will go to google.com and click on the link that makes a retrieve request to another site, such as www.googleexample.com.

  Tutorialandexample.com will place a cookie with the domain name Domain=googleexample.com.

Google.com now stores a third-party cookie from googleandex-ample.com.

With the following three values, the SameSite property defines whether third-party cookies are sent:

- **Strict**

  The strict value for the SameSite property will only be transmitted through a first-party cookie context. Third-party cookies will not be considered.

- **Lax**

  When a user hits a link with third-party navigation, the "Lax" value of a SameSite property is delivered. If the SameSite property is not explicitly specified on the third-party link, the default value is lax.

- **None**

  If the SameSite property is set to "None," cookies are transmitted in all contexts.

  We've spoken about cookies and their attributes; now let's look at the many sorts of cookies:

Varieties of Cookie

Cookies are classified into the following kinds based on their usage and behaviors:

First-Party Cookies

First-party cookies are those that are transmitted to the system directly from the server of the website that we are viewing. The visited website stores these cookies directly on our computer. Most websites send cookies to their visitors in order to collect useful information and analytics in order to improve the user experience.

Authentication is the greatest example of a first-party cookie. When a user registers in to an application, the server sends cookies to the client, which keeps them on the user's local machine. We do not need to enter the login credentials again the next time you check in to the program. The website cannot identify the user without first-party cookies and will not automatically log us in or remember our choices from previous sessions.

Third-Party Cookies

The third-party domains to which we are redirected create third-party cookies.

It is not created by the domain in which we are currently logged in.

These cookies are typically used for tracking and can be retained even after the browser is closed. Ad tracking from websites is an excellent example of a third-party cookie. We may have noticed that after browsing a few products from various eCommerce sites, we will begin to see ads for those products. Because we may have been exposed to third-party cookies from a domain other than that specific website while browsing the products.

When we close the browser or that specific website, a third-party cookie can be used to track our browsing details, such as which products you have seen and whether or not we have purchased them. After that, we'll have to start receiving emails about those products and seeing advertisements from various ad agencies.

Session Cookies

Session cookies are transient cookies that are deleted when the user closes the browser tab.

Session cookies are often utilized when a user inputs their login credentials and connects into an application. When session cookies are utilized, users must provide their credentials each time they attempt to log in to the application.

The shopping cart management on an eCommerce site is a good example of a session cookie.

Session cookies aid in the organization of a user's shopping cart.

If the site does not employ session cookies, users will have a more difficult time remembering the goods they have chosen.

Secure Cookies

The cookies include a Secure feature to prevent unwanted access from cookies given to a user as part of an HTTP response. When cookies are used in conjunction with the Secure property, all HTTP requests will contain the cookie only if it is communicated over a secure medium.

In 2002, Microsoft Internet Explorer introduced HttpOnly cookies. Cookies with the HttpOnly flag can be included in a Set-Cookie HTTP header. The HttpOnly property decreases the possibility of users clicking on a malicious link that exploits cross-site scripting vulnerabilities.

In general, attackers attempt to inject malicious scripts into a trusted website in order to obtain cookies and other sensitive information stored on the local system.

Zombie Cookies

The zombie cookies' names give us a hint. These cookies, like zombies, can come back to life after being killed. These cookies can be reactivated when the browser is closed or erased. Cookies from zombies can be stored anywhere other than the browser's dedicated storage.

In general, the zombie cookie can make a copy of the original cookie, store it somewhere else, and then reattach it to the user's cookie storage.

Few firms previously exploited the zombie cookie to track user activities and obtain personal information. Few states have prohibited the zombie cookie, which is considered an illegal violation of privacy.

FORM IN JAVASCRIPT

We will learn, examine, and understand the JavaScript form in this session. We will also learn how the JavaScript form is implemented for various reasons.[14]

In this session, we will learn how to access the form, obtain elements as the JavaScript form's value, and submit the form.

Overview to Forms

Forms are the foundation of HTML. In order to generate the JavaScript form, we need the HTML form element. The following sample code may be used to create a form:

```
<html>
<head>
<title> Form of Login </title>
</head>
<body>
<h3> LOGIN </h3>
<formform ="Loginform" onsubmit="submitform()">
<h4> USERNAME</h4>
<input type="text" placeholder="Enter email id"/>
<h4> PASSWORD</h4>
<input type="password" placeholder="Enter
password"/></br></br>
```

```
<input type="submit" value="Login"/>
<input type="button" value="SignUp"
onClick="create()"/>
</form>
</html>
```

In the program:

- The form name tag is used to define the form's name. The form is called "Loginform" in this case. This name will appear in the JavaScript form.

- The action element specifies the action that the browser will do when the form is submitted. We haven't done anything here.

- When the form is to be sent to the server, the method to take action can be either post or get. Both techniques have their own set of properties and regulations.

- The input type tag specifies the type of inputs that will be available in our form. We've set the input type to 'text,' which means we'll enter data into the textbox as text.

- Net, we've set the input type to 'password,' and the input value is password.

- Next, we choose the input type 'button,' and when we click it, the form's value is shown.

Aside from action and methods, the HTML form element also provides the following helpful techniques.

- submit (): The technique for submitting the form.

- The reset () technique is used to reset the form values.

Referencing Forms

Now that we've established the form element with HTML, we need to connect it to JavaScript. To do this, we employ the getElementById () function, which refers to the HTML form element in the JavaScript code.

The following is the syntax for utilizing the getElementById() method:

```
let form = document.getElementById('subscribes');
```

We may make the reference using the Id.

Submitting Form

The onSubmit() function is then used to submit the form by sending its value.

In general, we utilize a submit button to submit the value provided in the form.

The submit() function has the following syntax:

```
<input type="submit" value="Subscribes">
```

The action is executed shortly before the request is delivered to the server when we submit the form. It lets us to add an event listener to the form, allowing us to set multiple validations on it.

Finally, a combination of HTML and JavaScript code is used to complete the form.

Let us gather and use all of them to develop a Login form and a SignUp form, and then use both of them.

Login Form

```
<html>
<head>
<title> Form of Login </title>
</head>
<body>
<h3> LOGIN </h3>
<formform ="Loginform" onsubmit="submitform()">
<h4> USERNAME</h4>
<input type="text" placeholder="Enter email id"/>
<h4> PASSWORD</h4>
<input type="password" placeholder="Enter
password"/></br></br>
<input type="submit" value="Login"/>
<input type="button" value="SignUp"
onClick="create()"/>
</form>
<script type="text/javascript">
function submitform(){
```

```
alert("Successfully Login ");
}
function create(){
window.location="signup.html";
}
</script>
</body>
</html>
```

SignUp Form

```
<html>
<head>
<title> SignUp Page</title>
</head>
<body align="center" >
<h1> CREATE ACCOUNT</h1>
<table cellspacing="2" align="center" cellpadding="9"
border="0">
<tr><td> Name</td>
<td><input type="text" placeholder="Enter name"
id="n1"></td></tr>
<tr><td>Email </td>
<td><input type="text" placeholder="Enter email id"
id="e1"></td></tr>
<tr><td> Set Password</td>
<td><input type="password" placeholder="Set password"
id="p1"></td></tr>
<tr><td>Confirm Password</td>
<td><input type="password" placeholder="Confirm
password" id="p2"></td></tr>
<tr><td>
<input type="submit" value="Create"
onClick="createaccount()"/>
</table>
<script type="text/javascript">
function create_account(){
var n=document.getElementById("n1").value;
var e=document.getElementById("e1").value;
var p=document.getElementById("p1").value;
var cp=document.getElementById("p2").value;
```

```
//Code for the password validation
        var letters = /^[A-Za-z]+$/;
        var email_val = /^([a-zA-Z0-9_\.\-])+\@
(([a-zA-Z0-9\-])+\.)+([a-zA-Z0-9]{2,4})+$/;
//other validations required code
if(n==''||e==''||p==''||cp==''){
alert("Enter details correctly");
}
else if(!letters.test(n))
        {
                alert('Incorrect Name, must contain
alphabets only');
        }
else if (!email_val.test(e))
        {
                alert('Invalid format of email please
enter valid email id');
        }
else if(p!=cp)
{
alert("The Passwords not matching");
}
else if(document.getElementById("p1").value.length >
13)
{
alert("The Password maximum length is 13");
}
else if(document.getElementById("p1").value.length < 7)
{
alert("The Password minimum length is 7");
}
else{
alert("Our account has create successfully...
Redirecting to google.com");
window.location="https://www.google.com/";
}
}
</script>
</body>
</html>
```

VALIDATION OF JAVASCRIPT FORMS

It is critical to check the user-submitted form since it may include incorrect information.

As a result, validation is required to authenticate the user. Because JavaScript allows form validation on the client side, data processing is faster than server-side validation.[15]

JavaScript form validation is preferred by the majority of web developers.

We can validate name, password, email, date, cell numbers, and other data using JavaScript.

Example of Form Validation in JavaScript

In this example, we'll validate the name and password. The name cannot be blank, and the password cannot be less than seven characters long. On form submission, we validate the form.

The user will not be sent to the next page unless the values entered are correct.

```
<script>
    function validateform(){
    var name=document.my_form.name.value;
    var password=document.my_form.password.value;

    if (name==null || name==""){
      alert("Name cannot be blank");
      return false;
    }else if(password.length<7){
      alert("Password must be atleast 7 characters
long.");
      return false;
      }
    }
    </script>
    <body>
    <form name="my_form" method="post" action="abcd.
jsp" onsubmit="return validateform()" >
    Name: <input type="text" name="name"><br/>
    Password: <input type="password"
name="password"><br/>
    <input type="submit" value="register">
    </form>
```

Password Retype Validation in JavaScript

```
<script type="text/javascript">
    function matchpass(){
    var firstpassword=document.fm1.password.value;
    var secondpassword=document.fm1.password2.value;

    if(firstpassword==secondpassword){
    return true;
    }
    else{
    alert("password must same!");
    return false;
    }
    }
    </script>

    <form name="fm1" action="register.jsp"
onsubmit="return matchpass()">
    Password:<input type="password" name="password"
/><br/>
    Re-enter Password:<input type="password"
name="password2" /><br/>
    <input type="submit">
    </form>
```

Number Validation in JavaScript

Let us verify the textfield solely for numeric values. We're using the isNaN() method here.

```
<script>
    function validate(){
    var num=document.my_form.num.value;
    if (isNaN(num)){
      document.getElementById("numloc").
innerHTML="Enter Numeric value only";
      return false;
    }else{
      return true;
      }
    }
```

```
</script>
<form name="my_form" onsubmit="return validate()" >
Number: <input type="text" name="num"><span
id="numloc"></span><br/>
<input type="submit" value="submit">
</form>
```

Validation of JavaScript Using an Image

Let's look at an interactive JavaScript form validation example that shows the correct and incorrect image depending on whether the input is correct or incorrect.

```
<script>
    function validate(){
    var name=document.fm1.name.value;
    var password=document.fm1.password.value;
    var status=false;

    if(name.length<1){
    document.getElementById("nameloc").innerHTML=
    " <img src='checked.gif'/> Please enter name";
    status=false;
    }else{
    document.getElementById("nameloc").innerHTML="
<img src='unchecked.gif'/>";
    status=true;
    }
    if(password.length<7){
    document.getElementById("passwordloc").innerHTML=
    " <img src='checked.gif'/> Password must be at
least 7 char long";
    status=false;
    }else{
    document.getElementById("passwordloc").innerHTML="
<img src='checked.gif'/>";
    }
    return status;
    }
    </script>
```

```
<form name="fm1" action="#" onsubmit="return
validate()">
    <table>
    <tr><td>Enter the Name:</td><td><input type="text"
name="name"/>
    <span id="nameloc"></span></td></tr>
    <tr><td>Enter the Password:</td><td><input
type="password" name="password"/>
    <span id="passwordloc"></span></td></tr>
    <tr><td colspan="2"><input type="submit"
value="register"/></td></tr>
    </table>
    </form>
```

Email Validation in JavaScript

Using JavaScript, we can validate the email.

To validate the email address, several criteria must be met, including:

- The @ and. characters must appear in the email address.

- Before and after the @, there must be at least one character.

- There must be at least two characters following.(dot).

Let's look at a simple example of email validation.

```
<script>
    function validateemail()
    {
    var x=document.my_form.email.value;
    var atposition=x.indexOf("@");
    var dotposition=x.lastIndexOf(".");
    if (atposition<1 || dotposition<atposition+2 ||
dotposition+2>=x.length) {
        alert("Enter the valid email address \n
atpostion:"+atposition+"\n dotposition:"+dotposition);
        return false;
        }
    }
    </script>
    <body>
```

```
<form name="my_form"  method="post" action="#"
onsubmit="return validateemail();">
    Email: <input type="text" name="email"><br/>

    <input type="submit" value="register">
    </form>
```

WORKING WITH JAVASCRIPT APIS

An API is just a means of transferring data between interfaces. Assume we want to create an app that presents the user with real-time data retrieved from the server or even allows us to alter or add data to another endpoint. The API, or Application Programming Interface, makes this feasible.[16]

We'll use a basic public API that doesn't need authentication and lets us retrieve data simply querying the API with GET requests.

https://randomuser.me/ is a website that supplies us with fake data for random users to work with.

A request to https://randomuser.me/api/ will provide the result. The JSON answer that we receive is in the format shown below.

```
{
    "results": [
        {
            "gender": "Mmale",
            "name": {
                "title": "Mr",
                "first": "Nitin",
                "last": "Simka"
            },
            "location": {
                "street": {
                    "number": 230,
                    "name": "Erakon Roadd"
                },
                "city": "Jalandhar",
                "state": "Punjab",
                "country": "India",
                "postcode": 121001,
                "coordinates": {
                    "latitude": "81.1327",
```

```
                    "longitude": "104.4160"
                },
                "timezone": {
                    "offset": "+7:00",
                    "description":
        "Ludhiana, Amritsar, Chandigarh, Moga"
                }
            },
            "email": "nitin.simka@example.com",
            "login": {
                "uuid":
"bd0d135f-84df-4102-aa4f-5baaa41baf5c",
                "username": "redfrog722",
                "password": "abc",
                "salt": "q28gdiyN",
                "md5":
"291987daea22bb91775226574925b271",
                "sha1": "a0463a26ea5c2ff4f3ad498fd01c
                5994926e5021",
                "sha256":
"6583eb74ca08bfac50b3b29aa52c9f02ea5d9d017fef0e5a5a
6fae4f5225f928"
            },
            "dob": {
                "date": "1998-10-01T23:10:09.403Z",
                "age": 40
            },
            "registered": {
                "date": "2015-02-02T02:26:52.904Z",
                "age": 7
            },
            "phone": "(91)-234-7985",
            "cell": "(51)-984-9443",
            "id": {
                "name": "SSN",
                "value": "847-09-2973"
            },
            "picture": {
                "large":
" https://randomuser.me/api/portraits/women/61.jpg",
                "medium":
" https://randomuser.me/api/portraits/women/61.jpg",
```

```
            "thumbnail":
" https://randomuser.me/api/portraits/women/61.jpg"
            },
            "nat": "US"
        }
    ],
    "info": {
        "seed": "82a8d8d4a996ba17",
        "results": 1,
        "page": 1,
        "version": "1.3"
    }
}
```

Next, we'll need an HTML file for the frontend, where you'll show the obtained data.

We can use the "div" tag (block-level) or the "span" tag (inline-level) as a placeholder for the data.

We may obtain the needed "div/span" container where we need to insert the information by using the "id" property.

```
<html lang="en">

<head>
<meta charset="UTF-8" />
<meta name="viewport" content=
    "width=device-width, initial-scale=2.0" />

<link id="favicon" rel="icon"
    href="" sizes="17x17" />

<!-- To make the website more attractive, use the
font-awesome library -->
<link rel="stylesheet" href=
"https://cdnjs.cloudflare.com/ajax/libs/font-
awesome/4.7.0/css/font-awesome.min.css" />

<!—The Internal CSS styling -->
<style>
    .content {
    text-align: center;
```

```
    padding: 32px;
    margin: 0px auto;
    }

    .details {
    margin-left: auto;
    margin-right: auto;
    }

    img {
    border-radius: 6px;
    box-shadow: black;
    }

    table,
    td {
    border-collapse: collapse;
    margin-left: auto;
    margin-right: auto;
    text-align: center;
    padding: 12px;
    border: 2px solid black;
    }
</style>
</head>

<body>
<div class="content">
    <div class="head">
    <h1 id="head"></h1>
    </div>
    <div class="email">
    <i class="fa fa-envelope" style=
        "font-size: 16px; color: red;">
    <a href="" id="email"> </a>
    </div>
    <div class="phone">
    <i class="fa fa-phone" style=
        "font-size: 16px; color: red;">
    <a href="" id="phone"> </a>
    </div>
    <br />
```

```
     <div id="user-img"></div>
     <br />

     <div class="details">
     <table>
         <tr>
         <td>Age</td>
         <td><span id="age"></span></td>
         </tr>
         <tr>
         <td>Gender</td>
         <td><span id="gender"></span></td>
         </tr>
         <tr>
         <td>Location</td>
         <td><span id="location"></span></td>
         </tr>
         <tr>
         <td>Country</td>
         <td><span id="country"></span></td>
         </tr>
     </table>
     </div>
</div>
</body>

</html>
```

The script tag will have the code for making the API request and handling the response.

This should be included in the body tag or as a separate file.

We utilize the async/await method to ensure that data is presented even after the page has been loaded.

We may use the console.log(...) function to see if the user is obtaining the proper information.

To see the output, open the console window in our internet browser (Right Click -> Inspect -> Console or Ctrl+Shift+J in Chrome/Edge).

```
<script>
     const api_url = "https://randomuser.me/api/";
     async function getUser() {
```

```javascript
        // Make an API call (request)
        // and getting response back
        const response = await fetch(api_url);

        // Parsing it to the JSON format
        const data = await response.json();
        console.log(data.results);

        // Retrieve data from the JSON
        const user = data.results[0];
        let { title, first, last } = user.name;
        let { gender, email, phone } = user;
        let image = user.picture.large;
        let image_icon = user.picture.thumbnail;
        let age = user.dob.age;
        let { city, state, country } = user.location;

    let fullName = title + ". " + first + " " + last;
        document.title = fullName;

        // Accessing the div container and modifying/
        adding
        // items to it
        document.getElementById("head").innerHTML =
        fullName;
        document.getElementById("email").href =
        "mailto:" + email;
        document.getElementById("email").innerHTML =
        email;
        document.getElementById("phone").href = "tel:"
        + phone;
        document.getElementById("phone").innerHTML =
        phone;
        // accessing the span container
        document.querySelector("#age").textContent = age;
        document.querySelector("#gender").textContent
        = gender;

        document.querySelector("#location").textContent
                = city + ", " + state;

        document.querySelector("#country").textContent
= country;
```

```
        // Making a new element and adding
        // it to already made containers
        let img = document.createElement("img");
        let img_div = document.getElementById("user-img");
        img.src = image;
        img_div.append(img);

        const favicon = document.getElementById("favicon");
        favicon.setAttribute("href", image_icon);
    }

    // Call the function
    getUser();
    </script>
```

The final code is: It is the result of combining the preceding code parts.

```
<html lang="en">


<head>
<meta charset="UTF-8" />
<meta name="viewport" content=
    "width=device-width, initial-scale=2.0" />


<!-- To create the font-awesome library
more attractive website -->
<link rel="stylesheet" href=
"https://cdnjs.cloudflare.com/ajax/libs/font-
awesome/4.7.0/css/font-awesome.min.css" />

<!--The Internal CSS styling -->
<style>
    .content {
    text-align: center;
    padding: 32px;
    margin: 0px auto;
    }

    .details {
    margin-left: auto;
```

```
    margin-right: auto;
    }

    img {
    border-radius: 6px;
    box-shadow: black;
    }

    table,
    td {
    border-collapse: collapse;
    margin-left: auto;
    margin-right: auto;
    text-align: center;
    padding: 12px;
    border: 2px solid black;
    }
</style>
</head>

<body>
<div class="content">
    <div class="head">
    <h1 id="head"></h1>
    </div>
    <div class="email">
    <i class="fa fa-envelope" style=
        "font-size: 16px; color: red;">
    <a href="" id="email"> </a>
    </div>
    <div class="phone">
    <i class="fa fa-phone" style=
        "font-size: 16px; color: red;">
    <a href="" id="phone"> </a>
    </div>
    <br />
    <div id="user-img"></div>
    <br />

    <div class="details">
    <table>
```

```
        <tr>
        <td>Age:</td>
        <td><span id="age"></span></td>
        </tr>
        <tr>
        <td>Gender:</td>
        <td><span id="gender"></span></td>
        </tr>
        <tr>
        <td>Location:</td>
        <td><span id="location"></span></td>
        </tr>
        <tr>
        <td>Country:</td>
        <td><span id="country"></span></td>
        </tr>
    </table>
    </div>
</div>
</body>
<script>
const api_url = "https://randomuser.me/api/";

async function getUser() {

    // Make an API call (request)
    // and getting response back
    const response = await fetch(api_url);

    // Parsing it to the JSON format
    const data = await response.json();
    console.log(data.results);

    // Retrieve data from the JSON
    const user = data.results[0];
    let { title, first, last } = user.name;
    let { gender, email, phone } = user;
    let image = user.picture.large;
    let image_icon = user.picture.thumbnail;
    let age = user.dob.age;
    let { city, state, country } = user.location;
```

```javascript
    let fullName = title + ". " + first + " " + last;
    document.title = fullName;


    // Access the div container and modify/add
    // elements to containers
    document.getElementById("head").innerHTML =
fullName;
    document.getElementById("email").href = "mailto:"
+ email;
    document.getElementById("email").innerHTML =
email;
    document.getElementById("phone").href = "tel:" +
phone;
    document.getElementById("phone").innerHTML =
phone;
    // access span container
    document.querySelector("#age").textContent = age;
    document.querySelector("#gender").textContent =
gender;


    document.querySelector("#location").textContent
        = city + ", " + state;


    document.querySelector("#country").textContent =
country;

    // Create the new element and
    // appending it to previously created containers
    let img = document.createElement("img");
    let img_div = document.getElementById("user-img");
    img.src = image;
    img_div.append(img);


    const favicon = document.getElementById("favicon");
    favicon.setAttribute("href", image_icon);
}

// Call the function
getUser();
```

```
</script>
</html>
```

If we want to learn more about APIs and delve further into them, visit Public APIs, which provides a large variety of publicly available APIs to help us on our API discovery adventure.

To determine the type of answer sent by an API, Postman is a fantastic application that will meet all of our requirements. Another option is to use Postman APIs to perform the same action in the browser.

THE MOST WELL-KNOWN JAVASCRIPT LIBRARIES

The most popular JavaScript libraries are listed here.[17]

jQuery

jQuery is a traditional JavaScript library that is lightweight, quick, and feature-rich.

John Resig constructed it during BarCamp NYC in 2006. jQuery is MIT-licensed free and open-source software. It makes HTML page manipulation and traversal, animation, event management, and Ajax easier. According to W3Techs, jQuery is used on 77.6% of all websites (as of 23rd February 2021).

Features

- It offers a simple, minimalistic API.

- It makes use of CSS3 selectors to manipulate style attributes and discover elements.

- jQuery is small, needing only 30kb to gzip and minify, plus it includes an AMD module.

- It is simple to learn because its syntax is identical to that of CSS.

- Plugins allow for more customization.

- Versatility is provided through an API that works with different browsers, including Chrome and Firefox.

Use Cases

- CSS selectors are used to pick a node in the DOM based on certain criteria. These criteria contain the names of the elements as well as their properties (like class and id). DOM element selection using Sizzle (an open-source, multi-browser selector engine).

- Effects, events, and animations are created.

- Parsing JSON.

- Development of Ajax applications.

- Detection of features.

- Asynchronous processing may be controlled using Promise and Deferred objects.

React.js

React.js (also called as ReactJS or React) is an open-source JavaScript frontend library.

Jordan Walke, a software developer at Facebook, founded the app in 2013. It now has the MIT license; however, it was originally distributed under the Apache License 2.0.

React was created to make creating interactive user interfaces as simple as possible. Simply create a basic display for each state in our program. Following that, it will render and update the appropriate component as data changes.

Features

- The React code consists of components or entities that must be rendered to a specific element in DOM using a React DOM library.

- It employs a virtual DOM by constructing an in-memory cache in a data structure, calculating the difference and efficiently updating the display DOM in the browser.

- Because to this selective rendering, the app's efficiency improves while developers save time recalculating the page layout, CSS styles, and full-page rendering.

- It employs lifecycle methods such as render and componentDid-Mount to allow code execution at precise periods during the lifetime of an object.

- It supports JavaScript XML (JSX), which blends JavaScript with HTML. It facilitates the visual presentation of components that contain nested elements, attributes, JS expressions, and conditional statements.

Use Cases

- Serving as the foundation for mobile or single-page apps.

- Rendering and managing a state for the DOM.

- Creating effective user interfaces when creating web apps and interactive websites.

- Easier debugging and testing.

D3.js

Another well-known JS framework used by developers for data-driven document editing is Data-Driven Documents (D3) or D3.js.

In 2011, it was made available under the BSD license.

Features

- It places an emphasis on web standards and provides modern browser capabilities without forcing you to use a particular framework.

- A sophisticated data visualization tool is D3.js.

- Support for HTML, CSS, and SVG is available.

- Uses a data-driven method to modify the DOM.

- A quick framework called D3.js makes a variety of dynamic behavior and datasets for animation and interactivity possible.

- By reducing overhead, it permits more intricate graphics while still keeping high frame rates.

Use Cases

- Creating interactive and dynamic data visualizations.

- DOM data binding and data-driven transformations on the data. A numbers array may be used to generate HTML tables, for example, and then D3.js can be used to generate an SVG bar chart or a 3D surface plot.

- It may be used with a lot of modules because to its functional code.

- D3 has a variety of tools for altering nodes, including declaratively changing styles or attributes, adding, sorting, or removing nodes, as well as altering text or HTML content.

- To make animated transitions, complicated transitions using events, CSS3 transitions, and so on.

Underscore.js

Underscore is a JavaScript utility package that includes a number of functions for common programming tasks.

Jeremy Askenas produced it in 2009 and released it under an MIT license.

Lodash has now surpassed it.

Features

- Its capabilities are comparable to those of Prototype.js (another famous utility package), although Underscore is designed for functional programming rather than object prototype extensions.

- It includes about 100 functions that are classified into four kinds based on the datatypes they modify. These are the functions that can be manipulated:

  - Objects

  - Arrays

  - Arrays and objects both

  - Other features

- Underscore works with Chrome, Firefox, Edge, and other browsers.

Use Cases

- It offers functional tools like filters and maps, as well as specific functions like binding, rapid indexing, JavaScript templating, quality testing, and so on.

Lodash

Another JS toolkit that simplifies dealing with objects, arrays, strings, and numbers is called Lodash. Like Underscore.js, it was introduced in 2013 and uses functional programming.

Features

- It makes it easier to write concise and manageable JavaScript code.

- Mathematical operations, binding, throttling, decorating, constraining, debouncing, and other routine tasks are simplified.

- Simpler string operations include camel case, trimming, and upper case.

- Generation, modifying, compressing, and sorting of arrays.

- Additional operations on collections, objects, and sequences.

Use Cases

Its modular approaches can assist us in

- Arrays, strings, and objects are iterated through.

- Constructing composite functions.

- Value manipulation and testing.

Algolia Places

Algolia Places is a JavaScript package that allows us to use address auto-completion on our website in a simple and widespread manner.

It's a lightning-fast and incredibly accurate tool that can assist improve our site's user experience. Algolia Places uses OpenStreetMap's outstanding open-source database to cover international locations.

Features

- It speeds up checkouts by filling many inputs at once.

- We can easily utilize the nation or city selectors.

- We may see results fast by presenting real-time link recommendations on a map.

- Algolia Places can handle mistakes and present results appropriately.

- It returns responses in milliseconds by automatically routing all inquiries to the closest server.

Use Cases

- Allows us to include a map to display a certain place, which is quite handy.

- It allows us to use forms more effectively.

Anime.js

One of the best JavaScript animation libraries is Anime.js, which we can use to create animations to our website or application.

It was released in 2019 and is compact with a reliable yet straightforward API.

Features

- DOM attributes, CSS properties, SVG, CSS transformations, and JS objects are all supported by Anime.js.

- Works with a variety of browsers, including Chrome, Safari, Firefox, and Opera.

- Its source code is simple to understand and apply.

- Complex animation techniques like overlapping and staggered follow-through become simpler.

Use Cases

- On attributes and timings, we may utilize Anime.js' staggering mechanism.

- Create layered CSS modifications with multiple durations over one HTML element at the same time.

- Anime.js callbacks and controls functions are used to play, stop, trigger, reverse, and control events in a synchronized way.

Animate On Scroll (AOS)

For single-page parallax websites, Animate On Scroll is ideal. This open-source JS toolkit allows you to add nice animations to our sites that look great as we scroll down or up. It enhances our site design by allowing us to add fading effects, static anchor placements, and other features that will delight our users.

Features

- The library can identify element locations and apply appropriate classes when they appear in the viewport.

- It not only allows us to simply build animations, but it also allows us to adjust them in the viewport.

- It works well on a variety of devices, including a mobile phone, tablet, and PC.

- It has no dependencies because it is developed entirely in JavaScript.

Use Cases

- Animate one element based on the location of another.

- Animate items based on their position on the screen.

- On mobile devices, disable element animations.

- Create various animations such as fades, flips, slides, zooms, anchor placements, and so on.

Bideo.js

Do we want to incorporate full-screen videos into the backdrop of our website?

Try out Bideo.js.

Features

- Using this JavaScript package, we can easily add a video background.
- This feature looks great and works well on screens of all sizes and scales.
- Videos can be resized depending on the browser used.
- CSS/HTML makes it simple to implement.

Use Cases

- To incorporate responsive full-screen background videos into a website.

Chart.js

Is our website or project relevant to the field of data analysis?

Is it necessary to offer a large number of statistics? Chart.js is a fantastic JavaScript package to work with. Chart.js is a versatile and easy-to-use framework for designers and developers who want to quickly add stunning charts and graphs to their projects. It is open-source and licensed under the MIT license.

Features

- Basic charts and graphs may be added in an elegant and straightforward manner.
- As a result, responsive web pages are produced.
- Loading is light, and learning and implementing is simple.
- There are eight distinct sorts of charts.
- Excellent for beginners.
- Pages may be animated to make them more interactive.

Use Cases

- When diverse datasets are employed, mixed chart types provide clear visual representations.

- Plot sparse and complicated datasets on logarithmic, date, time, or user-defined scales.

Cleave.js

If we wish to format your text content, Cleave.js provides an intriguing approach.

Its invention seeks to make it simpler to boost the readability of the input field by formatting the inputted data. To format text, we no longer need to mask patterns or use regular expressions.

Features

- Improves user experience by providing consistent data for form submissions.

- We may format credit card numbers, phone numbers, dates, times, and numerals in a variety of ways.

- Custom blocks, prefixes, and delimiters should be formatted.

- Supports ReactJS components, among other things.

Use Cases

- Using CSS selectors, apply cleave.js to several DOM components.

- To make changes to a given raw value.

- To obtain the text field's reference.

- It is used in Vue.js, jQuery, and Playground with a redux form.

Choreographer.js

To efficiently animate complicated CSS, use Chreographer.js.

It may even include more custom functions for non-CSS animations. Install its package using npm or add its script file to utilize this JavaScript library.

Features

- Its Animation class is in charge of managing individual animation data.

- Each animation instance is configured through the animationConfig object.

- There are two built-in animation functions: 'change' and 'scale.'

- Scale is used to translate progressively measured values to a node's style parameter.

- The 'Change' command removes or adds style attributes.

Use Cases

- Make instant scroll animations.

- Create animations based on mouse movements.

Glimmer

Glimmer, which was released in 2017, has lightweight and fast UI components.

It makes use of the robust Ember CLI and can be used as a component with EmberJS.

Features

- Glimmer is a fast DOM rendering engine that may give exceptional render and update performance.

- It is adaptable enough to function with our existing technological stack without needing us to rewrite code.

Use Cases

- It may be used as a stand-alone component or integrated as a web component into existing systems.

- Rendering of the DOM.

- It aids in the differentiation between static and dynamic material.

- When we want the functionalities of Ember but in a lighter package, use Glimmer.

Granim.js

Granim.js is a JS framework that allows us to build dynamic and fluid gradient animations. We may make our site stand out by using colorful backgrounds.

Features

- Gradients can be used to cover pictures, work independently, slide beneath image masks, and so forth.

- Gradient directions may be customized using percentage or pixel values.

- Choose from diagonal, top-bottom, left-right, radial, and custom gradient directions.

- Set the length of the animation in milliseconds (ms) with changing states.

- Change the color and location of the gradient.

- Image modification based on canvas position, source, scale, and so forth.

- Other alternatives include setting callbacks, issuing events, gradient control methods, and so forth.

Use Cases

- Making a simple gradient animation using three gradients of two colors.

- Complex gradient animation with two gradients of three colors.

- Gradient animation using a single backdrop picture, two colors, and a single blending mode.

- Using a single picture mask, create gradient animations beneath a given form.

- Developing event-responsive gradient animations.

fullPage.js

fullPage.js, an open-source JS package, makes it simple to develop full-screen scrolling webpages or one-page websites. It is simple to use and allows us to include a landscape slider inside our site sections.

Features

- Provides several customization and setup possibilities.

- JavaScript frameworks such as react-fullpage, angular-fullpage, and vue-fullpage are supported.

- Allows for vertical as well as horizontal scrolling.

- A responsive design that adapts to different screen sizes and browsers.

- Page loads with auto-scrolling.

- Lazy video/image loading.

Use Cases

- To enhance the default functionality with the use of several extensions.

- To build full-screen scrolling websites.

- Making a one-page website.

Leaflet

Leaflet is one of the greatest JavaScript frameworks for incorporating interactive maps into our website. It is open-source and mobile-friendly, with a file size of roughly 39kb.

Leaflet powers the interactive maps in the MapPress Maps for WordPress plugin.

Features

- Performance improvements include mobile hardware acceleration and CSS support.

- Tile layers, popups, markers, vector layers, GeoJSON, and picture overlays are all examples of unique layers.

- Drag panning, pinch-zoom, keyboard navigation, events, and other interaction features.

- Layer switcher, attribution, scale, and zoom buttons are all available on the map.

- Browsers such as Chrome, Safari, Firefox, Edge, and others are supported.

- Customization options include OOP, HTML and image-based markers, CSS3 controls, and popups.

Case Studies

- Include a map with improved zooming and panning, smart polygon/polyline rendering, modular design, and tap-delay mobile animation on our website.

Multiple.js

Several.js allows background image sharing across multiple items by utilizing CSS or HTML and does not require JavaScript coordinate processing. As a result, it produces an eye-catching visual impact that encourages greater user involvement.

Features

- Multiple backgrounds are supported.

- Support for gradient opacity.

- Many mobile and web browsers are supported.

Use Cases

- To distribute background images.

Moment.js

Moment.js assists us in successfully managing time and date while working with multiple time zones, API requests, local languages, and so forth.

Dates and times can be streamlined by checking, parsing, formatting, or altering them.

Features

- It supports a large number of worldwide languages.

- Mutability of objects.

- Several internal characteristics like as epoch shifting and accessing native Date objects, are available.

- There are several suggestions for using its parser appropriately, such as strict mode, date formats, forgiving mode, and so on.

Use Cases

- To include a time stamp in a published article.

- Communicating with individuals from all around the world in their native tongue.

Masonry

Masonry is an outstanding JS grid layout framework.

This library assists us in positioning our grid items based on the amount of vertical space available. It's even utilized by some of the most popular WordPress picture gallery plugins.

Consider how a mason fits stones when constructing a wall.

Features

- The grid arrangement of masonry is built on columns and does not have a defined row height.

- Optimizes web page space by removing unwanted spaces.

- Sorting and filtering items while keeping the layout structure intact.

- Effects of animation.

- Dynamic components that alter the layout automatically for optimal structure.

Use Cases

- To make image galleries with different image sizes.

- List the most recent blog entries in many columns while keeping consistency, even if the summary lengths change.

- To represent portfolio items such as photographs, designs, projects, and so on.

Omniscient

Omniscient.js is a JS package that provides React component abstraction for immediate top-down rendering with immutable data. Because it is efficient and has fascinating features, this library may help us construct our project smoothly.

Features

- Reminds us of stateless React components.

- User interface functional programming.

- Component rendering from the top.

- Immutable data is supported by Immutable.js.

- Mixins provide tiny and composable components with shared functionality.

Use Cases

- To give component keys.

- Use auxiliary functions or constructs to communicate with parent codes.

- Overriding elements.

- Debugging and filtering.

Parsley

Do we want to include shapes into our projects? If so, Parsley may be beneficial to us.

It is a simple yet effective JS library for form validation.

Features

- Its simple DOM API accepts input straight from HTML tags without requiring you to write a single line of JS.

- Dynamic form validation is accomplished by dynamically detecting form alterations.

- There are over 12 built-in validators, an Ajax validator, and various extensions.

- We may modify Parsley's default behavior and provide a more UI and UX focused experience.

- Free, open-source, and extremely dependable, it is compatible with a wide range of browsers.

Use Cases

- Making a basic form.

- Performing difficult validations.

- Creating forms with several steps.

- Multiple inputs are being validated.

- Taking care of promises and Ajax requests.

- Creating excellent floating error labels by styling inputs.

Popper.js

Popper.js was intended to simplify positioning popovers, dropdowns, tooltips, and other contextual components that display near a button or other similar elements easier. Popper makes it easy to organize them, attach them to other site components, and make them work flawlessly on every screen size.

Features

- A little library of roughly 3kb in size.

- When we scroll inside the scrolling containers, the tooltip stays with the reference element.

- Advanced customizability.

- Uses a comprehensive toolkit to develop UIs, such as Angular or React, making integrations straightforward.

Use Cases

- To create a tooltip from the ground up.

- To neatly arrange these parts.

Three.js

Three.js can enhance our 3-D design experience. On contemporary browsers, it renders scenes using WebGL. If we are using IE 10 or below, try other CSS3, CSS2, and SVH renderers.

Features

- Chrome 9+, Opera 15+, Firefox 4+, Internet Explorer 11, Edge, and Safari 5.1 are all supported.

- Typed arrays, Blob, Promise, URL API, Fetch, and other JS capabilities are supported.

- We may make a variety of geometrics, objects, lighting, shadows, loaders, materials, arithmetic components, textures, and so on.

Use Cases

- To make a geometric cube, sphere, or other shape.

- Making a camera or a scene.

Screenfull.js

To add a full-screen element to our project, use Screenfull.js.

We will have no problems utilizing this JavaScript library because of its amazing cross-browser performance.

Features

- Make a page or element full-screen.

- Hide cell phone navigation UI.

- Using jQuery and Angular, add full-screen components.

- Detects full-screen changes, mistakes, and so forth.

Use Cases

- Including a full-screen feature on a website.

- Screenfull.js in a document.

- Toggling the full-screen mode and exiting.

- Event management.

Polymer

Polymer, a Google open-source JavaScript toolkit, is used to create web programs with components.

Features

- An easy method for creating custom components.

- Properties computed.

- Both one-way and two-way data binding are supported.

- Gesture occurrences.

Use Cases

- Using JS, CSS, and HTTP, you can construct interactive online apps using bespoke web components.

- It is utilized by popular websites and services like as YouTube, Google Earth, and Play, among others.

Voca

The aim of Voca is to alleviate the agony associated with dealing with JavaScript strings. It includes handy functions for easily manipulating strings such as changing case, padding, trimming, truncating, and more.

Features

- Because of its modular nature, the entire library or individual functions load rapidly while decreasing app construction time.

- Provides utilities for cutting, formatting, manipulating, querying, and escaping strings.

- There are no dependencies.

Use Cases

- Voca may be used in a variety of settings, including Node.js, Webpack, Rollup, Browserify, and others.

- To change the case of a topic to title case, camel case, kebab case, snake case, upper case, and lower case.

- To uppercase and lowercase the initial character.

- To enable an implicit/explicit chain sequence, construct chain objects to surround a subject.

- To conduct various operations such as character counting, string formatting, and so on.

We covered Asynchronous Development, DOM Manipulation, HTTP, and Forms in this chapter. We also talked about working with APIs and JavaScript libraries.

NOTES

1 How to Write Asynchronous Function for Node.js?: www.geeksforgeeks. org/how-to-write-asynchronous-function-for-node-js/?ref=lbp   Accessed on: 28 September 2022.

2 How to Create an Asynchronous Function in Javascript?: www.geeksfor-geeks.org/how-to-create-an-asynchronous-function-in-javascript/?ref=lbp Accessed on: 28 September 2022.

3 Synchronous and Asynchronous in JavaScript: www.geeksforgeeks.org/ synchronous-and-asynchronous-in-javascript/?ref=lbp Accessed on: 28 September 2022.

4 Explain Asynchronous vs Deferred JavaScript: www.geeksforgeeks.org/ explain-asynchronous-vs-deferred-javascript/?ref=lbp Accessed on: 28 September 2022.

5 Document Object Model: www.javatpoint.com/document-object-model Accessed on: 28 September 2022.

6 Javascript – document.getElementById() Method: www.javatpoint.com/document-getElementById()-method Accessed on: 28 September 2022.

7 GetElementsByClassName(): www.javatpoint.com/javascript-getelements-byclassname Accessed on: 28 September 2022.

8 Javascript – document.getElementsByName() Method: www.javatpoint.com/document-getElementsByName()-method Accessed on: 28 September 2022.

9 Javascript – document.getElementsByTagName() Method: www.javatpoint.com/document-getElementsByTagName()-method Accessed on: 29 September 2022.

10 Javascript – innerHTML: www.javatpoint.com/javascript-innerHTML Accessed on: 29 September 2022.

11 Javascript – innerText: www.javatpoint.com/javascript-innerText Accessed on: 29 September 2022.

12 5 Ways to Make HTTP Requests in JavaScript: https://livecodestream.dev/post/5-ways-to-make-http-requests-in-javascript/ Accessed on: 29 September 2022.

13 Http Cookies: www.javatpoint.com/http-cookies Accessed on: 30 September 2022.

14 JavaScript Form: www.javatpoint.com/javascript-form Accessed on: 30 September 2022.

15 JavaScript Form Validation: www.javatpoint.com/javascript-form-validation Accessed on: 30 September 2022.

16 Working with APIs in JavaScript: www.geeksforgeeks.org/working-with-apis-in-javascript/ Accessed on: 30 September 2022.

17 The 40 Best JavaScript Libraries and Frameworks for 2022: https://kinsta.com/blog/javascript-libraries/ Accessed on: 01 October 2022.

CHAPTER 4

The Clearer Picture

IN THIS CHAPTER

➤ The various uses of JS

- Frontend

- Backend

- Mobile

- Gaming

- Desktop

➤ Finding your Niche

- Which framework to learn and when?

- Combining JS skills with other programming languages

Let us now spend some time discussing JavaScript ecosystem as a whole.

A JAVASCRIPT FRAMEWORK IS WHAT?

A JavaScript framework is a group of prewritten programs designed to enable applications and give advantages that plain JavaScript cannot by itself. Consider a tent if the concept of frameworks is still unclear to us.

We construct a frame to serve as the tent's framework.[1] The tent's inside and outside may then be customized in anyway we choose.

DOI: 10.1201/9781003356578-4

Naturally, JavaScript frameworks aren't actual buildings like our tent, but the idea is the same.

Let's take a minute to address two frequently asked topics before moving on to the most well-known JavaScript frameworks.

What Distinguishes a JavaScript Framework from a JavaScript Library?

Libraries in JavaScript are collections of code created for certain use cases.

For instance, the Day.js package is devoted to making use of dates in JavaScript, which may be challenging even for experienced developers.

jQuery is a well-known JavaScript library that simplifies the syntax for DOM traversal, event handling, animations, and other typical operations. On the other hand, frameworks are designed to perform various tasks and serve as the foundation of a web application.

Like Angular, several frameworks design the complete site tree. In other words, they support the full application frontend. Some, like Vue.js, allow for gradual usage, allowing our application to make restricted use of the framework.

For particular use cases that our framework doesn't handle, we'll probably utilize libraries in our application. Remember those annoying dates with Day.js? This library is not required to be used in views that exclude dates.

However, regardless of the functionalities we use, if our application is created using Angular, the page template is written in Angular's syntax.

In contrast, Day.js may be called where it is necessary and not called where it is not.

Use a JavaScript Framework, But Why?

Because frameworks are constructed on top of JavaScript, we can accomplish any function a framework does using standard JavaScript.

But because the hard work has already been done, why go through all that bother again?

This underlines the fundamental advantage of using a JavaScript framework: More capability without the need for us to produce new code.

For instance, the virtual document object model is used by both React and Vue.js (DOM).

Because it only updates altered HTML components, the virtual DOM is quicker at handling HTML elements.

Contrarily, regular JavaScript will render the whole DOM once again regardless of the amount of the change.

React and Vue.js are thus quicker for websites and programs that have a lot of interactive elements.

Libraries and Frameworks for JavaScript

In programming, frameworks and libraries are crucial. This raises the issue, nevertheless, which is superior: JavaScript libraries or JavaScript frameworks?

One cannot replace the other nor is one better than the other. Nonetheless, a developer may choose which one to utilize based on the specifics of the project. Take into account the goals of the project you're working on. What, for instance, is the scope of our project?[2]

This might help us remove libraries and frameworks that are inappropriate for smaller applications from our list of options. Overall, although both libraries and frameworks need a fundamental knowledge of JavaScript, frameworks often demand more JS expertise and experience, making the learning curve for libraries a bit less difficult. And which library ought to should we use first? React is a logical first library option since creating and maintaining complex user interfaces is a major component of frontend web or app development, which is where most web developers start. Additionally, organizations place a great value on React expertise. The React team also provides extensive documentation and has a sizable community. The fact that you begin with a JavaScript library like React JS or jQuery does not exclude us from subsequently learning JavaScript frameworks, however.

On the contrary, if we start with one library, it will be a lot simpler to comprehend and ultimately go on to frameworks like Angular, Vue, or Ember JS.

Although learning to code is a process, we must start.

A programmer has access to the universal language known as JavaScript.

Its libraries and frameworks are very beneficial to programmers working in the web development industry. A framework inverts program control, which is the primary difference between it and a library.

It provides the developer with the necessary information. However, a library does not.

A programmer instead calls the library as and when needed. Overall, JavaScript offers great aesthetics and functionalities and is utilized in the majority of modern apps. Due to its superior functionality and simplicity of use, it is favored by web developers all over the globe.

TOP 7 JAVASCRIPT FRONTEND FRAMEWORKS

The best JavaScript frameworks for the contemporary web will be discussed first.[3]

1. React

One of the most well-known open-source JavaScript frameworks is React, which was developed in 2013 by a Facebook software developer called Jordan Walke.

On GitHub, the React community has received more than 180k stars.

React is used and adored by around 40% of developers globally.

Despite a minor decline in use satisfaction in 2020, React is still a popular option for new developers joining the IT industry.

It is simpler to learn, has stronger community support, and is lightweight.

Simform used React as well because of how lightweight it is to create a user-friendly component-driven frontend online application for the International Hockey Federation (FIH).

How It Operates

- Developers may include HTML snippets into JavaScript files thanks to React's usage of JSX.

- The React library integrates seamlessly with state management, routing, and APIs.

- The React library employs an in-memory cache to create a virtual DOM. The components' prior and subsequent states are compared by the virtual DOM. Based on that, only components whose statuses have changed are rendered by the actual DOM.

- Developers may nest by using the framework's one-way data binding, which is a unidirectional flow of data.

- When executing code, it makes use of lifecycle methods like componentDidMount.

Real-life examples

Popular websites like Facebook, Netflix, Asana, Pinterest, Airbnb, Reddit, UberEats, etc. have all been designed using React.

Popular React Components

- **Material UI:** A beautiful UI design may be produced with the material UI set of react components. It has several features, including stylistic elements for making widgets like forms, navigation, and layouts.

- **React Semantic UI:** Simple sentences are used by React Semantic UI to activate built-in functionality. Additionally, the interface has a wide variety of themes that provide developers total creative flexibility.

- **React Toolbox:** It is a collection of React components created in SASS that follows Google's guidelines for material design. To import SASS stylesheets, it makes use of CSS modules. The library offers adaptable and customizable solutions with easy integration with React webpack.

Advantages

- Facebook supports communities.

- Writing components without classes is possible.

- Recognized for its reusable code components.

- Suitable for beginners.

Disadvantages

- There is insufficient and credible documentation.

- Constant updates force developers to keep up with new developments.

- Learning JSX syntax may be difficult.

When Should We Utilize React?

React is the most effective option for creating Single-Page Applications because of its Virtual DOM features (SPAs). Additionally, React has a strong community and is a great choice for creating complex apps.

2. Vue.js

Vue.js is an open-source frontend framework created and maintained by Evan and his team that was first made available 7 years ago. These days, Vue.js is often used for lightweight frontend apps that must function on a

JavaScript framework. It came to the third place among frameworks in a Github poll done in 2021. By using this framework, close to 700k websites have been created. When developing code, Vue.js is a full framework that offers more flexibility. The framework is further renowned for its suitable size and quicker loading times.

How It Operates

- Virtual DOM is used by Vue.js to provide state updates and modifications.

- Both one-way and two-way data binding are supported by vue. js. Reactive two-way data binding is the term for this capability. It implies that React makes it simple to modify the data between a component class and its template.

- The ecosystem of Vue.js is rich. We may still create hybrid mobile apps with Quasar Framework, NativeScript, or Ionic even if it lacks its own mobile framework.

- JSX is also used by Vue.js. Vue.js can import and maintain customized components quickly by using JSX.

- As it provides a variety of methods to apply transition effects, Vue. js is feature-rich with CSS transitions and animations. Users of Vue. js may make use of the transition wrapper, unique transition classes, JavaScript hooks, and other features.

Real-Life Examples
Popular businesses like Alibaba, 9gag, Xiaomi, and others have used Vue. js for all of their frontend needs.

Popular Vue.js Components

- A Vue.js component library called Element UI has 500 active developers and strong community support. The component places a heavy emphasis on minute details, assisting both developers and designers in creating a beautiful and engaging user interface.

- Unofficial Vue.js material design framework Vuetify enables you to build reusable, squeaky-clean components that are compatible with

Server-Side Rendering, or SSR. Github now has 23k stars for it, and both the community and popularity are rapidly expanding. Over 400 people have contributed to the active Vuetify community, which has produced more than 20 plugins.

- A UI kit based on the Bootstrap library is called Bootstrap Vue.js. Developers may use this kit with Vue.js to create responsive, mobile-first apps using bootstrap version 4. The kit is jam-packed with a grid system, many UI elements, and themes.

Advantages

- The framework is simple for new users.

- Vue.js provides thorough documentation.

- Two-way data binding is supported.

- Is quite small and simple to incorporate.

Disadvantages

- Lacks a wide variety of plugins to choose from.

- The developer community is not very big.

- No tech giant is supporting the framework.

- Not appropriate for scaling.

When Should We Utilize Vue.js?

With Vue.js, we may use a framework that goes beyond a simple library and doesn't complicate code. Vue.js is the answer if you're searching for a forgiving design that yet keeps logic and view separate.

It assists in developing SPAs or launching smaller initiatives in terms of apps. Vue.js is the finest alternative on the market if we want a variety of developer-friendly capabilities like tree-sharking, code-splitting, etc.

3. Angular

Google created the TypeScript-based open-source web application framework known as Angular. This framework's version 2 included fundamental components including dependency injection, asynchronous compiles, RxJS, etc.

It has become very popular among developers. Nearly 60% of engineers have actual experience working with the Angular framework, according to a poll by Ideamotive. Simform specialists also used Angular to create the FoodTruck Spaces online application.

How It Operates

- A full-featured MVC framework is Angular. It helps in building an organized application.

- The architecture provides data flow in both directions. Using the controller, this functionality allows Angular to link the DOM to the model data. We may listen to events and change the data between parent and child components concurrently using bi-directional data flow.

- Despite its flaws, Angular's environment is amazing. We may use the numerous out-of-the-box solutions it offers to build quick and effective applications. For instance, nothing has to be installed or configured in order to use server-side rendering with Angular.

- All of the code components are very tested and reusable thanks to Angular's hierarchical dependency injection functionality.

- Due to its rapid mistake detection and useful feedback choices, Angular's debugging is often less difficult.

Real-Life Examples

Numerous Google services have been created using Angular.

Other well-known websites created using Angular include those from Forbes, LEGO, Autodesk, BMW, etc.

Popular Angular Components

- The Angular component library Ngx-bootstrap is perfect for incorporating bootstrap components into your project. For improved efficiency and a responsive user interface, the bootstrap components are created using Angular.

- Angular Material is a set of reusable UI components that draws inspiration from Google's Material Design. This toolkit offers a wide range of UI design elements, responsive grid layouts, and different themes.

Advantages

- The component-based design of Angular provides flawless model-to-view synchronization.

- Offers reusable, thoroughly tested components.

- Angular has a sizable development community and is supported by Google.

- Provides sophisticated features like dependency injection and directives.

Disadvantages

- The structure doesn't lend itself well to beginners. Users must get familiar with MVC before using the framework.

- Restricted SEO abilities.

- File sizes have increased significantly.

When Should We Utilize Angular?

Because it is a complete framework, Angular is appropriate for creating massive corporate applications. It also leverages MVC architecture, which enables smooth integration of sophisticated features.

4. jQuery

Prior to the creation of contemporary JavaScript libraries and framework, jQuery dominated the IT industry. It is one of the first open-source JavaScript libraries and is lightweight and feature-rich, having been released in 2006 by John Resign. One of the best JavaScript frontend frameworks, according to experts.

It is used by 95.5% of all websites that employ JavaScript, according to a W3Techs study. JavaScript scripts are recognized to be minimized by jQuery, which also provides strong assistance from its knowledgeable and mature community.

How It Operates

- For its event handling skills, jQuery is well-known. Even user actions like mouse clicks and keyboard presses are condensed into little pieces of code for simpler administration.

- The syntaxes of jQuery and CSS are pretty similar. Beginners may thus get practical experience with the framework rather quickly.

- The framework's most recent iteration now comes with jQuery Mobile for creating scalable mobile apps.

- It is a simple-to-use framework with a straightforward API that works with several browsers.

- One of the lightweight frameworks supporting AMD modules is jQuery, which has a 30kb zip size for a blank project. By using AMD modules, you can manage our UI dependencies without using Download Builder. The module also helps us load the source code for jQuery UI using an exclusive AMD loader like RequireJS.

Real-Life Examples
Twitter, Microsoft, Uber, Pandora, SurveyMonkey, and other well-known companies have used jQuery in their apps.

Popular jQuery Components

- A jQuery UI is a free library with a variety of UI elements for our next project. The library is an expansion of dynamic and interactive widgets that programmers may use to improve the user interfaces of their applications. Tree view, form widgets, color pickers, charts, RTL support, and other noteworthy elements are just a few. In addition, this library provides consistent performance across a range of browsers, platforms, and devices.

- A jQuery-based widget library for jQuery mobile is called Wijimo. JQuery is used to power the tool, which results in greater performance. It offers more than 30 themes, support for RTL, video widgets, animation widgets, etc. Additionally, this widget is compatible with both online and mobile platforms.

- A free plugin called Muuri allows us to build flexible layouts with jQuery. We have total control over the grid container's location and dimensions thanks to the plugin. When working with jQuery to create an intuitive UI, developers may unleash their inner designers thanks to the freedom.

Advantages

- All widely used web browsers are compatible with the framework.

- Offer exemplary community assistance.

- The learning curve for jQuery is not very severe.

- Provides a huge selection of plugins.

Disadvantages

- Because it contains all DOM events, effects, and AJAX components, the file size is enormous.

- DOM APIs are dated.

- Due to the lack of a data layer, DOM modification is a laborious and manual procedure.

When Should We Utilize jQuery?

jQuery is still the best option for delivering web-based and desktop JavaScript applications since it has cross-browser compatibility.

5. Svelte

Svelte is a framework that is an open-sourced frontend compiler, while the majority of the frameworks on this list are complete frameworks or libraries.

It was first shown in 2016 and quickly became well-liked by the developer community.

More than 25k websites have been created using it as of right now.

An application created using Svelte creates code to change DOM as it is only a compiler.

It is one of the frontend frameworks that are lightweight as a result.

How It Operates

- The MVC architectural concepts are used to segregate the template, logic, and view in the Svelte application. It enables numerous developers to collaborate on the same project at once.

- With Svelte, we can blend basic JavaScript with HTML, CSS, and TypeScript.

- Svelte uses minimal resources since it doesn't need anything extra to create a virtual DOM. It makes the total loading time of the program substantially faster.

Real-Life Examples

Many well-known companies have used Svelte to create their websites and benefited from its ease of use. A few examples are The New York Times, Absolute Web, Cashfree, Godaddy, and Razorpay.

Popular Svelte Components

- Svelte Material UI is a collection of TypeScript-written Material UI elements. SASS is used to style the Svelte Material UI. Developers may create unique user interface components using a variety of widgets and tools provided by SMUI (Svelte Material UI).

- Svelte-flow is a Flowbite-powered Svelte UI component that may help you design websites more quickly. Dark modes, buttons, modals, cards, a navbar, etc. are all included.

- Carbon Components Svelte—It is the Carbon Design System, an open-source design tool developed by IBM. It has about 7,000 icons, 700 pictograms, 20+ charts, and other things.

Advantages

- Code into vanilla JavaScript is converted.

- The structure is quite light.

- Provides support for component-based architecture.

Disadvantages

- A little ecosystem.

- There aren't many Svelte tools on the market.

- Is difficult to scale.

When Should We Utilize Svelte?
The USP of Svelte is simplicity. Svelte is best used for small-scale undertakings as a result. Its straightforward coding style makes it accessible to any beginner frontend developer.

6. Ember

Ember is a free JavaScript framework that supports both MVVM and MVC architectures. It was first released in 2011. By using the capabilities provided by Ember, more than 70k websites have been created.

One of the fastest rendering engines on the market, Glimmer, is the foundation around which Ember is based. Ember focuses primarily on creating web-based apps.

However, Ember has developed over time and currently provides whole support for creating mobile-based apps. Ember is one of the most reliable frameworks and is ideal for creating scalable one-page apps.

How It Operates

- Ember provides two-way data binding that instantly synchronizes display and model.

- Through its server-side DOM rendering, Ember uses fastboot.js to enhance the efficiency of complicated user interfaces.

- Ember's community is one of the busiest ones around right now.

- A large ecology exists in Ember. There is probably a plugin to make every function you ever find difficult to include easy. More than 1,500 add-ons are available for Ember to help anybody with their development endeavors.

Real-Life Examples
Ember was used by several well-known companies for their business requirements.

Ember has been utilized by companies including Apple Music, Square, LinkedIn, Netflix, Twitch, and others. Apple Music is one of the notable instances of a desktop application built using Ember.

Popular Ember Components

- The process of transforming naming conventions into classes, methods, and templates is carried out by the well-known plugin Ember Resolve. Usually, this is beneficial when Ember has to resolve its dependencies.

- Ember test helpers are a plugin that offers a number of utility methods to enhance your testing experience. DOM interaction helpers, routing helpers, rendering helpers, and other utility methods are included in the plugin.

- Ember-concurrency is a condensed plugin for Ember.js that enhances the concurrency/async functionalities. We may use the task primitive it provides, which has several advantages including permitting cancellation and exposing the underlying data.

Advantages

- Ember provides rendering on the server.

- Both TypeScript and JavaScript are supported.

- Ember features extensive and in-depth documentation.

- It has a solid data layer that is incorporated.

Disadvantages

- The structure may be a bit challenging for beginners.

- There is no way to reuse components.

- Provides no customization.

- Not suggested for little tasks.

When Should We Utilize Ember?
Component-based design and the abundance of plugins at our disposal might be the ideal partners for creating complicated mobile apps or single-page web applications.

7. Backbone.js
Backbone.js is a JavaScript library that was released as an open-source project in 2010 by Jeremy Ashkenas. It is renowned for being portable.

But for complete library compatibility, the framework largely relies on underscore.js and jQuery. Simform used the capabilities of backbone.js to create SenTMap, a sentiment analysis engine.

How It Operates

- One of the key aspects of Backbone.js is the ability to divide business logic from user input logic. This aids programmers in creating an application that is properly structured.

- Developers are urged by Backbone.js to turn data into models, DOM operations into views, and connect the two together via events.

- The framework gives client-side web applications powerful APIs with enumerable methods.

- Backbone.js automatically refreshes our application's HTML if the architecture's model changes.

Real-Life Examples

Backbone.js has been used by a number of well-known companies, including Uber, Pinterest, Reddit, Trello, and Tumblr, to fulfill application needs.

Advantages

- There are more than 100 extensions offered.

- The framework is simple for new users.

- Very portable.

- Data is kept in models rather than the DOM.

Disadvantages

- There is no two-way data binding functionality.

- At times, architecture seems to be complicated and hazy.

- More boilerplate code must be written by us.

- The developer community thinks that the framework is gradually getting outdated.

When Should We Utilize Backbone.js?

Backbone.js may be used for larger projects and is best suited for basic single-page apps.

How Can We Choose the Ideal JavaScript Framework for Our Next Project?

It is challenging to keep track of all the variations across frameworks.

The harder part is deciding which one to employ for our project.

Making the incorrect choice might be a terrible bet on our time and project money.

Unfortunately, it is difficult to tell which framework is the greatest suit for us.

Our company needs will determine the framework to use, but the following four considerations might aid in your choice.

Team Proficiency

The most common one is a framework, if there is such a thing.

However, developers won't be able to take full use of this framework if our current team isn't at ease utilizing it.

Choose a framework that our team has the greatest expertise with, or recruit remote workers to take advantage of market-leading frameworks.

Backward Compatibility

A frontend framework helps in coding the application, but the backend must also be taken care of.

For an application to be completely functional, the frontend and backend must communicate smoothly.

Choosing a frontend framework that complements your backend is a good idea if you have already established your backend.

If not, we will have to deal with difficulties such as integration problems, compatibility problems, etc.

Complexity

Choose a framework based on MVC architecture if you're creating a complicated web application with several sub-pages and capabilities. We will be able to divide your features into sections that can be developed concurrently by doing this. Our development time will be greatly shortened by doing this.

However, using a lightweight framework to create complicated applications might be disastrous. A less robust framework cannot manage the complexity and will eventually experience several issues.

Size and Functionality

Ideally, a framework shouldn't have a lot of features. Several frameworks may seem to be quite sophisticated yet are challenging to deploy. Focus on achieving maximum performance if we're creating a straightforward system with few features. As a rule of thumb, you should aim for a happy medium between performance and size when designing a framework.

5 Backend JavaScript Frameworks

The web is powered by JavaScript when it comes to web development.

JavaScript is in charge of websites' programmed behavior, including loading and reloading new page material without completely refreshing the page, animating page components, and verifying user input into online forms. HTML and CSS manage the style and data shown on a page.[4]

The popularity of JavaScript has led to the emergence of a wave of frameworks throughout time. For JavaScript developers, it feels like a new framework debuts every week, each claiming to be superior to the previous one.

There is a constant need for these items since millions of websites depend on third-party JavaScript libraries and frameworks.

What about the backend? We've previously covered some of the most well-liked frontend JS frameworks. Even while some frameworks are similar, it's best to avoid mixing together front- and backend programming, particularly when using something as important as JavaScript.

For instance, JavaScript is often used with server-side and other non-browser applications, which requires developers to approach their work fundamentally differently.

1. **Next**

    Although it first sounds a bit strange, the Next framework makes it incredibly simple to share JavaScript code across the project.

    This eliminates the need to write the same job in many languages of code.

    Nearly, the same component is used for displaying client-side markup and querying a datastore.

Everything about creating with Next becomes pretty intuitive once you master the fundamentals.

'With Next, we get highly well-maintained documentation as well as the same setup simplicity as we do with projects like create-react-app.

It is maintained by Vercel, a firm that was originally known as Zeit, and it contains a library of examples for almost every use case and integration that is currently in use.

Their deployment platform is something we also like.

Due to the fact that the API routes and pages we build are converted into lambda functions, Next was essentially built to be deployed with Now.

In my opinion, developers may save a tonne of time by concentrating more on application problems rather than AWS console issues.

Because we get a framework that handles server-side rendering, simple to configure API routes, and is generally a better create-react-app, we believe we would prefer Next over Gatsby or other Node backend tools. They're all beneficial in various ways, but because we tend to work alone on many projects, my choice for launching using Now seals Next for me.

It is marketed as a fantastic framework for everything production-related, from TypeScript and built-in CSS support to code-splitting and packaging. Next.js is now up to version 9.5. The first edition was released in October 2016.

2. Express

Express.js is a great option for developing online apps and server APIs, according to Kirill Onishuk, a full-stack web developer at OrangeSoft.

Its quickness, simplicity, and flexibility provide all the capabilities required for creating both simple and complicated programs.

Installing the necessary npm packages enables it to be readily extended, allowing for the solution of any issue.

Express offers a layer on top of node.js that does not restrict its functionality, allowing us to use its features quickly as well.

Because Express offers a wide variety of template engines, Onishuk said, 'it is appropriate for creating apps with server rendering' (for example, pug and handlebars).

It has several HTTP service methods and intermediary handlers for API development.

3. **Gatsby**

Gatsby may be used without a server since the pages can be developed locally and then pushed to an object store and CDN, according to Up Hail's founder Avi Wilensky (i.e., AWS S3 and Cloudfront). The design offers speedy performance while reducing expense and complexity.

With a vast library of more than 2,000 plugins, Gatsby is also scalable.

Gatsby, a React and GraphQI-based framework, works well for building relatively static webpages with services connected (via its plugins, of course).

The fact that Gatsby does not do server-side rendering makes webpages created with it very quickly, but it may also be restrictive.

4. **Node.js**

'At Riseapps, Node.js is the preferred JavaScript backend architecture.

We choose this architecture mostly because it allows us full-stack JS development.

This makes it easy to reuse code on both the frontend and the backend, which is a major benefit given how often we utilize React and Vue.js.

A web application that uses JavaScript on bothends loads extremely rapidly and fluidly. 'The applicability of Node for real-time applications, particularly those for communication, would be the next justification.

A framework that makes software quickly responsive is essential as we develop several applications with calling and messaging features.

Apps created with Node.js may also effectively manage numerous user requests.

'At long last, this JS design enables the development of scalable apps. This framework's nature makes the software it produces efficient and readily adaptable to changing needs.

For developers of all stripes, Node.js provides a wide range of applications.

In the context of AWS, where you may use it to launch EC2 instances, it is quite helpful.

It is used by businesses including IBM, Microsoft, Netflix, and Walmart as part of their infrastructure and web servers. In other words, you should study it if we want to work for a large organization that primarily relies on cloud infrastructure.

5. **Meteor**

Another framework that resembles a platform a little more is Meteor.

Christian Fritz, the company's founder and CEO, provides an excellent summary: 'Meteor has a package system, capabilities for building and deploying, and testing support.

Even while it has certain features in common with other frameworks like next.js or gatsby, it is nevertheless unique in a number of important ways.

The DDP protocol, which is exclusive to Meteor, is used for data synchronization.

Simply described, DDP selectively synchronizes collections in the client-side minimongo database and the server-side mongo database.

This eliminates the need for the developer to write API code for data transmission between the client and server, as I would if I were to use Express, and it does it in a very beautiful way: It uses reactive behavior on the client so that when new data comes, the page changes reactively using either React or another reactive framework. It only transmits patches, preventing the needless sending of repetitive data (Vue, Angular, Blaze).

Although many users now utilize GraphQL to reduce the need to write API code, Meteor still stands out for its live and reactive characteristic of the data 'just being there.'

This is ideal for any online application where users add to or modify material since it allows users to share their work in real time and smoothly with other users.

'The other thing I haven't seen in that form anywhere else yet is the possibility to create packages that have both a client and a server part.

Account management is the finest illustration of how this functionality is important.

For user management and authentication, a developer often has to choose two libraries—one for the frontend and one for the backend—and then figure out how to integrate them.

There are several hazards and it typically needs the developer to understand a little bit more about both of the selected libraries than they would want.

This is easy to do using Meteor.

For example, if you install the 'accounts-password' package, you get a user database on the server with (hashed) passwords and the necessary UI with login/signup/forgot-password/etc. capabilities on the client, and all the communication is already taken care of.

We may install further packages like 'accounts-google' for single sign-on with Google (and a similar package for Facebook or other social logins) just as easy.

Because it is developed in Node.js and interacts with MongoDB, a well-liked cross-platform database engine, Meteor is very beneficial for developers creating business solutions.

THE EIGHT TOP JAVASCRIPT GAME ENGINES

Scripting language JavaScript is cross-platform and interpretive. It is renowned for creating websites. It is also used in a lot of settings outside of browsers.[5] Both client-side and server-side development can be done with JavaScript. This session will examine the top 8 JavaScript gaming engines that every JS developer should be familiar with.

1. **PixiJS**

   PixiJS is a 2D rendering library that is very quick and versatile.

   We can make interactive, aesthetically beautiful visuals using PixiJS, which also supports cross-platform apps. Without prior WebGL experience, programmers may use the Pixi renderer to take advantage of hardware acceleration (it also supports a Canvas Fallback).

   It does not, however, have a built-in physics engine.

   It is a completely free open-source library, and a very supportive community is what fuels its development.

2. **Phaser**

   The creation of cross-platform gaming apps is a breeze using Phaser. Amazingly, it employs both a WebGL and a Canvas renderer internally and can switch between them dependent on browser support. Canvas is used for devices that don't support WebGL.

A sizable community of game creators using Phaser and a variety of plugins are both behind it. It is among the most popular gaming frameworks and engines right now on GitHub. For development, JavaScript or TypeScript may be utilized.

3. **Babylon.js**

Babylon JS is a stunning, effective, and straightforward rendering engine.

It provides programmers the ability to build nearly anything in your browser, from animated logos to fully interactive 3D games. Since it was created particularly for visualization, it isn't really a rendering engine for games, but you can still create strong games with it.

Due to its active and supportive developers, it has great community support.

It has a playground so that you may experiment before moving further with development.

4. **PlayCanvas WebGL Game Engine**

Without the requirement for a plugin, it leverages HTML5 and WebGL to run gaming apps and any other interactive 3D content on any mobile or desktop browser.

This indicates that you will be using their platform to write code, test it, and set up your scenes by quickly exporting your games. In contrast to Babylon JS, it places more emphasis on the Game Engine than the Rendering Engine.

The 3D rigid-body physics engine ammo.js makes it incredibly simple to add physics to your game.

5. **Melon.js**

It is a highly effective, lightweight, and user-friendly HTML5 game engine that enables designers and developers to concentrate on content by including the well-liked Tiled map format. Its major goal is to provide a user experience without plugins (It needs nothing but an HTML5-capable browser to function). To guarantee minimal CPU demands, it uses lightweight physics. It is a free open-source project that is backed by a vibrant group of dedicated developers.

6. **GDevelop**

It is an open-source, fully functional game production tool with a primary emphasis on 2D game development, although it may be used to create any kind of game.

Events is a tool that allows you to intuitively design the game logic without any prior knowledge of any particular programming language, and that is what distinguishes it from other game engines.

The Web, Windows, Android, iOS, macOS, and Linux are just a few of the platforms on which GDevelop games may be published and played.

It may be instantly exported to Android.

7. **Kiwi.js**

For creating games that function in HTML5 browsers, an open-source game framework is very simple to utilize.

Given that WebGL rendering has been increased, speed is its primary concern.

For the purpose of distributing games to mobile devices as native applications, the Cocoon.js framework is used.

8. **Three.js**

This project's primary objective is to simplify WebGL use.

You can work with WebGL with a lot less lines of code when using three.js.

It supports Canvas 2D, CSS3D, and SVG renderers in addition to WebGL as the default renderer.

10 MAJOR JAVASCRIPT FRAMEWORKS FOR DEVELOPING MOBILE APPS

JavaScript, which was formerly fundamental to the creation of dynamic webpages on the World Wide Web, is now a popular choice among app developers.

Businesses and developers now have a streamlined option to create dynamic UI, with less lines of code, thanks to JavaScript frameworks for designing mobile applications.

The amount of developers using JavaScript to create mobile applications has increased recently.[6]

There are hundreds of JavaScript frameworks to choose from for developing online, desktop, and mobile apps due to the language's widespread use.

Here are the top 10 JavaScript frameworks that let programmers create native and hybrid mobile applications that run on several platforms.

1. React Native

In 2015, Facebook unveiled React Native, an open-source framework for creating native applications that can run on several platforms.

Mobile applications developed using React and JavaScript are indistinguishable from those written in Objective-C, Swift, or Java.

The React library, written in JavaScript, is used to construct user interface components for websites; React Native is an offshoot of this framework.

When compared to the hundreds of other JS frameworks available, this one stands out due to its premium features, such as its declarative programming approach, virtual DOM, and reusable components to develop UI.

In What Ways Is React Native Superior?

- To create scalable applications, developers may mix and match React Native code with native code written in Objective-C, Swift, or Java.

- By contrast, developers who are well-versed in JavaScript will find learning React and creating React Native applications to be a breeze.

- For the development of portable programs that can run on several platforms, check out this JavaScript framework. Because they share 80% of their code across the Android and iOS platforms, React Native apps save developers a tonne of time and effort when it comes to building complex mobile applications.

2. NativeScript

NativeScript is a free and open-source framework for developing cross-platform native applications using Angular, Vue.js, TypeScript, or JavaScript.

It enables web developers to use their existing skill set to create native mobile experiences.

NativeScript allows developers to create native mobile applications using Vue CLI, VueX, and other Vue framework capabilities. NativeScript also combines with recent Angular full-stack capabilities including router support, code generation, interaction with the Angular CLI, and so on.

Why Is NativeScript Used?
NativeScript allows developers to use existing plugins from npm, CocoaPods (iOS), Gradle (Android), as well as hundreds of NativeScript plugins.

A single codebase may be developed and distributed across different platforms (Android and iOS). Angular or Vue.js may be utilized for code sharing. Web developers may construct native mobile applications using their current web expertise (JavaScript, CSS, Native UI Markup).

3. Ionic
Ionic is another well-known javascript framework for creating hybrid applications.

Understanding the framework of an Ionic app is simple for developers who are familiar with web technologies and web app development. Users are unaware that hybrid applications are running in a full-screen browser called WebView.

They may use native capabilities of mobile devices such as cameras and touch ID without connecting the core code to the device by using customizable native plugins.

Why Is Ionic Used?
A hybrid app codebase may be utilized across multiple platforms (Android and iOS), lowering development costs (as compared to native applications) and time to market.

When developing hybrid applications with Ionic, developers may use Cordova plugins to access a mobile device's hardware and software functionalities. Existing web development skills (HTML, CSS, and JavaScript) may be used to create mobile applications.

4. Apache Cordova
Apache Cordova (formerly PhoneGap) is a hybrid app development platform that encapsulates HTML or JavaScript programs in a native container.

A plethora of technologies, frameworks, and cloud services are available to improve Cordova's speed.

Popular names include Visual Studio, Ionic, Framework7, Monaca, Mobiscroll, and others.

Given the potential of Cordova, the contributors to this framework include tech titans such as Adobe, Microsoft, Blackberry, IBM, Intel, and others.

Why Was Cordova Chosen?

There is a large community of Cordova plugin developers.

As a consequence, the framework enables developers to access a large variety of plugins, allowing them to access device functions and so expand the scope and size of the program. It is feasible to deliver code for several platforms (iOS, Android) with Cordova, making app development more cost-effective.

5. OnSenUI

OnSen UI is a JS framework that allows you to create hybrid mobile applications using HTML, CSS, and JavaScript. Onsen UI is compatible with AngularJS and Angular 2+, React, Vue, and jQuery, allowing developers to transition between libraries and frameworks when creating interactive user interfaces.

Why Use OnSen UI?

OnSen UI includes a vast collection of sophisticated UI components that are particularly built for mobile applications. Monaca and OnSen UI get along swimmingly.

Monaca provides a robust command-line tool and desktop interface to help with complex tasks.

6. jQuery Mobile

With so many smartphones on the market, it is critical to be cautious while building a mobile application that not only loads quicker but is also customizable and usable across several platforms.

When it comes to developing a faster-loading app, jQuery Mobile tops the list when compared to other frameworks.

- Cross-platform apps may be created more quickly by developers.

- It is a low-cost hybrid mobile app development.

- HTML5 and CSS3 are utilized to create a more touch-friendly user interface.

- Because it is a lightweight framework, the software loads quicker.

- Navigation driven by Ajax with dynamic page transitions.

- A consistent user interface across all platforms and devices.

7. Mobile Angular UI

Mobile Angular UI is an HTML5 framework that uses AngularJS and Bootstrap 3 to create highly interactive mobile applications. If we like Angular, this is the Framework for us.

This framework not only provides crucial mobile components such as switches, sidebars, and overlays, but it also assists the website in becoming responsive in the form of an application.

- Aids in the quicker and easier binding of data.

- Modifications will be reflected in the model immediately.

- Reduces the load on server CPUs by facilitating caching and other tasks.

- More rapid application prototyping.

8. Sencha Touch

Sencha Touch allows you to tailor precisely how users interact with the program based on their preferences by adding a slew of features.

Sencha Touch is a popular HTML-based framework used to design apps that run quickly on all platforms without the need to update the code for each one.

- Provides apps with high-level responsiveness.

- It works with the most recent versions of Android, iOS, and BlackBerry.

- The program is loaded as quickly as possible.

9. Titanium

Titanium, an ancient framework for hybrid mobile app development, gives straightforward and transparent access to most native capabilities.

Developers may create native apps as well as hybrid and web apps using web technologies such as JavaScript and CSS.

- Developers may quickly create apps that are compatible with Android, iOS, and other platforms.

- Functional entities enable the development of high-performance applications.

- Because it comes with an integrated environment, we can create rapid prototypes.

- Open-source alternative that is very cost-effective.

- Because it supports sophisticated web technologies, the code structure has been simplified.

10. Meteor

Meteor is a platform that is free and open source. It is a popular JavaScript for mobile applications. This JavaScript framework not only allows for quick prototyping and cross-platform coding, but it also provides us control over our application.

- JavaScript code may be modified without any programming knowledge.

- Meteor is well-known for its speed and ease of deployment.

- Removes bugs that most new programs seem to have.

- Provides a lot of versatility between platforms and devices.

- External libraries and a variety of plugins may be used.

THE BEST JS FRAMEWORKS FOR DESKTOP APPLICATIONS

A cross-platform program is one that operates on many operating systems.

This is incredibly handy for both the client and the developer: developing a cross-platform solution saves time and money, and makes the program simpler to maintain.[7]

Desktop apps may also be cross-platform, but they need a unique methodology to account for all of the quirks of desktop PC operating systems.

Are Cross-Platform Apps Interchangeable with Desktop Programs?

The correct response to this question is 'both' and 'neither.' A cross-platform program, it seems, is a platform that works on several operating systems. This is incredibly handy for both the client and the developer: developing a cross-platform solution saves time and money, and makes the program simpler to maintain.

Desktop apps may also be cross-platform (as discussed further in the article), but they need a unique methodology to account for all of the quirks of desktop PC operating systems.

The cross-platform desktop app is a high-quality, quick system that satisfies the user and, as a result, provides considerable advantages to the client.

The Advantages and Disadvantages of a Standalone Level vs a Cross-Platform App

A standalone application is a software that runs locally on the device and does not need anything more than the required level to work.

Because all logic is embedded inside the program, it does not need an Internet connection or any additional installed services or tools in most circumstances.

A cross-platform application is one that adapts to and runs on several operating systems, as well as one that integrates online technology with tools for designing operating software for smartphones and desktop computers.

Everything, however, relies on your goal: what is the objective of the application we are developing? Is the platform in need of upgrades, internet access, or hyperlinks? Can it stand alone as an introduction platform and so function without an online connection?

Are Desktop Apps Supported by React and NodeJS?

Yes will be the succinct response. But let us begin at the beginning.

ReactJS is a free and open JavaScript library for building user interfaces.

The method addresses the issue of partial updating of a web page's content, which is faced in the creation of single-page apps.

React is a powerful framework developed in JavaScript.

The open-source framework is used to create interactive interfaces for React desktop applications.

ReactJS is ideally suited for handling the design layer of complicated apps, web apps, and even websites.

Node.js allows us to execute JavaScript programs on the server and provide the results to the user. JavaScript has become a mainstream language with a significant developer community thanks to the Node.js platform.

Node is a server-side framework that is powered by Google Chrome's V8 JavaScript Engine.

This open-source platform is also used to develop networking and backend applications.

Node JS desktop apps are simple to use, high quality, and speedy.

Top Five JS Frameworks for Desktop Applications (Desktop Apps)

1. Electron

This is an open-source framework. GitHub built it 7 years ago for the editor of the JS desktop application Atom.

This library will enable the development of a high-quality cross-platform desktop application.

Electron makes use of web technologies such as JavaScript, HTML, and CSS.

The Electron program has the benefit of allowing us to create desktop apps that function similarly to online applications while also allowing us to read and write data in our computer's file system. The Electron framework was used to construct the desktop platform Skype for the Linux operating system.

2. NodeGUI

This is another open-source framework for developing cross-platform desktop apps using CSS and JavaScript. It is possible to construct native apps with the aid of this framework.

Here we will discover a collection of fee-based developer tools and widgets that may be used to construct built-in UI platform pieces. There is also a React-based variant.

3. Proton Native

This is a relatively 'new' program on the market. Proton Native allows you to create programs on the PC. This is comparable to what React Native did for mobile devices. We may use the framework to construct interfaces without interruption and manage the progress of cross-platform apps. This is what distinguishes Proton Native as one of the finest JS frameworks for creating apps for a variety of OS systems. Proton Native develops the program using just native tools, takes very minimal computer space, and does not use many resources.

The framework employs the same syntax as React Native and is compatible with the React and Redux frameworks. Another benefit is that it is Node.js compatible.

4. NW.js

This is also a good JavaScript framework for desktop apps. It is open-source Intel, which combines the Node.js framework with the Chromium engine, previously known as Webkit.

With this high-quality combination, we can build an application on the NW.js framework that not only loads the local webpage in the program window but also connects to the operating system through the JavaScript API.

This solution allows you to customize the size of windows, toolbars, and menu items.

NW.js will also allow us to access files on our local PC. The framework supports all browser features and may secure our JavaScript source. NW.js is available for Linux, Mac OS, and Windows.

5. AppJS

This is a simple-to-use yet very powerful tool for developing cross-platform apps. When developing an application, you do not need to learn a new language. If we know the fundamentals of HTML, CSS, and JavaScript, we can easily design applications for a smartphone.

Because AppJS is built on Chromium, the developer has access to the most recent HTML5 APIs. AppJS may also be used to construct visually appealing apps ranging from word processors to 3D games. In the default mode, there are no GUI widget limits; therefore, the creation of user interfaces is now limited only by our creativity.

HOW TO SELECT THE BEST JAVASCRIPT FRAMEWORK FOR OUR PROJECT

Many JavaScript frameworks are created and updated on a regular basis, making it difficult to stay up with the times and choose which framework is appropriate for our project. Before selecting any of these for our web application, evaluate the unique needs of our project as well as the framework's strengths and limitations. IT businesses in Ukraine can assist with project creation and selecting the optimal framework.[8]

Before beginning project execution, it is typically required to undertake preliminary research to choose the best technology for our needs. Before beginning any project, it must be thoroughly analyzed and evaluated. However, there are several crucial factors by which we may estimate the choice of a particular technology for development in advance:

Development Speed and Simplicity of Use, as well as Project Support

The speed of development is determined by the technology utilized in our project. If your project already makes use of technologies such as TypeScript or JSX, Angular is a better fit. However, if we are beginning a project from scratch, Vue.js is the ideal choice because it adheres to standards.

Trends

These frameworks are well-liked and will take the lead in the development industry in the next few years. Vue, on the other hand, is fast gaining popularity, followed by the React framework.

Scalability and Mobility

If we've decided to move a project from one framework to another, Vue.js is the finest option. Because developers would most likely need to convert TypeScript or JSX code to standard JavaScript and HTML if they wish to rewrite Angular or React applications.

The Frequency of Updates

Another critical consideration is the frequency with which the framework is updated. Every 6 months, Angular is extensively upgraded. Vue is as reliable as it can be in this sense, with big changes every few years.

This session will discuss the three most popular JavaScript frameworks, Angular, React, and Vue. They are the most well-known JavaScript frameworks nowadays.[9]

Angular	React	Vue
If we are an extremely structured person who likes to keep everything distinct, Angular is for you. Each component and functionality has its own set of HTML, CSS, and TypeScript files.	If we want to have everything under the control, from the row of a table to the location of the buttons, and want to reuse components, then React is for us.	If we are a nice and clean person who prefers easy organization and does not want to navigate between files, the Vue with its extremely simple data binding is ideal for us.
If we don't want to deal with the hassle of installing third-party packages, Angular's built-in packages are ideal. This built-in package includes packages for routing and forms, among other things.	React allows us to install packages of our choosing for a variety of reasons. For instance, there are several packages available for routing, but whatever package we choose is determined by our expertise with the package.	Vue includes some built-in packages as well, but we may easily add third-party packages based on our preferences.
If the project is fairly huge and there are many features to be created, then Angular is the way to go because it follows the MVC pattern, and managing the code for an Angular Project is quite simple.	If the project is small to medium in scope and many components are reusable, we should select React for that type of project since component reusability and component-based thinking will enhance productivity significantly.	Vue is utilized when the application is small to medium in size and speed and performance are the most important aspects of the project or application.
Data management is a key notion in Angular, and you can do it totally raw using RXJS, or we can utilize the NGRX framework and Akita as well.	The Redux framework may be used to manage data in React.	In the case of Vue, we may handle the data via VUEX.

Which JavaScript Framework Should We Start With?

That is dependent on our aim. To begin, decide whether we want to work on frontend or backend development. Are we interested in performing all of the functions of a web app and coding behind the scenes?

Each JavaScript framework has its own official site where we may download and start using the product (for example, React.js or Node.js). Our framework classes will lead us through the following steps and how to use all of the capabilities.[10]

React.js

React.js was the most extensively used web framework if you eventually want to focus on frontend programming. And it's easy to see why React.js is a frontend favorite: it allows us to create scalable, dynamic, and interactive online apps.

There is a considerable discussion regarding whether React.js is a 'framework' or a 'library,' which is a collection of previously published code that we may use to create our own code. Because both libraries and frameworks contain pre-written code that allows us to do anything, the small distinction may make our head spin. While both libraries and frameworks may be useful, frameworks often provide overall web programs with more structure.

Node.js

For those interested in backend programming, it's 'Node.js all the way.' Node.js is a framework for developing desktop apps as well as a JavaScript runtime environment (which implies it runs a server in the language). Node.js can support asynchronous JavaScript code, which implies it can run programs while waiting for a longer-running job to finish.

JAVA VS. JAVASCRIPT

JavaScript is a lightweight computer language that is utilized to make web webpages dynamic. It has the ability to inject dynamic text into HTML. The browser's language is another name for JavaScript. JavaScript (JS) is not connected to or similar to Java. Both languages have a C-like syntax and are extensively used in client-side and server-side Web applications, but the similarities end there.[11]

JavaScript has the following features:

- JavaScript was originally designed for DOM manipulation. Previously, websites were primarily static; but, with the advent of JS, dynamic Web sites were established.

- In JS, functions are objects. They, like any other object, can have attributes and methods. Other functions can take them as arguments.

- Date and time can be handled.

- Although the forms are produced in HTML, it does Form Validation.

- A compiler is not required.

Example: This is the most basic JavaScript example.

```
<script>
    console.log("Welcome to Home");
</script>
```

Java is an object-oriented language of programming with a virtual machine platform that lets us develop compiled programs that run on almost any platform. 'Write Once, Run Anywhere,' Java promised.

Java has the following features:

1. **Platform Independence:** The compiler turns source code to byte-code, which is subsequently executed by the JVM. This bytecode is platform-independent.

2. **Object-Oriented Programming Language:** Object-oriented programming is a way of structuring a program in which each object represents a unique instance of a class. The OOP concept is built on four pillars:

   - Encapsulation

   - Abstraction

   - Polymorphism

   - Inheritance

3. **Simplicity:** Java is a simple language because it lacks sophisticated features such as pointers, operator overloading, multiple inheritance, and explicit memory allocation.

4. **Robust:** The Java programming language is robust, which implies it is dependable. It is designed in such a manner that it makes every attempt to find faults as early as possible, which is why the java compiler can detect errors that other programming languages cannot.

5. **Secure:** Because we don't have pointers in Java, we can't access out-of-bound arrays; if we do, we get an ArrayIndexOutOfBoundException.

6. **Distributed:** Using the Java programming language, we may develop distributed applications. For developing distributed Java applications, Remote Method Invocation and Enterprise Java Beans are employed.

7. **Multithreading:** Multithreading is supported by Java. It is a Java feature that permits the concurrent execution of two or more portions of a program in order to maximize CPU usage.

Example: Here we have a basic Java program as an example.

```
// Import required classes
import java.io.*;

// the Main class
class PFP {

    // method of main driver
    public static void main(String[] args)
    {
        // Print-statement
        System.out.println(
            "Welcome to Home");
    }
}
```

The following is the distinction between Java and JavaScript

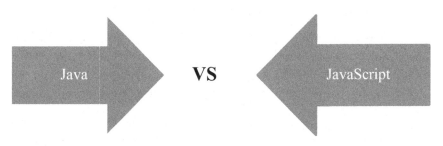

The distinction between Java and JavaScript

Java	JavaScript
Because Java is a tightly typed language, variables must be declared before they may be used in the program. The type of a variable is verified at build time in Java.	JavaScript is a weakly typed language with permissive syntax and rules.
Java is a computer language that is object-oriented.	JavaScript is a scripting language that is object-oriented.
Java programs may execute in any virtual machine (JVM) or browser.	JavaScript code used to only run in the browser, but it can now run on the server thanks to Node.js.
Java objects are class-based, and we can't write a program in Java without first establishing a class.	JavaScript Objects are built on prototypes.
The Java application has the file extension '.Java' and converts source code into bytecodes that are then executed by the JVM (Java Virtual Machine).	JavaScript files have the file extension '.js' and are interpreted rather than compiled; every browser has a JavaScript interpreter for executing JS code.
Java is a stand-alone programming language.	if it is incorporated into a web page at build time and combines with its HTML content
Concurrency in Java is handled by threads.	Concurrency in JavaScript is handled by an event-based technique.
Multithreading is supported by Java.	Multi-threading is not supported by JavaScript.
Java is mostly used for backend applications.	JavaScript is utilized for both the frontend and the backend.
Java consumes more RAM.	JavaScript makes use of less Memory.
To run the code, Java requires a Java Development Kit (JDK).	JavaScript may be executed in any text editor or browser terminal.

PYTHON VS. JAVASCRIPT

We will discuss about the difference between Python and JavaScript below.

What Is JavaScript?

An interactive website can be written in JavaScript, a scripting language.

In accordance with client-side programming principles, it executes locally within the user's web browser, bypassing the requirement for server-side processing. JavaScript is also compatible with other technologies, such as REST APIs, XML, and more.[12]

These days, JavaScript also uses Node js and other modern technologies.

What Is Python?

Python is an advanced, object-oriented language with a high level of usability.

It's great for creating apps quickly because of its pre-built data structures and dynamic binding and typing.

Python's module and package support further the system's modularity and facilitates code reuse. Due to the low barrier to entry (line count), it is a rapid programming language. It's perfect for newcomers because it prioritizes clarity and ease of use. Key distinctions between Python and JavaScript are outlined here.

Differences of Most Significance

- JavaScript is a scripting language that facilitates the creation of interactive web pages, whereas Python is a high-level object-oriented programming language that is suitable for quick application development due to its in-built data structures, dynamic binding, and typing.

- Mutable and immutable data types exist in Python but not in JavaScript.

- JavaScript requires UTF-16 encoding due to its lack of in-built functionality for handling raw bytes, but Python source code is ASCII unless a different encoding is specified.

- Curly brackets are used in JavaScript whereas indentation is used in Python.

- We may construct a property for a JavaScript object by composing its underlying attributes, and in the Python programming language, attributes are defined by use of the getter and setter methods.

- JavaScript may be used to create a website or native app, but Python is better suited to more mathematically complex activities like data analysis, machine learning, and scientific computing.

Features of JavaScript

JavaScript's primary capabilities are as follows:

- It's popular for both client and server-side development because of its portability between platforms.
- Methodology that is well-suited to testing.
- Quickly get started with coding and learn the language.
- Gives us more options to rely on.

Features of Python

Python's primary capabilities are as follows:

- A breeze to pick up and keep in good shape
- It has portability and uses the same interface regardless of the hardware platform it's installed on.
- The Python interpreter may be expanded using low-level modules.
- Python's robust framework and community make it a great choice for large-scale software projects.
- Automatic garbage collection is a feature available in Python.
- Tests and fixes may be performed in real time.
- It allows dynamic type verification and provides access to high-level dynamic data types.
- Python code is compatible with C, C++, and the Java programming languages.
- Goroutines provide convenient support for several threads running at once.
- Quick times for compilation
- Simple-to-deploy, statically-linked binaries

Comparison between Python vs Java Script

The primary distinction between Python and JavaScript is as follows:

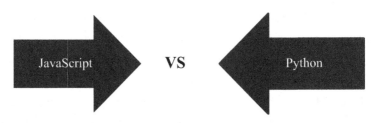

The distinction between Python and JavaScript

JavaScript	Python
JavaScript does not understand the terms mutable and immutable.	Python supports both mutable and immutable data types.
Because JavaScript lacks built-in functionality for processing raw bytes, it should be encoded as UTF-16.	Unless you provide an encoding format, Python source code is ASCII by default.
JavaScript only supports floating-point integers.	There are several numeric types in Python, such as int and fixed-point decimal.
Curly brackets are used in JavaScript.	Python employs indentation.
JavaScript contains fewer modules such as date, arithmetic, regexp, and JSON.	Python has a large number of modules.
JavaScript objects contain properties that are made up of underlying attributes that allow us to specify a property.	Getter and setter functions are used to define attributes in the Python programming language.
JavaScript employs an inheritance paradigm based on prototypes.	Python employs a paradigm of class-based inheritance.
JavaScript is a fantastic choice for mobile development in addition to frontend and backend programming.	Python is unsuitable for creating mobile apps.
JavaScript may be used to create a website or a native application.	Python is used for data analytics, machine learning, and other math-intensive activities.
TOBIE has a rating of 7.	TOBIE has a rating of 3.
In the United States, the average annual income for a JavaScript developer is $114,856.	The annual compensation for a python developer is $120,255.

JQUERY VS. JAVASCRIPT

We will discuss about the difference between jQuery and JavaScript below:

What Exactly Is jQuery?

A free and open-source Javascript library for creating, navigating, and modifying the HTML DOM. A DOM is a tree-like structure used to represent webpage elements. jQuery allows web designers to quickly use JavaScript code on their websites. The sophisticated jQuery technique allows for the creation of powerful dynamic websites and online apps.[13]

jQuery's syntax is intended to make things simple, such as

- A document's navigation
- DOM element selection
- Making animations
- Event management
- Creating Ajax apps

Among all other libraries, jQuery is one of the most extensively used, with the following key features:

- Selection of DOM elements
- Sizzle allows for traversal and manipulation (the selector engine).
- Developing a new programming style
- DOM data structures and algorithms are combined.

jQuery, on the other hand, enables developers to build plug-ins on top of the JavaScript library. Abstractions for low-level interaction and animations can also be created by developers.

The Distinction between jQuery and JavaScript

Although jQuery is a component of JavaScript, the following variances may exist:

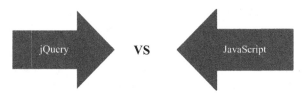

The distinction between jQuery and JavaScript

jQuery	JavaScript
It is a library for JavaScript.	It is a dynamic and interpreted programming language for web development.
Only the relevant jQuery code has to be written by the user.	The whole js code must be written by the user.
It requires less time.	It takes longer since the entire screenplay must be written.
Handling multi-browser compatibility concerns is not required.	Developers write their own code to handle cross-browser compatibility.
The header of the page must contain the URL of the jQuery library.	Every browser has support for JavaScript. No other plugins are necessary.
Because it is a JavaScript library, it is dependent on JavaScript.	In JavaScript, jQuery is present. As a result, jQuery may or may not be used in the js code.
It merely only has a few lines of code.	The code might be difficult and lengthy.
It is a basic, quick, and easy method.	It is a programming method with weak typing.
jQuery is a web design method that has been optimized.	JavaScript, which introduced jQuery, is one of the most popular web design programming languages for developers.
DOM is created faster with jQuery.	JavaScript creates DOM slowly.

JAVASCRIPT VS. PHP

We will discuss about the difference between PHP and JavaScript below:

What Exactly Is PHP?

Adds support for the Hypertext Preprocessor. It's the most popular web development language. It's generally referred to be an open-source scripting language.[14]

PHP code may be inserted in HTML documents. The code is written in-between <?php> and?> the start and finish processing instructions. PHP is also a basic language for beginners.

Although both PHP and JavaScript are utilized in web development, they serve quite distinct goals and perform very different jobs.

PHP and JavaScript may even collaborate to accomplish a same objective in certain instances. When the two languages interact, JavaScript handles the frontend of the website while PHP handles the backend. However, when they operate separately, each may contribute significantly to web development. Most popular and trending websites, such as Facebook, Yahoo, and Flickr, are developed using a combination of JavaScript and PHP.

The Distinction between JavaScript and PHP

The following table compares and contrasts JavaScript with PHP.

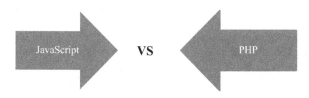

The distinction between JavaScript and PHP

JavaScript	PHP
It is currently a full-stack programming language. It may therefore serve both client and server sites.	It is a scripting language for the server. It simply serves the website's backend.
It is speedier, but it is more difficult to learn.	It is slower yet simpler to learn.
It is an asynchronous language of programming that does not wait for input–output operations to complete.	It is a programming language that is synchronous. As a result, it waits for the input–output activities to complete.
Every web browser, including Mozilla, Google Chrome, and many more, supports it.	It is compatible with systems such as Windows, Linux, and Mac. IIS, Apache, and Lighttpd web servers all support it.
It contains less secure code.	PHP code is quite secure.
It requires an environment in order to access the database.	It provides quick and easy access to the database.

(Continued)

JavaScript	PHP
The code is enclosed by <script>...<script> tags.	The program written inside <?php....?> tag.
Previously, JavaScript could generate interactive sites for clients. However, it can now create real-time games and apps, as well as mobile applications.	A PHP code may build dynamic pages, transmit and receive cookies, collect form input, and so on.
It is a single-threaded programming language. As a result, each input–output process is performed concurrently.	It is a multi-threaded programming language. As a result, it will block if numerous input–output procedures are performed.
The.js suffix is used to store an external JavaScript file.	The '.php' extension is used to store files.
The js code may be embedded in HTML, XML, and AJAX.	Only HTML allows us to embed PHP code.
It has fewer features.	When compared to JavaScript, it provides more sophisticated functionalities.
Popular JavaScript frameworks include Angular, React, Vue.js, Meteor, and more.	PHP frameworks that are popular include Laravel, Symfony, FuelPHP, CakePHP, and many others.
Twitter, LinkedIn, Amazon, and other websites created on JavaScript are examples.	Wordpress, Tumblr, MailChimp, iStockPhoto, and more websites created with PHP are examples.

DART VS. JAVASCRIPT

We will discuss about the difference between Dart and JavaScript below:

JavaScript and Dart are the greatest cross-platform mobile app development languages. Dart is a newer language than JavaScript, but it offers several really useful features and good Google support. When it comes to cross-platform mobile application and server-side application development, JavaScript was at the pinnacle of its popularity.[15]

In this section, we will compare and contrast Dart with JavaScript. But, before we get into the specifics, we'll learn about Dart and JavaScript.

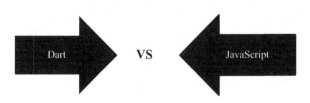

The distinction between Dart and JavaScript

What Exactly Is Dart?

Dart is a client-optimized programming language that was created by Google in 2011 and is meant to build rapid apps for any platform. It was initially used internally by Google to construct web, server, and mobile apps. Dart compiles source code in the same manner that other programming languages like C, JavaScript, Java, and C# do.

It also has its own virtual machine (VM), Dart VM, for running the native application. It also includes its own package management, called Pub. It gained popularity with Google's launch of Flutter for cross-platform mobile application development.

The primary reason for this is that Flutter is entirely focused on Dart. Dart, on the other hand, may be learnt rapidly by developers with prior familiarity with OOPS languages.

Benefits and Drawbacks of Dart

Dart has the following benefits and drawbacks:

Advantages

- It is a client-oriented, open-source computer program.

- It is very scalable across projects.

- It was created by Google and works effortlessly on the Google Cloud Platform.

- It is simple to learn if we are already familiar with JavaScript since it is comparable to JavaScript.

- It's faster than JavaScript.

- It is mostly used to create mobile apps.

Drawbacks

- It just has one object class.

- It is a very new programming language that is not commonly used in the industry.

- We can't rename a function in Dart without creating a new assignment statement.

- Because there are few internet resources, it is difficult to discover answers to difficulties.

What Is JavaScript?

To create dynamic HTML sites with interactive effects, programmers turn to JavaScript, a small, object-oriented programming language.

The creation of games and mobile apps both benefit greatly from the usage of JavaScript.

As its name implies, it is a scripting language whose code is interpreted and run only in a web browser. Node.js might be used to execute the code outside of the browser.

Client-side and server-side programming are both possible with this language, which is also known as the language of browsers. Brendan Eich of Netscape created it, and in 1995 it was first made available to consumers. Prior to being renamed JavaScript, the language went by the name LiveScript. As a scripting language, JavaScript borrows extensively from C in terms of syntax. JavaScript code is saved in a file with the.js extension.

The Benefits and Drawbacks of Using JavaScript

These are some of JavaScript's benefits and drawbacks:

Advantages

- It's a lightweight, quick, and adaptable open-source framework.

- Cross-compilation is possible.

- It's compatible with classes, interfaces, and modules.

- Since it's utilized for both front- and backend work, it might be compatible with a wide range of devices.

- We can utilize this to create interactive user interfaces that change in response to a mouse hover.

- Because of its compatibility with other languages, JavaScript may be used in a wide variety of programs.

- Creating complex programs may need us to enhance JavaScript.

Drawbacks

- It relies on limited libraries.

- Client-side there is no way to create or read files with JavaScript. For reasons of safety, it has been kept.

- There's a risk that one mistake might take down the whole website.

- Because of the dynamic quality of the language, serious errors by programmers are not uncommon.

- Only a single inheritance is supported, not numerous ones. This characteristic of object-oriented languages may be necessary for certain applications.

Important Distinction between Dart and JavaScript

Here, we'll contrast Dart with JavaScript in terms of their most distinguishing features:

Simplicity of Use

JavaScript has been around for a while and is a mature and powerful language.

JavaScript is easy to use. It contains a number of frameworks and libraries that are freely accessible online. Developers may save time and effort by making use of these frameworks to create new software with little rework.

Dart, on the other hand, is a new language for most developers outside of Google. Despite Google's attempts to explain the Dart programming language, finding answers to particular issues remains tough for developers. It features a writing style and grammar comparable to Java, so developers with OOPS knowledge should be able to learn and utilize Dart once they understand the fundamentals.

Speed

Because JavaScript is an interpreted language, it is lighter and quicker than other computer languages. It outperforms Java and other compiled languages.

Dart, on the other side, is substantially quicker than JavaScript. Dart can be compiled in both JIT and AOT modes, which aids app development in a variety of ways. JIT compilation, for example, may be used to accelerate development, while AOT compilation can be used to optimize the release process.

Type Security

As an interpreted language, JavaScript offers both dynamic and duck-typing.

Because it can type any code, JavaScript is not a type-safe language.

Mistakes in the code can only be found during runtime. Alternatively, Dart allows for both loose and strict prototyping. The bulk of programming problems is identified during the compilation phase since Dart is a compiled language. It is type-safer than JavaScript.

Popularity

JavaScript may be found almost everywhere. JavaScript is supported by almost every machine. JavaScript is now used to build code for the web, mobile, and server side.

There are about 2.5 million questions regarding JavaScript on Stack Overflow. Because of its ubiquity, the JavaScript ecosystem has grown enormously, and it currently dominates the 'market' for reusable components, thanks to the development of cloud component hubs. Frontend developers would prefer an alternative option.

Dart, on the other side, is gaining traction, but it is no match for JavaScript. Dart was nowhere to be seen until Google announced Flutter. Dart has attracted developers who were previously averse to JavaScript. Dart currently has around 45K Stack Overflow questions labeled.

The Learning Curve

JavaScript is not an easy language to learn for novices, but understanding the principles of programming makes JavaScript straightforward. For developers who wish to learn JavaScript, there are several online courses and tutorials accessible.

Dart, on the other side, might be a difficult exercise for beginners since it is not a frequently used programming language. Online, there are extremely few Dart programming classes or books.

Web vs. Mobile

With its multiple frameworks, JavaScript has dominated both online and mobile app development. With the release of Facebook's React Native, designing mobile and web applications for small companies became a no-brainer. There are still several JavaScript frameworks, such as Agular, Vue.js, and others, that may be used to create websites, PWAs, and hybrid mobile apps.

However, Dart may be used to build both mobile and web-based applications. The cross-platform mobile app development capabilities of Dart and the Flutter framework caused them to rise to prominence.

Frontend vs. Backend

JavaScript is used for frontend development in conjunction with HTML and CSS.

However, since the Node.js platform has grown in popularity, it is now routinely utilized for backend and server-side programming. Dart, on the other side, is now being used in conjunction with Flutter to create the frontend of cross-platform mobile apps. Dart may also be utilized for web development; however, no mention of it being used for backend development is mentioned.

Commercial Usage

JavaScript is widely utilized in industry, especially large-scale projects. It is used in the creation of network and cross-platform applications. In Facebook's online and cross-platform applications, React and React Native, JavaScript is utilized. The eBay, Airbnb, Slack, and more companies utilize JavaScript as well.

Dart, on the other side, was created at Google. As a consequence, it was first used internally.

Following the launch of Flutter, major companies such as Alibaba started adopting Flutter and Dart to develop cross-platform apps.

The following comparison table demonstrates the head-to-head comparison between Dart vs JavaScript:

Features	Dart	JavaScript
Simplicity of use	Dart features a Java-like syntax and writing style, making it easy to use for developers with OOPS expertise.	JavaScript is simple to use, and it has a variety of frameworks and libraries available online, allowing developers to reuse preexisting code to develop apps more quickly.
Editor and IDE support	Dart code may be written in simple editors such as Sublime or VIM. The most popular IDEs for Dart application development are IntelliJ IDEA and Android Studio, both of which include the Dart plugin.	It has several great editors and IDEs for developing apps. A full-fledged IDE is not necessarily required; instead, developers can utilize lightweight editors such as VIM, Sublime Text, Emacs, or Atom. Some IDEs, such as WebStorm and Visual Studio Code, may help us create JavaScript applications.

(Continued)

Features	Dart	JavaScript
Popularity	Dart and Flutter have a tiny community in addition to various internet communities. Despite good documentation, many experienced developers are nevertheless perplexed by Dart.	Because it is a simpler, lightweight, dynamic language, it is easier for new developers to learn. It boosts developer productivity by offering a variety of JavaScript frameworks and thousands of conveniently accessible web packages.
Type safety	Because it supports both loose and strong prototyping, it is more type-safe than JavaScript.	Because it allows both duck-typing and dynamic, it is not a type-safe language.
The Learning Curve	Because Dart is not a commonly used programming language, it might be difficult for novices. Online, there are extremely few Dart programming classes or books.	JavaScript is not a simple language to learn for novices, but knowing the principles of programming makes JavaScript straightforward.
Commercial Usage	Dart is backed by Google and is utilized by a number of well-known companies, including Blossom, WorkTrails, Whale, Mobile, and others.	JavaScript is frequently utilized to construct online and cross-platform mobile apps in huge organizations such as Instagram, Slack, Reddit, eBay, and Airbnb.
Speed	Dart can be compiled in both JIT and AOT modes, allowing for the creation of apps in a variety of methods. Dart is significantly quicker than JavaScript.	Because JavaScript is an interpreted language, it is lighter and quicker than other computer languages. It outperforms Java and other compiled languages.
Web vs. Mobile	Dart may be used to create online and mobile applications.	JavaScript can be used with various frameworks to construct online and mobile apps.

JAVASCRIPT VS. ANGULAR JS

The client's web browser executes JavaScript, a lightweight, object-oriented programming language used to create dynamic HTML pages with interactive effects.[16]

It's a kind of scripting language that runs in the browser and adds interactivity and dynamism to websites. The contrasting Angular JS is a framework written in JavaScript that adds functionality to HTML. Creating dynamic and single-page web apps is its primary purpose (SPAs). Differences between JavaScript and Angular JS will be covered here. First, we'll become acquainted with JavaScript and Angular JS before we dive into their differences.

The distinction between Angular JS and JavaScript

What Is JavaScript?

JavaScript is a tiny, object-oriented programming language that allows developers to construct dynamic HTML pages with interactive effects.

Using JavaScript is very beneficial for the development of games and mobile applications.

It is a scripting language whose code is only understood and executed on a web browser, as its name suggests.

Code may be executed outside of the browser using Node.js. It is the language browsers utilize. It is handy for developing client and server applications.

Brendan Eich of Netscape designed and published it to the public for the first time in 1995.

Before it was renamed JavaScript, the language was known as LiveScript.

JavaScript as a scripting language draws heavily from C in terms of syntax.

A file with the.js extension is where JavaScript code is kept.

JavaScript Features

There are several JavaScript features. Among them are the following:

- Originally, JavaScript was built for DOM manipulation. Previously, the majority of websites were static; however, JS allows for the creation of interactive webpages.

- In JavaScript, functions are objects.

- They may have the same attributes and methods as regular objects, and they can be provided as parameters to other functions.

- JavaScript requires no compiler.

- Date and time may be handled by JavaScript.

What Is Angular Js?

It is an open-source framework for frontend web development with excellent features and support. The Angular team at Google initially introduced it in 2010.

It is a framework that is always evolving and extending to include more effective techniques for constructing online applications. It typically creates applications using the model view controller (MVC) paradigm and enables both data binding and dependency injection.

Since AngularJS is mostly derived from HTML and JavaScript, there's no need to study a foreign language or grammar. The function converts static HTML to dynamic HTML. It expands HTML's capabilities by introducing built-in attributes and components and by allowing easy JavaScript creation of additional attributes.

Angular JS features

There are several angular JS functionalities. Among them are the following:

- AngularJS enables us to work with modules that facilitate their reuse, saving time, and code.

- Angular JS's usage of JavaScript, HTML, and CSS makes it user-friendly.

- A template is sent to the DOM and then the AngularJS compiler, while AngularJS itself is mostly plain HTML.

- It then travels through the templates and becomes usable.

Major Distinctions between JavaScript and Angular JS

There are a number of significant distinctions between JavaScript and Angular JS. Among them are the following:

- JavaScript is a server-side and client-side scripting language for online application development. AngularJS, on the other hand, makes web apps rapid and simple from the start.

- JavaScript reduces the time required to fix widespread flaws and faults. Compared to JavaScript, AngularJS requires more time to do the same task.

- JavaScript is one of the most efficient approaches for developing websites and constructing online apps. In contrast, AngularJS has been mostly used as a JS framework for constructing web apps.

- JavaScript is a programming language used to control the Document Object Model (DOM) (Document Object Model). AngularJS, on the other hand, augments its capabilities with several technologies.

- JavaScript doesn't allow dependency injection. AngularJS, on the other hand, enables data binding and dependency injection.

- JavaScript coding is rapid and efficient. In contrast, Angular JS applications often become slow.

- JavaScript has used the same method for a number of years. On the other side, AngularJS has been upgraded for typescript, resulting in lighter and more engaging apps.

- The comprehensive user interface of JavaScript includes sliders and other features. AngularJS, on the other hand, is a data-driven framework used to develop online apps.

- JavaScript is a robust and intricate programming language. In contrast, AngularJS is a straightforward and effective framework.

Comparative Analysis of JavaScript and Angular JS

Here, we will examine a head-to-head contrast between JavaScript vs Angular JS:

Features	JavaScript	Angular JS
Definition	It is a scripted object-oriented language used to create mobile and dynamic web apps.	It is an open-source framework for creating dynamic web pages and big single-page online apps.
Developed	It was created by Netscape Communications in 1995.	It was primarily created by Google in 2010.
Syntax	Its syntax is far more sophisticated than that of Angular JS.	Its syntax is basic and straightforward.
Programmed	The interpreters are developed in the C and C++ programming languages.	It is written in the JavaScript programming language.
Filters	The filters are not supported.	Filters are supported.
Learnability	It is not easy to learn.	It is simple to learn if you have a basic understanding of JavaScript.
Concept	It is based on the notion of dynamic typing.	To construct apps, Angular JS uses the model view controller approach.
Dependency injection	It does not allow for dependency injection.	It allows data binding as well as dependency injection.

JAVASCRIPT VS. NODE.JS

JavaScript is a lightweight, object-oriented programming language used to construct dynamic HTML web pages with interactive effects.[17]

Node.js, on the other hand, often displays a list of objects and functions that JavaScript code may access when executed in the V8 engine or through the node interpreter.

This session will focus on the distinction between JavaScript and Node.js. However, before examining the differences, we shall get familiar with JavaScript and Node.js.

The distinction between Node JS and JavaScript

What Is JavaScript?

JavaScript is a compact, object-oriented programming language that lets developers add interactivity to static HTML pages via scripting. When making video games or mobile applications, JavaScript comes in quite handy.

Simply said, it is a scripting language whose code can only be read and executed on a web browser. Node.js allows code to be executed in environments other than a web browser.

Browsers communicate using this language. It can help you build both client and server applications. Brendan Eich of Netscape developed it and made it available to the general public for the first time in 1995. In the past, this language was known as LiveScript, but it has since been renamed JavaScript. The syntax of the programming language JavaScript is heavily inspired by C. JavaScript code is saved in a file with the extension.js.

JavaScript's Benefits and Drawbacks Are Discussed

These are some of JavaScript's benefits and drawbacks:

Benefits

- It is a lightweight, speedy, and versatile open-source framework that supports cross-compilation.

- It works with classes, interfaces, and modules.

- It is used for both frontend and backend development, enabling cross-device interoperability.

- We can use this to construct interactive user interfaces that respond to mouse hovers.

- JavaScript may be utilized in a wide range of projects due to its interoperability with other languages.

- Creating complicated applications may necessitate the use of JavaScript enhancements.

Drawbacks

- It is reliant on limited resource pools.

- There is no mechanism to create or read files using JavaScript on the client side. It has been retained for safety reasons.

- There is a chance that a single error will bring the entire website down.

- Why because the language is dynamic, developers may make fatal mistakes rapidly.

- Only one inheritance is supported, not many ones.

- This feature of object-oriented languages may be required for specific applications.

What Is Node.js?

Node.js is a free and open-source server-side JavaScript runtime environment that may be used across several platforms. Node.js makes it possible for JavaScript to be executed in environments outside of web browsers.

Node.js is mostly used for web development and comes with a wide variety of modules. It's possible to use it with Windows, Linux, Mac OS, and other computers. For the development of scalable JavaServer Pages (JSP) applications, it offers a cross-platform runtime environment that features event-driven, non-blocking (asynchronous) I/O.

Ryan Dahl created and first released Node.js in 2009. Web apps, real-time chat apps, command-line apps, and REST API servers are just some of the many types of applications that may be built using Node.js. However, its primary use is in the creation of server-side network applications like web browsers. A common Node.js filename extension is.js.

How Does Node.js Work, and What Are Its
Benefits and Drawbacks?

The benefits and drawbacks of Node.js come in many forms.

Benefits

- A free and open-source framework, js is distributed under the MIT license.

- It's a minimalist framework; therefore, it just has a few components. Depending on the specifics of a given use case, more modules may be necessary.

- This framework is compatible with several operating systems, including Windows, Mac OS X, and Linux.

- JavaScript is a programming language used to create backend systems and services.

- No data was ever buffered in a js app before. Applications written in Node.js simply send out data in bite-sized pieces. All of the APIs in the Node.js library operate in a non-blocking, asynchronous manner. This basically denotes that a server written in Node.js will not hold its breath for an API to deliver data. A Node.js notification mechanism helps the server get a response from an API after it has called it and moved on to the next API.

- js is a library for rapid program execution based on Google Chrome's V8 JavaScript Engine.

Drawbacks

- Consistency issues are a major drawback of using Node.js. To keep their code compatible, developers must make adjustments to the API all the time, which just adds to their workload. It isn't keeping up with the advancement of resource-intensive apps and does not enable multi-threaded programming.

- JavaScript, unlike many other programming languages, does not have a robust library system.

- Users are therefore compelled to seek out a standard library for processing images, parsing XML, performing Object-Relational Mapping (ORM), managing databases, etc. It complicates even the most fundamental of programming jobs with Node.js.

Comparing JavaScript with Node.js: Key Distinctions

Here, we'll contrast JavaScript with Node.js by highlighting their key distinctions:

- Typically used for client-side scripting, JavaScript is a small, portable, platform-independent, interpreted computer language. Java and HTML both include it by default. However, Node.js is a server-side programming language built on the same V8 engine that powers Google Chrome. Therefore, it is utilized to create apps focused on the network. It's a decentralized system for processing large amounts of data in real time.

- JavaScript is a scripting language that may be executed in any browser that has the JavaScript Engine installed. The alternative option is Node.js, which is an implementation of the JavaScript programming language. To be more practical, it requires libraries that can be accessed without much hassle while writing in JavaScript.

- Any engine, such as V8, Safari's JavaScript Core, Firefox's Spider Monkey, or any other, may execute JavaScript (Google Chrome). Because of this, developing with JavaScript is straightforward, and any operating environment functions as effectively as a browser. However, Node.js only works on Google Chrome since it relies on the browser's proprietary V8 engine. Contrarily, JavaScript code produced by any developer may be executed in any environment, regardless of whether or not the V8 engine is available.

- Getting into any OS requires completing a certain nonblocking job. JavaScript has a few standard objects, but they are entirely platform-dependent. As an example, ActiveX Control is a program that can only be used on a Windows computer. However, Node.js is allowed to execute non-blocking OS-specific operations from any JavaScript code. It does not include any constants that are unique to any one operating system. Node.js is proficient at making a clean connection with the file system, enabling the developer to access and modify files on the disc.

- When developing a single web app, JavaScript is often utilized for all client-side responsibilities. Business validation, the periodic display of a dynamic page, or even a basic Ajax request might all be part of a single action. These have a fixed lifetime in each given web application. However, Node.js is often used to make any operating system accessible or executable in a non-blocking manner. Non-blocking operations on an OS include things like creating or running a shell script, receiving specific hardware-related information with a single call, retrieving data about certificates already installed on the machine, and carrying out a huge number of predefined actions.

- The key benefits of using JavaScript are the flexibility it provides in terms of interface and interaction, as well as the appropriate amount of server connectivity and direct input for visitors. However, Node.js can process several requests at once and features a node package manager with more than 500 modules. Its unique abilities include support for micro-service architecture and Internet of Things.

In-Depth Analysis of JavaScript vs. Node JS

Here, we'll contrast JavaScript and Node JS, two popular server-side scripting languages:

Features	JavaScript	Node JS
Definition	It is a cross-platform, accessible, interpreted, lightweight scripting computer language used to create dynamic and web applications.	It's a cross-platform, accessible JavaScript runtime environment that lets us run JavaScript on the server.
Type	It is a kind of computer language. It is compatible with any browser that has a functional browser engine.	It's a JavaScript interpreter and environment with several useful libraries for JavaScript programming.
Dedicated Server	It is commonly used on client-side servers.	It is often utilized on the server.

(Continued)

Features	JavaScript	Node JS
Community	The node community does not care about all of the JavaScript.	The JavaScript community is represented by all node projects.
Running Engines	Any engine, including Spider Monkey, V8, and JavaScript Core, can run JavaScript.	Node JS is only enabled by the V8 engine, which is typically used by Google Chrome. Any JavaScript program built using Node JS will be executed in the V8 engine.
Used for	It is intended for the development of network-centric applications.	It is intended for data-intensive real-world applications that operate across several platforms.
Languages	It's a new variant of the ECMA script that operates on Chrome's C++-based V8 engine.	It makes use of C, C++, and JavaScript.
Modules	TypedJS, RamdaJS, and other JavaScript frameworks are examples.	Nodejs modules include Lodash and Express. All of these modules must be imported from npm.
Companies' Uses	Google, Shopify, Udacity, Sendgrid, Groupon, Okta, Instacart, and more firms employ JavaScript.	Node Js is used by a variety of firms, including Netflix, Hapi, Walmart, Paypal, Linkedin, Trello, Medium, and eBay.

We discussed the many uses and frameworks of JS Frontend, Backend, Mobile, Gaming, and Desktop in this chapter.

Furthermore, we explored which framework to learn and when, as well as how to combine JS abilities with other programming languages.

NOTES

1 The 5 Best JavaScript Frameworks of 2022 [+ How to Pick the Right One]: https://blog.hubspot.com/website/javascript-frameworks Accessed on: 03 October 2022.

2 JavaScript Library vs JavaScript Frameworks – The Differences: www.microverse.org/blog/javascript-library-vs-javascript-frameworks-the-differences Accessed on: 03 October 2022.

3 7 Frontend JavaScript Frameworks Loved by Developers in 2022: www.simform.com/blog/javascript-frontend-frameworks/ Accessed on: 03 October 2022.

4 5 Backend JavaScript Frameworks Experts Love: https://insights.dice.com/2020/08/21/5-backend-javascript-frameworks-experts-love/ Accessed on: 04 October 2022.

5 8 Best Javascript Game Engines: www.geeksforgeeks.org/8-best-javascript-game-engines/ Accessed on: 04 October 2022.

6 10 Popular Javascript Frameworks for Mobile App Development: https://insights.daffodilsw.com/blog/5-popular-javascript-frameworks-for-mobile-app-development Accessed on: 04 October 2022.

7 One for All and All for One: JS Frameworks for Desktop Applications and the Best of Them: https://luxnet.io/blog/the-best-of-js-frameworks-for-desktop-applications Accessed on: 06 October 2022.

8 How to Choose the Best Javascript Framework: https://wiredelta.com/how-to-choose-the-best-javascript-framework-2/ Accessed on: 06 October 2022.

9 How to Choose a Right JavaScript Framework for Your Project?: https://dev.to/abdurrkhalid333/how-to-choose-a-right-javascript-framework-for-your-project-2501 Accessed on: 06 October 2022.

10 How to Choose a JavaScript Framework for Beginners: www.codecademy.com/resources/blog/what-javascript-framework-to-learn-beginner/ Accessed on: 06 October 2022.

11 Difference between Java and JavaScript: www.geeksforgeeks.org/difference-between-java-and-javascript/ Accessed on: 06 October 2022.

12 Python vs JavaScript: Key Difference between Them: https://www.guru99.com/python-vs-javascript.html#:~:text=KEY%20DIFFERENCES%3A-,JavaScript%20is%20a%20scripting%20language%20that%20helps%20you%20create%20interactive,choice%20for%20rapid%20application%20development. Accessed on: 06 October 2022.

13 jQuery vs. JavaScript: www.javatpoint.com/jquery-vs-javascript Accessed on: 07 October 2022.

14 jQuery vs. PHP: www.javatpoint.com/javascript-vs-php Accessed on: 07 October 2022.

15 Dart vs. JavaScript: www.javatpoint.com/dart-vs-javascript Accessed on: 07 October 2022.

16 JavaScript Vs. Angular Js: www.javatpoint.com/javascript-vs-angularjs Accessed on: 07 October 2022.

17 JavaScript vs. Node.js: www.javatpoint.com/javascript-vs-nodejs Accessed on: 08 October 2022.

CHAPTER 5

Frontend Development

IN THIS CHAPTER

➢ React

➢ Express

➢ Vue.js

In the previous chapter, we covered frameworks for gaming, desktop, frontend, backend, and mobile, and in this chapter, we will discuss frontend development.

FRONTEND VS BACKEND

Frontend and backend are the two terms used in web development most frequently.

These words are crucial for web development even if they are very different from one another.[1] Each side must work together and communicate with one another as a single unit in order to improve the website's functionality.

FRONTEND DEVELOPMENT

The part of a website that users engage with directly is referred to as the frontend.

It is frequently referred to as the 'client side' of the program. It encompasses all of the elements that consumers view and utilize right away, including button colors, text styles, images, graphs, and tables.

DOI: 10.1201/9781003356578-5

HTML, CSS, and JavaScript are the three languages used for frontend programming.

The structure, design, behavior, and content of everything seen on browser displays when websites, online applications, or mobile apps are viewed are all put into practice by frontend developers. Performance and responsiveness are the main objectives of the frontend.

Frontend Languages

The languages listed below are used to build the frontend portion:

- **HTML:** In HTML, 'Hypertext Markup Language' is denoted. It is used to develop the frontends of web pages using a markup language. HTML is an abbreviation for Hypertext Markup Language. The connection between web pages is defined by hypertext. The written documentation included inside the tag that specifies the structure of web pages is defined using markup language.

- **CSS:** Cascading Style Sheets, sometimes known as CSS, is a straightforwardly written language that makes it easier to display web pages. Applying styles to web pages is possible using CSS. More importantly, CSS enables us to do this without having to rely on the HTML that each webpage is made up of.

- **JavaScript:** JavaScript is a well-known programming language that is used to work on websites so that users may interact with them. It is utilized to increase a website's functionality so that exciting games and web-based programs may be employed on it. Being a good developer requires knowledge of JavaScript, which can be utilized in both the frontend and the backend. For example, Dart for Flutter, JavaScript for React, and Python for Django are just a few of the other languages that may be used for frontend development, depending on the framework.

Frontend Frameworks and Libraries

- **AngularJS:** AngularJs is a JavaScript open-source frontend framework that is mostly used to create single-page web applications

(SPAs), frontend frameworks, and libraries. It is a framework that constantly develops and grows and provides better techniques to create Internet applications. Dynamic HTML is created by converting static HTML. The open-source undertaking has a free variant. HTML and data are related because directives expand HTML attributes.

- **React.js:** React is a declarative, efficient, and flexible JavaScript toolkit for building user interfaces. ReactJS is a free frontend library with component architecture that is solely in charge of the application's view layer. Facebook takes care of it. Frontend development is also extremely easy with React JS.

- **Bootstrap:** Bootstrap is a free and open-source framework for creating responsive webpages and online applications. For building flexible, mobile-first websites, the framework is the most popular combination of HTML, CSS, and JavaScript.

- **JQuery:** Streamlining interactions between JavaScript and the Page Object Model (DOM) of an HTML/CSS document is accomplished via the open-source JavaScript framework known as JQuery. To elaborate, jQuery facilitates DOM animations, Ajax interactions, traversal and manipulation of HTML pages, and JavaScript programming for cross-browser usage. SASS is the trustworthy, advanced, and powerful CSS extension language. It may be used to quickly add inheritance, nesting, and variables to an existing CSS style sheet on a website.

- **Flutter:** The open-source Flutter UI development SDK is overseen by Google. It is powered by the programming language Dart. From a single code base, it produces effective and visually beautiful natively developed applications for desktop, web, and mobile (IOS, Android). Thanks to native speed and UI, Flutter's main selling point is the simplicity, expressiveness, and flexibility of flat development. In March 2021, Flutter will release Flutter 2, an upgrade that will let programmers create and share web apps while desktop programs are still being developed.

- A few instances are Semantic-UI, Foundation, Materialize, Backbone.js, Ember.js, and more libraries and frameworks.

BACKEND DEVELOPMENT

The server side of a website is called the backend.

It also ensures that everything on the client side of the website functions properly while storing and organizing data. It is the portion of the website that you are unable to see and use.

It is the part of the program that consumers do not directly interact with.

Users indirectly access the components and features created by backend designers via a frontend application. The backend also includes tasks like developing APIs, building libraries, and interacting with system elements devoid of user interfaces or even systems of scientific programming.

Backend Languages

The following list of languages is used to build the backend portion:

- **PHP:** PHP is a programming language used on servers that was created primarily for creating websites. PHP is referred to be a server-side scripting language since PHP code is executed on the server.

- **C++:** It's a widely used language for a wide variety of programming tasks, and it's especially popular in the professional arena. In addition, it serves as a backend language.

- **Java:** One of the most well-liked and often used platforms and computer languages is Java. It can scale up quite well.

- **Python:** Python is a programming language that enables rapid work and more effective system integration. It is also a crucial language for the backend, and Python Programming Foundation—Self-Paced course may help us learn it. This course is suitable for beginners and will assist you in laying a solid foundation for Python.

- **Node.js:** JavaScript code may be executed outside of a browser using the Node.js runtime environment, which is free and cross-platform. We must keep in mind that NodeJS is neither a programming language nor a framework. The majority of folks are perplexed and realize it's a computer language or framework. For creating backend services like APIs for web apps or mobile apps, we often employ Node.js. Large corporations like PayPal, Uber, Netflix, Walmart, and others utilize it throughout production.

Backend Frameworks

- **Express:** Express is a Node.js framework for server-side and backend programming. Single-page, multi-page, and hybrid web apps may all be created with it. We may manage a variety of various HTTP requests with its assistance.

- **Django:** Django is a model-template-views-based web framework written in Python. It is used to create expansive and intricate web applications. It has the qualities of being quick, secure, and scalable.

- **Ruby on Rails:** Model-view-controller architecture is used by the server-side framework known as Ruby on Rails. It offers pre-built structures including databases, online services, and web pages.

- **Laravel:** Laravel is a reliable PHP web application framework called Laravel. Reusing the components of many frameworks while building a web application is its best feature.

- **Spring:** This server-side framework, called Spring, supports Java applications' infrastructure. It supports a variety of frameworks, including Hibernate, Struts, and EJB. Additionally, it offers addons that make it simple and rapid to create Java apps.

- C#, Ruby, GO, and other backend programming and scripting languages are a few examples.

Difference between Frontend and Backend Development

Frontend and backend development are two facets of the same problem, yet they differ significantly from one another. The backend controls how everything functions, whereas the frontend is what users see and interact with.

The frontend of a website is the portion that visitors can see and interact with. It includes the design, menus for navigation, texts, photographs, and videos, as well as the graphical user interface (GUI) and command line. Contrarily, the backend is the portion of the website that visitors cannot access or interact with.

Frontend refers to the elements of the website that visitors can view and interact with visually. On the other side, the backend is responsible for everything that takes place in the background.

The frontend is written in HTML, CSS, and JavaScript, and the backend is written in Java, Ruby, Python, and .Net.

REACTJS

We will about ReactJS below with its definition, installation, and syntax.

WHAT DOES THE 'REACT' MEAN?

React is a JavaScript toolkit for building user interfaces that is managed by Facebook and a developer community that uses open-source software. React has been widely adopted in the field of web development despite the fact that it is not a language because of its large library of practical tools.[2]

Although it didn't debut until May 2013, this library has quickly become a standard for web designers and developers. Beyond the realm of user interface development, React provides a number of architectural support extensions like Flux and React Native.

The Question Is, 'Why React?'

At now, no other frontend framework comes close to competing with React's widespread adoption. We'll explain the reason:

- The building of dynamic web apps is simplified with React since it takes less code and provides more capability than JavaScript, which may rapidly become convoluted.

- React's usage of virtual DOM makes developing web apps more quickly. When a change is made to a component in a web application, the virtual DOM compares it to its prior state and only updates the elements in the Real DOM that have changed.

- Components are the foundation of a React project, and many different kinds of components may be found in a single app. With their own dedicated logic and controls, these modules may be utilized throughout the program, thus cutting down on development time.

- There is only one path for data to go in React. It follows that developers would often stack kid components atop parent components when building a React app. Since data only moves in one way, it's much simpler to pinpoint exactly where an issue is originating inside an application.

- React has a shallow learning curve since it mostly builds on familiar principles from HTML and JavaScript, with a few helpful additions. Still, we need to put in some effort to learn the ins and outs of React's library, just as you would with any other tool or framework.

- It's useful for creating both online and mobile applications: Although it is common knowledge that web apps are built using React, it is far from its only purpose. React Native is a popular framework for developing high-quality mobile apps; it is based on the original React library. To that end, it's important to note that React is as at home when developing for the web as it is for mobile devices.

- Facebook has created a Chrome plugin that can be used to debug React apps, providing dedicated tools for simple debugging. Because of this, fixing bugs in React web apps is a breeze.

React Features

It's no secret that ReactJS is quickly becoming the preferred JavaScript framework among today's most cutting-edge websites.[3]

It's doing some very important work for the frontend ecosystem right now. Some of ReactJS's most notable characteristics are listed here.

- JSX

- Components

- One-way Data Binding

- Virtual DOM

- Simplicity

- Performance

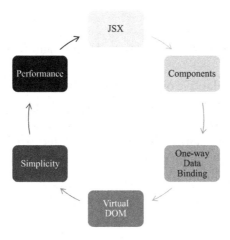

Features of React

JSX

JavaScript XML is what JSX refers to. It's a new addition to the JavaScript syntax.

ReactJS employs a syntax that's similar to XML or HTML.

Calls to the React Framework's Java API are generated from this syntax. By enhancing ES6, it allows HTML-like text to coexist with JavaScript react code. In ReactJS, JSX is not required but is highly encouraged.

Components

Components are the backbone of ReactJS. Each individual 'component' in a ReactJS program has its own set of rules and data processing capabilities. Because of their modular nature, these parts may be reused, making it easier to manage the codebase of large-scale projects.

Data Binding, One Way Only

Due to its architecture, ReactJS only supports one-way data binding and flows in just one direction. Using one-way data binding, you may exert more command over the whole program.

If information is flowing in the other way, then supplementary capabilities are needed.

This is due to the fact that data included inside components should be immutable. The flux pattern is useful for ensuring that your data flows in just one way. The application's newly discovered flexibility is the main cause of the higher efficiency.

Virtual DOM

A DOM object that exists only in a computer's memory is called a 'virtual DOM object.'

The effect is similar to a one-way data binding.

If there are any changes made to the web app, the complete user interface will be re-rendered in a virtual DOM representation. Then, it compares the old DOM representation to the new one. Afterward, just the modified elements will be reflected in the true DOM. This eliminates memory waste and speeds up the program.

Simplicity

Because it is written in JSX files, ReactJS is easy to learn and implement.

We all know that since ReactJS is a component-based approach, the code may be reused as many as we want. This makes it easy to pick up and get started with.

Performance

There is widespread agreement that ReactJS is a speed demon. As a result of this improvement, it is now the best framework available. Because it controls a DOM that exists only in the computer's memory, this is the case. HTML, XML, and XHTML are all supported by the Document Object Model (DOM), a programming API that works across platforms.

The DOM is purely virtual. This is why we avoid explicitly altering the DOM whenever we build new components. Instead, we're focusing on developing virtual components that can be easily transformed into DOM for improved speed.

Benefits and Drawbacks of ReactJS

The most popular open-source JavaScript library nowadays is called ReactJS. It's useful for quickly building high-quality web applications with nothing in the way of custom code. ReactJS's primary goal is to help programmers create faster app interfaces.[4]

The following are some major benefits and drawbacks of using ReactJS:

Benefits

1. **ReactJS is simple to learn and use**

   As opposed to other similar frameworks, ReactJS is far less complicated to learn and use. There is a tonne of help material like guides and videos included. Any developer with a JavaScript experience may quickly grasp and begin designing web applications using React.

   It's a JavaScript framework that represents the view in the Model-View-Controller (MVC) design pattern. It is not fully featured, but it has the benefit of an open-source JavaScript User Interface (UI) library, which aids in job execution.

2. **It is now easier to create dynamic web applications**

   It was difficult to construct a dynamic web application particularly using HTML strings since it required extensive code, but React JS eliminated that problem and made it easy. It requires less code while providing greater features. The JSX (JavaScript Extension) syntax is used, which is a notation for building HTML elements using HTML tags and HTML citations. Further, it simplifies the process of making codes that computers can read.

3. **Components that may be reused**

A ReactJS web application is composed of many components, each with its own logic and controls. These parts are responsible for generating a small, modular chunk of HTML code that may be dropped in wherever it's needed. You may easily plan and manage your apps with the help of the code that can be reused. These components may be layered onto one another to form complex software systems. ReactJS uses a method based on a 'virtual DOM' to add elements to the HTML DOM. In order to save time, the virtual DOM only updates the data for the specific nodes that have changed, rather than the whole DOM.

4. **Improving Performance**

ReactJS is quicker because of the virtual DOM. The DOM provides a consistent API for developing applications that work with HTML, XML, and XHTML regardless of the platform. This bug slowed down development time for most programmers when the DOM was updated. Virtual DOM is how ReactJS dealt with this problem.

The React Virtual DOM is a version of the web browser's DOM that resides completely in memory. As a result, we did not write directly to the DOM while creating a React component.

Instead, we're creating virtual components that will respond to the DOM, resulting in smoother and quicker performance.

5. **The Use of Handy Tools**

React JS has also grown in popularity owing to the availability of a useful collection of tools.

These tools help developers comprehend and simplify their work. The React Developer Tools are Chrome and Firefox dev extensions that enable you to investigate the React component hierarchies in the virtual DOM. We may also pick certain components and analyze and update their current properties and state.

6. **Well-known for being SEO-friendly**

Traditional JavaScript frameworks have a problem with SEO. JavaScript-heavy apps are usually difficult for search engines to read.

Many site developers have often complained about this issue. ReactJS solves this issue, allowing developers to be readily found on search engines. This is because React.js applications may run locally on the server and the virtual DOM can render and deliver a web page to the browser.

7. **The Advantages of Having a JavaScript Library**

The majority of web developers now use ReactJS. It is because it provides a highly comprehensive JavaScript library. The JavaScript library gives web developers greater freedom to pick how they wish to work.

8. **Test Scope for the Codes**

ReactJS apps are really simple to test. It provides a platform for developers to test and debug their programs using native tools.

Drawbacks

1. **The rapid rate of development**

The quick pace of growth has benefits and drawbacks. In the event of a disadvantage, since the environment is always changing, some developers may not feel comfortable relearning new methods of doing things on a frequent basis.

With all of the constant upgrades, it may be difficult for them to absorb all of these changes.

It is incumbent upon them to continually improve their skills and get familiar with cutting-edge practices.

2. **Inadequate documentation**

It is just another drawback of rapidly evolving technology. The rate of advancement and expansion of React technologies makes it impossible to offer thorough documentation. To solve this, developers create their own instructions when new versions and tools are added to their present projects.

3. View Part

ReactJS just covers the app's UI layers and nothing more. As a result, we will still need to choose some additional technologies in order to have a comprehensive tools set for development in the project.

4. SX as a barrier

ReactJS makes use of JSX. Because of this syntactic extension, HTML and JavaScript may cohabit. Although this method has benefits of its own, some members of the development community consider JSX to be a barrier, especially for novice developers.

Developers complain about the complexity of the learning curve.

Version of React

A detailed React release history is shown here. On GitHub, we may also get complete documentation for latest versions.[5]

SN	Version	Release Date	Significant Changes
1.	0.3.0	29/05/2013	Initial Public Release.
2.	0.4.0	20/07/2013	\<div\>{/* */}\</div\> support for comment nodes Server-side rendering APIs have been improved. React. autoBind has been removed. Support for the main point, Formal improvements, Bugs have been fixed.
3.	0.5.0	20/10/2013	Increase memory use, Assistance with Selection and Composition events, In mixins, getInitialState and getDefaultProps are supported. React.version and React.isValidClass have been added. Windows compatibility has been improved.
4.	0.8.0	20/12/2013	Support for rows and cols, defer & async, loop for \<audio\> & \<video\>, and autoCorrect attributes has been added. onContextMenu events have been added. jstransform and esprima-fb utilities have been upgraded. Browserify has been upgraded.
5.	0.9.0	20/02/2014	Added support for crossOrigin, download and hrefLang, mediaGroup and muted, sandbox, seamless, and srcDoc, scope attributes, Added any, arrayOf, component, oneOfType, renderable, shape to React. PropTypes, Added support for onMouseOver and onMouseOut event, Added support for onLoad and onError on \<img\> elements.

(Continued)

SN	Version	Release Date	Significant Changes
6.	0.10.0	21/03/2014	Added support for srcSet and textAnchor attributes, add update function for immutable data, Ensure all void elements don't insert a closing tag.
7.	0.11.0	17/07/2014	Improved SVG support, Normalized e.view event, Update $apply command, Added support for namespaces, Added new transformWithDetails API, includes pre-built packages under dist/, MyComponent() now returns a descriptor, not an instance.
8.	0.12.0	21/11/2014	New features have been added. The spread operator ({...}) was created to replace this. transferPropsTo, acceptCharset, classID, manifest HTML attributes, and React.addons.batched are now supported. API updates, @jsx React.DOM is no longer necessary, CSS Transitions problems have been resolved.
9.	0.13.0	10/03/2015	Deprecated patterns that were warned about in 0.12 no longer work, the sequence of ref resolution has altered, and this._pendingState and this._rootNodeID have been removed. Classes in ES6 are supported. API React. findDOMNode(component) has been added, as well as support for iterators and immutable-js sequences. New features have been added. Deprecated React.addons. createFragment method React.addons.classSet.
10.	0.14.1	29/10/2015	Support for srcLang, default, sort, and color attributes has been added. Legacy.props access on DOM nodes has been ensured. scryRenderedDOMComponentsWithClass was fixed. React-dom.js has been added.
11.	15.0.0	07/04/2016	Instead of producing HTML, the first render now utilizes 'document.createElement'. No more additional <span>s. SVG support has been improved, ReactPerf. getLastMeasurements() is now opaque, and New deprecations are announced with a warning. React DOM now supports the citation and profile HTML attributes, as well as the cssFloat, gridRow, and gridColumn CSS properties.
12.	15.1.0	20/05/2016	Repair a batching bug, Use the most recent object-assign, Resolve the regression, Remove the usage of the merge utility. Some modules have been renamed.
13.	15.2.0	01/07/2016	Include information about the component stack, Stop validating props at mount time, add React.PropTypes. symbol, add onLoad and onError handling to <link> and <source> elements, add isRunning() API, fix performance regression.

(Continued)

SN	Version	Release Date	Significant Changes
14.	15.3.0	30/07/2016	Include React. PureComponent, Fix nested server rendering problem, add xmlns and xmlnsXlink to support SVG attributes and referrerPolicy to HTML attributes, update React Perf Add-on The ref problem has been resolved.
15.	15.3.1	19/08/2016	Enhance the performance of development builds. Internal hooks should be cleaned. Improve fbjs, React's startup time should be reduced. Fix a memory leak in server rendering, as well as the React Test Renderer. Convert the trackedTouchCount invariant to a console. error.
16.	15.4.0	16/11/2016	React package and browser build no longer contain React DOM, improved development efficiency, fixed infrequent test failures, updated batchedUpdates API, React Perf, and ReactTestRenderer.create().
17.	15.4.1	23/11/2016	Reorganize variable assignment, Handling of fixed events, The browser build is now compatible with AMD setups.
18.	15.4.2	06/01/2017	Build difficulties have been resolved. Missing package dependencies were added. Error messages have been improved.
19.	15.5.0	07/04/2017	React-dom/test-utils have been added. peerDependencies were removed. Fixed an issue with the Closure Compiler and added a React deprecation notice. React.PropTypes and createClass Chrome problem was fixed.
20.	15.5.4	11/04/2017	Enzyme compatibility is improved by presenting batched data. Updates to the shallow renderer, proptypes, and the react-addons-create-fragment package to support the loose-envify transform.
21.	15.6.0	13/06/2017	Add CSS variable support to the style attribute and Grid style properties. Fix AMD support for addons that rely on react. Remove any undue reliance. Add a React deprecation warning. helpers for createClass and React. DOM
22.	16.0.0	26/09/2017	Improved error handling with the addition of "error boundaries, " React DOM now supports supplying non-standard attributes, minor changes to setState behavior, and the removal of the react-with-addons.js build React.createClass is added as a create-react-class, React.PropTypes is added as a prop-type, React.DOM is added as a react-dom-factory, and the scheduling and lifecycle methods' behavior is changed.

(Continued)

SN	Version	Release Date	Significant Changes
23.	16.1.0	9/11/2017	Bower Releases are being discontinued. Fix an unintentional superfluous global variable in UMD builds. Fix the onMouseEnter and onMouseLeave events, Replace the <textarea> placeholder, Remove any unneeded code. Replace a missing package.json reliance, Add React DevTools support.
24.	16.3.0	29/03/2018	Add a new context API that is officially supported. Include a new package. When attempting to create portals using SSR, prevent an endless loop. Fix a problem with this. state, Resolve an IE/Edge problem.
25.	16.3.1	03/04/2018	Prefix private API with, In development mode, fix performance regression and error handling problems. Consider peer dependence. When utilizing Fragment, IE11 displays a false positive warning.
26.	16.3.2	16/04/2018	Repair an IE crash, Labels in User Timing measurements should be fixed. Add a UMD build, and use nesting to improve the efficiency of the unstable_observedBits API.
27.	16.4.0	24/05/2018	Include support for the Pointer Events standard. Allow for the specification of propTypes. Correct the reading context, Fix the getDerivedStateFromProps() functionality. Fix a crash in testInstance.parent. Add the React.unstable_Profiler component to track performance. Change the names of internal events.
28.	16.5.0	05/09/2018	Include support for the React DevTools Profiler. Handle failures in additional edge circumstances with grace. Include react-dom/profiling. Browsers should have a onAuxClick event. To mouse events, add movementX and movementY fields. Pointer event now has tangentialPressure and twist fields.
29.	16.6.0	23/10/2018	Add contextType support. Priority levels, continuations, and wrapped callbacks are all supported. Enhance the fallback method. Remove the gray overlay from iOS Safari. Add React.lazy() to separate code components.
30.	16.7.0	20/12/2018	Improve the speed of React.lazy for lazy-loaded components. To minimize memory leaks, clear fields after unmounting. Fix the problem with SSR. Resolve a performance decline.
31.	16.8.0	06/02/2019	Include Hooks, For batching updates, add ReactTestRenderer.act() and ReactTestUtils.act(). Allow React to be supplied synchronous thenables. Improve useReducer Hook's lazy initialization API with lazy().
32.	16.8.6	27/03/2019	In useReducer(), rectify an improper bailout, Resolve iframe issues in Safari DevTools, and alert if contextType is set to Context. Instead of Context, use Consumer and warn if contextType is set to an incorrect value.

SETUP OF THE REACT ENVIRONMENT

We will understand how to set up a development platform for a ReactJS application in this part.[6]

Prerequisite for ReactJS is as follows:

- NodeJS and NPM

- React and React DOM

- Webpack

- Babel

REACTJS INSTALLATION METHODS

There are two approaches to prepare an environment for a ReactJS application to run successfully.

The list of them is as follows:

- By use of the npm command

- Use the command create-react-app

1. By Use of the npm Command

Install NPM and NodeJS
The platforms required to create any ReactJS application are NodeJS and NPM.

By clicking the link provided below, we may install NodeJS and the NPM package manager.

We will talk about the NodeJS installation in Chapter 6.

Utilize the command indicated in the code below to confirm NodeJS and NPM.

```
$ node -v

$ npm -v
```

Get React and React DOM Installed
On the desktop or anywhere you choose, create a root folder with the name reactApp.

On the PC, we make it here. The folder may be created manually or by using the command shown below.

```
$ mkdir reactApp

$ cd reactApp
```

Create a package.json file right now. A package.json file must be generated and stored in the project folder in order to construct any module. We must execute the following command, as seen below, to do this.

```
javatpoint@root:~/Desktop/reactApp> npm init -y
```

We must install react and its DOM packages using the npm command below in the terminal window after generating a package.json file.

```
javatpoint@root:~/Desktop/reactApp>npm install react
react-dom --save
```

The aforementioned command may also be used independently, as seen in the example below.

```
javatpoint@root:~/Desktop/reactApp>npm install react
--save
javatpoint@root:~/Desktop/reactApp>npm install react-
dom --save
```

Install Webpack
Automation of the development and production pipelines is accomplished using Webpack.

Webpack-dev-server will be used for development, Webpack will be used to produce builds, and Webpack CLI offers a number of commands. These are combined by Webpack into a single file (bundle). Utilize the command described below to install Webpack.

```
javatpoint@root:~/Desktop/reactApp>npm install webpack
webpack-dev-server webpack-cli --save
```

The following command may also be used independently, as seen in the example below.

```
javatpoint@root:~/Desktop/reactApp>npm install webpack
--save
javatpoint@root:~/Desktop/reactApp>npm install
webpack-dev-server --save
javatpoint@root:~/Desktop/reactApp>npm install
webpack-cli --save
```

Install Babel

Babel is a JavaScript transpiler and compiler used to translate different source code.

React JSX and ES6 are converted into ES5 JavaScript, which may be used with any browser.

Babel-preset-react enables our browser to immediately update whenever any changes are made to our code without losing the state of the app. We require babel-loader for JSX file types.

Babel preset babel-preset-env is necessary for ES6 functionality. Use the command as indicated in the below code to install Webpack.   .

```
javatpoint@root:~/Desktop/reactApp>npm install babel-
core babel-loader babel-preset-env babel-preset-react
babel-webpack-plugin --save-dev
```

The following command may also be used individually, as seen in the example below.

```
javatpoint@root:~/Desktop/reactApp>npm install babel-
core --save-dev
javatpoint@root:~/Desktop/reactApp>npm install babel-
loader --save-dev
javatpoint@root:~/Desktop/reactApp>npm install babel-
preset-env --save-dev
javatpoint@root:~/Desktop/reactApp>npm install babel-
preset-react --save-dev
javatpoint@root:~/Desktop/reactApp>npm install babel-
webpack-plugin --save-dev
```

Creation of Files

To finish the installation procedure, the following files must be added to our project folder.

indexs.html, Appl.js, main.js, webpack.config.js, and.babelrc are these files.

We may manually generate these files or use the command prompt.

```
javatpoint@root:~/Desktop/reactApp>touch indexs.html
javatpoint@root:~/Desktop/reactApp>touch Appl.js
javatpoint@root:~/Desktop/reactApp>touch main.js
javatpoint@root:~/Desktop/reactApp>touch webpack.
config.js
javatpoint@root:~/Desktop/reactApp>touch .babelrc
```

2. Set React Application Compiler, Loader, and Server

Configure Webpack

We may configure webpack by including the following code to the webpack.config.js file.

It specifies our app's entry point, build output, and automatically resolved extension.

Additionally, it sets the development server's port to 8080.

It specifies the loaders for processing the different file formats used by our application and adds plugins required for development.

webpack.config.json

```
const path = require('path');
const HtmlWebpackPlugin = require('html-webpack-plugin');

module.exports = {
    entry: './main.js',
    output: {
        path: path.join(__dirname, '/bundle'),
        filename: 'indexsbundle.js'
    },
    devServer: {
        inline: true,
        port: 8080
    },
    module: {
        rules: [
```

```
        {
            test: /\.jsx?$/,
            exclude: /node_modules/,
        use: {
                loader: «babel-loader»,
            }
        }
    ]
},
plugins:[
    new HtmlWebpackPlugin({
        template: './indexs.html'
    })
]
}
```

Now, open the package.json file, remove "test" "echo\ "Error: no test specified\" && exit" from the "scripts" object, and replace it with the start and build commands. Because we will not do any testing on this application.

```
{
    "name": "reactApp",
    "version": "1.0.0",
    "description": "",
    "main": "indexs.js",
    "scripts": {
        "start": "webpack-dev-server --mode development
--open --hot",
        "build": "webpack --mode production"
    },
    "keywords": [],
    "author": "",
    "license": "ISC",
    "dependencies": {
        "react": "^16.8.6",
        "react-dom": "^16.8.6",
        "webpack-cli": "^3.3.2",
        "webpack-dev-server": "^3.3.2"
    },
    "devDependencies": {
        "@babel/core": "^7.4.3",
```

```
    "@babel/preset-env": "^7.4.3",
    "@babel/preset-react": "^7.0.0",
    "babel-core": "^6.26.3",
    "babel-loader": "^8.0.5",
    "babel-preset-env": "^1.7.0",
    "babel-preset-react": "^6.24.1",
    "html-webpack-plugin": "^3.2.0",
    "webpack»: "^4.30.0"
  }
}
```

HTML Webpack Template for the index.html File

Using the HtmlWeb-packPlugin plugin, we can add a custom template to produce indexs.html.

This allows us to add a viewport element to provide responsive scaling of our app on mobile devices. In addition, it adds the indexsbundle. js script, which is our packaged app file, and sets the div id="app" as the root element for our app.

```
<!DOCTYPE html>
<html lang = "en">
  <head>
    <meta charset = "UTF-8">
    <title>React App</title>
  </head>
  <body>
    <div id = "app"></div>
    <script src = 'indexsbundle.js'></script>
  </body>
</html>
```

App.jsx and main.js

This is the first React component, sometimes known as the app entrance point.

It will display "Hello, Everyone."

App.js

```
import React, { Component } from 'react';
class App extends Component{
```

```
render(){
    return(
        <div>
            <h1>Hello Everyone</h1>
        </div>
    );
    }
}
export default App;
```

Import this component and display it to our App's root element so that it is visible in the browser.

Main.js

```
import React from 'react';
import ReactDOM from 'react-dom';
import App from './App.js';

ReactDOM.render(<App />, document.
getElementById('app'));
```

Creation of .babelrc file
Create a file named.babelrc and paste the code below into it.

.babelrc

```
{
    "presets":[
    "@babel/preset-env", "@babel/preset-react"]
}
```

Running Server
After installing and configuring the application, we may start the server by using the following command.

```
javatpoint@root:~/Desktop/reactApp>npm start
```

It will display the port number that must be opened in the browser. After opening it, the output will be shown.

Create the Bundle
Now, produce the application's bundle.

Bundling is the process of integrating imported files into a single file, called a 'bundle.' This bundle may then be added to a website to load an application in its entirety. To construct this, we must execute the build command indicated below in command prompt.

```
javatpoint@root:~/Desktop/reactApp> npm run build
```

This command creates the bundle in the current folder (to which our application belongs) and displays it.

3. Use the Command create-react-app

If we do not want to install react using webpack and babel, we may install react using create-react-app. The 'create-react-app' function is administered by Facebook.

This is appropriate for novices who do not want to manually deal with transpiling technologies such as webpack and babel. This section demonstrates how to install React using the CRA tool.

Install NodeJS and NPM
NodeJS and NPM are the required development platforms for every ReactJS application.

We may download NodeJS and the NPM package manager in the next chapter.

Installation of React
We may install React using the npm package manager using the command below. Do not stress about the potential difficulties of installing React. The necessary functionality is included in the create-react-app npm package.

```
javatpoint@root:~/>npm install -g create-react-app
```

Develop a New React Project
After installing React, the create-react-app command may be used to build a new React project. Here, we pick the project name jtp-reactapp.

```
javatpoint@root:~/>create-react-app jtp-reactapp
```

```
javatpoint@root:~/>npx create-react-app jtp-reactapp
```

The above code will install react and generate a new project called jtp-reactapp. This application includes the subfolders and files that will be shown by default.

To begin, enter the src folder and make modifications to the required file. By default, files are stored in the src folder.

For instance, we will open App.js and make the code modifications indicated below.

App.js

```
import React from 'react';
import logo from './logo.svg';
import './App.css';

function App() {
  return (
    <div className="App">
      <header className="App-header">
        <img src={logo} className="App-logo"
alt="logo" />
        <p>
          Welcome Everyone.

      <p>Get started, edit src/App.js and save to the
reload.</p>
        </p>
        <a
          className="App-link"
          href="https://reactjs.org"
          target="_blank"
          rel="noopener noreferrer"
        >
          Learn React
        </a>
      </header>
    </div>
  );
}

export default App;
```

Running Server

After installation is complete, we may start the server by using the following code:

```
javatpoint@root:~/Desktop>cd jtp-reactapp
javatpoint@root:~/Desktop/jtp-reactapp>npm start
```

COMPARISON BETWEEN ANGULARJS VS REACTJS

We will discuss AngularJS and ReactJS below.

AngularJS

The open-source JavaScript framework AngularJS is used to create dynamic web applications. In 2009, Misko Hevery and Adam Abrons created AngularJS, which is currently maintained by Google.[7]

The most recent version of Angular as of March 11, 2019 is 1.7.8. It is mostly used for creating single-page applications and is based on HTML and JavaScript. It may be added to an HTML document using a <script> tag. It enhances HTML by adding built-in attributes using directives and connects data to HTML using Expressions.

Characteristics of AngularJS

- **Data binding:** AngularJS follows the two-way data binding pattern. The synchronization of data is done between model and display components.

- **POJO Paradigm:** AngularJS employs the POJO (Plain Old JavaScript) model, which delivers objects that are both spontaneous and well-planned. The POJO concept makes AngularJS autonomous and simple to utilize.

- **Model-View-Controller Framework:** MVC is a software design pattern used in the development of online applications. AngularJS's working paradigm is built on MVC principles. AngularJS's MVC architecture is simple, flexible, and dynamic. MVC facilitates the development of client-side applications.

- **Services:** AngularJS offers various built-in services, such as $http for XMLHttpRequest creation. In AngularJS, user interfaces are constructed using HTML. This declarative language includes shorter tags and is straightforward to interpret. It delivers a structured, organized, and fluid interface.

- **Dependency Injection:** AngularJS's built-in dependency injection subsystem facilitates the creation, comprehension, and testing of applications.

- **Community activity on Google:** AngularJS gives tremendous community support. Since Google maintains AngularJS, this is the case. Therefore, if you have maintenance concerns, there are several forums where we may have our questions answered.

- **Routing:** Routing is the process of transitioning from one view to another. Routing is the most important feature of single-page applications, in which all content appears on a single page. When a user clicks the menu, the developers do not want to send them to a different website. The developers want for the content to load on the same page regardless of the URL.

ReactJS

User interfaces for single-page applications are created using the free and open-source JavaScript package ReactJS. It is exclusively responsible for the application's view layer.

It enables developers to assemble complicated user interfaces using tiny, isolated pieces of code known as 'components.' ReactJS consists of two parts: components, which are the elements that include HTML code and what we want to see in the user interface, and an HTML page where all your components are presented.

It is developed by Jordan Walke, a former software developer at Facebook. Initially created and managed by Facebook, it was eventually included in major products like WhatsApp and Instagram. ReactJS was created by Facebook in 2011 for the newsfeed area, although it was not made available to the public until May 2013.

Characteristics of ReactJS

- **JSX:** JSX is a syntactic extension for JavaScript. The JSX syntax is converted into React Framework JavaScript calls. It extends ES6 so that HTML-like text may coexist with React code written in JavaScript.

- **Components:** Components are fundamental to ReactJS. Multiple components make up a ReactJS application, and each component has its own logic and controls. These components are reusable, which makes it easier to maintain the code in bigger projects.

- **One-way Data Binding:** ReactJS uses unidirectional data flow, or one-way data binding. The one-way data binding provides more application-wide control. If the data flow is in the other direction, then extra characteristics are required. This is because components are intended to be immutable and their data cannot be modified.

- **Virtual DOM:** A virtual DOM object is a representation of a physical DOM object. When any changes are made to a web application, the complete user interface is re-rendered in virtual DOM form. The difference between the existing DOM representation and the new DOM is then examined. Once complete, the actual DOM will only update the modified elements. It speeds up the program and eliminates memory waste.

- **Simplicity:** ReactJS utilizes the JSX file, which makes the application easy to both create and comprehend. In addition, ReactJS is a component-based framework that allows code to be reused as required. It makes it easy to use and understand.

- **Performance:** ReactJS is renowned for its excellent performance. This is because it has control over a virtual DOM. The DOM is purely memory-based. As a result, when we construct a component, we do not immediately write to the DOM. Instead, we are developing virtual components that will transform into the DOM, resulting in a more efficient and fluid user experience.

AngularJS vs. ReactJS

	AngularJS	ReactJS
Author	Google	Facebook Community
Developer	Misko Hevery	Jordan Walke
Initial Release	October 2010	March 2013
Latest Version	Angular 1.7.8 on 11 March 2019.	React 16.8.6 on 27 March 2019
Language	JavaScript, HTML	JSX
Type	Open-Source MVC Framework	Open-Source JS Framework
Rendering	Client Side	Server Side
Packaging	Weak	Strong
Data Binding	Bi-directional	Unidirectional
DOM	Regular DOM	Virtual DOM
Testing	Unit and Integration Testing	Unit Testing
App Architecture	MVC	Flux
Dependencies	Requirements are automatically managed by it.	To handle dependencies, extra tools are needed.
Routing	For its router setup, it needs a template or controller that must be manually maintained.	Although it contains several routing modules, such as react-router, it does not handle routing.
Performance	Slow	fast thanks to virtual DOM.
Best For	Single-page apps that refresh a single view at a time work best with it.	The ideal use cases are single-page apps that update several views simultaneously.

COMPARISON BETWEEN REACTJS AND SVELTE

What Is Svelte?

Svelte is a frontend compiler that is free and open-source, and it was created by Rich Harris in 2016. Svelte assembles HTML templates to produce original code that directly modifies the Document Object Model.[8]

In contrast to React and other conventional JavaScript frameworks, Svelte does not incur virtual DOM cost. Svelte's methods result in less transmitted files and higher client performance. The application code is processed by the compiler, which also redraws UI components impacted by the data and inserts calls to automatically update the data.

The TypeScript programming language, a superset of JavaScript, is used to create Svelte.

When Need One Use Svelte?

Svelte's code is recognized for being straightforward since Vanilla JavaScript is quite similar to it. Svelte enables developers to accomplish their goals with less code. If website developers want to create an extremely minimal package size, they should utilize Svelte.

Svelte-written programs are practical for usage in low-capacity or low-power devices. Better control over state management, routing, and the development of specialized infrastructure is offered by nimble tools and frameworks. DOM manipulation, reactive frameworks, and growing markets may all benefit from Svelte.

Which Companies Utilize Svelte?

Major corporations rely on Svelte for their websites, including Yahoo, Rakuten, Bloomberg, Facebook, Apple, The New York Times, Square, ByteDance, Spotify, Reuters, Ikea, Brave, and others. Because Svelte turns the application's code to optimum JavaScript while it is being coded, businesses like it. As a result, the performance of programs created in Svelte is not hampered by framework abstractions.

What Is React?

React is a frontend JavaScript library that developers use to create user interfaces.

The UI elements are maintained by the Meta (Facebook), and a group of organizations and developers collaborate to create updated versions. The foundation for creating webpages, mobile applications, and server-rendered apps is React. React is helpful for managing state and rendering it onto the DOM.

React application development necessitates the use of extra libraries. To create React components, you need to be familiar with design patterns, client-side code, and routing.

When Should React to Be Used?

The component library React is versatile and ideal for state management. As a result, data may be sent between apps and websites that employ React components without refreshing the page. For user interfaces that need a lot of user involvement, React should be employed.

React is the model-view-'view' controller's component. React makes it simple to manage lower-level algorithms, and just the view model of the user interface needs to be coded. The Virtual DOM of React speeds up loading times and enhances website performance.

Which Companies Utilize React?

React is used to create user interfaces by hugely popular companies including Facebook, Instagram, Salesforce, Shopify, Discord, Skype, and Pinterest.

Companies prefer React to build the frontend portion of their websites since it is easy to find developers internationally. React is a popular option among developers and businesses because it is quick, simple to use, and scalable.

React vs Svelte: Which Is Superior?

Svelte is a more recent framework than React and requires no additional tools. Multiple variables and preferences may influence a developer's decision between these frameworks.

Let's compare their distinctions so you can select the appropriate JavaScript framework for our applications.

Performance

Traditional Document Object Model (DOM) necessitates an update for each code change, which degrades the efficiency of the application. Virtual DOM accelerates the process by functioning as temporary memory storage for user interface modifications.

A procedure called as diffusion or reconciliation delays updates until they can be successfully updated and rendered.

React utilizes virtual DOM to decompose an application's code as the code is run.

VDOM improves React's performance over conventional JavaScript languages. However, Svelte improves efficiency by avoiding the VDOM diffing procedure. Svelte is a compiler that renders DOM documents using reactive programming. The DOM is updated whenever an assignment causes a change in the component stage. As a serverless-first framework, Svelte is therefore seen as more reactive than React.

Bundle Size

The.gzip version of Svelte has a size of 1.6 kilobytes. When paired with ReactDOM, React.gzip has a total size of 42.2 kilobytes. Svelte's decreased bundle size assures faster loading times, enhanced responsiveness, and reduced bandwidth costs.

Testing

End-to-end tests are able to be performed on React code. The application's React code is tested in a realistic browser environment. This decreases the time to market (TTM) and increases the value of your software. The Svelte testing library is available for unit testing. The Svelte testing library is more compact than React and provides straightforward calculations. Thus, Svelte can assist developers in maintaining code that is clean, functional, and compact.

Community Assistance

React has a large developer community since it is one of the most popular JavaScript platforms in the world. The community of React developers contributes tutorials, guidelines, updates, components, and more in order to maintain the library's usefulness. The fact that a huge corporation like Facebook (Meta) maintains React increases the need for React engineers. Svelte is uncommon, but developers that employ it report high levels of satisfaction. Svelte's enterprise-level support is relatively new, as Sveltekit 1.0 has not yet been published. Compared to the more than 287k active React developers, the Svelte community consists of just 11k developers.

Who Succeeds?

The Svelte vs. React debate is simple when the project needs are well-defined. Utilize Svelte in our applications to obtain a lower bundle size, manageable code, and outstanding performance without the VDOM. Due to the framework's simplicity, Svelte helps developers to prepare websites more quickly.

Utilizing React for our projects will facilitate the recruitment of software professionals.

React facilitates the maintenance of application stability. An active community of React developers assists in resolving development-related questions and issues.

Using React with Svelte to produce robust software solutions necessitates the hiring of seasoned software engineers.

REACT JSX

All React components have a render method, as we have previously seen. A React component's HTML output is defined by the render function. A React plugin called JSX (JavaScript Extension) enables the creation of JavaScript code that resembles HTML.[9]

To put it another way, JSX is an extension of ECMAScript utilized by React to allow HTML-like syntax to coexist alongside JavaScript/React code. Preprocessors (also known as transpilers, such as babel) employ the syntax to convert HTML-like syntax into typical JavaScript objects that a JavaScript engine can interpret.

In the same file where we write JavaScript code, JSX enables us to write HTML/XML-like structures (such as DOM-style tree structures). A preprocessor will subsequently convert these expressions into JavaScript code. JSX tags contain a tag name, attributes, and children much as XML/HTML tags do.

Example

In this section, we'll put JSX syntax in a JSX file and examine the associated JavaScript code that a preprocessor converts (babel).

JSX File

```
<div>Hello Everyone</div>
```

Output

```
React.createElement("div", null, "Hello Everyone");
```

The code above creates a react element with three arguments, the first of which is the element's name, "div," the second of which is the attributes supplied in the div tag, and the third of which is the content we supply, "Hello Everyone."

Why Use JSX?

- Because it conducts optimization when converting the code to JavaScript, it is quicker than standard JavaScript.

- React employs components that combine markup and functionality rather than splitting technologies by placing them in distinct files. Components will be covered in a later section.

- The majority of the mistakes may be identified during compilation since it is type-safe.

- Making templates is made simpler.

JSX Nested Elements

We must enclose it in one container element if we want to utilize more than one element.

In this case, the div element serves as a container for three nested items.

App.JSX

```
import React, { Component } from 'react';
class App extends Component{
    render(){
        return(
            <div>
                <h1>Everyone</h1>
                <h2>Training Center</h2>
                <p> The greatest CS lessons may be found
on this website.</p>
            </div>
        );
    }
}
export default App;
```

Attributes in JSX

Like standard HTML, JSX uses attributes with HTML components.

Because class is a reserved term in JavaScript, JSX employs camelcase naming conventions for attributes rather than the conventional naming convention of HTML. For example, a class in HTML becomes className in JSX.

In JSX, we may also utilize our own unique custom characteristics.

Data- prefix must be used for custom attributes.

In the instance below, the p> tag's custom attribute data-demoAttribute has been utilized as an attribute.

Example

```
import React, { Component } from 'react';
class App extends Component{
    render(){
        return(
            <div>
                <h1>Everyone</h1>
                <h2>Training Institutes</h2>
                <p data-demoAttribute = "demo"> The
greatest CS lessons may be found on this website.</p>
            </div>
        );
    }
}
export default App;
```

There are two methods to define attribute values in JSX:

1. **As String Literals:** Double quotes may be used to express the values of attributes.

```
var element = <h2 className = "firstAttribute">Hello
Everyone</h2>;
```

Example

```
import React, { Component } from 'react';
class App extends Component{
    render(){
        return(
            <div>
                <h1 className = "hello" >Everyone</h1>
                <p data-demoAttribute = "demo"> The
greatest CS lessons may be found on this website.</p>
            </div>
```

```
        );
    }
}
export default App;
```

2. **As Expressions:** Curly braces {} can be used to define attribute values as expressions:

```
var element = <h2 className = {varName}>Hello
Everyone</h2>;
```

Example

```
import React, { Component } from 'react';
class App extends Component{
    render(){
        return(
            <div>
                <h1 className = "hello" >{45+10}</h1>
            </div>
        );
    }
}
export default App;
```

Comments in JSX

Similar to how JSX expressions are used, JSX enables us to utilize comments that start with /* and conclude with */ and enclose them in curly brackets. The JSX sample below demonstrates how to utilize comments.

Example

```
import React, { Component } from 'react';
class App extends Component{
    render(){
        return(
            <div>
                <h1 className = "hello" >Hello
Everyone</h1>
```

```
        {/* This is the comment */}
        </div>
    );
  }
}
```

Styling in JSX

React consistently advises using inline styles. We must use camelCase syntax to set inline styles. On some elements, React automatically permits appending px after the number value. The element's style may be seen in use in the instance below.

Example

```
import React, { Component } from 'react';
class App extends Component{
  render(){
    var myStyle = {
        fontSize: 50,
        fontFamily: <Courier>,
        color: <#004400>
    }
    return (
        <div>
            <h1 style = {myStyle}>www.example.com</h1>
        </div>
    );
  }
}
export default App;
```

Example

```
import React, { Component } from 'react';
class App extends Component{
  render(){
    var x = 6;
    return (
        <div>
```

```
            <h1>{x == 1 ? 'True!' : 'False!'}</h1>
        </div>
    );
    }
}
export default App;
```

EXPRESS.JS

We will about Express.js below with its definition, installation, and syntax.[10]

WHAT IS EXPRESS.JS?

Express is a Node.js web framework that is quick, forceful, necessary, and modest. We might imagine express as a layer added to Node.js that assists in managing a server and routes. It offers a complete collection of tools for creating online and mobile apps.

Here are a few of the key components of the Express framework:

- Single-page, multi-page, and hybrid web apps may all be created with it.

- It enables middleware configuration for HTTP request responses.

- According to the HTTP method and URL, it defines a routing table that is utilized to carry out various operations.

- It enables the dynamic rendering of HTML pages by using template parameters.

Why Employ Express?

- Very fast I/O.

- Single threaded and asynchronous.

- MVC-style organization.

- Routing is simple with a robust API.

How Does Express Appear?

See a simple Express.js application.

basic_express.js
```
var express = require('express');
var app = express();
app.get('/', function (req, res) {
  res.send(‹Welcome to Everyone›);
});
var server = app.listen(8000, function () {
  var host = server.address().address;
  var port = server.address().port;
  console.log(‹Instance app listening at
http://%s:%s›, host, port);
});
```

Prerequisite

We must have a working grasp of JavaScript and Node.js before studying Express.js.

Audience

Both learners and experts may benefit from the information in our Express.js lesson.

Problem

We guarantee that there won't be any issues with this Express.js lesson. However, if there is a mistake, please report it using the contact form.

Benefits of Express.js

- Enables quick and simple creation of Node.js web applications.

- Simple to adjust and personalize.

- Enables us to specify application routes based on HTTP methods and URLs.

- Includes a number of middleware modules that we may use to add extra request and response-related functions.[11]

- Simple integration with several template engines, such as Jade, Vash, and EJS.

- Allows us to provide a middleware for handling errors.

- It's simple to provide static files and application resources.

- Enables the creation of REST API servers.

- Simple connection to databases like MongoDB, Redis, and MySQL.

SETTING UP EXPRESS

Using npm, we can put it in. Inspect our installation of npm and Node.js.[12]

Step 1: The first step is creating a directory for our project and making that directory our working directory.

```
$ mkdir pfp
$ cd pfp
```

Step 2: Making a package using the npm init command. For our project, a json file.

```
$ npm init
```

This command lists all of our project's dependencies. The document will be updated as more Setting up Express

Step 3: Type the below command line in our pfp(name of our folder) folder:

```
$ npm install express --save
```

Let's now use an example to better grasp how express.js works.

Example

In app.js, enter the following code.

```
var express = require('express');
var app = express();
```

```
app.get('/', function (req, res) {
res.send("Welocme to Everyone");
});
app.listen(4000);
```

Run the program by entering the following code in the run window.

```
node app.js
```

The Early Stages

Unbelievably, Node.js is 12 years old. The Internet is 32 years old, but JavaScript is 26 years old. Ryan Dahl created Node.js in 2009. Node.js initially only supported Linux and Mac OS X.[13]

Dahl oversaw its creation and upkeep, while Joyent subsequently provided sponsorship.

Because it had to manage a lot of connections simultaneously, Dahl criticized the Apache HTTP Server, the most popular web server at the time, for having restricted capabilities in 2009 (up to 10,000 and more).

The problem was handled by writing code using sequential programming when there was any halted code throughout the whole process or when there was an implied multiple execution stack in the event of simultaneous connections.

The Node.js project was introduced by Dahl on November 8, 2009, at the first European JSConf.

The V8 JavaScript Chrome engine, a basic I/O API, and an event loop are all components of Node.js.

Its Evolution

JavaScript engines improved a lot as browsers vied to provide consumers with the greatest performance.

Major browsers put a lot of effort into figuring out how to make JavaScript run more quickly and provide better support.

Node.js was thus created at the appropriate time and location.

Numerous methods for JavaScript server-side programming were established, as well as creative thinking that has benefited many developers.

The fact that Node.js supports hundreds of open-source libraries, the bulk of which are available on the npm website, is one of the main reasons for its popularity among developers.

A large number of developer conferences and events, such as Node.js Interactive, Node.js Summit, and NodeConf, as well as additional local events, are held in the Node.js community.

The Node.js open-source community created web frameworks to hasten the creation of apps.

Connect, Sails.js, Koa.js, Express.js, Feathers.js, socket.io, Derby, Hapi.js, Meteor, and several more frameworks are among them.

BASICS OF NODE.JS

JavaScript is supported by Node.js. Thus, JavaScript syntax in Node.js is comparable to JavaScript syntax in browsers.[14]

Types of Primitive

These basic types are available in Node.js:

- String

- Boolean

- Number

- Undefined

- Null

- RegExp

Everything else in the Node.js is an object.

Loose Typing

Like JavaScript in browsers, Node.js JavaScript enables loose typing. To define a variable of any type, use the var keyword.

Object Literal

The object literal syntax is the same as JavaScript in browsers.

```
var obj = {
    authorName: 'Shiya Sham',
    language: 'Node.js'
}
```

Functions

Similar to JavaScript in browsers, Node's JavaScript treats functions as first-class citizens.

Additionally, a function may have characteristics and attributes. In JavaScript, it is comparable to a class.

```
function Display(k) {
    console.log(k);
}

Display(200);
```

Buffer

Buffer is an extra data type in Node.js that is not offered by JavaScript in browsers.

When reading from a file or receiving packets over the network, buffer is mostly utilized to hold binary data.

Process Object

A process is used to execute each Node.js script. To get all the details about the Node.js application's current process, it contains a process object. The example that follows demonstrates how to use a process object to get process information in REPL.

```
> process.execPath
'C:\\Program Files\\nodejs\\node.exe'
> process.pid
1234
> process.cwd()
'C:\\'
```

Defaults to Local

When it comes to global scope, Node's JavaScript differs from JavaScript in browsers.

Variables defined without the var keyword become global in the browser's JavaScript. Everything becomes local by default with Node.js.

Utilize Global Scope

Global scope in a browser refers to the window object. Global object in Node.js is a representation of the global scope. We must export anything using export or module.export in order to add it to the global scope. To access modules or objects from the global scope, use the need() method to import them.

Use exports.name=object, for instance, to export an object in Node.js.

```
exports.log = {
    console: function(msg) {
        console.log(msg);
    },
    file: function(msg) {
        // here log to file
    }
}
```

We can now use the log object anywhere in our Node.js project by importing it using the require() method.

VUEJS

We will about VueJS below with its definition, installation, and syntax.

WHAT IS VUEJS?

An open-source, progressive JavaScript framework called VueJS is used to create dynamic web interfaces. One of the well-known frameworks for streamlining web development is this one. The view layer is where VueJS focuses.[15]

It may be seamlessly incorporated into large frontend development projects. VueJS installation is pretty simple to begin with. Interactive web interfaces are simple to comprehend and quick to construct for any developer.

Former Google employee Evan You is the creator of VueJS. VueJS's first version was published in February 2014. It is now rated 64,828 stars on GitHub, making it highly well-liked.

Features

The characteristics of VueJS are listed below.

- **DOM virtual**
    Virtual DOM is a technique utilized by VueJS and other frameworks such as React and Ember.

Instead of altering the DOM itself, a duplicate of it is built and placed in the form of JavaScript data structures. Every time a change has to be performed, the JavaScript data structure is modified and then compared to the original data structure. The actual DOM, which the user will see altering, is then updated with the final adjustments. This is advantageous for optimization since it costs less and allows for quick modifications.

- **Binding of data**
  With the aid of a binding directive called v-bind that is included with VueJS, the data binding functionality assists in manipulating or assigning values to HTML attributes, changing the style, and assigning classes.

- **Components**
  One of VueJS's key features, components enable the creation of unique elements that may be reused throughout HTML.

- **Event handling**
  In VueJS, the DOM elements include a property called v-on that makes it possible to listen to events.

- **Animation/Transition**
  When HTML elements are added, changed, or deleted from the DOM, VueJS offers a variety of techniques to apply transition. For the transition effect, an element must be wrapped in the built-in transition component of VueJS. The interface may be made more interactive and third-party animation libraries are simple to add.

- **Computerized Property**
  One of VueJS's key characteristics is this. It's critical to pay attention to UI element changes and perform the necessary computations. Additional code is not required for this.

- **Templates**
  The DOM is bound to the Vue instance data through HTML-based templates that are provided by VueJS. The templates are converted by Vue into simulated DOM Render functions. We may utilize the

render function template, but we must swap out the template with the render function in order to do so.

- **Directives**

    The built-in directives in VueJS may be used to carry out a variety of frontend tasks, including v-if, v-else, v-show, v-on, v-bind, and v-model.

- **Watchers**

    Data that changes is given watchers. For instance, form input components.

    We don't need to add any further events in this case. The code is made easy and quick by the watcher, which takes care of processing any data changes.

- **Routing**

    With the aid of vue-router, pages may be navigated between.

- **Lightweight**

    The performance and weight of the VueJS script are both quite quick.

- **Vue-CLI**

    Using the vue-cli command line interface, VueJS may be installed via the command line. Using vue-cli makes it simple to build and compile the project.

Comparative Assessment of Other Frameworks

Let's now evaluate VueJS in comparison to other frameworks like React, Angular, Ember, Knockout, and Polymer.

VueJS vs React

DOM Virtual   The DOM tree is represented virtually by virtual DOM. A JavaScript object that is identical to the actual DOM is constructed using virtual DOM. Every time a modification to the DOM is required, a new JavaScript object is formed and the modifications are made. Later, the final modifications are updated in the actual DOM after a comparison of the two JavaScript objects. Both VueJS and React employ virtual DOM, which speeds things up.

JSX vs. a Template   Separate html, js, and css are used by vuejs. The VueJS style is relatively simple for a novice to comprehend and adapt. The VueJS template-based method is fairly simple. React uses the jsx method. For ReactJS, everything is JavaScript. JavaScript includes both HTML and CSS.

Tools for Installation   VueJS utilizes vue-cli, the CDN, and npm, whereas React uses build react app.

Both are quite simple to use, and the project has been set up to meet all the prerequisites. VueJS does not need webpack for the build, but React requires. Using the CDN library, we may begin writing VueJS code anywhere in jsfiddle or codepen.

Popularity

More people use React than VueJS. React offers more employment opportunities than VueJS.

React is more well-known since it is backed by a well-known company, namely Facebook.

React employs the finest JavaScript practices since it exploits the language's fundamental idea. Anyone who uses React will undoubtedly be quite knowledgeable about all the JavaScript fundamentals.

The framework VueJS is under development. Currently, compared to React, VueJS has less career possibilities. A poll indicates that many individuals are adjusting to VueJS, which might increase its popularity relative to React and Angular. A strong community is developing VueJS's many features. This community updates the vue-router on a regular basis. VueJS is a strong library that was created by combining the best elements of Angular and React. Due to its lightweight library, VueJS is considerably quicker than React/Angular.

VueJS vs Angular

Similarities

Angular and VueJS are quite similar to one another. V-if and V-for directives are nearly identical to Angular's ngIf and ngFor. Both of them offer a command line interface that is used to install and build the project.

Both Angular and VueJS require angular-cli. Both provide server side rendering, two-way data coupling, etc.

Complexity

Vuejs is really simple to use and learn. As was previously said, a newbie may use the VueJS CDN package to get started with codepen and jsfiddle. For Angular, we must follow a set of procedures for installation, and getting started with Angular might be a bit challenging for novices. It employs TypeScript for coding, which is challenging for anyone with a background in JavaScript's fundamentals. However, users with a background in Java and C# find it simpler to learn.

Performance

The users will determine the performance. Compared to Angular, VueJS is substantially less in file size. The following URL: http://stefankrause.net/js-frameworks-benchmark4/webdriver-ts/table.html compares the performance of the frameworks.

Popularity

Currently, Angular is more widely used than VueJS. Angular is widely used by many businesses, making it quite well-known. For those with Angular expertise, job prospects are also more plentiful. VueJS, on the other hand, is gaining ground and may be seen as an excellent rival to Angular and React.

Dependencies

Many functionalities are included by default with Angular.

To begin, we must import the necessary modules, such as @angular/animations and @angular/form.

VueJS relies on third-party libraries to function since it lacks several of Angular's built-in functionality.

Flexibility

Any other large project may be seamlessly combined with VueJS without any problems.

It won't be simple to start using Angular with any other project that already exists.

Reverse Compatibility

AngularJS, Angular2, and Angular4 have all been around. The two Angular frameworks, JS and v2, vary greatly.

Due to fundamental incompatibilities, project applications created in AngularJS cannot be transferred to Angular2. VueJS 2.0 is the most current version, and it has strong backward compatibility. It has excellent documentation that is extremely simple to read.

Typescript

For its coding, Angular uses TypeScript. To use Angular, users need to be familiar with TypeScript. But with the CDN library, we may begin writing VueJS code anywhere in jsfiddle or codepen. Standard JavaScript is available for use and is a great place to start.

ENVIRONMENT SETUP FOR VUEJS

VueJS may be installed in a number of ways. A few methods for doing the installation are covered in the sections that follow.[16]

Directly Use the <script> Tag in an HTML File

```
<html>
   <head>
      <script type = "text/javascript" src = "vue.min.
js"></script>
   </head>
   <body>
</body>
</html>
```

Visit the VueJS home page at https://vuejs.org/v2/guide/installation.html and download the necessary version of vue.js. Production version and development version are the two versions available for use. As demonstrated in the accompanying screenshot, the production version is minimized but the development version is not. Debug mode and warnings will be supported by the development version while the project is being developed.

By Using the CDN

In our application, we may also utilize the Vue.js file from the CDN library. We may acquire the most recent version of Vue.js by using this URL in our application: https://unpkg.com/vue inside <script> element.

Example 1

```html
<!DOCTYPE html>
<html>
<head>
  <title>Out first Vue app</title>
  <script src="https://unpkg.com/vue"></script>
</head>
<body>
  <div id="app">
    {{ message }}
  </div>
  <script>
    var app = new Vue({
      el: '#app',
      data: {
        message: 'Vue.js instance with the CDN'
      }
    })
  </script>
</body>
</html>
```

In addition, we may get Vue.js via jsDelivr (https://cdn.jsdelivr.net/npm/vue/dist/vue.js) and cdnjs (https://cdnjs.cloudflare.com/ajax/libs/vue/2.4.0/vue.js).

Example 2

```html
<!DOCTYPE html>
<html>
<head>
  <title>Our first Vue app</title>
<script src="https://cdn.jsdelivr.net/npm/vue/dist/
vue.js"> </script>
</head>
<body>
  <div id="app">
    {{ message }}
  </div>
  <script>
    var app = new Vue({
```

```
      el: '#app',
      data: {
        message: 'Vue.js second instance with the CDN'
      }
    })
  </script>
</body>
</html>
```

By Using the NPM

If we want to create a big-scale application with VueJS, NPM is advised. If we want to install Vue.js via the npm package, use the following line. It includes Webpack and Browserify in addition to other essential technologies that facilitate development.

```
npm install vue
```

By Using the CLI Command Line

Additionally, we may use the CLI to install Vue.js and launch the server activation process. Using the CLI, run the following command to install Vue.js:

```
npm install --global vue-cli
```

The installation of Vue.js cli will take a little while. When finished, it will display the Vue.js CLI version.

```
+ vue-cli@2.9.6
added 238 packages from the 205 contributors in 346.282s
```

Creating a Project with Webpack

The command below may be used to start a Webpack project. Here, we'll make a project called "myproject."

```
vue init webpack myproject
```

We will be prompted to input Y/n at several points during this process. Type Y to continue.

All requirements and the template will be downloaded automatically. We'll notice a message following the successful creation of our project.

Start the Project, Then the Server

The project has now been started. Enter the project directory using the command below:

```
cd myproject
```

The Server may be started by using the command:

```
npm run dev
```

We can see that the Server is launched after executing the npm run dev command. Open Google Chrome or any suitable browser and execute localhost http://localhost:8080/#/ to launch our project.

UNDERSTANDING VUE.JS

There are several ways to use and install Vue.js in our project, as we saw previous.

This session will cover how to verify the Vue.js version, the benefits and drawbacks of utilizing Vue.js in our project, the first example, and an explanation of all the underlying concepts.[17]

Advantages of Using Vue.js

Vue.js is among the most cutting-edge software frameworks for creating websites and single-page applications. The name suggests that the user interface (UI) or 'view side' of a project is where it is most often applied. Evan You (a former Google employee who was working on Angular at the time) created this framework so that rich client-side applications may be built with JavaScript. Let's examine the advantages of integrating Vue.js into our project:

The benefits of utilizing Vue.js include the following:

Extremely Small in Size
Small footprint is one of Vue.js's main selling points.

This interesting JavaScript plugin is only 18–21 KB, so it can be downloaded and used in no time at all.

Simple to Comprehend and Code
The Vue.js framework has a very straightforward structure that is easy to grasp.

It is one of the reasons for the framework's popularity.

We can simply develop in Vue.js if we are comfortable with HTML and JavaScript.

Because of its basic structure, users may quickly include Vue.js in their web projects and construct apps.

Integration with Existing Applications Is Simple
Vue.js offers many components for everything and can be rapidly integrated with existing apps. It may be integrated with any JavaScript-based application.

Nature Is Adaptable
The flexibility of Vue.js also makes it simple to grasp for developers of React.js, Angular.js, and any other modern JavaScript framework.

We have a significant amount of flexibility to use virtual nodes to create HTML files, JavaScript files, and pure JavaScript files.

Components
In Vue.js apps, we may construct reusable custom components.

Documentation That Is Simple, Thorough, and Detailed
Vue.js provides highly simple, extensive, and clear documentation, allowing developers with little knowledge of HTML and JavaScript to code with it.

DOM Virtualization
Vue.js employs virtual DOM, as do other existing frameworks such as ReactJS, Ember, and others. Virtual DOM is an in-memory tree version of the actual HTML DOM that may be modified without impacting the original DOM.

Two-Way Communication
Vue.js's MVVM design allows for two-way communication, making HTML blocks relatively straightforward to manage.

Companies That Use Vue.js

Vue.js is gaining popularity as more and more well-known firms begin to employ it in real time. Several businesses are effectively utilizing Vue.js in the real world.

Here are several examples:

- **Facebook:** Facebook is the most successful corporation that uses Vue.js in their real-world projects. This framework is being used by Facebook for the marketing side of their Newsfeed.

- **Adobe:** Adobe's Portfolio product makes use of Vue.js. The organization has already moved its current software to the Vue.js framework, taking advantage of its ease of integration.

- **Xiaomi:** Xiaomi is also employing Vue.js to construct its product catalog in order to give consumers a dynamic experience.

- **Alibaba:** Vue.js has been adopted by Alibaba, one of China's most important public corporations.

Other famous firms that use Vue.js in their projects include:

- Grammarly

- Laracast

- Behance

- Netflix

- Codeship

- Livestorm

- Gitlab

- Euronews

- Wizzair, etc.

Examine the Vue.js Version We Have Installed

If we're already familiar with Node.js and have the Vue.js CLI installed on our machine, we can use the Node.js command prompt to verify the version of our installed Vue.js:

- Run the following command in the Node.js command prompt:

```
vue --version
```

- If it replies favorably, go to the next step in creating our new project. Vue.js version 2.9.6 is successfully installed in the preceding instance. To create a new project, use the following command:

Syntax:

```
vue create <ourAppName>
```

- To build an app called, use the vue create firstapp command.
- We encountered an error stating that the vue create command is only compatible with Vue CLI 3, and we are using an earlier version. Now, use the command below to uninstall the previous version and install the new one.

```
npm uninstall -g vue-cli
npm install -g @vue/cli
```

- The outdated version of Vue.js is clearly removed. Install the newest version now.
- The latest version of Vue CLI is now installed. The vue—version command may be used to determine the Vue CLI version.
- We can see that the most recent Vue CLI version has been installed. Run the vue create firstapp command to make a new app named.

INSTANCES IN VUEJS

We must use the Vue method to create a new Vue instance in order to launch a Vue application. The main.js file's default activation of the Vue instance occurs whenever we start a new Vue project. Another name for it is a root Vue instance.[18]

Syntax:

```
var vm = new Vue({
    // option
  })
```

The MVVM pattern informed the design of Vue's application. To refer to our Vue instance, we must use the variable vm (short for ViewModel). When creating a Vue instance, we must include an options object.

Let's look at an illustration to see what the Vue constructor must provide.

Indexs.html file:

```
<html>
    <head>
        <link rel="stylesheet" href="indexs.css">
        <script src="https://cdn.jsdelivr.net/npm/vue/
dist/vue.js"></script>
    </head>
    <body>
<div id = "app">
        <h1>Firstname is: {{firstname}}</h1>
        <h1>Lastname is: {{lastname}}</h1>
        <h1>{{mydetails()}}</h1>
    </div>
        <script src="indexs.js"></script>
    </body>
</html>
```

Indexs.js file:

```
var  vm = new Vue({
    el: '#app',
    data: {
        firstname : "Alisha",
        lastname : "Singla",
        address : "delhi"
    },
    methods: {
        mydetails : function() {
            return "I am "+this.firstname +" "+ this.
lastname +" from "+ this.address;
        }
    }
})
```

Let's utilize a simple CSS file to enhance the output's visual quality.

Indexs.css file:

```
html, body {
    margin: 6px;
    padding: 0;
}
```

Example Explanation
We can notice that we utilized a parameter named el in the example above. The id of the DOM element is carried by this 'el' argument. We have the id #app in the aforementioned example. The div element's id is what is displayed in the Indexs.html file.

```
<div id = "app"></div>
```

Now, the logic of the aforementioned program will only have an impact on the div element and nothing else.

We have defined the data object after specifying the id. We have specified certain values, including firstname and lastname, in the data object. The <div> element contains a definition for this as well. For instance,

```
<div id = "app">
   <h1>Firstname : {{firstname}}</h1>
   <h1>Lastname : {{lastname}}</h1>
</div>
```

The Firstname: {{firstname}}value defines the first name of the data object's stored data.

When we run the program, the value assigned in the data object, Alisha, will be substituted inside the interpolation, i.e. '{{}}'.

The same is true for the final name as the Lastname: {{lastname}} value provides the last name of the data object's stored data.

When you run the program, the value assigned in the data object, i.e., '{{}}' Singla, will be substituted inside the interpolation.

Following the definition of the data object, we have methods with a function named "mydetails" and a return value.

It is also specified within the <div> element as

```
<h1>{{mydetails()}}</h1>
```

As a result, we can see that within {{}} a call to the function mydetails is made. As we can see, the value returned in the Vue instance is printed within {{}}.

TEMPLATE IN VUE.JS

In this, we will learn how to get an output on the screen in the form of an HTML template.

Vue.js employs an HTML-based template syntax that allows Vue.js developers to declaratively connect the displayed DOM to the data of the underlying Vue instance.

All Vue.js templates are valid HTML that can be processed by browsers and HTML parsers that support the standard.[19]

If we use the simple interpolation approach, i.e., double curly brackets, to display the HTML text on the web browser, the output will be incorrect.

To fully grasp this notion, consider a simple example and examine the result.

Indexs.html file:

```
<html>
   <head>
```

```
    <title>Vue.js Template</title>
    <link rel="stylesheet" href="indexs.css">
        <script src="https://cdn.jsdelivr.net/npm/
vue/dist/vue.js"></script>
    </head>
    <body>
      <div id = "app">
          <h1>Firstname is: {{firstname}}</h1>
          <h1>Lastname is: {{lastname}}</h1>
          <div>{{htmlcontent}}</div>
      </div>
      <script src="indexs.js"></script>
    </body>
</html>
```

Indexs.js file:

```
var vm = new Vue({
    el: '#app',
    data: {
        firstname : "Alisha",
        lastname : "Singla",
        htmlcontent : "<div><h1>This is the Vue.js
Template Instance</h1></div>"
    }
```

Let's utilize a simple CSS file to enhance the output's attractive appearance.

Indexs.css file:

```
html, body {
    margin: 6px;
    padding: 0;
}
```

In the above instance, we can see that the html content is not shown on the browser as we would like. The html content is shown in the manner we specify in the htmlcontent variable.

This is not what we are looking for. We want it to appear in the browser as standard HTML text.

To address this problem, we will need to employ the v-html directive.

When we apply the v-html directive to the html element, Vue.js understands that it must output HTML content.

Now, insert the v-html directive into the.html file and compare the results in the following instance.

Syntax:

```
<div v-html = "htmlcontent"></div>
```

Example 2

Indexs.html file:

```
<html>
    <head>
        <title>Vue.js Template</title>
        <link rel="stylesheet" href="indexs.css">
            <script src="https://cdn.jsdelivr.net/npm/
vue/dist/vue.js"></script>
    </head>
    <body>
        <div id = "app">
            <h1>Firstname : {{firstname}}</h1>
            <h1>Lastname : {{lastname}}</h1>
            <div v-html = "htmlcontent"></div>
        </div>
        <script src="indexs.js"></script>
    </body>
</html>
```

Indexs.js file:

```
var vm = new Vue({
    el: '#app',
    data: {
        firstname : "Alisha",
        lastname : "Singla",
        htmlcontent : "<div><h1>This is the Vue.js
Template instance</h1></div>"
    }
})
```

In the above instance, we can see that the v-html directive correctly adds an HTML template to the DOM. Let's look at how to add properties to the existing HTML components now.

Attributes Should Be Added to HTML Elements

Assume we have an image element in the HTML file and want to assign src, which is a Vue.js component. Consider the following:

Indexs.html file:

```
<html>
    <head>
        <title>Vue.js Template</title>
        <link rel="stylesheet" href="indexs.css">
            <script src="https://cdn.jsdelivr.net/npm/
vue/dist/vue.js"></script>
    </head>
    <body>
        <div id = "app">
            <h1>Firstname : {{firstname}}</h1>
            <h1>Lastname : {{lastname}}</h1>
            <div v-html = "htmlcontent"></div>
            <img src = "" width = "310" height = "280" />
        </div>
        <script src="indexs.js"></script>
    </body>
</html>
```

Indexs.js file:

```
var vm = new Vue({
    el: '#app',
    data: {
        firstname : "Alisha",
        lastname : "singla",
        htmlcontent : "<div><h1>This is the Vue.js
Template instance</h1></div>",
        imgsrc : "https://www.fiordalisa.ch/
wp-content/uploads/2017/12/IMG_40.jpg"
    }
})
```

Example 3

Indexs.html:

```html
<html>
    <head>
        <title>Vue.js Template</title>
        <link rel="stylesheet" href="indexs.css">
        <script src="https://cdn.jsdelivr.net/npm/
vue/dist/vue.js"></script>
    </head>
    <body>
        <div id = "app">
            <h1>Firstname : {{firstname}}</h1>
            <h1>Lastname : {{lastname}}</h1>
            <div v-html = "htmlcontent"></div>
            <img v-bind:src = "imgsrc" width = "310"
height = "280" />
        </div>
        <script src="indexs.js"></script>
    </body>
</html>
```

Indexs.js:

```js
var vm = new Vue({
    el: '#app',
    data: {
        firstname : "Alisha",
        lastname : "singla",
        htmlcontent : "<div><h1>This is the Vue.js
Template instance</h1></div>",
        imgsrc : "https://www.fiordalisa.ch/
wp-content/uploads/2017/12/IMG_40.jpg"
    }
})
```

In this chapter, we covered installation, advantages, disadvantages, basic syntax of React, Express, and Vue.js.

NOTES

1 Frontend vs Backend: www.geeksforgeeks.org/frontend-vs-backend/#:~: text=The%20visual%20aspects%20of%20the,%2C%20Ruby%2C%20 Python%2C%20and%20. Accessed on: 11 October 2022.

2 The Best Guide to Know What Is React: www.simplilearn.com/tutorials/ reactjs-tutorial/what-is-reactjs Accessed on: 10 October 2022.

3 React Features: www.javatpoint.com/react-features Accessed on: 10 October 2022.

4 Pros and Cons of ReactJS: www.javatpoint.com/pros-and-cons-of-react Accessed on: 10 October 2022.

5 React Version: www.javatpoint.com/react-version Accessed on: 10 October 2022.

6 React Environment Setup: www.javatpoint.com/react-installation Accessed on: 10 October 2022.

7 Difference between AngularJS and ReactJS: www.javatpoint.com/reactjs-vs-angularjs Accessed on: 11 October 2022.

8 Svelte vs React: Which JavaScript Framework Is Better?: www.turing.com/ blog/svelte-vs-react-which-javascript-framework-should-you-choose-in-2022/#:~:text=Svelte%20is%20a%20free%20and,components%20to%20 design%20UI%20elements. Accessed on: 11 October 2022.

9 React JSX: www.javatpoint.com/react-jsx Accessed on: 12 October 2022.

10 Express.js Tutorial: www.javatpoint.com/expressjs-tutorial Accessed on: 12 October 2022.

11 Express.js: www.tutorialsteacher.com/nodejs/expressjs Accessed on: 12 October 2022.

12 Express.js: www.geeksforgeeks.org/express-js/ Accessed on: 12 October 2022.

13 The History of Node.js: www.section.io/engineering-education/history-of-nodejs/ Accessed on: 12 October 2022.

14 Node.js Basics: www.tutorialsteacher.com/nodejs/nodejs-basics Accessed on: 12 October 2022.

15 VueJS – Overview: www.tutorialspoint.com/vuejs/vuejs_overview.htm Accessed on: 12 October 2022.

16 Vue.js Installation: www.javatpoint.com/vue-js-installation Accessed on: 13 October 2022.

17 Getting Started with Vue.js: www.javatpoint.com/getting-started-with-vue-js Accessed on: 13 October 2022.

18 Vue.js Instance: www.javatpoint.com/vue-js-instance Accessed on: 13 October 2022.

19 Vue.js Template: www.javatpoint.com/vue-js-template Accessed on: 13 October 2022.

CHAPTER 6

Backend Development

➤ Node.js

➤ MongoDB

➤ Server-side JS

In the previous chapter, we covered frontend development, and in this chapter, we will discuss backend development.

WHAT IS BACKEND DEVELOPMENT?

Server-side development is referred to as backend development. It focuses on databases, programming, and website design. It describes the operations that take place behind the scenes when a user performs any activity on a website.[1]

It might be logging into an account or completing an online transaction.

Backend developers write code that allows browsers to interface with database information.

NODE.JS

We will discuss introduction to node.js and its installation process below:

What Is Node.js, and How Does It Work?

Node.js is a fascinating combination of front- and backend technologies in the context of application stacks. Node.js is based on JavaScript, which

DOI: 10.1201/9781003356578-6

is often used for the frontend, client-side of a web application; however, Node.js extends the capabilities of JavaScript so that it may run on the backend, server-side component of web application architecture or in a serverless architecture.[2]

The server-side processing is handled by Node.js's native runtime environment.

Node.js is similar to Java in that both languages have their own runtime environment in which to execute programs.

Node.js is a runtime environment that is meant to be fast and lightweight, with features like non-blocking I/O and a package management that simplifies the process of creating applications.

The Node.js package manager is known as npm. Its objective is to act as an index of libraries created by the Node.js developer community that can be readily shared and imported by other projects. These packages give useful answers to common functions and code, making it easier to construct new applications and improve existing ones.

Why Should We Use Node.js?

Node.js is a suitable option for a wide range of use scenarios.

Node.js, as a predominantly server-side framework, lends itself to applications on the backend of the technological stack. Here are a few examples of why Node.js makes sense to utilize.

Fast, Lightweight Applications with Real-Time Communication

Understanding the size of your product is critical to selecting the appropriate technology to develop it with. Node.js's flexibility and efficiency make it ideal for developing small, quick, and scalable apps. One example is real-time apps such as instant messaging and collaboration tools. This, along with Node.js's quick synchronization capabilities, makes it suitable for event-based applications. WebSockets and WebRTC apps are examples of this.

Serverless and Microservice Design

Node.js is ideal for developing serverless and microservice-based applications due to its flexibility. These design choices are both highly popular for conserving resources and managing application lifecycles efficiently. Serverless architecture is popular due to its potential to reduce computing expenses by using only the resources required for the application to execute with no additional overhead. These are stateless and lightweight programs.

As a result, Node.js integration with serverless architecture is an excellent match.

When the server demand is variable, there are npm packages for serverless design, and constructing a serverless Node.js application works well with an overall microservice architecture in C2C and B2C use cases.

The Internet of Things

Node.js excels at handling several connections at once. Because IoT is based on multiple devices generating little signals that must be handled rapidly, Node.js is an excellent backend for these types of applications, including serverless architecture and real-time communication capability.

Processing of Audio/Video

Node.js is considerably better at handling asynchronous input and output than other technologies. As a result, when paired with other media tools, Node.js may be used to process and handle multimedia data.

A streaming configuration, for example, may be readily configured using Node.js.

Quick Development

Because Node.js is built on standard web languages, it is incredibly easy to use and has very short ramp-up times. New items may be developed swiftly and promptly brought to market.

As a result, the quantity of engineering resources necessary to do so is lowered.

This case study demonstrates how Node.js may assist in meeting tight deadlines.

The product, an online marketplace for hail damage repair companies and customers, was supposed to go live before the peak season.

When deciding between PHP and Node.js, we chose Node.js to match both functional needs and timeframes. We were able to cut development time by using isomorphic architecture.

Code Integration with C++

Node.js may work in tandem with existing C++ libraries. This is due to the fact that the Node.js runtime is based on a C++ server that runs on the host node. As a result, Node.js can rapidly transport data between C++ and application code.

The Downsides of Node.js

Heavy Calculation Activities Cause Performance Constraints

Even today, the most significant limitation of Node.js is its inability to handle CPU-bound activities.[3]

But, in order to comprehend the underlying causes of this problem, we need some context.

Let's start with the fundamentals: JavaScript. Node.js, as we know, is a server-side runtime environment that runs JavaScript. JavaScript, as a frontend programming language, processes work on a single thread. Threading is not necessary since JavaScript tasks are lightweight and consume minimal CPU.

Returning to Node.js, we now understand why it is deemed single threaded:

It executes JavaScript in a single thread.

A non-blocking input/output architecture means that Node.js responds to the client call to start a request and processes the job as soon as the callback is fired, as the task is ready.

Node executes JS code on an event basis on its single thread while processing jobs asynchronously. That is referred to as an event loop.

The issue arises when Node.js gets a CPU constrained task: if a big request arrives in the event loop, Node.js will set all available CPU to handle it first, before answering other requests queued. Because of the sluggish processing and overall latency in the event loop, Node.js is not recommended for intensive computing.

However, with the 10.5.0 upgrade in 2018, multithreading was added as an experimental capability in Node.js.

A new feature called the worker threads module allows you to employ extra threads from a thread pool to carry out CPU-bound activities.

However, this is only possible on machines with several cores, because Node.js still enables us to use one core for one thread.

This means that hefty parallel tasks can be run on a separate thread.

This functionality is still experimental in Node.js version 12; however, it has been greatly improved.

Callback Hell Is a Problem

Because of its asynchronous nature, Node.js mainly relies on callbacks, which are routines that execute when each job in the queue is completed.

Keeping a multitude of queued jobs in the background, each with its own callback, may result in callback hell, which has a direct influence on code quality.

Simply described, it's a "situation in which callbacks are nested within other callbacks several levels deep, possibly making understanding and maintaining the code challenging."

However, this is sometimes interpreted as an indication of poor coding standards and a lack of knowledge with JavaScript and, in particular, Node.js.

Tooling Immaturity

Although the core Node.js modules are relatively stable and mature, many tools in the npm registry are either of poor quality or are not fully documented/tested.

Furthermore, the register isn't well-structured enough to provide tools depending on their ranking or quality.

As a result, without understanding what to look for, it may be difficult to identify the ideal option for our needs.

The fact that the Node.js ecosystem is primarily open source also has an effect.

There Is a Growing Need for Skilled Experts

Contrary to popular perception, not all JavaScript developers are also Node.js engineers.

Mastering server-side JavaScript coding takes considerable work and an experience in backend development. The number of Node.js engineers is much smaller than the overall number of JS professionals due to the steep learning curve.

As the buzz around Node.js grows, so does the need for skilled individuals in this industry.

As a result, with millions of JavaScript engineers available, it may be difficult to locate a knowledgeable Node.js expert for our project.

We definitely don't want to limit our search to just one nation in this scenario.

In the IT business, sourcing technical expertise from other countries has long been the standard.

Where Can We Use Node.js?

Following are some examples of when Node.js has shown to be a valuable technological asset.[4]

- Applications that are I/O bound

- Applications for Data Streaming

- Data Intensive Real-time Applications

- Applications based on JSON APIs

- Applications on a Single Page

Where Should We Not Use Node.js?

Node.js should not be used for CPU-intensive applications.

SETUP OF THE NODE.JS ENVIRONMENT

If we still want to set up our Node.js environment, we will need the two following software on our computer: (a) a text editor and (b) the Node.js binary installable.[5]

Text Editor

This is where we will type our program.

Some editors are Windows Notepad, the OS Edit command, Brief, Epsilon, EMACS, and vim or vi.

On various operating systems, the name and version of the text editor may change.

Notepad, for example, will be used on Windows, while vim or vi may be used on both Windows and Linux or UNIX.

Source files are files that we produce with your editor that contain program source code.

The source files for Node.js apps are usually suffixed with ".js."

Before we begin programming, make sure we have a text editor and enough expertise to develop a computer program, store it in a file, and then run it.

Node.js Runtime

The source code in the source file is only JavaScript. Our JavaScript code will be interpreted and executed using the Node.js interpreter.

The Node.js distribution is available as a binary installable for SunOS, Linux, Mac OS X, and Windows operating systems that support the 32-bit (386) and 64-bit (amd64) x86 CPU architectures.

The section that follows will show us how to install the Node.js binary distribution on different operating systems.

Get the Node.js Archive

Visit https://nodejs.org/download to obtain the most recent installable archive file for Node.js. The versions that are available on various OS as of the time this guide was written are listed below.

OS	Archive Name
Windows	node-v6.3.1-x64.msi
Mac	node-v6.3.1-darwin-x86.tar.gz
Linux	node-v6.3.1-linux-x86.tar.gz
SunOS	node-v6.3.1-sunos-x86.tar.gz

Installation on SunOS, Mac OS X, Linux, and UNIX

Install and extract the node-v6.3.1-osname.tar.gz archive into /tmp according to the OS architecture for our computer, and then move the extracted contents into the /usr/local/nodejs directory. For instance:

```
$ cd /tmp
$ wget http://nodejs.org/dist/v6.3.1/node-v6.3.1-
linux-x64.tar.gz
$ tar xvfz node-v6.3.1-linux-x64.tar.gz
$ mkdir -p /usr/local/nodejs
$ mv node-v6.3.1-linux-x64/* /usr/local/nodejs
```

Add the PATH environment variable to the path /usr/local/nodejs/bin.

OS	Output
Mac	export PATH=$PATH:/usr/local/nodejs/bin
Linux	export PATH=$PATH:/usr/local/nodejs/bin
FreeBSD	export PATH=$PATH:/usr/local/nodejs/bin

Setup on a Windows Computer

To install Node.js, use the MSI file and follow the on-screen instructions. The installer by default makes use of the Node.js package located at C:\

Program Files\nodejs. The C:\Program Files\nodejs\bin directory should be added to Windows' PATH environment setting by the installation. Any open command windows must be restarted for the modification to take effect.

Executing a File Will Verify Installation

Create a main.js file with the following code on our computer (Windows or Linux).

```
/* Hello, Everyone! program in node.js */
console.log("Hello, Everyone!")
```

To view the outcome, run the main.js file using the Node.js interpreter now.

```
$ node main.js
```

FIRST APPLICATION OF NODE.JS

Let's first look at the components of a Node.js application before building a real "Hello, Everyone!" application. The following three crucial parts make up a Node.js application:

- Import required modules: Use the need directive to load the necessary Node.js modules.

- Create server: Create a server that responds to client requests in a manner similar to the Apache HTTP Server.[6]

- Read request and return response: The server constructed in a previous stage will read the HTTP request sent by the client, which can be a browser or a console, and deliver the response.

Creation of Node.js Application

Step 1: Import the necessary module.

The following is how we load the http module using the need directive and save the resulting HTTP instance into an http variable:

```
var http = require("http");
```

Step 2: Create a server

Using the newly formed http instance, we execute the http.create-Server() function to create a server instance, and then we bind it to port 8081 by using the server instance's listen method. Send it a function with request and response arguments. Make the example implementation return "Hello Everyone!" every time.

```
http.createServer(function (request, response) {
    // Send HTTP header
    // HTTP Status: 200 : OK
    // Content Type: text/plain
    response.writeHead(200, {'Content-Type': 'text/
plain'});

    // Send response body as "Hello Everyone!"
    response.end('Hello Everyone!\n');
}).listen(8081);

 // Console will print message
 console.log('Server running at
http://127.0.0.1:8081/');
```

The aforementioned code is sufficient to build an HTTP server that listens on the local machine's port 8081, or waits for a request.

Step 3: Testing Request & Response.

Let's combine steps 1 and 2 in a file named main.js and launch our HTTP server as seen below.

```
var http = require("http");

http.createServer(function (request, response) {
    // Send HTTP header
    // HTTP Status: 200 : OK
    // Content Type: text/plain
    response.writeHead(200, {'Content-Type': 'text/
plain'});

    // Send response body as "Hello Everyone!"
    response.end('Hello Everyone!\n');
}).listen(8081);
```

```
// Console will print message
console.log('Server running at
http://127.0.0.1:8081/');
```

Execute "main.js" now to launch the server in the manner shown below.

```
$ node main.js
```

MongoDB

We will discuss introduction to MongoDB and its installation process below:

What Is MongoDB

MongoDB is a free document-oriented database that can hold a big amount of data while also allowing us to deal with it extremely efficiently.

It is classified as a NoSQL (Not simply SQL) database since data in MongoDB is not stored and retrieved in the form of tables.

MongoDB is a database that was created and operated by MongoDB. Inc under the SSPL (Server-Side Public License) and was first published in February 2009.

It also offers official driver support for all prominent programming languages such as C, C++, C#, etc.[7]

Programming languages such as Net, Go, Java, Node.js, Perl, PHP, Python, Motor, Ruby, Scala, Swift, and Mongoid are just a few examples.

As a result, we may write an application in any of these languages.

Nowadays, numerous firms, like Facebook, Nokia, eBay, Adobe, and Google, utilize MongoDB to store massive amounts of data.

How Does It Work?

Now we'll look at what goes on behind the scenes.

As we all know, MongoDB is a database server that stores data in databases.

In other words, the MongoDB environment provides you with a server on which we may launch MongoDB and build several databases.

The data is kept as collections and documents due to the NoSQL database.

As a result, the database, collection, and documents are linked as follows:

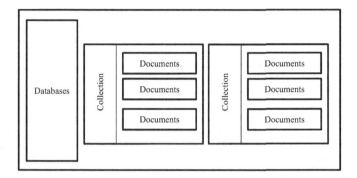

Working of MongoDB

- Collections exist in the MongoDB database in the same way that tables exist in the MYSQL database. We are permitted to build several databases and collections.

- We now have papers within the collection. Because we are schemaless, documents do not have to be comparable to one another, and the data we want to store in the MongoDB database is included inside documents.

- The fields are used to build the documents. Fields in documents are key-value pairs, similar to columns in a relational database. The fields' values can be of any BSON data type, such as double, string, and Boolean.

- The data in MongoDB is saved in the form of BSON documents. BSON is an abbreviation for binary representation of JSON documents. In other words, the MongoDB server turns JSON data in the backend into a binary version known as BSON, which is then stored and searched more effectively.

- It is possible to store nested data in MongoDB documents. Because of data layering, complex data associations may be built and stored in a single document, making data management and retrieval considerably faster than using SQL. To get data from tables 1 and 2, we must use complicated SQL joins. The BSON document can be up to 16MB in size.

MongoDB Data Modeling

As we saw in the introduction, MongoDB data has a flexible structure.[8]

Unlike SQL databases, which require you to define the schema of a table before entering data, MongoDB's collections do not impose document structure.

This kind of adaptability is what makes MongoDB so effective.

Keep the following points in mind when modeling data in Mongo.

- What are the application's requirements?—Examine the application's business requirements to determine what data and the sort of data it requires.

- As a result, ensure that the structure of the document is determined appropriately. What are data retrieval patterns?—If we anticipate a high volume of queries, consider including indexes in our data model to boost query performance.

- Are there frequent inserts, updates, and deletions in the database? To increase the overall efficiency of our MongoDB system, reconsider the usage of indexes or add sharding if necessary in your data modeling strategy.

What Distinguishes MongoDB from RDBMS?

The following are some significant differences between MongoDB and RDBMS:

MongoDB	RDBMS
It is a document-oriented, non-relational database.	The database is a relational one.
It is appropriate for storing hierarchical data.	It is not appropriate for storing hierarchical data.
Its schema is dynamic.	It already has a schema.
The CAP theorem is at its core (Consistency, Availability, and Partition tolerance).	It focuses on the characteristics of ACID (Atomicity, Consistency, Isolation, and Durability).
It performs significantly better than RDBMS in terms of speed.	It performs worse than MongoDB in terms of speed.

MongoDB Features Include

- **Schema-less Database:** MongoDB offers a nice feature called schema-less databases. A schema-less database allows several types of documents to be stored in a single collection. That is to say, in the MongoDB database, several documents of varying field counts, content types, and sizes may coexist in the same collection. It is not required for one document to be comparable to another, as in relational databases. MongoDB's interesting feature gives databases a lot of flexibility.

- **Oriented to Documents:** As MongoDB, all data is kept in documents rather than tables like in RDBMS. In these documents, data is kept in fields (key-value pairs) rather than rows and columns, making the data far more flexible than in RDBMS. And each document has a distinct object id.

- **Indexing:** Every field in the documents in the MongoDB database is indexed with main and secondary indices, making it easier and taking less time to obtain or search data from the pool of data. If the data is not indexed, the database must search each document individually with the supplied query, which takes a long time and is inefficient.

- **Scalability:** MongoDB offers horizontal scalability via sharding. Sharding is the process of distributing data over numerous servers. A huge quantity of data is partitioned into data chunks using the shard key, and these data pieces are distributed evenly across shards that exist across many physical servers. It will also add additional machines to an already active database.

- **Replication:** With the aid of replication, MongoDB enables high availability and redundancy by creating several copies of the data and sending these copies to a separate server so that if one server fails, the data may be accessed from another server.

- **Aggregation:** It allows us to conduct actions on aggregated data to obtain a single or calculated output. It is analogous to the SQL GROUPBY clause. It offers three types of aggregations: aggregation pipelines, map-reduce functions, and single-purpose aggregation techniques.

- **High Efficiency:** MongoDB has superior speed and data permanence when compared to other databases due to capabilities such as scalability, indexing, and replication.

MongoDB Has the Following Advantages

- It is a NoSQL database with no schema.
- When working with MongoDB, we do not need to design the database schema.
- The join operation is not supported.
- It gives the fields in the papers a lot of leeway.
- It contains a variety of data.
- It has a high level of performance, availability, and scalability.
- It effectively supports Geospatial.
- It is a document-oriented database that stores data as BSON documents.
- It also allows for multiple documents ACID transitions (string from MongoDB 4.0).
- There is no need for SQL injection.
- It is simple to integrate with Big Data Hadoop.

MongoDB Disadvantages

- It stores data in a large amount of memory.
- We may not save more than 16MB of data in the documents.
- Data nesting in BSON is similarly limited; we cannot nest data more than 100 layers.

GETTING STARTED WITH MongoDB

Terminology

A MongoDB Database may be thought of as a container for all collections.[9]

- As MongoDB, documents are stored in collections. It's quite similar to relational database management system tables.

- There are fields in this document. It's like an RDBMS tuple, except the schema may change on the fly. Even within the same collection, documents need not contain a uniform set of fields.

How to Get Started

After installing MongoDB, we can find all of the installed files under C:\ ProgramFiles\MongoDB\ (default location).

There are a number of executables in the C:\Program Files\MongoDB\ Server\3.2\bin directory and a brief summary of them is as follows:

```
mongo: A command-line tool for interacting with
databases.
mongod: This is the database, mongod. configures the
server.
mongodump: It removes the database's binary data (BSON)
mongoexport: The document is exported using
mongoexport in the JSON and CSV formats.
mongoimport: To add data to the database.
mongorestore: To restore everything that you've
exported, use mongorestore.
mongostat: Database statistics
```

We may now start the MongoDB server. Open a Command Prompt and go to the location of the MongoDB executables (C:\Program Files\MongoDB\ Server\3.2\bin\, however this path may change in the future). Simply typing "mongod" will result in an error stating that the path \data\db does not exist.

This signifies that the default storage path C:datadb was not discovered. So we may create the directory C:datadb manually or with the mkdir program. We may also alter the default path by using the "mongod" command with the switch –dbpath <path>.

After creating this directory, rerun the "mongod" command to start the server on port 27017.

We must now launch our customer. In order to modify the directory to the MongoDB path, create a new terminal. Once we type "mongo," our client will start up and attempt to connect to the server.

To communicate with and manage the databases, use this CLI. This shell resembles a JS console somewhat. We may experiment with various JS commands to see how it works. Now that our customer is operational, we can begin working on the database. We can see that the active database is called "test." We may switch to different databases, such as "local," by saying "use <dbname>," and you can examine the databases by typing "see dbs."

There are no collections currently in existence. By entering the command "display collections," this may be viewed.

Start by entering some information into our database. By using the method db.createCollection(name, { size : ..., capped : ..., max : ... }), we can create a collection.

However, we have constructed a json file (with employee data) that was generated at random, and we would import it into our database by entering

```
mongoimport --jsonArray --db test --collection
employeedata <
C:\mongoJson\employeedata.json
```

This might import the Employee data json file that is referenced by the path in the database "test" collection titled "employeedata."

We may now type "display collections" in the shell to confirm that the collection has been imported. Count(), find(), and findOne() are a some of the very basic querying techniques we may employ with our document.

As we can see, each document contains a field named "_id" that was absent from the data imported. The explanation is because every document in MongoDB is guaranteed to have a unique "_id" by default, which is a 12-byte hexadecimal integer. Even though changing this "_id" field is possible, doing so is not advised.

Indexing: If our query returns more than one document, we may utilize indexing.

For example, db.employeedata.find() retrieves all of the documents in the collection, but if we just want the 7th one, use db.employeedata.find() [6] to get it. [Note: Indexing begins at 0 here.]

Projections: Assume we want just certain specified information for a query rather than the whole set of details in the document. We can do these using projections.

Simply set the required fields to 1 after our query object, and the rest will be presumed to be 0. However, keep in mind that the "_id" field is always expected to be 1 implicitly, and if we don't want to see the unsightly "_id" field, we must specify this in our projection by "_id: 0"

Queries

1. Determine the company's personnel count for "PEEKS FOR PEEKS."

```
> db.employeedata.find( { company= "PEEKS FOR
PEEKS" } ).count()
```

2. Display all of the employees called "Sanjana Jain" in detail

```
> db.employeedata.find( { name: "Sanjana Jain" }
```
All of the papers that match the supplied name would appear here.

3. Display the "Harshit Gupta" employee's age, gender, and email address but not their "_id." (Presume there is just one worker with the name Harsh Sharma.) Employing projections

```
> db.employeedata.find( { name: "Harsh Sharma" }, {
_id:0, age:1, gender:1, email:1 } )
```
The results of questions may also be saved in variables, which can then be used to create intriguing inquiries.

4. List every female employee's name in print.

```
> var femaleEmp = db.employeedata.find( { gender:
"female" } )

for ( var x = 0 ; x < femaleEmp.count() ; x++){

print ( femaleEmp[i].name)

}

> db.employeedata.find( { gender: "female" }, {
_id:0, name:1 } )
```

HOW CAN MongoDB BE INSTALLED ON WINDOWS?

MongoDB is an open-source document-oriented database that can hold a big amount of data while also allowing you to deal with it extremely efficiently.

It is classified as a NoSQL (Not Only SQL) database since data in MongoDB is not stored and retrieved in the form of tables.[10]

This has been a broad introduction to MongoDB; now we will learn how to install MongoDB on Windows.

MongoDB may be installed in two ways: as a msi package or as a zip archive.

We'll go through how to install MongoDB using msi in this section, so pay attention to each step:

Step 1: Download MongoDB Community Server from the https://www.mongodb.com/try/download/community2 MongoDB Download Center.]

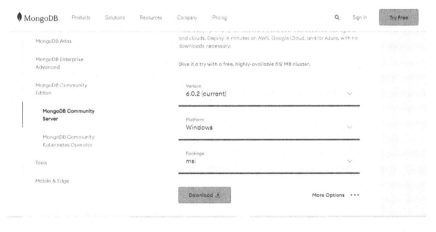

Download MongoDB

We may choose any version, Windows, and package based on our needs. For Windows, we must select:

- Version: 4.2.2

- OS: WindowsOS

- Package: msi

Step 2: Once the download is complete, open the msi file and go to the starting page by clicking the next button:

Installation Step 2

Step 3: Go ahead and click the next button after accepting the end-user license agreement.

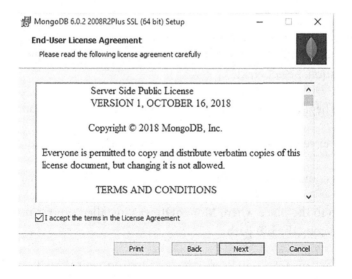

Installation Step 3

Step 4: To install every function of the application, choose the entire option. Use the Custom option if we wish to install only particular software features and choose the installation location in this case:

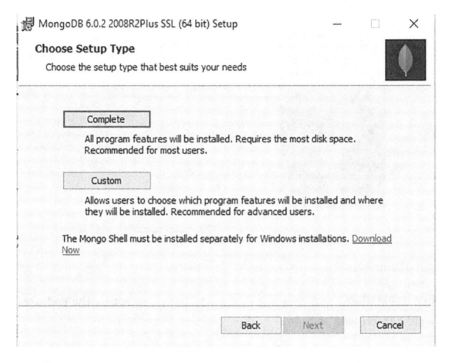

Installation Step 4

Step 5: Choose "Run service as Network Service user" and note the directory's location. Select Next.

Step 6: To begin the installation process, press the Install button:

Step 7: After selecting the install option, MongoDB is installed:

Step 8: To complete the installation procedure, click Finish now:

Step 9: Go to the place where MongoDB was installed on our machine in step 5 and copy the bin path.

Step 10: Next, open System Properties, << Environment Variable << System variable << path << Edit Environment variable paste the copied URL into

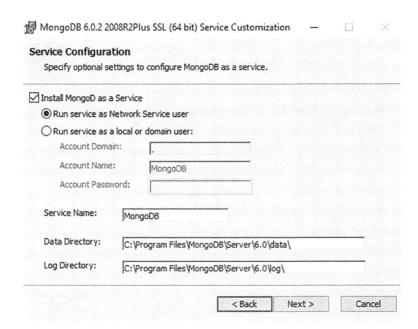

Installation Step 5

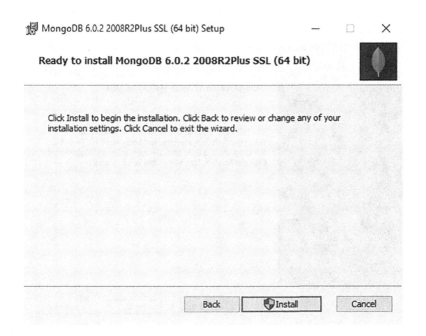

Installation Step 6

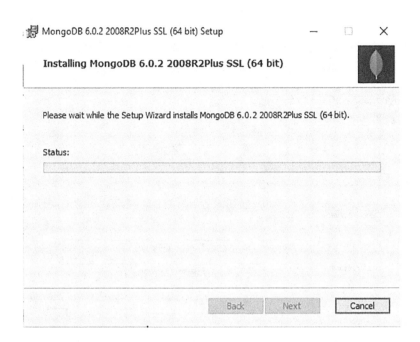

Installation Step 7

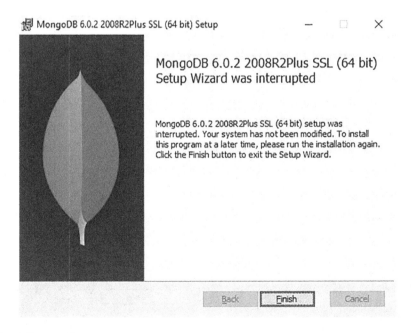

Installation Step 8

our environment system, and then click OK to establish an environment variable.

Step 11: Following the setup of the environment variable, mongod, the MongoDB server, will be started. Run the following command after starting the command prompt:

```
mongod
```

An error message stating "C:/data/db/ not found" may appear when we perform this program.

Step 12: Next, open C drive and make a folder called "data" inside of which we should make another folder called "db." these folders have been created. Run the following command after once again opening the command prompt:

```
mongod
```

Now, the MongoDB server (also known as mongod) will operate correctly.

Run Mongo Shell

Step 13: At this point, we'll connect the mongo shell to our server (mongod). Therefore, keep the mongod window open and type mongo in a new command prompt window. Our mongo shell will now connect successfully to the mongod.

Important Notice: Do not close the mongod window; doing so may cause our server to cease functioning and prevent it from connecting to the mongo shell.

We may now start creating queries in the mongo Shell.

Example

In our shell, we may now create new databases, collections, and documents. An illustration of creating a new database is shown below.

The use Databasename creates a new database in the system if one doesn't already exist and utilizes an existing database if one does.

```
use pfp
```

Our database for the name pfp is now ready.

The student collection is created in the pfp database using the db.Collection name command, and the document is added using the insertOne() method:

```
db.student.insertOne({Ankita:400})
```

SERVER-SIDE JS

We will discuss introduction to Server-side JS and its installation process below:

Server-Side Website Programming

The Dynamic Websites—Server-side programming subject is comprised of a set of modules that demonstrate how to develop dynamic websites, or websites that serve personalized content in response to HTTP requests.[11]

The majority of significant websites employ server-side technologies to dynamically display data on demand. Consider, for instance, how many things are accessible on Amazon and how many Facebook postings have been published. It would be extremely inefficient to display all of these on separate static pages; so instead, these sites display static templates (built using HTML, CSS, and JavaScript) and dynamically update the data displayed within those templates when necessary, such as when we want to view a different product on Amazon.

In the present world of web development, it is strongly suggested to have knowledge in server-side development.

Server-side programming is typically less daunting than client-side development for new developers because most dynamic websites use web frameworks that simplify common web server operations like retrieving data from a database and displaying it in a page, validating user-entered data and saving it to a database, checking user permissions and logging users in, etc. The ability to program (or familiarity with a certain programming language) is helpful but not required.

To the same extent, we don't need to be a coding pro to work effectively with the team building our website's frontend.

Web browsers run JavaScript, a Web programming language that is largely used on webpages and web apps. But because JavaScript is a general-purpose language, it may also be used for other kinds of programming. It may be utilized on the server side, which in this context refers to all locations other than the web browser.

Engines That Run JavaScript

JavaScript has several engines that implement it. JavaScript code is read by JavaScript engines, which then carry it out. Web browsers make heavy use of these, but they also have other possible host environments, such as web servers.

The public API that JavaScript engines make available allows for the language to be embedded in other applications and systems (like web browser, web server, and database).

SpiderMonkey: Mozilla Foundation maintains SpiderMonkey, the original JavaScript engine developed by JavaScript's developer, Brendan Eich.

C/C++ code serves as the implementation. Originally designed for use with Netscape Navigator, Mozilla Firefox is now the browser of choice for many.

Mozilla Foundation also maintains the Rhino JavaScript engine. It was developed using the Java programming language. Because of Rhino, the Java API is available to JavaScript.

JavaScript has the ability to interact with Java through calling Java methods, setting Java properties, and converting JavaScript values to Java values.

Chrome V8 utilizes the JavaScript framework that the Chrome team maintains.

It is a C++ program.

JScript & Chacra: Microsoft's Internet Explorer and Edge use two engines—JScript and Chacra.

JavaScriptCore (Nitro): Safari uses Apple's custom-built JavaScriptCore (Nitro) engine.

Runtime Environment

To put it simply, a JavaScript Runtime Environment is a container that houses the JavaScript engine and executes scripts. Because of its embedded nature, JavaScript often requires extra libraries.[12] These further objects and capabilities are made available by the Runtime Environment. Web browsers include a number of other things, such as the window and the page.

Uses of Server-Side JavaScript

Here are some instances of server-side JavaScript usage:

Document-oriented database MongoDB utilizes the SpiderMonkey engine.

NoSQL database CouchDB, powered by SpiderMonkey.

Riak is a distributed, SpiderMonkey-powered key-value database.

SpiderMonkey is the engine used by Thunderbird, an email client.

Use the SpiderMonkey engine for Flash, Reader, and Adobe Acrobat.

GNOME is a desktop environment that utilizes the SpiderMonkey engine and runs on UNIX-like operating systems.

Java API is used by Rhino to transform JavaScript scripts into Java classes. We may run scripts in batch mode using Rhino shell.

We may run JavaScript code on the server side using the Node.js JavaScript runtime environment. Built around a V8 engine. Building scalable network applications requires the usage of Node.js. It is built on asynchronous, event-driven communication, which enables us to successfully manage heavy loads.

MERN STACK

Full-stack online applications may be deployed more quickly and with less effort with MERN Stack, a JavaScript stack. There are four technologies that make up the MERN Stack: MongoDB, Express, React, and Node. js. The whole point of it is to streamline and simplify the development procedure.[13]

Each of these four potent technologies plays a significant role in the creation of web apps and offers a comprehensive environment for programmers to use.

As a jumping off point, consider: Make a new folder for the project first. Next, open a command prompt or terminal and go to the project's folder; then, run the following command to create a package.json file. (Ensure that npm is set up)

```
npm init
```

Acquainting Oneself with MERN Stack Components
1. MongoDB: Cross-Platform Document-Oriented Database
MongoDB is a NoSQL database in which each record is a document consisting of key-value pairs comparable to JSON (JavaScript Object Notation) objects.

MongoDB is adaptable and lets users design schema, databases, and tables, among other things.

Documents that can be identified by a primary key are the fundamental unit of MongoDB.

Once MongoDB has been deployed, users may also use the Mongo shell.

Through the JavaScript interface provided by Mongo shell, users may communicate and perform activities (eg: querying, updating records, deleting records).

Why Should We Create Mobile and Web Applications with MERN Stack?

- **Cost-effective:** All four of the above-mentioned technologies, MERN (MongoDB, Express.js, React.js, and Node.js), are utilized in MERN Stack, which is based on JavaScript. This makes it cost-effective, and with less cost investment, the user will be able to get greater outcomes.

- **SEO friendly:** Here, SEO (Search Engine Optimization) friendly implies that Google, Yahoo, and other scan engines can efficiently and simply search each page on the website, understand and correlate the content with the searched text, and readily index it in their database. As websites developed with MERN technology are always optimized for search engines.

- **Better performance:** Better performance refers to the quicker reaction between the backend, the frontend, and the database, which eventually increases the website's speed and delivers better performance, hence facilitating a seamless user experience.

- **Improves Security:** It mostly relates to the security of MERN-generated apps; web application security refers to the techniques, methods, and technologies used to safeguard web servers and different online applications, such as APIs (Application user interface), against internet-based attacks. Generally speaking, secure hosting companies can easily incorporate MERN-based apps. For additional or enhanced protection, Mongo DB and Node.js security solutions are also used.

- **Give the quickest delivery:** Web and mobile apps generated with MERN Stack are developed much quicker, allowing us to provide speedier delivery to our customers.

- **Provides quicker Adjustments:** MERN stack technologies offer rapid modifications in mobile and web apps per client request.

- **Open Source:** MERN's four constituent technologies are all open source. This functionality enables developers to get answers to questions arising from open portals during development. Consequently, it will eventually be advantageous for a developer.

- **Easy to switch between client and server:** Because it is developed in a single language, MERN is highly simple and quick, making it easy to move between client and server. Additionally, switching between client and server is fairly simple.

Why Employ MongoDB?

- Being a document-oriented database, indexing documents is simple. Consequently, a quicker reaction.

- Scalability—Large data sets may be managed by distributing them over several computers.

- Utilization of JavaScript—The greatest benefit of MongoDB is that it utilizes JavaScript.

- Any form of data is included in a distinct document.

  - JSON data consists of Objects, Object Members, Arrays, Values, and Strings.

  - JSON syntax is quite simple to use.

  - JSON has broad browser compatibility.

  - Sharing Data: It is simple to exchange data of any size or form (video, audio).

- Simple Environment Configuration—Setting up MongoDB is a breeze.

- Flexible Document Model—MongoDB offers the document model (tables, schemas, columns, and SQL), which is quicker and more convenient.

- Creating a database: Easily achieved with the "use" command:

```
use databasename;
```

- Constructing a table If the collection or table does not already exist, one will be made:

```
db.createCollection("collectionname");
```

- Recordings being added to the collection:

```
db.collectionname.insert

(

    {

        "id" : 101,

        "Name" : "Karan",

            "Department": "Tech",

            "Organization": "Peeks For Peeks"

    }

);
```

- A document's query:

```
db.collectionname.find({Name : "Karan"}).
forEach(printjson);
```

2. Express: Backend Framework

Express is a Node.js framework used as a backend framework. Express allows building the backend code simpler and easier than using Node.js and producing several Node modules. Express supports the creation of excellent web applications and APIs. Because Express offers so many middlewares, writing code is quicker and simpler.

Why Use Express?

- Single-threaded and asynchronous.

- Effective, quick, and scalable.

- 'Node.js' has the largest community.

- Express' integrated router encourages code reuse.

- Robust API.

- Create a new folder to house our express project, then enter the command below to create a 'package.json' file at the command prompt. Accept the defaults and go on.

```
npm init
```

- Then, install express by using the command shown below. Finally, create a file called index.js within the directory.

```
npm install express --save
```

- To establish an example server, enter the following code in index.js instantly.

```
const express = require('express'),
http = require('http');

const hostname = 'localhost';
const port = 8080;
const app = express();

app.use((req, res) => {
console.log(req.headers);
res.statusCode = 200;
res.setHeader('Content-Type', 'text/html');
res.end('<html><body><h1>This is the test server</
h1></body></html>');
```

```
});
const sampleserver = http.createServer(app);

sampleserver.listen(port, hostname, () => {
console.log(`Server running at
http://${hostname}:${port}/`);
});
```

- Update the package.json file's "scripts" section.

- Then execute the command below to start the server.

```
npm start
```

- Now that the server is operating, we may access the output by opening the browser.

3. React: Frontend Library

A JavaScript package called React is used to create user interfaces. Because React can manage quickly changing data, it is used to create single-page apps and mobile applications. JavaScript coding is supported by React, and UI components may be made.

Why Use React?

- Virtual DOM—A virtual DOM object is a DOM object's representation. The virtual DOM is an exact replica of the original DOM. Any changes to the web application result in a complete re-rendering of the virtual DOM. The difference between the original DOM and the virtual DOM is then compared, and adjustments are applied to the original DOM appropriately.

- JSX—Abbreviation for JavaScript XML. It is a React-specific HTML/XML JavaScript Extension. Facilitates and simplifies the creation of React components.

- Components: Components are supported by ReactJS. Components are the building elements of UI, with each component having its own logic and contributing to the UI as a whole. These components also increase code reuse and simplify the overall web application's readability.

- High Performance—Features like virtual DOM, JSX, and Components make it much quicker than other available frameworks.

- Developing Android/iOS Apps—With React Native and understanding of JavaScript and ReactJS, we can simply create Android-based or IOS-based apps.

- Install "create-react-app" using npm or yarn in order to launch your React application.

```
npm install create-react-app --global
```

OR

```
yarn global add create-react-app
```

- After that, we may use to build a new React app.

```
create-react-app appname
```

- Then, to launch our application, browse to the "appname" folder and execute yarn start or npm start.

- Update the index.js file.

```
ReactDOM.render(
<h1>Hello EVERYONE!!</h1>,
document.getElementById('root')
);
```

- Use the commands listed below to execute our program.

```
npm start
```

OR

```
yarn start
```

4. Node.js: JS Runtime Environment

The JavaScript Environment provided by Node.js enables users to run their code on the server (outside the browser). The user may select from thousands of free packages (also known as node modules) to download using the Node Pack Manager, or npm.

Why Use Node.JS?

- JavaScript Runtime Environment is available for free.

- Follows a single-threaded model; single threading.

- Data Streaming Quickly—Node.js has a quick code execution and is built on the JavaScript Engine of Google Chrome.

- High Scalability.

- Start a Node.js application by entering the command shown below in the command window. Embrace the default settings.

```
npm init
```

- Make a file with the name indexs.js.
    Example: A simple Node.js example for calculating a rectangle's area and perimeter.

```
var rectangle = {
    perimeter: (j, Ky) => (2*(j+k)),
    area: (j, k) => (j*k)
};

function Rectangle(l, b) {
    console.log("A rectangle with l = " + l + "
and b = " + b);

    if (l <= 0 || b <= 0) {
        console.log("Error! Rectangle's length &
breadth should be greater than 0: l = "
            + l + ", and b = " + b);
    }
    else {
```

```
        console.log("The Area of a rectangle: " +
rectangle.area(l, b));
        console.log("The Perimeter of a rectangle:
" + rectangle.perimeter(l, b));
    }
}

Rectangle(2, 6);
Rectangle(5, 14);
Rectangle(-7, 2);
```

- Run the command shown below in the command window to launch the node application.

```
npm start
```

What Is the MERN Stack's Structural Makeup and How Does It Operate?

The 3-tier architecture system at MERN primarily consists of three layers. The following are these layers:

- Web as frontend tier

- Server as the middle tier

- Database as backend tier

Its four components- MongoDB, Express.js, React, and Node.js are already known to us.[14]

Let's examine these three stages that were discussed before in greater detail:

Web or Frontend Layer

React.js is primarily responsible for the top tier of the MERN stack. When building websites, it is one of the most used open-source frontend JavaScript libraries. It is known for its ability to create dynamic client-side applications. React facilitates the construction of sophisticated interfaces from individual components. It also links these sophisticated interfaces to the backend server's data. React is used to construct online apps and mobile applications (React Native). React enables the reusability of code and can easily support it, which has several advantages and saves a great deal of time.

It allows users to develop massive web apps that can quickly modify page data without requiring a page refresh.

Server or Middle Tier

It is the next level down from the top layer and is mostly managed by Express.js and Node.js from the MERN stack. Express.js maintained the Server-side framework while operating within the Node.js server, allowing these two components to manage it concurrently. When it comes to backend development in JavaScript, Express.js is among the most widely used frameworks. It makes it easier and simpler for developers to create sophisticated APIs (Application Programming Interface) and web servers.

It also provides useful functionality to HTTP (HyperText Transfer Protocol) objects in Node.js. In contrast, Node.js plays a significant role in and of itself.

It is an open-source server environment and cross-platform runtime environment for running JavaScript code outside of a web browser. Node.js consistently employs JavaScript; hence, it enables a computer user to rapidly develop any web service or web or mobile application.

Database as Backend Tier

The database as the backend layer

It is one of the most significant tiers of the MERN Stack and is mostly managed by MongoDB; a database's primary function is to store all the data linked to your application, such as content, statistics, information, user profiles, and so on. It keeps all the data primarily for safety reasons. It keeps an accurate record, which provides the data to the user whenever necessary. Primarily, it saves data in the database. It makes at least two copies of the files to ensure that, even if the originals are lost, you can still get your hands on the data you need.

It means that MongoDB is not structured like a relational database with tables.

In contrast, it offers a whole separate system for retrieving and storing data. Mongo DB is the most popular open-source document-oriented NoSQL (NoSQL or Non-Structured Query Language) database. NoSQL often refers to a non-relational database that does not need a set structure or relational tables in order to hold the essential data. MongoDB stores data in a structure distinct from relational tables, which comprise rows and columns.

MEAN	MERN
The stack technology includes Angular.js, Express.js, Node.js, and MongoDB.[15]	Stack technology includes MongoDB, React.js, Express.js, and Node.js.
The JavaScript framework Angular.js is part of the MEAN stack.	JavaScript library React.js is part of the MERN stack.
Typescript is used by Angular.js in the MEAN stack.	React.js uses JSX and JavaScript in the MERN stack.
It boosts productivity.	It is not very productive.
Compared to the MERN stack, it is more challenging to master.	It is significantly easier to learn because of the superior documentation.
It helps with code management and rendering.	The virtual DOM makes it possible for fluid rendering.
The data flow is bidirectional.	It only allows one way data transmission.
It is incompatible with apps for mobile devices.	With mobile apps, it is compatible.

MERN VS MEAN

What Are MERN Stack Developers' Futures?

It goes without saying that the future isn't set in stone. However, given on the market data we now have, we can certainly make a reasonable analysis of the growth that MERN stack developers will see in the future. What are the benefits for developers of understanding the MERN Stack?[16]

1. Open source: The best aspect of MERN is that the four technologies that comprise the stack are open source (open-source). This makes it simpler for developers to obtain quick answers from the accessible open portals and successfully resolve any problems that may emerge throughout the development process.

2. Cost-Effective: MERN stack developers are in high demand since this stack utilizes just one language, JavaScript. It is considerably more advantageous for businesses to invest in MERN-savvy personnel. This is a more efficient approach, both financially and in terms of time, than recruiting experts for each technology.

3. Simple to switch between client and server: With MERN Stack, everything is written in a single language, which makes it much easier for developers to know the language (within 4–6 months with dedicated learning). It is also simple to switch between client and server, providing developers with additional expansion opportunities.

4. UI rendering and performance: React JS has shown to be the finest solution for UI layer abstraction, rendering, and performance to date.

Why? It allows developers to construct and arrange application code in accordance with their vision.

In this chapter, we covered backend development where we discussed Node.js, MongoDB, and Server-side JS.

NOTES

1 What Is Backend Developer? Skills Need for Web Development: www.guru99.com/what-is-backend-developer.html Accessed on: 13 October 2022.

2 Using Node.js for Backend Web Development in 2022: https://mobidev.biz/blog/node-js-for-backend-development Accessed on: 13 October 2022.

3 The Good and the Bad of Node.js Web App Development: www.altexsoft.com/blog/engineering/the-good-and-the-bad-of-node-js-web-app-development/ Accessed on: 13 October 2022.

4 Node.js – Introduction: www.tutorialspoint.com/nodejs/nodejs_introduction.htm Accessed on: 14 October 2022.

5 Node.js - Environment Setup: www.tutorialspoint.com/nodejs/nodejs_environment_setup.htm Accessed on: 14 October 2022.

6 Node.js - First Application: www.tutorialspoint.com/nodejs/nodejs_first_application.htm Accessed on: 14 October 2022.

7 What Is MongoDB – Working and Features: www.geeksforgeeks.org/what-is-mongodb-working-and-features/ Accessed on: 14 October 2022.

8 What Is MongoDB? Introduction, Architecture, Features & Example: www.guru99.com/what-is-mongodb.html Accessed on: 14 October 2022.

9 MongoDB: Getting Started: www.geeksforgeeks.org/mongodb-getting-started/?ref=lbp Accessed on: 14 October 2022.

10 How to Install MongoDB on Windows?: www.geeksforgeeks.org/how-to-install-mongodb-on-windows/ Accessed on: 14 October 2022.

11 Server-Side Website Programming: https://developer.mozilla.org/en-US/docs/Learn/Server-side Accessed on: 15 October 2022.

12 Server-Side Javascript: www.javascriptinstitute.org/javascript-tutorial/server-side-javascript/ Accessed on: 15 October 2022.

13 MERN Stack: www.geeksforgeeks.org/mern-stack/ Accessed on: 15 October 2022.

14 MERN Stack: www.javatpoint.com/mern-stack Accessed on: 15 October 2022.

15 What Is the MERN Stack and Why It Is the Best to Fit for Web Development: www.groovyweb.co/blog/what-is-the-mern-stack-and-why-it-is-the-best-to-fit-for-web-development/ Accessed on: 15 October 2022.

16 Future of MERN Stack Developers in 2022: Fewer Risks, More Rewards: www.cybersuccess.biz/future-of-mern-stack-developers/#:~:text=MERN%20 is%20a%20free%20and,end%20or%20server%2Dside%20development. Accessed on: 15 October 2022.

CHAPTER 7

JavaScript for Mobile Usage

IN THIS CHAPTER

➤ React Native

➤ NativeScript

In the previous chapter, we covered backend development, and in this chapter, we will discuss JS for mobile usage.

WHY IS JAVASCRIPT REGARDED AS ONE OF THE FINEST PROGRAMMING LANGUAGES FOR MOBILE APPS IN 2022?

Due to the prevalence of smartphones in everyday life, the development of mobile apps will be one of the industries with the highest demand in 2022. The process of creating a mobile app involves a variety of technologies and procedures.[1]

Coding, which uses a range of languages to accomplish the process, is one of the most important components. JavaScript is a computer language that has long been favored by developers due to a wide range of advantages. Major developers always include JavaScript in their tech stack when creating high-quality apps.

DOI: 10.1201/9781003356578-7

JavaScript's Importance in the Development of Mobile Applications

When creating a robust and collaborative UI/UX that meets the needs of the customer, mobile app developers benefit from a wide range of JavaScript coding advantages.

It has been demonstrably shown that developing mobile apps with JavaScript is quicker than with other languages.

Extremely Responsive

One of the bothersome problems in the development sector is the network's slowness.

The problem becomes more serious when a slow network is combined with the time it takes to send server queries, which results in delayed page loads.

If an app can function better with fewer server bytes, users will benefit from a faster-acting app.

JavaScript can greatly enhance the scenario by pushing XML or JSON data instead of other sorts of data. There will be little interaction with the server, quick output, and full HTML rendering in the browser.

Consequently, using Java Script in the development has additional benefits. Without further server connectivity, any modifications to the UI that do not affect the data can be made. As a result, our app will be very user-responsive and provide the finest experience.

Frontend Rich Platform

Whatever server technology is used, Java Script ensures that users will have access to a robust frontend platform.

This will increase the frontend development's usability and make it more resistant to the server's changing characteristics.

Backend tasks can be accommodated and successfully carried out by rewriting the server-side code.

As a result, by determining the server's capability, developers can select the best platform for all future tasks.

We can be guaranteed to acquire the ideal platform to complete your work if JavaScript has a precise frontend.

Up until the JSON is covered, the frontend will be the best place to execute all the functionality.

Offline Assistance

The hard requirement of communicating with the server following each user interaction is present in server-related programming. As the server is down, the software becomes unusable. But even in the absence of the internet, JavaScript development is still quick and responsive. Compared to the standard server-oriented development approach, it offers a significant advantage.

In JavaScript development, the frontend uses locally cached data to update the application until connectivity is restored. This will facilitate local change tracking and force modifications to one side after connectivity is restored.

It differs from other apps in that it carries out the essential activities without the need for ongoing server connections. A user interface (UI) built using Java Script loads and runs on a screen without the use of a network connection. JavaScript can provide options that conventional server-side frontend programming cannot.

Suitable for All Kinds of Developers

The environment configuration for JavaScript is not very specific.

All you need is a browser to start the programming process by going to developer tools.

Therefore, it is favored by developers of all stripes and levels of experience.

Even beginners in the field can quickly learn and master it, resulting in widespread acceptance.

JavaScript Frameworks for Mobile Apps

Using JavaScript frameworks, you can complete all important client-side tasks.

To create high-quality JavaScript apps, developers can use a variety of frameworks, depending on the need.

PhoneGap

This makes it easier to construct a variety of platforms with a single JavaScript code base that can serve a variety of target clients.

Ionic

The Ionic framework can be used by programmers to create, test, monitor, and publish high-performance mobile apps. It is among the most widely used JavaScript frameworks available, out of all of them.

React Native

With its navigable design features, this well-known open-source framework makes it easier for developers to create mobile apps.

jQuery

It is never easy for developers to create apps for all kinds of mobile devices. As there are many different topics that need to be covered, this is not an easy job for app engineers. However, jQuery enables us to create quick, highly responsive software that works with a variety of mobile and desktop platforms.

Native Language

Native script framework is a vital tool for effectively creating apps for both iOS and Android.

The native script framework codes help to get improved user interface functionalities in the finished product, as the name implies.

Tabris.js

Even this framework enables the creation of native iOS or Android apps by just a single JavaScript piece of code. It is also mentioned as one of the most popular frameworks used by programmers to create native apps.

SHOULD WE USE JAVASCRIPT WHEN DEVELOPING FOR MOBILE?

It is totally fair to be concerned whenever we consider developing a mobile app, especially if we want it to function on both iOS and Android and since we might later encounter technological difficulties. However, since we won't have to learn how to accomplish it in an entirely new development language, things need not be that horrible. We'll be able to steer clear of the choppy waters up front with the assistance of an experienced development company like Kambda.[2]

One of the most important technological advancements nowadays is the creation of mobile apps. These days, the proliferation of smartphones and the app market have had a significant impact on every area of technology. The main languages for creating all kinds of coding are HTML, CSS, and JavaScript, while many other languages are also utilized. These three coding systems work well together. HTML is the markup that instructs the browser how to display a website's text and images. CSS is the style sheet, which means it gives the entire website a consistent appearance. JavaScript improves the user experience by generating an interactive and dynamic interface that enables web pages to respond to a variety of variables, including events, variables, the user's browser, effects, and so on.

Despite what was just stated, JavaScript is not generally used for creating apps because it is the language used to create and maintain websites. Additionally, even though there are ways to create apps solely using JavaScript, there are other, more effective ways to do so.

Nevertheless, JavaScript (JS) has one significant benefit that can help us save time: we can reuse your code for both the frontend and the backend (Node.js).

Another benefit of JS is that it works well across all browsers, which makes the development process simpler.

The popularity of the JS framework is growing daily. Even large corporations like Apple and IBM use JS. The angularJS team now collaborates with Google and Microsoft, continuing the trend. JavaScript makes it simple to create apps because we only need to develop them once to release them across all platforms (Android, iOS, and Windows).

Key Attributes of JavaScript

- One of the simplest languages.

- Quick and effective.

- Since it runs client-side, it avoids using the server and conserves bandwidth.

- Used to add dynamic elements and motion to otherwise boring websites.

While jQuery and other JavaScript libraries can be used to add more sophisticated dynamic features to webpages, plain JavaScript is still frequently recommended for basic client-side operations. A professional JavaScript app can be made using a variety of frameworks, including PhoneGap, jQuery Mobile, and Ionic.

Native React

This framework was created recently, primarily by Facebook. It is a viable alternative for those looking to develop a single program that works on both Android and iOS gadgets. It provides excellent performance, perhaps even better than some of the other frameworks discussed above.

JQuery

The 'write less, do more' maxim is taken to a new level by the jQuery Mobile framework, which enables us to create a single, highly branded responsive website or application that will run on all widely used smartphone, tablet, and desktop platforms.

PhoneGap

By using PhoneGap, we can 'easily create hybrid applications built with HTML, CSS, and JavaScript using existing web development expertise.'

Create cross-platform experiences from a single codebase to connect with our audience on any device.

Ionic

Ionic 'helps us design, deploy, test, and monitor apps easier than ever before, from open source to professional services.' Although there are many more frameworks for creating mobile apps using JavaScript, JQuery and React Native are the most popular ones among developers.

BENEFITS OF USING JAVASCRIPT WHEN DEVELOPING MOBILE APPS

Since smartphones are so close to people, mobile app development has begun to influence the world. A vast variety of languages, primarily JavaScript, CSS, and HTML, are utilized to construct all types of coding. The development of mobile apps is now one of the most important areas of current technology developments thanks to JavaScript coding. Despite not being seen as a key language for app development, JavaScript offers a number of techniques to create applications. The JavaScript framework has had a significant impact on the creation of mobile apps recently. Let's look at a few of the key advantages of using JavaScript in mobile applications.[3]

Since smartphones are so close to people, mobile app development has begun to influence the world. A vast variety of languages, primarily JavaScript, CSS, and HTML, are utilized to construct all types of coding. The development of mobile apps is now one of the most important areas of current technology developments thanks to JavaScript coding.

Despite not being seen as a key language for app development, JavaScript offers a number of techniques to create applications. The JavaScript framework has had a significant impact on the creation of mobile apps recently. Let's look at a few of the key advantages of using JavaScript in mobile applications.

The programming language known as JavaScript is used to carry out sophisticated operations on web pages. The app uses JavaScript to improve the UI/UX and to deliver recent scrolling video jukeboxes, the most recent content updates, animated 2D/3D visuals, interactive maps, and other features. JavaScript has the ability to validate, manipulate, and calculate data as well as edit and modify CSS and HTML.

Using a JavaScript codebase, Meteor is the platform for developing mobile and web applications. JavaScript makes it simple to create new mobile applications, and it may be appropriate for all platforms, including Android and iOS. Let's look at some of the main characteristics of JavaScript that make it useful for creating mobile applications.

- Recognized as the world's easiest language.

- Able to conserve bandwidth while performing client-side operations.

- Utilized in the construction of dynamic animations.

- Rapid and organized growth.

REACT NATIVE

We will discuss about the setup, scope, benefits of React Native below:

Setting Up a React Native Environment

Depending on the operating system we use, there are many alternatives for setting up (installing) the React Native environment.[4]

Each development and target operating system has a somewhat distinct set of instructions.

In this session, Windows will serve as the development platform while Android will serve as the final operating system.

It takes Node, the React Native command line interface, Python 2, JDK, and Android Studio to create an app utilizing the React Native framework.

Here, we use the Windows version of the popular package management Chocolatey.

We may use this to install the latest versions of Java SE Development Kit and Python (JDK).

How to Install React Native Environment in Steps

1. Go to the https://chocolatey.org/ website, click "Install Chocolatey Now," and a new URL will open.

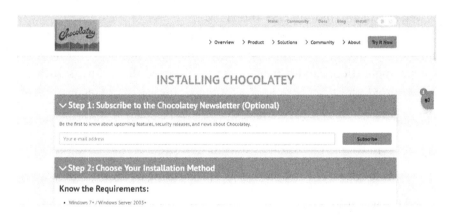

Installation of chocolatey

2. Run the chocolaty setup program, and then copy the code under the Install using cmd.exe section.

```
@"%SystemRoot%\System32\WindowsPowerShell\v1.0\
powershell.exe" -NoProfile -InputFormat None
-ExecutionPolicy Bypass -Command "iex ((New-Object
System.Net.WebClient).DownloadString('https://
chocolatey.org/install.ps1'))" && SET
"PATH=%PATH%;%ALLUSERSPROFILE%\chocolatey\bin"
```

3. Enter this code into our Command Prompt after opening it in Administrative mode (right-click Command Prompt and choose "Run as Administrator").

It'll set up Chocolatey.

4. Paste the code and execute it in command prompt's Administrative mode (install Node.js, Python, and JDK).

If we've already installed JDK, make sure it's version 8 or newer, and if we've previously installed Node.js, make sure it's version above 8.

```
choco install -y nodejs.install python2 jdk8
```

5. We may install React Native using Node's npm (Node Package Manager).

Run the code provided:

```
npm install -g react-native-cli
```

Install Android Studio

1. Download Android Studio from the https://developer.android.com/studio/ website.

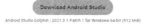

Android Studio provides the fastest tools for building apps on every type of Android device.

Installation of Android Studio

2. Run the Android Studio Set (.exe) file we downloaded and follow the instructions.

3. Decide which functionality to install.

4. Decide where to put the device.

5. Click Next to let the installation continue.

6. To finish the installation, click Finish.

When the installation is complete, the Android Studio home screen will show up.

Set Up the Android SDK and the Java JDK

1. First set the JDK path.

2. In the System variables section, change the Android SDK path to My Computer > Properties > Advanced system settings > Environment Variables.

Then, add Android Home and Android SDK to the "New..." screen appears.

3. Install the necessary components by selecting them from Tools Android > SDK Manager > SDK platforms and installing them.

4. Permit the installation to continue, then click Finish when it is complete.

5. To create an Android emulator, a virtual Android device, pick the device type under Tools > Android > AVD Manager > Create Virtual Device.

6. Choose the Android emulator's API level.

7. Enter the device's name and configure its settings by selecting Show Advanced Settings.

8. Begin using the emulator.

FUTURE SIGNIFICANCE OF REACT NATIVE IN THE DEVELOPMENT OF MOBILE APPS

Facebook's introduction of the React Native framework for mobile app development has sparked wonderful enthusiasm in the app community. To ensure the success of their projects, business and technical professionals must fully grasp the significance of React Native.

The engineers at Facebook and Instagram manage the famous JavaScript framework ReactJS, which has a native counterpart called React Native. React Native has gained tremendous popularity within the developer community in just 2 years. It has received so many stars that it is currently GitHub's fourteenth most popular project of all time.

These days, the react native development firm is using this technology. According to Google trends, more people have searched for 'React Native' than for 'iOS development' or 'Android development.'[5]

Software developers are working hard to produce mobile apps that perform fast and efficiently in the present digital environment, where speed, efficiency, and rapid tools are vital for every mobile application

The engaging user experience and straightforward development have convinced mobile app developers to use JavaScript, HTML5, CSS, or React Native to build the app.

The leading mobile app development companies view React Native as the future of app development for a variety of reasons.

These factors include:

1. **Cross-Platform Support**

    Given that the bulk of React Native APIs are cross-platform, one component will work on both iOS and Android.

    We can build complete, completed applications that function, look, and feel natively without writing a single line of platform-specific code. We do, however, occasionally need to be platform-specific. For instance, the effects of design are different on iOS and Android.

    React offers remedies for such circumstances with its platform module and platform-specific file extensions. The platform module's capacity to recognize the OS being used by the app allows for the definition of platform-specific implementations. By employing platform-specific file extensions, we may designate files for various platforms. React automatically chooses the appropriate date based on the operating system that the app is running on.

2. **Open Source**

    We are all aware with the idea that open-source projects are made up of a huge number of contributors that work tirelessly to improve the projects.

Similar to this, there is a huge developer community that is always striving to enhance functionality, fix issues, and make React Native simpler to use.

Every time we wish to design anything that is typical of mobile apps, there is a strong possibility that React Native members have already done it.

3. Reduced Development Time

React Native modifies the mobile app development life cycle. Since it is open source, a lot of individuals in the community identify with it. Many different mechanisms can be combined with it. The state management tool Redux was used, which also greatly improved development. When there is a single shared data layer for iOS and Android, it goes more quickly and has a lower failure rate.

4. Code Push and Live Updates

When developing native mobile applications, employing React Native has several advantages, including Live Updates. Developers may transmit the updates directly to the user's phone without going via the app store update cycle. This is now possible since JavaScript is so widely used. Live updates for IOS are authorized more gradually.

But if we update all of our users' applications at once, we can be confident that you won't have to deal with problems with older versions. The live updating feature of Microsoft

We can publish changes to our React Native project using the Code Push SDK thanks to integration with React Native. The only thing that can be changed is the JavaScript file and the assets, which is a drawback. The standard App Store or Play Store update procedure will need to be followed for any update that affects the Native OS side.

5. UI and Performance

It's common practice to create hybrid mobile applications using JavaScript, HTML, and CSS.

These applications will maintain their excellent performance without having their functionality altered because of Reacts' independence from the user interface.

6. **Employ the Same Code When Creating Apps for Different Platforms**

The usage of React Native by mobile app developers allowed them to create applications for several platforms using the same code.

The main shortcoming is recovered in this way.

What could be more advantageous for developers than the ability to create cross-platform applications utilizing and mastering only one set of tools?

7. **Reduces the Time It Takes to Write Code**

The ability to reuse previously created code is truly a huge deal in the world of software development. We can get to that precise capacity with the help of React Native. We don't mean to imply that React Native allows you to 'write once and use everywhere.'

As a developer, we must create new code to create a user interface (UI) that adheres to the standards and best practices of each platform so that it seems and feels natural.

The nicest aspect is that there is some shared UI code that can be utilized on both platforms.

8. **Quickly Accessible Resources**

It is easy and quick to locate developers that can construct mobile apps using React Native with an emphasis on efficiency since React Native uses JavaScript, one of the most well-liked and quickly growing computer languages.

9. **A Single Framework for Various Platforms**

React Native enables full codebase replication between iOS and Android (or just a portion of it). In practice, certain changes may require a complete rewrite, and other features will be included as in-app packages. The react native developer community actively supports the framework by releasing new tools as open source.

10. **Quick Reloads**

By introducing Hot Reload, React Native increases productivity and decreases total development time. It allows a developer to continue working on new versions and UI changes while the app is still running.

11. **A Better Environment for Development**

Developers are more effective in the React Native environment.

By removing the time-consuming rebuild and deployment from the iteration cycle, a pleasant development experience is generated. React native uses the Flexbox layout engine for mobile apps on both platforms. This suggests that just one layout engine has to be understood in order to design for both iOS and Android.

12. **Includes Two Important Ecosystems**

iOS and Android have very distinct ecosystems. The creation of these platforms is challenging and challenging. Therefore, making native apps for them is said to be the greatest nightmare of developers. Similar to building iOS applications, Swift or Objective C expertise is essential. On the other hand, developing Android applications necessitates a thorough knowledge of Java and the Android SDK. We will also have to put up with the inconvenience of keeping up with the most recent features that these two important ecosystems have to offer. But with modern technology, no issue persists indefinitely.

Why Is React Native so Popular?

Because of its excellent performance, improved user experience, and wide range of accessibility, React Native is receiving high praise from the industry. Facebook supports the sophisticated backend development language, ensuring its endurance throughout actual development. React Native exclusively focuses on UI, in contrast to MeteroJS and AngularJS. The user interface of React Native apps is incredibly responsive. Our app will load faster and have a smoother feel thanks to React Native and the native environment of the device.

Additionally, React Native works with third-party plugins. Download a third-party plugin and attach it to a native module in order to include Google Maps features into our project. In addition to making the life of mobile app developers easier worldwide, Facebook's React Native is a mobile framework that helps them create ground-breaking applications for their customers. Additionally, our app effortlessly makes advantage of the device's features like rotation, zoom, and compass.

Building React Native Apps

1. **Skype Using React Native**

    When the Skype app first started having a lot of issues, it was announced that a new application using React Native development was being introduced.

    Skype had a complete redesign, down to the icons, so that both old and new capabilities could benefit users of the application's cutting-edge appearance. Microsoft announced that React Native would not only be considered as a platform for the PC version of Windows but also for the creation of mobile applications after realizing the effectiveness of React Native. Additionally, Microsoft acquired the astonishing benefits of React Native from the GitHub repository.

2. **React Native Facebook Ads**

    Before React Native began supporting social networking sites, it began with Facebook advertisements as a mobile app for Android users under Facebook's wing.

    It might deal with problems caused by the numerous business logic needs required to handle variations in time zones, ad formats, date formats, currency conventions, currencies, and many other things. Other developers were inspired to try and implement React Native technologies that were freshly released or incorporated into Facebook advertisements.

3. **Using React Native, Facebook**

    As a simple feature, Facebook intended to make its online version available to its customers on mobile so they could enjoy a smooth user interface when using their smartphone applications. Facebook intended to use a single team to create its mobile application offerings. React Native was therefore used in the creation of Facebook's mobile app for both iOS and Android users.

    The development team for React Native verified and examined the new features' tested performance. This crucial modification determines whether the user will abandon or continue using the program. It is but one example of how changes were made using React Native, but many other aspects were also extensively used by users.

4. **Tesla Using Native React**

Tesla, the most well-known manufacturer of electric vehicles in the world, has joined the react-native community in order to create an application for its electric vehicles and Powerwall batteries. They did it by using Facebook's trending structure as a guide.

The Tesla app has a few restricted functions that allow for smartphone-based car operation, including the ability to analyze a vehicle and pinpoint its precise location.

Although their application development is not entirely known, clients have given the concept a positive response.

5. **Using React Native with Instagram**

Instagram is one among them while discussing react native app development services.

It started with transforming the basic view to an excellent UI to overcome the hurdle of integrating react-native into their existing project.

Due to the elegant user interface, it does not require a separate navigation infrastructure.

Even though the development team encountered several challenging jobs when integrating React Native app features into Instagram, they were able to steadily boost the app's velocity.

Approximately 80%–90% of the codes are exchanged between iOS and Android, which is a huge time saver for an app development team.

6. **Shine with React Native**

One of the top native React apps for users who are stressed out, unmotivated, or lack motivation is Shine. It provides relaxing articles, encouraging quotations, and mottos.

When users log in from their day, the app's inspirational and spiritual audio made by specialists helps them deal with daily stress. This software was initially made available to iOS users with a focus on the American market because Apple phones had a significant market share. They quickly created the app for Android, which is why they used React Native because the technology makes it simple to transfer code from iOS to Android.

Benefits of React Native App Development

React Native has several advantages for creating mobile apps.

1. **More Flexibility**

   Any team member may hop right to the work that was left before and continue performing it thanks to the type of interface utilized by each native development service.

   With this team, flexibility is growing and the processes for updating and upgrading the mobile app are greatly facilitated.

2. **It Saves Time and Money**

   Businesses may now have apps for both the Android and iOS platforms thanks to React Native, which also saves time for the developers.

   This is so because they may save time and effort by developing just a single app that will work on both the Android and iOS markets.

   As a result, money that would have been spent on creating different apps is also saved.

3. **Excellent Performance**

   The central processing unit (CPU), which powers the majority of OS operations, is employed here, but React Native apps also make use of the GPU, the graphics processing unit, to aid improve speed. However, due to the programming language's specialization for mobile devices, React Native apps run almost as quickly as native apps created specifically for the Android or iOS platform.

4. **Immediately Changed Views**

   Reacts Native's live or hot reloading feature enables developers to examine their changes in real time in a live preview window while simultaneously viewing their changes in the code.

   Additionally, the developers benefit greatly from this since they receive real-time feedback as each step is completed.

5. **Movable**

   React Native is claimed to give a lot of flexibility to the procedures being used, making this one of the biggest advantages of adopting it for mobile app development.

   These properly export applications from React Native and transfer them to Android Studio or XCode before continuing.

Cons of React Native

We discussed a few advantages of React Native above, but we all know that anything that has advantages also has disadvantages. The disadvantages (drawbacks) of React Native are therefore listed below.[6]

1. **Insufficient Framework**

   Every new update or release, as we all know, brings with it a number of significant changes that might eventually be difficult for the developers to handle.

   React Native is the speedier and newer alternative in this situation, but in an effort to move quickly, the framework tends to lose its commitment to credibility and, as a consequence, becomes too immature for any type of iOS and Android apps.

2. **It Is Difficult to Define the User Interface**

   Choosing React Native for your app development is not worth it at this moment if your mobile application requires capabilities like animation, numerous screen transitions, and interactions.

3. **Complicated Debugging**

   Debugging procedures and how React Native-developed mobile applications are challenging to troubleshoot. Most of the credit for this goes to the programming languages Java, JavaScript, and C/C++.

CREATE A MOBILE APPLICATION USING REACT NATIVE

Businesses have been forced to consider moving their business models from traditional platforms to digital platforms as a result of the fast changing environment across the globe. Businesses are beginning to create extremely efficient corporate apps that function flawlessly on iOS and Android.

However, their ability to invest in mobile app development is constrained by the rising cost of app development. However, given that mobile applications have grown so prevalent across all industries from communication to retail, healthcare, and entertainment businesses have realized how difficult it would be to compete in the next decades without having a strong online presence. Although there is an app for nearly everything, which provides a seamless user experience and guarantees easy user navigation, businesses are still unsure about which technology to utilize to develop successful solutions.

The Leading Cross-Platform Framework, React Native

React Native is a cross-platform framework built on JavaScript that has been extensively used to develop mobile apps that look and feel native on iOS and Android.

React Native, although being introduced by Facebook in 2015, has swiftly risen to prominence as the leading open-source framework.

After powering several applications like Skype, Instagram, Facebook, and others, it eventually became well-known as the greatest app development option.

It was the ideal platform for app creation because of the advantages of reusability of scripts, rapid testing capabilities, and running apps on both iOS and Android platforms.

Why Should We Use React Native When Developing Mobile Apps?

Undoubtedly, 42% of developers worldwide like React Native, however when it comes to investing in an app development project, many organizations are perplexed as to why React Native is the top option.

Here are a few justifications for using React Native for app development.

Saves both Money and Time

The main benefit of using React Native for app development is the time, money, and effort it saves. Developing two native apps for several platforms will cost us more money than utilizing React Native and a single codebase to create an app.

Therefore, using React Native, developers can easily release the same update for both iOS and Android platforms without the added work of utilizing a distinct codebase, saving money on paying mobile app developers to create two native apps.

High Quality

Businesses' top priorities are almost usually related to the app's performance.

Additionally, React Native apps are just as good as native Android and iOS apps.

React Native uses GPU to do computations, as opposed to other cross-platform frameworks that use CPU. This is a key factor in the better performance of React Native apps.

Over-the-Air Updates

React Native's ground-breaking OTA update capability enables developers to make changes to the backend while users are actively using the app.

Once completed, the modifications will appear immediately in the app.

In other words, consumers frequently have the option to update an app without visiting the app store.

The entire process of upgrading the app is made simple and quick thanks to React Native's functionality.

The Main Advantage Is Open-Source Software

For those who want to personalize the lovely application, React Native offers a wide range of freely available native-like UI capabilities.

Since React Native enables developers to smoothly export scripts from Android Studio to Xcode, developers do not have difficulties porting React Native projects from one platform to another.

NATIVESCRIPT

We will discuss about the introduction, setup, scope, benefits of NativeScript below:

What Is NativeScript?

An open-source framework called NativeScript is used to build native mobile apps for iOS and Android. This framework is JIT compiled. On the JS virtual computer, NativeScript code is executed.[7]

Both the Android and iOS platforms employ the V8 engine runtime. For development, NativeScript makes use of XML, JS, and CSS. It has a web-based IDE called PlayGround. This PlayGround includes a user-friendly working interface, straightforward project management, hot reloading, and device debugging. NativeScript enables programmers to build native, cross-platform applications fast and effectively while reducing the expenses of testing, development, and training. Therefore, Native applications will remain powerful and rich for years to come, making them better and simpler to use.

Why NativeScript Is Preferred for the Creation of Android Applications

These days, developers may choose from a wide range of frameworks to create stunning and scalable mobile applications.

Developers may take advantage of both smartphone features and their web development expertise thanks to the widespread adoption of the hybrid app development idea in the market.

This is where NativeScript enters the picture because of all the advantages it offers businesses searching for an Android app development solution.

As the name implies, Native Script enables JavaScript developers to create flawlessly native apps.[8]

Surprisingly, the length of time it takes to build an app as a whole is cut without sacrificing quality. Additionally, programmers can utilize alternative frameworks like TypeScript and Angular. Applications created using Native Script run incredibly well, have a great user experience, and can connect to several devices.

Here are all the key justifications to use Native Script in the event that we are considering doing so for our projects.

What Is NativeScript? What Are Its Main Advantages and Disadvantages?

A well-known open-source frontend framework called Native Script is used to create native and cross-platform mobile apps that have outstanding performance and user experience features. When it was introduced in 2014, it soon gained a reputation for great usability and platform-specific programming capabilities.

The most important benefit of using Native Script is providing users with an engaging native user experience across platforms like Android, iOS, and the web. Android developers can benefit from the simple access to native Android features through native Android APIs to build a user-centric app regardless of the niches.

Advantages of Native Apps

1. **Native Apps Provide Quickness**

   Because they are native to the platform, native apps operate more quickly. There are many preloaded elements. Since they leverage the built-in features of the device, they are quick because the user data is fetched from the web rather than the complete application.

2. **The Use of Native Apps Offline**

Even without internet access, native apps function. Therefore, native apps are usable while we're stranded in a place with poor or no connectivity, like an airline, underground tunnel, or metro.

3. **Native Applications Offer a Recognizable Interface and Feel**

The default apps on their device have been enhanced with native applications. Because the program is similar to other apps already installed on the smartphone, when a user does several actions, they rapidly know the natural flow of the application.

Native apps have an advantage in this situation because mobile applications that attempt to mimic the appearance and feel of native apps frequently wind up succumbing to the phenomenon known as the 'uncanny valley effect,' which was named by robotics professor Masahiro Mori.

4. **Native Apps**

Maintain aspect ratios the width to height ratio of various screens is known as an aspect ratio. It is a significant element that affects how good an image is.

Changing the size and form of the device causes many apps to break and function incorrectly.

The orientation, size, and resolution of an app can be more precisely controlled with native apps.

Layout features are available to developers as they create native apps.

A native app keeps the aspect ratio on its own regardless of the screen it is running on after setting the screen size. Both iOS and Android have tools called Constraint Layout and Auto Layout that assist in keeping the aspect ratio on their respective devices. Along with maintaining aspect ratios, these capabilities offer various DPI (dots per inch) for each screen to preserve the visual quality.

Limitations with Native Apps

1. **Lengthy Downloading Process**

Native applications are ready to use only after consumers download them from the app store (Google Play or Apple App Store).

This entails a number of steps going to the app store, selecting the program, accepting its terms and conditions, and then eventually installing it. Many folks don't have the time and patience to follow all the steps to download an app. We lose 20% of consumers at each level in an app funnel.

2. **Absolute Rigidity**

There is little freedom for developers when choosing the platform on which to build native applications. One platform at a time, with separate development for Android and iOS, is required of developers. We'll often need to employ two teams of developers if you're recruiting app developers for our native app idea: one for Android and one for iOS.

3. **Costly Development**

Native app developers are hard to find since the coding they utilize is fairly difficult. As a result, native app development takes longer to complete and costs more money. It also costs more money and takes longer to build native applications since they need distinct codes for each platform.

Additionally, the expense of maintaining native applications is relatively expensive.

Upkeep accounts for 15%–20% of total app development costs. For instance, a simple native app that costs $25,000 would need roughly $5,000 in upkeep. The maintenance expenses of a native app will increase along with its development expenditures.

4. **Development That Takes Time**

Because each platform, like iOS and Android, has a unique set of codes, it takes longer to develop for each platform because it's like creating for two new applications.

A high-quality native app has to be developed in roughly 18 weeks. Depending on how difficult the project is, the time grows.

Setups for NativeScript Environment

How to install NativeScript on our computer is described in this section.

Prerequisites

We require the following requirements before beginning installation:

- Node.js

- Android

- iOS

Verify Node.js

Node.js is a JavaScript runtime engine constructed on top of Google Chrome's internal JavaScript engine, v8.

NativeScript utilizes Node.js heavily for different purposes like building the beginning template application, compiling the application, etc.

It is required to have Node.js on our PC. Hopefully, we have installed Node.js on our system.

If it is not installed then visit the website, https://nodejs.org/ and get the latest LTS package and install it.

To test if Node.js is correctly installed, enter the below command on our terminal:

```
node --version
```

The version was visible. The most recent 'LTS' stable version of node is 12.14.0.

CLI Setup

We may construct and develop NativeScript applications using the NativeScript CLI, a terminal/command line program.

NativeScript CLI is installed on our computer via the Node.js package manager npm.

Run the command shown below to install NativeScript CLI.

```
npm install -g nativescript
```

setupcli

The most recent version of the NativeScript CLI, tns, is installed on our system. Enter the following command into our terminal now.

```
tns
```

cli

Without any further setup, we can construct and develop applications using tns.

However, we were unable to deploy the program on actual hardware.

Instead, we may use the NativeScript Playground iOS and Android app to launch the program.

Setting Up the NativeScript Playground Application

Search for NativeScript Playground on the Google Play Store or the iOS App Store.

Click the install button when the program is displayed in the search results.

The NativeScript Playground app will be installed on our device.[9]

Without actually publishing the program to a real device or emulator, we may test our apps on Android or iOS devices using the NativeScript Playground application.

This will speed up the process of developing the application and provide a simple approach to get it going.

Setup for Android and iOS

Let's learn how to set up the system to create and launch iOS and Android apps on either a real device or an emulator.

Step 1: Dependency on Windows

Run the command below as administrator at our Windows command prompt.

```
@powershell -NoProfile -ExecutionPolicy Bypass
-Command "iex
((new-object net.webclient).DownloadString('https://
www.nativescript.org/setup/win'))"
```

Following this command, downloaded scripts install their dependencies and are configured.

Step 2: Dependency on macOS

We must check whether Xcode is installed before we can install on macOS.

NativeScript requires the use of Xcode.

If Xcode isn't already installed, go to https://developer.apple.com/xcode/, download it, and then install it. In our terminal, run the following command to begin.

```
sudo ruby -e "$(curl -fsSL https://www.nativescript.
org/setup/mac)"
```

The script will install the necessary prerequisites for developing for both iOS and Android after running the aforementioned command. Close our terminal and restart it after it's finished.

Step 3: Android reliance

The following requirements should be set up, hopefully:

- JDK 8 or higher

- Android SDK Build-tools 28.0.3 or higher

- Android Support Repository

- Google Repository

- Android SDK

- Android Studio

If the following requirements are not set up, go to https://developer.android.com/studio/install and install it. Finally, add the environment variables JAVA_HOME and ANDROID_HOME.

Step 4: Verify dependencies

Everything is finished at this point. This dependence may be verified using the command provided below.

```
tns doctor
```

Top NativeScript Usage Cases

For years, feature-rich and performant apps have employed Native Script across all platforms.

The key selling point of the framework continues to be its customary capacity to influence native user experience. Let's quickly review some of the most prominent and well-known use cases of Native Script from various angles.

- Popular social networking platforms including Facebook, Twitter, WhatsApp, and a number of others employ Native Script.

- NativeScript is used by several popular GPS map and location apps, including Field Trip, Banjo, Glimpse, and others.

- Numerous popular news and entertainment applications, like Buzzfeed, Reddit, SmartNews, Feedly, and others, also employ Native Script.

- Native Script Live is used by a number of well-known gaming applications, including Drop7, Crossy Road, Real Racing 3, Robot Unicorn Attack 2, and others. Live feed apps, including Livestream, Broadcast me, Periscope, and numerous more, also utilize Nativescript.

- NativeScript is used by streaming music and video applications like Apple Music, iHeartRadio, and others.

- Native Script is also used by popular chat and social messaging apps like Skype, Snapchat, Messenger, and others.

Key Benefits of Developing Android Apps Using NativeScript

NativeScript has established itself as a go-to framework for creating robust, captivating, and high-performing native Android apps throughout the years. For their Android app projects, developers may take use of a number of fantastic benefits provided by Native Script.

Let's quickly review the main advantages of utilizing Native Script while creating Android apps.

Performance of Native Apps

Accessing the native UI through a specific Android API is the main benefit of utilizing NativeScript for Android programming. NativeScript, in contrast to many other frameworks, can access native UI without using WebViews or a middle JavaScript bridge.

NativeScript is likely to begin running native code in all areas of the app as soon as the developers have specified the native feature and capability.

As long as this natural UI building ability is present. The user interface may be further modified by Android developers to suit the needs of a certain device.

This is crucial for a complex and varied device ecosystem like Android because Native Script, like other native Android programming languages like Kotlin or Java, can enable fast app performance and a completely platform-specific user experience without compromising the code's reusability. The user interface and user experience characteristics stay naïve when the same code is reused across different platforms.

Reusable Program

We can easily utilize and reuse the same codebase across iOS, Android, the web, and other platforms when using NativeScript. Additionally, Native Script includes a number of native Android capabilities that programmers may employ right away in their app projects.

By integrating with a variety of other top JavaScript frameworks, including React, Angular, Vue, and others. While preserving the platform-specific user experience, Native Script can assist with platform-specific code reuse.

The Very Low Learning Curve

By utilizing the Native Script framework, any app developer may quickly hone and expand their programming talents. Native Script enables us to get a head start while learning to develop Android features from scratch if we are just getting started with the platform.

We may create a whole Android app with the aid of some basic understanding of popular web development languages like JavaScript, CSS, and Android UI.

Along with facilitating simple access to platform-specific APIs for iOS and Android.

The framework is renowned for its simplicity in integrating with other frameworks and SDKs.

Every plugin, template engine, and API that Android developers utilize in their various app projects are supported by the framework. The Android SDK is also fully supported by it. The ability to integrate with various technologies guarantees that developers have the greatest amount of flexibility and creative freedom to create a distinctive and interesting user experience.

Substantial Community Support

The team behind the creation of Native Script was made up of professionals with years of expertise in creating native apps for various platforms.

They are familiar with the difficulties experienced by developers working on the iOS and Android platforms.

Additionally, the framework has widespread support from the developer community.

Last but not least, the company that created Native Script offers enterprise-level assistance for projects that include developing mission-critical apps.

COMPARISON BETWEEN NATIVESCRIPT AND REACT NATIVE

It's not easy to pick one framework from two JS-based frameworks. Both provide benefits that are relatively comparable due to being cross-platform. However, React Native truly shines in particular industries. The performance, learning curve, popularity, and development community of the two frameworks, as well as other important characteristics, are briefly compared here.[10]

Performance of NativeScript and React Native

Both frameworks offer native app performance to start. Both take a long time to load. But this is where React Native takes center stage. NativeScript renders pages slowly. To be really honest, delayed rendering is unacceptable in a society when every second matters. This is the very situation when React Native is useful. React Native uses native SDKs to render apps while rendering dynamic components. All because of the Virtual DOM, this transforms React Native into a very fast framework.

Learning Curves for NativeScript and React Native

NativeScript and React Native cannot be handled by a developer with only JS skills.

Let's consider this. Initially, NativeScript will be simpler for developers with an Angular background. Programmers with a React background, on the other hand, will find the shift to React Native easier.

It is important to remember that JavaScript is used by both systems. For frontend developers, this is a fantastic chance. At these times, it is somewhat simpler to perceive these frameworks. Choosing React Native means that all we need is JavaScript, whereas NativeScript provides assistance through its declarative coding approach.

Development Community for React Native vs NativeScript

React Native has a larger developer community than NativeScript, which is utilized by 11% of programmers, with 42% of programmers. React Native is also very popular since tech behemoths like Instagram and Tesla selected it over PhoneGap or NativeScript to create their applications.

The importance of considering community support is vital while deciding on the best structure.

Even though it may seem odd, NativeScript has existed for a lot longer than React Native.

React Native was published on March 26, 2015, whereas NativeScript was first made available in 2014.

Although the 1-year gap may appear to be an advantage, NativeScript is increasingly being replaced with React Native.

React Native records 533k downloads on npm weekly, compared to around 7k downloads per week for NativeScript as of the publication date.

Speaking of contributions, React Native beats out NativeScript with more than 2,200 contributors on GitHub. NativeScript has 208 contributors.

On GitHub, React Native is really utilized by 720k developers, whereas NativeScript is used by greater than 3.5k.

These margins show the developer community's widespread acceptance of React Native, which has an effect on the amount of third-party libraries, replies, and bug solutions on StackOverflow. Overall, React Native triumphs in this case.

Popularity of NativeScript vs React Native

Both NativeScript and React Native were developed using JavaScript.

The competition is never far apart. According to a 2019 StackOverflow study, JavaScript was the most widely used technology.

React.js has surpassed Angular.js/Angular and Vue.js when it comes to web frameworks.

It appears that developers favor React.js more. React Native is simultaneously used by 10.5% of all respondents. In addition to becoming more popular than NativeScript, React Native also attracts more attention.

Which Should We Use between React Native and NativeScript?

It may be difficult to decide between these two well-known technologies because each has advantages and drawbacks of its own. The best technology for us will mostly rely on the needs of our project. The proper times to utilize NativeScript and React Native have been determined, nevertheless.

Select NativeScript if

- We want to create a cross-platform program.

- Using the free and built-in plugins and templates, we want to create extendable APIs.

- Instead of creating complex, inaccessible, and distracting user interfaces, we don't require webViews.

- Avoid performance problems at all costs.

Select React Native if

- We want to quickly develop an MVP.

- We want to create real-time apps that communicate updates in real-time.

- We want to make mobile apps with a certain UI.

- Without third-party plugins, our platform must be created.

In this chapter, we covered advantages, disadvantages, scope, popularity and comparison of React Native, and NativeScript.

NOTES

1. Why Is JavaScript Considered One of the Best in Mobile App Development for 2022?: www.linkedin.com/pulse/why-javascript-considered-one-best-mobile-app-?trk=pulse-article_more-articles_related-content-card Accessed on: 17 October 2022.
2. Should You Use JavaScript for Mobile Development?: www.kambda.com/should-use-javascript-mobile-app-development/ Accessed on: 17 October 2022.

3. Benefits of Using JavaScript for Mobile App Development: https://medium.com/@rohithaelsa/benefits-of-using-javascript-for-mobile-app-development-e1e71aa94e21 Accessed on: 17 October 2022.

4. React Native Environment Setups: www.javatpoint.com/react-native-environment-setup Accessed on: 19 October 2022.

5. Future Scope of React Native for Mobile App Development: https://richest-soft.com/blog/future-scope-of-react-native-for-mobile-app-development/ Accessed on: 17 October 2022.

6. The Pros and Cons of Native Apps: https://clutch.co/app-developers/resources/pros-cons-native-apps Accessed on: 18 October 2022.

7. NativeScript Tutorial: www.tutorialspoint.com/nativescript/index.htm Accessed on: 18 October 2022.

8. Why Nativescript Is Preferred for Android App Development: www.cisin.com/coffee-break/technology/know-why-nativescript-is-preferred-for-android-app-development.html Accessed on: 18 October 2022.

9. NativeScript – Installation: www.tutorialspoint.com/nativescript/nativescript_installation.htm Accessed on: 19 October 2022.

10. NativeScript vs React Native for Native App Development in 2022: www.bacancytechnology.com/blog/nativescript-vs-react-native Accessed on: 18 October 2022.

JavaScript for Desktop Apps

In the previous chapter, we covered JS for mobile usage, and in this chapter, we will discuss the usage of JS for Desktop Apps.

The design of desktop programs has improved in recent years, with more and more apps taking on the appearance and feel of today's cutting-edge websites.

Electron is the technology that has allowed desktop programs to go to this next level.

It's a breeze to use, loads quickly, and streamlines production.

Previously, JavaScript was the preferred language for creating websites and online applications, in large part because JavaScript frameworks like React, Vue, and Angular were so well-liked. However, with the advent of Node.js in 2009, JavaScript gained the ability to operate outside the browser.

Because of this, we can now utilize JavaScript for a lot more than simply websites, including the development of desktop apps using Electron.js.

DOI: 10.1201/9781003356578-8

Electron is a runtime that provides a wide range of native (operating system) APIs, allowing us to write desktop apps in pure JavaScript.

We may think of it as a fork of the Node.js runtime tailored specifically for desktop programs as opposed to web servers.

HOW CAN WE USE DESKTOP APPLICATIONS?

The term 'desktop application' refers to software designed to be used only on personal computers. These programs are installed for one single function and serve no other reason.

Microsoft Word, which we use to write and edit documents, is an example of a desktop program. Web browsers, Visual Studio Code, and Adobe Photoshop are further examples of widespread desktop apps.

Desktop apps are distinct from online programs in that they need installation prior to use and, in some cases, may not even require an active internet connection to function.

However, web applications need constant connectivity to the internet and can only be accessed by going to the URL where the app is located.

The following are some examples of frameworks used while creating desktop applications:

1. Java

    Java is an object-oriented, class-based programming language that was created with the goal of requiring as little from the underlying implementation as feasible.

    As a result, generated Java code may run on any systems that accept Java without the need for recompilation, allowing application developers to 'write once, run everywhere' (WORA).

2. JavaFX

    As stated on their website, it is a Java-based, open-source, next-generation client application platform for desktop, mobile, and embedded devices.

3. C#

    C# is a general-purpose, multi-paradigm programming language that supports a wide range of programming paradigms, including strong typing, lexically scoped, imperative, declarative, functional, generic, object-oriented, and component-oriented.

4. .NET

.NET is a free, open-source, and cross-platform development environment that may use to create a wide variety of software.

When using.NET, developers have access to a wide variety of tools and frameworks for creating applications for the web, mobile devices, desktop computers, video games, and the Internet of Things.

WHAT IS AN ELECTRON?

Electron is a free and open-source software environment for creating desktop software.

The project, originally known as 'Atom shell,' is built and supported by GitHub.[1]

With it, we can create desktop apps that run on several platforms with only HTML, CSS, and JavaScript. This implies that a same set of codes may be used to create desktop programs for several platforms, including Windows, MacOS, and others.

It was built using Node.js and Chromium. Many well-known programs, including the Atom text editor, Visual Studio Code, WordPress for desktop, and Slack, were developed using Electron.

Installation

Use the NPM package manager to add Electron to our project.

```
npm install electron --save-dev
```

If we intend on working with electron applications extensively, we may install it globally with this command:

```
npm install electron -g
```

WHICH APPS USE ELECTRON?

Electron provided several advantages to numerous businesses.[2]

1. WebTorrent Desktop Application

Let's face it: We all love torrents, whether they're downloaded on our phones or our computers. However, this sort of software still seems obsolete and out of date, which is why the folks at WebTorrent decided to take action—adopting Electron JS as their primary development tool.

WebTorrent is the first torrent client that works in the browser, is entirely built-in JavaScript, and leverages WebRTC for peer-to-peer transmission. WebTorrent connects the user to a decentralized browser-to-browser network that provides efficient file sharing without the need for plugins, extensions, or installs.

Why Is Electron Used by WebTorrent for Desktop?

Electron enters the fray with the WebTorrent desktop client, making it as light, ad-free, and open source as possible. It also helps with streaming and functions as a hybrid client, connecting the program to all of the prominent BitTorrent and WebTorrent networks.

2. WordPress Desktop Application

WordPress, as the undisputed monarch of content management systems, needed a dependable and automatic desktop version. It joined the list of desktop applications utilizing Electron JS—as an open-source framework that enables users to manage WordPress content—thanks to Electron JS.

We've all heard about WordPress and how to use it in our browsers. WordPress for desktop, on the other hand, is something altogether new: desktop software built on the Electron framework that delivers a seamless cross-platform experience, enabling users to concentrate on their content and design without being distracted by browser tabs.

Why Does the WordPress Desktop App Make Use of Electron?

WordPress for desktop is a desktop program that uses Electron as a foundation and JavaScript with React as the primary language in this new desktop technology.

3. Ghost Electron Application

We are not alone if you have never heard of Ghost. Ghost is essentially an open-source platform that allows users to create and manage contemporary web publications.

Ghost is entirely hackable and has a significant influence on the future of online media, from blogs to magazines and journals. This is mostly due to the easier and more focused authoring experience, which is clearly a result of the JavaScript desktop framework, among other technologies.

Why Does the Ghost Desktop App Make Use of Electron?

In that spirit, Ghost for desktop is a desktop program built with Electron JS that enables authors to maintain many blogs at the same time while focusing on their content.

If we're a writer, we're surely aware that basic things like keyboard shortcuts may be difficult to implement in a browser. The Ghost desktop program, on the other hand, makes it simpler than ever.

Ghost for desktop is one of the Electron-based applications that provide a better user experience by using JavaScript and Node.js on both the backend and frontend.

4. The Electron App Beaker Browser

Are we looking for a dependable peer-to-peer web browser? If so, we've just discovered it. Beaker Browser is a collaborative browser for hackers. Beaker Browser, originally developed as a hackable product, transforms the Web to an open-source format and allows hackers, modders, and creative types to make the most of their digital abilities.

Why Is Electron Used by Beaker Browser?

The Electron framework makes it much simpler to construct Beaker.

It assisted the Electron design process with minimum iterations and in the best manner possible as a toolset for developing browsers. In a word, Beaker Browser is an open-source online browser and a solution that enables social hacking simpler and more effective than ever before.

5. Pexels Electron App

Pexels is a lifesaver for many authors, designers, and publicists.

As a site with thousands of royalty-free stock pictures, it clearly needed to be improved.

That is how the Pexels desktop app, developed using Electron JS, came to be.

Why Does the Pexels Desktop App Make Use of Electron?

With just one click, this software makes it simpler than ever to copy a snapshot to your clipboard. The picture may then be pasted into any software and used as a stock image for an article, infographic, or social media post. There are no downloads, therefore there are no issues, and finding new photographs is simple due to the Pexels desktop software.

6. Slack Desktop Application

Slack desktop app for macOS is another amazing program that makes use of this JavaScript technology.

Why Does the Slack Desktop App Make Use of Electron?

It was created using the Electron framework, which is clearly noticeable due to its speedier performance and frameless appearance, as opposed to the browser experience.

Slack for desktop is the software of choice for many organizations seeking for an improved organization or a more focused workplace. Although Slack for desktop uses a mixed method, the majority of their assets and code are loaded remotely, using the Chromium rendering engine and the Node.js runtime and module system.

7. WhatsApp Electron Application

WhatsApp, the most downloaded chat software, is another prominent desktop program that uses ElectronJS.

Why Does the WhatsApp Desktop App Make Use of Electron?

The Electron framework helped WhatsApp developers cover everything at once and wrap the desktop experience of WhatsApp behind a more streamlined and revolutionary framework—the Electron. This resulted in less labor and more contribution.

WHY DO SO MANY BUSINESSES CHOOSE ELECTRON TO CREATE CROSS-PLATFORM DESKTOP APPS?

There are many important reasons why businesses choose Electron to create desktop apps:

Electron enables developers to create desktop programs using JavaScript specifically, developers leverage web technologies such as HTML, CSS, and JavaScript.

Electron allows developers to create cross-platform programs that run on Mac, Windows, and Linux—it removes the requirement for developers to be skilled in technologies required to develop for these platforms natively.

What Is the Significance of This?

At the highest level, we can see Mac, Windows, and Linux. That's already quite a lot. On a deeper level, though, such systems come in a variety of flavors. Each has unique characteristics, and each one that is still in use should be considered during product creation.

Furthermore, each platform has its own peculiarities.

To meet this development challenge, we must employ professionals, which might take a long period. Furthermore, developing three distinct applications is a time-consuming procedure.

From a commercial standpoint, in many circumstances, that is not a realistic answer.

BENEFITS OF ELECTRON

Nowadays, most developers choose Electron to create cross-platform apps due to the following remarkable benefits[3]:

Single Codebase

Electron offers a versatile abstraction for native operating system functionality.

As a result, developers may keep a single codebase for their cross-platform application, which will work on the majority of popular platforms.

Quick Feature Delivery

Creating user interfaces in Electron using HTML and CSS is simple; these web technologies allow us to construct any custom GUI element.

Furthermore, Node.js offers a vast ecosystem of libraries, allowing us to easily add native-like capabilities.

Framework Maturity

Because Electron was first launched about 8 years ago, it has a large user base and community.

There are also useful built-in features such as auto updates.

Reputable firms like Microsoft use Electron to develop cross-platform apps.

Electron was used to build applications such as Visual Studio Code, Teams, and Skype.

Electron Has Several Unresolved Concerns

While the Electron framework is generally amazing, it has numerous key speed concerns.

Electron includes Chromium and Node.js in the final application package, thus even if we write a basic and lightweight app by carefully selecting frontend libraries and frameworks, our project will become bloated.

Chromium and Node.js are large projects, and their modules will need more resources than usual on our machine.

In other words, Electron-based apps will need a large amount of physical memory and disc space. Furthermore, because of their high resource usage, Electron programs rapidly deplete our laptop's battery. Electron-based cross-platform apps often become bloatware as a result of the severe performance difficulties discussed above. This disadvantage may be hidden from the common user by powerful hardware. However, if users begin running many Electron apps, they will quickly notice this hidden performance disadvantage.

ALTERNATIVES FOR ELECTRON

Several alternatives, such as Electrino and DeskGap, appeared as remedies to Electron's performance difficulties some time ago.

Both efforts attempted to decrease the size of the final bundle by utilizing the operating system's webview rather than Chromium.

Unfortunately, the developed Electron framework could not finish these two projects.

However, there are two popular lightweight Electron alternatives: Tauri and Neutralino.js.

Both projects attempt to address Electron's performance problem by replacing Chromium and Node with better, lighter alternatives.

Instead of Chromium, both projects utilize the well-known webview library to render HTML and CSS. The webview library renders using the current web browser component.

It will, for instance, utilize gtk-webkit2 on Linux systems, Cocoa Webkit on macOS, and Edge/MSHTML on Windows.

DRAWBACKS OF ELECTRON.JS FRAMEWORK

There are some disadvantages to using electron.js, which are listed below[4]:

Excessive Volume

Electron programs use their own version of the Chromium browser.

This browser is quite large and comprises millions of lines of code.

In fact, since the Chrome browser is the same size as an operating system, it takes up a lot of hard disk space on a computer.

However, given that current computers often offer users with 2 tera-bytes of memory space, the huge number of electron applications isn't a major concern.

Electron.js Framework Consumes a Lot of Resources

The Electron.js framework consumes ROM and system resources, as well as battery power fast if utilized on a laptop.

Indeed, the Electron application is optimized to function on many systems, and since the platforms vary, application optimization necessitates more energy.

Because native apps are platform-specific, their resources are superior.

Specific Customer Needs

Electron.js apps typically operate the same on all platforms, but programmers may struggle if users have a different design for each device.

In reality, developers must devote more effort to creating unique features to each platform, which will inevitably raise expenses. Most crucially, this will not work; as a result, application owners must plan ahead of time for their product identification.

SIGNIFICANCE OF USING THE ELECTRON.JS FRAMEWORK

The Electron JS framework is used by developers to create high-quality cross-platform apps.

But why do you believe programmers choose this framework over other tools?

First and foremost, this framework supports all accessible platforms, making it very user-friendly for developers. In addition, developers will be able to create Cross-Platform apps using the Electron.js framework and other JavaScript frameworks.

Another reason for the Electron framework's success is that its apps are genuinely web applications. In other words, Electron.js is a web technology that allows us to simply convert a desktop program to a web version.

DISTINCTION BETWEEN THE MAIN AND RENDERER PROCESSES

By establishing BrowserWindow instances, the main process generates web pages.

The web page is rendered in its own renderer process by each BrowserWindow instance.

The related renderer process is ended when a BrowserWindow instance is destroyed.

The main process is in charge of all web pages and their associated renderer processes.

Each renderer process is isolated and is solely concerned with the web page that is executing in it.

HELLO EVERYONE CODE IN ELECTRON

For our project, we built a package.json file. Now we'll use Electron to build our first desktop app.[5]

Make a new file named main.js. Fill in the following code:

```
const {app, BrowserWindow} = require('electron')
const url = require('url')
const path = require('path')

let win

function createWindow() {
    win = new BrowserWindow({width: 700, height: 500})
    win.loadURL(url.format ({
        pathname: path.join(__dirname, 'index.html'),
        protocol: 'file:',
        slashes: true
    }))
}

app.on('ready', createWindow)
```

Make a new file named index.html, this time in HTML. Enter the code below into it.

```
<!DOCTYPE html>
<html>
    <head>
        <meta charset = "UTF-8">
        <title>Hello Everyone!</title>
    </head>
```

```
<body>
    <h1>Hello Everyone!</h1>
    We are using the node <script>document.
write(process.versions.node)</script>,
    Chrome <script>document.write(process.versions.
chrome)</script>,
    and Electron <script>document.write(process.
versions.electron)</script>.
  </body>
</html>
```

Use the following command to launch this app:
```
$ electron ./main.js
```

HOW DOES THIS APP FUNCTION?

We made a primary file as well as an HTML file.

Two modules are used in the main file: app and BrowserWindow. The app module manages our application's event lifecycle, while the BrowserWindow module creates and manages browser windows. We built a createWindow function that creates a new BrowserWindow and associates it with a URL. When we launch the program, this is the HTML file that is rendered and shown to us. In our html file, we utilized a native Electron object process.

This object extends the Node.js process object, retaining all of its functionality but adding many more.

BUILDING UIs WITH ELECTRON

Electron applications' user interfaces are constructed using HTML, CSS, and JS.

As a result, we can use all of the existing tools for frontend web development here as well.

To create the applications, we may utilize technologies like Angular, Backbone, React, Bootstrap, and Foundation.[6]

We may handle these frontend dependencies using Bower. Bower should be installed via

```
$ npm install -g bower
```

Bower now provides access to all available JS and CSS frameworks, libraries, plugins, and so forth.

For example, to get the most recent stable version of bootstrap, use the following command:

```
$ bower install bootstrap
```

This will download the bootstrap component from bower components.

We may now use this library in our HTML. Let's build a basic page using these libraries.

Let us now use the npm command to install jquery.

```
$ npm install --save jquery
```

This will also be needed in our 'view.js' file. We already have a 'main.js' file as seen below.

```
const {app, BrowserWindow} = require('electron')
const url = require('url')
const path = require('path')

let win

function createWindow() {
    win = new BrowserWindow({width: 700, height: 500})
    win.loadURL(url.format ({
        pathname: path.join(__dirname, 'index.html'),
        protocol: 'file:',
        slashes: true
    }))
}
app.on('ready', createWindow)
```

Open our index.html file and add the following code:

```
<!DOCTYPE html>
<html>
    <head>
        <meta charset = "UTF-8">
        <title>Hello Everyone!</title>
        <link rel = "stylesheet"
            href = "./bower_components/bootstrap/dist/
css/bootstrap.min.css" />
    </head>

    <body>
        <div class = "container">
            <h1>This page use Bootstrap and jQuery!</h1>
            <h3 id = "click-counter"></h3>
            <button class = "btn btn-success" id =
"countbtn">Click</button>
            <script src = "./view.js" ></script>
        </div>
    </body>
</html>
```

Create a view.js file and add the click counter logic to it.

```
let $ = require('jquery')  // jQuery loaded and
assigned to $
let count = 0
$('#click-counter').text(count.toString())
$('#countbtn').on('click', () => {
    count ++
    $('#click-counter').text(count)
})
```

Use the following command to launch the app:

```
$ electron ./main.js
```

We may create our native app in the same way that we create webpages. If we do not want users to be limited to a certain window size, we may utilize responsive design to enable them to use our app in a flexible way.

In this chapter, we examined desktop apps built using electron.js, as well as their merits and downsides, as well as how to install electron.js.

NOTES

1 Building Desktop Apps with Electron and Vue: www.smashingmaga-zine.com/2020/07/desktop-apps-electron-vue-javascript/ Accessed on: 19 October 2022.

2 7 Famous Electron App Examples (JavaScript Desktop Apps): https://brainhub.eu/library/electron-app-examples Accessed on: 19 October 2022.

3 Why You Should Use an Electron Alternative: https://blog.logrocket.com/why-use-electron-alternative/ Accessed on: 19 October 2022.

4 Introducing the Electron.js Framework, Its Advantages and Disadvantages: https://ded9.com/introducing-the-electron-js-framework-its-advantages-and-disadvantages/ Accessed on: 20 October 2022.

5 Electron – Hello World: www.tutorialspoint.com/electron/electron_hello_world.htm Accessed on: 20 October 2022.

6 Electron – Building UIs: www.tutorialspoint.com/electron/electron_build-ing_uis.htm Accessed on: 20 October 2022.

CHAPTER 9

Appraisal

WHAT EXACTLY IS JAVASCRIPT?

JavaScript was first developed with the intention of "bringing online pages to life."

Scripts are what you name the programs written in this language. They may be written directly in the HTML of a web page and will execute themselves as soon as the page loaded.

Scripts are sent in plain text format and run in that format. They may be run without any further preparation or compilation being necessary.

JavaScript is a programming language that is executed on the client side of the web and may be used to create and program how web pages react when a certain event takes place. JavaScript is a popular choice since it is both accessible and strong as a programming language. It is most often used to control the behavior of web pages.

JavaScript is not 'Interpreted Java,' despite the widespread belief that this is what it is. JavaScript is a dynamic programming language that supports prototype-based object building. This is the gist of what JavaScript is. Because learning this language requires familiarity with a significant number of novel ideas, the fundamental grammar was designed to be conceptually comparable to Java and C++. Constructs of the language such as if statements, for and while loops, switch and try... catch blocks have the same functionality in each of these languages (or nearly so).

The programming language JavaScript may operate in both a procedural and an object-oriented mode. In contrast to the syntactic class declarations that are prevalent in compiled languages such as C++ and Java,

DOI: 10.1201/9781003356578-9

objects in JavaScript are formed programmatically. This is accomplished by adding methods and attributes to objects that are otherwise empty at the time of execution. After the construction of an item, that item might serve as a model (or prototype) for the construction of more items of the same kind.

JAVASCRIPT'S PAST AND ITS FUTURE

JavaScript was first developed by Brendan Eich in 1995 for use with Netscape Navigator, which was the most popular web browser at the time. JavaScript made it possible for web developers to create more dynamic websites by allowing for the modification of visual components on the screen in real time in response to the actions of site visitors. There were a number of name changes made over JavaScript's first half year of existence. It was at first known as Mocha, and afterward as LiveScript, before finally being given the name JavaScript.

In spite of its name, the programming language JavaScript has no connection to the Java programming language. This is a fun fact. The cooperation that existed between Netscape and Sun Microsystems, the company that was responsible for developing Java, led to the creation of the term.

These days, JavaScript is used for a far wider variety of purposes than only as a programming language for the web. Because it is a powerful and adaptable language that can be used in a number of different ways, you may write in JavaScript as you choose, whether you like imperative programming, a more object-oriented style, a functional approach, or even an event-driven model.

WHAT MAKES JAVASCRIPT UNIQUE?

At a minimum, JavaScript has the following three wonderful qualities:

- Complete incorporation of HTML and CSS.

- Things that are simple can be accomplished with ease.

- All of the main browsers provide support for it, and it is turned on by default.

JavaScript is the only technology available for browsers that combines all three of these features.

This is what sets JavaScript different from other languages. Because of this, it is the tool that is used the most often for the creation of browser interfaces.

Having stated that, JavaScript may be used in the creation of servers, mobile apps, and other types of software.

Languages That Are "Superior" To JavaScript

There are certain people for whom the syntax of JavaScript is not suitable. The preferences of various individuals might vary greatly.

This is to be anticipated given the fact that each person's projects and needs are unique to them.

Therefore, in recent times a variety of new languages have emerged; in order for these languages to operate in a browser, they must first be transpiled, or converted, to JavaScript.

These days, modern technologies make the translation process incredibly quick and easy to understand, which enables programmers to write code in one language while having it automatically converted 'under the hood.'

These languages are some examples:

- CoffeeScript is often referred to as the 'syntactic sugar' of JavaScript. It does this by introducing shorter syntax, which in turn enables us to create code that is more clear and exact. Ruby developers, on the whole, are fond of it.

- TypeScript is focused on implementing 'strict data typing' to facilitate the creation and maintenance of complicated systems. Microsoft is the company that created it.

- Data type is likewise added by Flow, but in a different manner. Facebook was the developer behind this.

- Dart is a standalone programming language that operates in non-browser settings (like mobile applications), but it can also be transpiled to JavaScript for use in browsers. Its engine runs natively on the Dart platform. Designed and built by Google.

- The use of Brython, which is a transpiler for Python to JavaScript, makes it possible to write apps in Python alone, without the need for JavaScript.

- Kotlin is a cutting-edge programming language that is terse, safe, and current. It may be used to target either the browser or Node.

There are further ones. Even if we utilize one of these transpiled languages, to fully grasp the situation, we still need to be well-versed in JavaScript.

In Comparison to Other Languages, JavaScript

When it was initially released, JavaScript was nothing more than an additional Turing-complete option that had been introduced to Netscape's browser. The majority of programmers laughed it off as a game, something that might be used to assess the accuracy of the information in the form or to add irritating popup windows. They missed the opportunity to seize the potential. Before it pushed forward-thinking features like lambdas and functions as first-class objects into the mainstream, not many people recognized the significance of the language's innovative characteristics.

It has been almost 20 years since then, and throughout that time, everything has changed. JavaScript serves as the basis for the vast majority of people's interactions with the computer world, which takes place via web apps. Programmers are increasingly turning to Node.js for greater performance as well as the ability to execute the same code on the server as they do on the client. As a result, even server applications are increasingly built in JavaScript.

The following is a quick comparison of JavaScript with some of the other main programming languages, written as a bulleted list for ease of reading.

JavaScript Contrasted with C

- Compilation of C takes place in advance. Just-in-time (JIT) compilers are used to understand JavaScript during runtime, and the language is also sometimes built at this point.

- C is statically typed. JavaScript is a dynamically typed programming language.

- The C programming language needs its users to create and release chunks of memory. This is taken care of automatically by JavaScript.

- When moving C code to a new processor, it is necessary to recompile the code. There is no need for JavaScript to be.

- Through the use of pointers, C is built to facilitate direct interaction with the memory of the computer. This ability is hidden behind JavaScript.

- C is a programming language that is often used for embedded computers and applications that call for high levels of performance, such as operating systems. In the beginning, JavaScript was only included in web pages, but now it is being used in Node.js server applications, which is a relatively new use for the technology.

- C provides users with explicit control over threads, but JavaScript encourages users to juggle several jobs by partitioning activities into asynchronous functions that are executed when data is available. C provides users with this level of control, whereas JavaScript does not.

The Contrast between Java and JavaScript

- Compilation of Java results in bytecode, which is an intermediate form that is later executed by a JIT compiler. In the past, JavaScript was only ever executed via an interpreter; however, these days, a JIT compiler is often used.

- To put it simply, Java is not a dynamically typed language, while JavaScript is a dynamically typed programming language.

- In contrast to JavaScript, Java is a tightly typed programming language.

- Java is built to serve massive applications and provides a strong namespace for these programs. JavaScript doesn't supply it directly, therefore programmers have synthesized it.

- Java was originally used in browsers as well as servers, although nowadays, it is mostly used on servers. Previously, JavaScript could only be executed in browsers; however, it is now very often employed on the server side.

- Java and JavaScript both support a wide variety of other languages. Cross-compilers are able to translate a wide variety of languages such that they may be executed on Java's JVM or JavaScript engines.

- Java 8 has included a method for embedding JavaScript, allowing the programming language to take use of numerous of JavaScript's advantages.

- Java provides the programmer with direct control over the threads. The call-and-response function structure of JavaScript helps to conceal a significant portion of this.

When Compared to C#, JavaScript Is

- The C# programming language is reduced down to a form called bytecode, which is an intermediate form that is later executed by a JIT compiler. Once upon a time, the only way to process JavaScript was via interpretation. These days, however, a JIT compiler is often used.

- JavaScript is dynamically typed, in contrast to the statically typed nature of C#.

- JavaScript is not highly typed, in contrast to C#, which is.

- JavaScript has different libraries that can cover this capability, one of which being Underscore.js. While C# has LINQ, a powerful.NET component that offers native data querying capabilities, JavaScript has independent libraries that can cover this feature.

- The computer language C# provides precise control over the threads. The call-and-response function structure of JavaScript helps to conceal a significant portion of this.

- Overloading of operators and conversions is available in C#. JavaScript does not.

JavaScript Compared to the Programming Language Python

- The initial purpose of JavaScript was to provide support for HTML sites inside browsers. Python was designed to be executed through the command line in order to enable server environments (and desktops).

- The communities that speak both languages are now much bigger. The field of social research has seen significant adoption of Python as a data processing language. There are now instances of JavaScript on servers and in other places.

- JavaScript denotes sections of code with brackets shaped like curly braces. Indentation and whitespace are used by Python.

- Python's argument blocks for methods may be as flexible as the user wants them to be, but JavaScript requires that every parameter be defined.

- The execution of JavaScript code is often triggered by events such as clicks of the mouse or keystrokes. Calls made to functions are acknowledged by Python.

- The processing and analysis of data are the primary emphases of many Python libraries, while the manipulation of HTML in a browser is the primary focus of many JavaScript tools.

When Compared to PHP, JavaScript Is

- Both of these scripting languages were initially interpreted at run-time, but nowadays, a JIT compiler is often used to do the necessary transformations.

- Both have variables that may be written dynamically.

- In the beginning, PHP was created to be used on servers to compile HTML pages, whereas JavaScript was meant to run inside of browsers on client computers. At this time, JavaScript is also capable of constructing HTML files on the server.

- PHP is almost never used for anything other than putting together HTML. The ever-more-complex interfaces in the browser and server-side stacks that integrate business logic and databases rely on JavaScript as their basis.

- PHP is a programming language that is designed to get data from databases and format it using HTML. It is a very straightforward language. JavaScript is evolving into a language that may be used for a wider range of applications, including general computing and interaction with browsers.

JavaScript Compared to the Programming Language Ruby

- In the past, operating JavaScript was restricted to the client's browser, whereas Ruby was executed on the server in conjunction with the Rails framework.

- The Ruby on Rails framework provides an inspiration for many of the principles that are used in JavaScript while it is executing in Node.js on the server.

- Ruby and JavaScript are both examples of dynamically typed programming languages.

- In Ruby, the term 'end' is used to denote the end of a block, while curly brackets are used in JavaScript.

- Ruby takes more of its syntax from Perl and Smalltalk, whereas JavaScript takes a significant portion of its syntax from Java and C.

- Ruby is mainly confined to server applications that use its Rails framework; nevertheless, some administrators like Ruby for their server-supporting command-line programs. On the other hand, JavaScript is transitioning to become a general-purpose programming language.

As can be seen, JavaScript diverges significantly from a good number of the other common programming languages. Its first version was created in only 10 days, but it included a number of forward-thinking improvements that allowed it to survive into the present decade. These innovations let it survive into the current decade.

There are many problems, yet, it seems that it will continue to be a key language for frontend developers for as long as it is the only language that all browsers understand.

Opportunities for Professional Development in JavaScript

Frontend Web Developer
It entails the construction of a user-facing and visually appealing portion of a website. This position will mostly include working with HTML, CSS, JavaScript, and a basic backend. You probably have a good understanding

of several ideas that go beyond the fundamental technologies, such as performance testing or regression testing.

The following is a list of the duties of a Frontend Developer:

- Develop new software applications from the idea to conclusion, including frequent testing and maintenance.

- In order to construct normal programs and libraries for the future applications.

- Ensure that the technical capabilities of the UI/UX design are met.

- Before sending any user inputs to the backend service team, it is imperative that all of those inputs be checked for authenticity.

- Collaborate with the other members of the team as well as the investors.

Designer and Developer of Web Applications

Developing software applications that run on the web, such as interactive online forms, shopping carts, word processing and spreadsheet programs, video and picture editors, file converter tools, scanning programs, and email software.

Desktop programs that are cross-platform are often created on platforms such as Adobe AIR, whereas ELECTRON makes use of JavaScript.

In the process of developing interactive web pages. It would be preferable to use a JavaScript framework such as jQuery that extends your JavaScript capabilities in order to make this JavaScript simpler.

This role is distinct from that of a Frontend Developer since there is less emphasis placed on design and more on the principles behind programming.

Developer Skilled in JavaScript

It is the responsibility of a JavaScript developer to connect this newly generated element with the services that are already in place on the backend. In most cases, the developer will get assistance from the backend web designer, who is liable for the whole of the server-side application logic. Together with other frontend web developers who focus on the application's HTML and aesthetics, a JavaScript developer often collaborates on projects with these colleagues. Programming and application development are the responsibilities of a JavaScript developer. In addition to that, he is accountable for

- Creating new features for, and improving, the primary frontend website platform.

- Developing new functions that are focused on the end user.

- Helping out with frontend work on other programs (HTML/CSS/JavaScript in Ruby and Python application), along with the designing and programming of new frontend applications for a variety of different platforms.

- Performing code analysis, analysis of requirements, analyses of system risk and software dependability, and identification of code metrics.

UX/UI Designer

It is the process of analyzing and investigating how people use a certain website. The next step is to test the outcome of the system after implementing improvements that will make it better. A rich earning potential may be attained by possessing knowledge of both user experience designing and JavaScript.

They are also quite proficient in the design tools of choice; however, their skill set may simply include HTML and CSS. In addition to being familiar with JavaScript, the employee should have expertise in interface design. The people who are responsible for the user interface might also be referred to as visual designers.

DevOps Engineer

This position helps to close the communication gap between IT and developers. In addition to that, they are investigating things like server software, version control, deployment, build procedures, and testing servers and processes.

The following is a list of the tasks of a DevOps Engineer:

- Putting out updates and addressing any technical problems that may have arisen.

- Developing tools to reduce the number of errors that users encounter while also enhancing their overall experience.

- Developing software to work in coordination with existing backend systems inside the organization.

- Carrying out an investigation into the underlying causes of production problems.

- Developing scripts in order to automate the process of visualization.

- Developing processes for debugging the system and doing general maintenance on it.

Developer Who Works on All Layers
It is comparable to the work done on the frontend and the backend. The company is looking for persons with very high levels of expertise, since this is a very prestigious position.

For the position of Full Stack Developer in JavaScript, the following responsibilities and competencies are required:

- Create a blueprint for the whole structure of the web application.

- Collaborating with the technical team to develop new features via design and testing.

- Having experience in developing for both mobile and desktop platforms is advantageous.

- The skills and understanding to secure sensitive information.

- Should have prior knowledge with languages used for backend development (Example: JavaScript, Ruby, PHP, Python, Java, .NET, etc.).

- A history of collaboration with graphic designers and experience translating concepts into visual components.

What Is the Most Appropriate Framework for JavaScript?
An abstraction, a web development framework enables software to offer broad functionality and be tailored in specific ways with the addition of user-written code. These modifications may be made in a variety of ways. One definition of a JavaScript framework is an application framework written in JavaScript that may be customized by developers for their own needs.

Because frameworks are more malleable for use in web design, the vast majority of website developers choose to work inside them. Frameworks simplify and streamline the process of working with JavaScript, opening up possibilities such as making apps more responsive to the device being used.

Therefore, Vanilla js is considered to be one of the greatest frameworks for JavaScript.

Vanilla js

Plain JavaScript is what's referred to as Vanilla js, and you'll notice that developers utilize Vanilla js to produce JavaScript code that doesn't need the assistance of any libraries. You will see that Vanilla js is a scripting language that does not impose any restrictions or guidelines on the developers about the manner in which the data in the application may be defined. There is a possibility that apps written with vanilla.js may not always provide the most optimal outcomes for the application.

You will see that Vanilla js is very popular among developers. This is because it is widely acknowledged as one of the simplest frameworks, making it accessible to developers of all levels.

Why Do We Believe That Frameworks Written in JavaScript Are so Awesome?

They alleviate your burden by simplifying the difficult and convoluted code.

They allow you to ship code more quickly and boost the pace of your work.

They challenge you to concentrate more on the value of your app rather than the execution of it.

Collaboration is, in our opinion, the JS framework that offers the best potential return on investment. Because of their standardized user interface and methodologies, software engineers from different countries, such as Canada, the United States, and Brazil, are able to communicate with one another and collaborate effectively.

When the time comes, you will be able to discover an experienced developer who can confidently step into the project codebase if you are creating an app using [insert your preferred framework]. This individual will be able to begin working on features without you having to spend time explaining every aspect of your software architecture to them.

Practice is yet another important reason why frameworks should be used. They will make you practice on and off throughout the day. That's fantastic news! Whatever it is that you're working for, mastery can only be achieved via consistent practice.

Appendix I

JavaScript Cheat Sheet

W E MUST JOIN THE JavaScript file to the HTML file in order to utilize JavaScript on the website. Including comments in the coding process will help us produce better code overall. One may use either single-line or multi-line comments.

- In order for the browser to recognize that your code is written in JavaScript and execute it, you must enclose the code in [delete] tags and paste it into your HTML page.

  ```
  <script type="text/javascript">
    // Your js code goes here
  </script>
  ```

- An outside JavaScript report also can be written one after the other and blanketed inside our HTML report the usage of the script tag as:

  ```
  <script src="filename.js"></script>
  ```

- JavaScript comments are very useful for explaining JavaScript code, understanding what is happening in the code, and making it easier to read.

1. Single-line comments: It starts with "//".

2. Multi-line comments: Enclose comments that span multiple lines with /* and */.

INSTANCES OF JAVASCRIPT VARIABLES

JavaScript variables are merely the names of data storage areas. As such, we may utilize them as surrogate values in our JavaScript programs and still accomplish a wide range of tasks. You have three options when working with variables in JavaScript.

- When it comes to JavaScript, var is by far the most used variable. Only inside the scope of a function may it be redeclared and its value transferred. Variables declared using var will rise to the top of the stack when the JavaScript code is executed. This is an example of a variable declared with the "var" keyword in JavaScript:

  var x = 140; // x may be redeclared and given a new value at any time

- To avoid unexpected results, const variables in JavaScript must be declared in the body of the code before they may be utilized. They cannot be redeclared or have their values changed in any way over the course of the program's execution. Listed below is an example of a JavaScript variable defined using the "const" keyword:

  const x = 5; // It's not possible to change the value of the variable x

- similar to the const variable, the let variable cannot be redeclared. However, their worth may be changed. The following is an example of a variable defined using the "let" keyword in JavaScript:

  let x = 202; // The variable x cannot be redeclared, although its value may be changed, as in let x = 202;

DATATYPES IN JAVASCRIPT

JavaScript variables may hold a wide variety of data. The equals (=) sign operator is used to assign values to variables in JavaScript. JavaScript supports the following data types:

- **Variables:** The variable data type may take on a wide range of values since, well, it's called a variable. Below is an example of a variable's data type: var y

- **Strings:** Multi-character sequences of varying lengths that make up JavaScript's string data type. You can see how the string data type is used in the following code snippet: var demoString = "Hello World."

- **Numbers:** These are only figures. All integers and real numbers are equally acceptable. Here's an example of the numeric data type in action: var id = 100

- **Operations:** You may also attach operations in JavaScript to variables.

- **Objects:** Objects in JavaScript are storage locations for a set of named values known as properties. They are responsible for their own informational components and procedures. Below is an example of the objects data type: var name = "name:"Jon Snow", id:"AS123"

- **Boolean value:** A Boolean value is one that may be either true or false. Below is a code snippet demonstrating the use of the boolean data type: var booleanValue = true.

- **Constant numbers:** Data types with a constant value are called "constant numbers." The following is an instance of the constant data type: const g = 9.8

OPERATORS OF JAVASCRIPT

You can use JavaScript operators on variables to perform a wide range of operations. These are the numerous kinds of operators that may be used in JavaScript:

JavaScript's fundamental operators allow for elementary arithmetic operations like addition and multiplication to be carried out. Here is an index of all JavaScript's primitive operators:

- To add two integers together, use the plus sign (+).

- To do a subtraction operation, utilize the "Subtraction Operator (–)."

- Multiple numbers may be multiplied with the help of the MultiplicationOperator (*).

- In order to do a division, we need to utilize the Division Operator (/).

- By enclosing an expression or sub-expression in parenthesis with the (...) grouping operator, the order of evaluation of the operators is changed such that the ones with lower precedence are evaluated first.

- When dividing by another integer, the residual may be found with the help of the Modulus operator (%).

- To add one to an integer, use the Increment operator (++).

- When using the Decrement operator (--), the value of a number is reduced by 1.

Bitwise Operators

Using JavaScript's bitwise operators, you can execute any operation that involves a number's bits. Here's a rundown of all the bitwise operators available in JavaScript:

- The bitwise AND operator, (&), produces a result of 1 for every bit location where the corresponding bits in both operands are 1.

- Wherever bits in each or both operands are 1, the bitwise OR operator (|) delivers a 1.

- Bitwise NOT is an operator (~) that flips the bits in the operand. Like other bitwise operators, it converts the operand to a signed 32-bit integer.

- Each bit location in which the corresponding bits of both operands are 1s but not both is returned by the bitwise XOR operator (^).

- The left shift operator (≪) moves the bits of the first operand to the left by the amount specified.

- By providing a positive integer, the right shift operator (≫) will shift the first operand to the right by that many bits.

Comparison Operators

JavaScript has a number of comparison operators, all of which are listed below.

- Whenever its two operands are equal, the equality operator (==) will return a true or false result.

- When its two operands are of the same type and equal in value, the equivalent operator (===) returns a Boolean.

- The inequality operator (!=) returns a boolean if the two operands are not equal.

- If the two operands are not the same type, or if they are not equal, the inequal operator (!==) will return a Boolean result.

- In JavaScript, only the conditional (ternary) operator accepts three operands: a condition followed by a question mark (**?**), an expression to run if the condition is true followed by a colon (:), and a final expression to execute if the condition is false.

- If the left operand has a smaller value than the right operand, then the Lesser than operator (<) will return true.

- The (>=) operator evaluates to true if and only if the left operand is greater than or equal to the right operand.

- Less-than-or-equal-to (=) is an equality operator (<=) that evaluates to true if the left operand is less than or equal to the right operand.

Logical Operators

The whole set of JavaScript logical operators is as follows:

- The logical AND operator (**&&**) for a collection of Boolean operands evaluates to true if and only if all of the operands are true.

- The logical OR (logical disjunction) operator (**||**) indicates that a set of operands is true if and only if any of the operands is true.

- The NOT operator (logical complement, negation) (**!**) turns the truth into a lie.

JAVASCRIPT FUNCTION

A function in JavaScript is a predefined piece of code that may be used to accomplish a certain goal. As soon as it is called or invoked, it begins running. To save retyping the same code again and over, you may save it as a function and call it as necessary. The functions keyword in JavaScript is used to define new functions. JavaScript is capable of many things, including:

FUNCTION AND DESCRIPTION

parseInt(): It is a function that takes a string and returns an integral value that represents the string.

parseFloat() is a function that takes an input and returns a floating-point representation of that value.

isNaN(): To test whether a value is Not a Number, programmers may use the isNaN() method.

Number(): This function, called Number(), takes an input and returns the corresponding number.

eval(): JavaScript code in string form may be evaluated using the eval() method.

prompt(): Use the prompt() method to generate a text box asking the user for input.

encodeURI(): Using this method, you may convert a URI to the Unicode (UTF-8) format.

match() is a built-in JavaScript function that can be used to check if a string matches a given regular expression.

ARRAY IN JAVASCRIPT

It's common practice in many languages to store data in arrays. They may be used to classify things like variables and characteristics. An array is a sequence of items all of the same kind. A collection of automobiles, written in JavaScript:

var cars = ["Tesla", "Toyota", "Honda"];

With our newfound knowledge of array construction, we can apply various transformations to the resulting data. Check out the many APIs in JavaScript for manipulating arrays:

- **push():** It is utilized at the end of an array for adding a new element.

- **pop():** It is for eliminating the last element of the array.

- **concat():** It is used to join several arrays into one.

- **splice():** It is used for adding elements in a particular way and position.

- **shift():** It is for eliminating the first element of the array.

- **reverse():** It is used for preserving the order of the elements in the array.

- **slice():** It is for pulling a copy of a part of an array into a new array.

- **unshift():** It is utilized for adding new elements at the starting of the array.

- **toString():** It is used for converting the array elements into strings.

- **valueOf():** It is used for returning the primitive value of the given object.

- **join():** It is used for combining elements of an array into one single string and then returning it.

- **lastIndexOf():** It is used for returning the final index at which a given element appears in an array.

- **sort():** It is used for sorting the array elements based on some condition.

- **indexOf():** It is used for returning the first index at which a given element is found in an array.

STRINGS IN JAVASCRIPT

Strings, as we've already established, are just sequences of characters that may be put to various uses. Since Strings are so versatile in JavaScript, we've decided to devote their own section to them in this reference guide. Let's have a look at JavaScript's string functions and the numerous escape sequences it supports.

In the fields of computers and communications, a 'special character' known as a 'escape character' is a character that, when followed by other characters in a string, alters the meaning of those characters. Escape characters make up a subset of the metacharacters that are available. The surrounding context of a character will determine whether or not that character may be used as an escape character. To encapsulate strings, JavaScript may use either single quotes or double quotes. You will need to make use of special characters in order to include quote marks into a string. For instance, the following is a selection of escape sequences that might be used in JavaScript:

- \\—Backslash

- \"—Double quotes

- \'—Single quotes

- \t—Horizontal tab

- \n—Newline

- \v—Vertical tab

- \r—Carriage return

- \b—Backspace

- \f—Form feed

DOM, OR THE JAVASCRIPT DOCUMENT OBJECT MODEL

A website's code is arranged according to the Document Object Model (DOM). JavaScript has a large range of options for building and changing HTML components, which may be accessed via the language (called nodes).

Node Properties

Let's start with an examination of some of the attributes of a node in the JavaScript DOM:

- **attributes:** Obtains a real-time collection of all the attributes of an element.

- The **baseURI** attribute, when applied to an HTML element, will return the element's primary URI.

- **childNodes:** Provides access to an element's child nodes as a list.

- **firstChild:** Returns the first child node of the element.

- **lastChild:** The last child node of an element.

- **nextSibling:** Node at the same level in the tree as the current node is returned by nextSibling.

- **nodeName:** The name of a node is returned by calling the node-Name method.

- **nodeType:** Obtains the node's type and returns it.

- **nodeValue:** A node's value can be set or retrieved using the node-Value method.

- **ownerDocument** is the root document object of this node.

- **Parent Node:** This function returns the Node that is the parent of the current element.

- **previousSibling:** Using the previousSibling technique, this command retrieves the node that came before the current node in the tree.

- **textContent:** Stores or retrieves the textual content of a node and its children.

Node Methods

Let's look at some of the Node Methods supplied by JavaScript to work with these DOM nodes:

- **appendChild():** A new child node is appended to an element as its final child node using the appendChild() method.

- In HTML, **cloneNode()** is a function used to create a copy of an existing node.

- The **compareDocumentPosition()** method is used to examine the similarities and differences between the document locations of two elements.

- The feature's APIs are implemented by the object returned by **getFeature()**.

- **hasAttributes():** Whether the element contains characteristics is determined by the value returned.

- If an element has any child nodes, the **hasChildNodes()** method will return true, otherwise it will return false.

- An additional child node is inserted to the left of the current node using the **insertBefore()** method.

- If the passed-in namespaceURI is the default, **isDefaultNamespace()** will return true; otherwise, it will return false.

- Function to test if two nodes are equivalent **isEqualNode()**.

- If two elements have the same node, **isSameNode()** returns true.

- A feature can be tested to see if it is supported by calling the **isSupported()** method on the element.

- The **lookupNamespaceURI()** method gets the namespace URI for a given node and returns it.

- For a given namespace URI, **lookupPrefix()** will return a DOMString with the prefix if it exists.

- The **normalise()** method merges adjacent text nodes in an element and gets rid of any that are empty.

- Child() method's **removeChild()** method removes a child node from an element.

Element Methods

This function substitutes a child node of an element with another.

Here are a few examples of the element methods available in JavaScript:

- The **getAttribute()** method retrieves the attribute's value from a node in an element.

- Input a namespace and the name of an attribute, and **getAttributeNS()** will return that attribute's value as a string.

- When called, getAttributeNode() will give you back the node you passed in as an attribute.

- The **getAttributeNodeNS()** function retrieves the attribute node associated with the given namespace and attribute name.

- This function, called "**getElementsByTagName()**," returns a collection of all child elements with the specified tag name.

- When called with a tag name, **getElementsByTagNameNS()** returns a live HTMLCollection of elements from the given namespace.

- With **hasAttribute()** if the element has attributes it returns true, otherwise false.

- **hasAttributeNS()** evaluates whether the given attribute is present on the current element in the given namespace and returns true or false accordingly.

- The **removeAttribute()** method is used to get rid of an attribute from an element.

- Invoking **removeAttributeNS()** on an element in a given namespace will remove that attribute from that element.

- To set or alter an attribute node, use **setAttributeNode()**.

- Adding a new namespaced attribute node to an element is as simple as calling **setAttributeNodeNS()**.

TRANSFORM DATA USING JAVASCRIPT

Using higher-order functions, data transformation is possible in JavaScript. Functions that take in other functions as arguments and return another function are said to be higher-order functions in JavaScript. Map(), Filter(), and Reduce are the Only Higher-Order Functions That Accept Functions as an Input (). Now, let's examine the applications of these features. All of these operations can be performed on arrays without resorting to any intermediate variables or collections because they are built into the JavaScript Array prototype.

map() Method

A function is applied to each array element using the map() method. The array's contents are passed one by one to the callback method, which then generates a new array with the same dimensions. This function can be used to apply a uniform operation or transformation to each array element and return a new array of the same length containing the resultant updated values.

filter() Method

The filter() method is used to delete data from an array if it does not match a certain condition. Each item in the array is passed along to the callback function. The element will be added to the new array if and only if the callback function returns true after each iteration.

reduce() Method

It is possible to combine the results of many members of an array into a single value by using the reduce() function. Prior to making a call to reduce, the starting value of the accumulator is required to be supplied (final result). In the course of each cycle, we carry out an operation in the callback, and the results of that operation are accumulated in a variable.

Date Objects

In JavaScript, the date object is a built-in datatype. Dates and times can be managed and modified with its help. The new Date() operator is used to construct date objects, which can be declared in 1 of the 4 possible ways.

Syntax

new Date()
new Date(milliseconds)
new Date(dataString)
new Date(year, month, date, hour, minute, second, millisecond)

JavaScript provides a number of functions for accessing and generating date and time information. These strategies include, but are not limited to:

Method and Description

- This function, called '**getDate()**,' returns a numeric representation of the day inside a given month (1–31).

- Using **getTime()**, you may find out how many milliseconds have passed since January 1, 1970.

- **getMinutes()** is the function that gets the current minute (0–59).

- The current year, in four digits, can be retrieved with the help of the **getFullYear()** function (yyyy).

- **getDay()** gives you back a number from 0 to 6 that represents the day of the week.

- **parse()** takes a date in string form and returns the number of milliseconds since January 1, 1970.

- In numerical form, **setDate()** gives you today's date (1–31).

- When the time needs to be changed, use the **setTime()** function (milliseconds since January 1, 1970).

JAVASCRIPT BROWSER OBJECTS

In addition to HTML components, JavaScript may also monitor the user's browser behavior and incorporate its properties into the code.

A number of Window attributes that JavaScript can use are detailed below.

- **window.history:** Returns the History object for the window.

- **innerHeight:** The window's internal height in pixels.

- **innerWidth:** The width of the content area's innermost margin.

- **closed:** If a window has been closed, closed will return true, otherwise it will return false.

- **pageXOffset:** The pixel distance from the page's center. It appears that you have used your mouse to scroll horizontally across this page.

- **pageYOffset:** The vertical distance in pixels from the page's center. A vertical scroll was made in the document.

- **navigator:** the window's Navigator object (navigator) is returned.

- **opener:** Using opener will return a pointer to the parent window that initiated the current window's creation.

- **outerHeight:** The overall height of the window, including the title bar and any toolbars.

- **outerWidth:** The total width of a window, including the borders and any other components.

- **defaultStatus:** If you want to modify or restore the status bar's default text, use the defaultStatus command.

- **document:** The document object associated with the current window is returned.

- **frames:** This will return every iframe in the current window.

- **location:** Brings back the location object for the window.

- **name:** Specifies or returns the window's label.

- **parent:** This refers to the window that is the parent of the active window.

- **screen:** Obtains the Screen object for the current window.

- **screenLeft:** The left horizontal position of the window (relative to the screen).

- **screenTop:** The top vertical position of the window.

- **self:** Returns the active window.

- **status:** To modify or restore the text in a window's status bar, use the status command.

- **top:** Brings back the window that's at the top of the screen in your browser.

- **screenX** is equivalent to the standard screenLeft attribute, but is necessary in specific browsers.

- **screenY** is equivalent to screenTop but is required by some browsers.

The following are some examples of JavaScript methods that can be used in the user's browser:

- To warn the user and provide them the option to dismiss the warning, the **alert()** method presents a dialogue box.

- You may often test out an expression or run a function with the help of the **setInterval()** method.

- **setTimeout():** After a given amount of time has elapsed, a function or expression is executed.

- To stop a timer that was set with setInterval(), use **clearInterval()**.

- When called, **clearTimeout()** will cancel any timers that were previously created using setTimeout() ().

- With **open()**, a new tab or window will open in your browser.

- The **print()** function prints the contents of the active window.

- Removes the focus from the active window via the **blur()** function.

- With **moveBy()**, you can reposition a window relative to its current location.

- Using the **moveTo()** method, you can relocate a window to a new position.

- If you use **close()** on a window, it will close and the program will exit.

- **confirm():** invokes a dialog box containing a message and OK and Cancel buttons.

- The **focus()** function is used to concentrate the active window.

- The **scrollBy()** method will move the document down by the specified number of pixels.

- The **scrollTo()** method takes a pair of x, y coordinates and scrolls the document to that location.

- **prompt():** Displays a dialogue box requesting input from the site visitor.

- Input a number of pixels, then **resizeBy()** will make that amount the new width and height of the window.

- **resizeTo()** Sets the window's width and height to the parameters you provide.

- The **stop()** function cancels the loading of the current window.

This section provides a list of Screen attributes that can be considered by JavaScript.

    height: The full vertical distance of the display.

    screen width: The total horizontal distance between two adjacent display elements.

    colorDepth: Gives back the bit depth for each palette color.

availableHeight: Returns the height of the display when available-Height is called (excluding the Windows Taskbar).

availableWidth: Replies with the width of the display.

ALGEBRA AND COMPUTATION

A number of Number and Math-related properties and methods are available in JavaScript.

Some of the characteristics of numbers are their maximum or minimum values, whether they are positive or negative infinity, or whether they are NAN (not a number). JavaScript provides a variety of functions for working with numeric values, including:

- **valueOf()** It gives back the raw form of a number.

- the **toString()** method converts an integer into a string.

- **toFixed()** returns the string representation of a number with the given precision.

- It takes an integer and returns a string of a given length using the **toPricision()** method.

- Use **toExponential()** to get a string representation of a rounded number in exponential form.

The number manipulation is simplified thanks to the mathematical functions provided by the math object of the JavaScript programming language. Mathematical objects have a variety of numerical properties, such as the logarithm, Euler's number, the square root, and the square root of PI. The following is a list of some of the mathematical property manipulation tools that are available via JavaScript:

- Returns the greatest value in a range **max(x, y, z…n)**.

- The function **min(x, y, z,…)** returns the least-significant of a given set of numbers.

- To get the exponential value of x, just type **exp(x)**.

- Natural logarithm (in base E) of x; **log(x)** returns this value.

- To get the square root of an input value, use the function **sqrt(x)**.

- The result of calling **pow(x, y)** is x raised to the yth power.

- **round(x)**: It adjusts x to the next whole number.

- When you type **sin(x)**, you get x's sine value back (x is in radians).

- the tangent of an angle is given by **tan(x)**, which in this case would be x.

Appendix II
Brief Guide to TypeScript

T HE INCORPORATION OF STATIC types into JavaScript is one of the many features that TypeScript brings to the table, making it much simpler for us to build large applications.

JavaScript was created to be utilized by a wide variety of people, including software developers as well as individuals who are not developers. It was made to be user-friendly and straightforward enough so that even inexperienced people could comprehend it. This ultimately resulted in the establishment of a magnificent language for the production of prototypes and projects on a scale that falls in between small and large. Programming with JavaScript, on the other hand, might be difficult to scale up when it comes to the building of large applications. This is mostly due to the fact that the components of our application cannot have their contracts specified openly.

AN OUTLINE OF THE TYPESCRIPT PAST

JavaScript, which is also known as ECMAScript, was a straightforward programming language for online browsers that was where it all started. At the time that it was being created, it was thought that it would be used for small snippets of code that would be embedded in a web page. Writing more than a few hundred lines of code would have been regarded pretty strange at the time. Because of this, the execution of this kind of code was carried out by older versions of web browsers in a somewhat sluggish manner. On the other hand, throughout the course of time, JS has amassed a greater following, and web developers have begun using it in order to create interactive experiences.

The developers of web browsers responded to the increasing demand for JS by enhancing the performance of their execution engines via dynamic compilation and expanding the range of uses for the language (adding APIs). Web developers were thus motivated to use it even more as a result of this. When you go to modern websites, your web browser is probably running programs that include tens of thousands to hundreds of thousands of lines of code. This happens every time you go to a new page. This exemplifies the gradual and consistent development of what we now refer to as 'the web,' which started out as a simple network of static pages but has now grown into a platform on which a wide variety of complex applications may be executed.

In addition, JS has garnered sufficient popularity to be used in situations other than browsers, such as the development of JS servers via the use of node.js. This is an example of how JS has expanded its application outside the realm of browsers. Because it can be used on any platform, JS is a fantastic choice for developing applications that can be used across several platforms. The majority of today's workforce in the information technology industry writes all of their stack code in JavaScript.

FOUNDATIONAL ELEMENTS OF TYPESCRIPT

The language, the compiler, and the language service may be considered the three primary pillars upon which Typescript is founded.

Language of TypeScript

- This includes the syntax of TypeScript, as well as its keywords and type annotations.

- The syntax of TypeScript is comparable to, but not identical to, the syntax of JavaScript.

Compiler for TypeScript

- The TypeScript code must first be compiled into JavaScript before the compiler may begin its work.

- In fact, what takes place is not exactly compilation but rather transpilation.

- It is also the job of the TypeScript compiler to delete any information that is connected to types while the program is being compiled.

In JavaScript, types are not regarded as genuine features since they are not used. Because TypeScript has to be changed into regular JavaScript first, everything that has to do with types has to be removed before the code can be regarded genuine JavaScript and submitted to the browser to be executed. This is because TypeScript has to be converted into normal JavaScript.

In addition to this, the Typescript compiler is responsible for doing code analysis. Errors and warnings will be generated if there is a sufficient foundation for the system to do so.

Language Department

The task of extracting type information from the source code is within the purview of the language service.

The development tools may use this information to give IntelliSense type suggestions, and alternative refactorings once they have processed it.

A STATIC TYPE CHECKER DEFINED BY TYPESCRIPT

Earlier, we said that there are some programming languages that would never, under any circumstances, permit the execution of programs that include defects. Static checking is the method of discovering errors in computer code without actually running the program itself. The process of identifying whether or not something constitutes an error based on the kinds of values that are being acted on is referred to as 'static type checking,' and it is referred to as 'checking' for short.

Because TypeScript does its error checking before the execution of a program by examining the various kinds of values, it is referred to as a static type checker. For instance, there is an error in the very last example that was provided before because of the kind of object. The error that TypeScript pointed out is as described below:

```
const obj = { width: 10, height: 15 };
const area = obj.width * obj.heigth;
```

Property 'height' does not exist on type '{ width: number; height: number; }'. Did you mean 'height'?Property 'height' does not exist on type '{ width: number; height: number; }'. Did you mean 'height'?

A Typed Expansion of the JavaScript Language

However, what is the connection between TypeScript and JavaScript?

Syntax

How we compose text into the shape of a program is referred to as its syntax. As TypeScript is a superset of JavaScript, it is compatible with the syntax of JS. To provide just one example, this line of code has a syntax error since it is missing an a):

```
let a = (4
')' expected.')' expected.
```

There is no JavaScript code that will be flagged as an error by TypeScript due to the language's grammar. This indicates that you can take any functional JavaScript code and place it in a TypeScript file without worrying about how the code is written.

Types

TypeScript, on the other hand, is a typed superset that extends the rules that control how different kinds of values may be applied. It does this by extending the rules that govern how values are applied. The issue that had been occurring before with obj.height was not due to a syntax error; rather, it was an error that happened as a result of the incorrect application of some sort of value (a type).

Another example of this would be the piece of JavaScript code that follows, which, when run in a web browser, would record a value as follows:

```
console.log(4 / []);
```

This grammatically correct software keeps track of infinity. TypeScript, on the other hand, will throw an error if you try to divide a number by an array since it deems this to be a meaningless operation.

```
console.log(4 / []);
```

On the right side of an arithmetic operation, you are free to use any type that is numeric, bigint, or enum. On the right hand side of an arithmetic operation, you may use a type that begins with "any," "number," or "bigint," or you can use an enum type.

There is a chance that dividing a number by an array was not something you intended to do. It is possible that you intended to divide a number by an array, maybe to find out what would happen if you did so, but in the vast majority of situations, this is a mistake in the code. The objective of the built-in type checker in TypeScript is to allow correct programs to execute while identifying as many common programming errors as is reasonably possible under the circumstances.

When you move some code from a JavaScript file to a TypeScript file, you can discover type issues in the TypeScript file depending on how the code was written in the JavaScript file. It's conceivable that these are legitimate problems with the code, but it's also possible that TypeScript is being too cautious for no good reason. In this post, we will demonstrate how to include a range of TypeScript syntax in order to eliminate errors such as these.

Behavior During Runtime

While JavaScript is being performed, another programming language known as TypeScript keeps the functionality that JavaScript provides intact. In JavaScript, for example, the operation of division by zero produces the value infinite rather than causing an error to occur during the execution of the program. The execution of JavaScript code will not be affected in any significant way by TypeScript, as a general rule.

Because of this, when you migrate code from JavaScript to TypeScript, even if TypeScript deems the code to have type errors, it is assured that the code will run in the same manner as it did in JavaScript. Both JavaScript and TypeScript make use of the same grammar, which is why this is the case.

One of the most important guarantees made about TypeScript is that it will keep the same runtime behavior as JavaScript. This indicates that you will be able to transition between the two languages in a smooth manner without having to worry about any little modifications that may cause your application to stop operating properly.

Erased Types

When the TypeScript compiler has completed checking your code and is ready to build the "compiled" version of the code, it will often erase all of the types. This is done in preparation for the next step in the process. This indicates that the simple JS code that is created when your code is compiled does not contain any type information.

Since of this, TypeScript will never change the way your program works based on the types it has derived from the data you supply because it can't access that information. The most important thing to remember is that even while you may see type difficulties during the compilation process, the type system does not in and of itself have any bearing on how your program functions when it is being run. This is the bottom line.

In conclusion, the package that contains TypeScript does not include any additional runtime libraries. Because your apps will utilize the same standard library (or more libraries) as JavaScript programs, there is no additional TypeScript-specific framework that you will need to learn how to use. This is because your applications will use the same libraries.

TYPESCRIPT'S PRIMARY ATTRIBUTES AND FUNCTIONS

TypeScript's Support for Type Annotations

The process of assigning a type to a variable or function is what is known as type annotation.

```
const birthdayGreeter = (name: string, age: number):
string => {
return 'Happy birthday ${name}, you are now ${age}
years old!';
};

const birthdayHero = "Jane User";
const age = 22;
console.log(birthdayGreeter(birthdayHero, 22));
```

The above example shows how to construct a function with two arguments: name and age. We give the name field a type of string and the age field a type of number.

The value that is returned by a function may also have types assigned to it. In this particular instance, our function is going to return a value of the string data type.

```
const birthdayGreeter=(name: string, age: number):
string => { };
```

If we sent in arguments of a type that was different from the type that Typescript anticipates, we would get an error.

TypeScript's Support for Structural Typing

The programming language TypeScript is a structurally typed language, which means that in order for two items to be deemed to be of the same type, they must have equivalent and similar properties.

Inference of Type Utilizing TypeScript

In the event that no explicit type is supplied, the TypeScript compiler may make an attempt, based on its own logic, to infer the type information. This suggests that TypeScript is able to give a type to a variable or function based on the initial values of the variable or the application of the function, respectively.

When you create variables, set default values, or figure out the type of the result that a function should return, you are most likely engaging in some kind of type inference.

```
const platform = 'freeCodeCamp';
const add = (a: number, b: number) => a + b
```

In the example that was just shown, the variable platform is given the type string even though we did not do so explicitly. Additionally, the return value of the function add is assumed to have the type number.

Deleted Characters in TypeScript

During compilation, TypeScript eliminates the following constructs of the type system:

Input
let x: someType;

Output
let x;

WHY SHOULD YOU USE TYPESCRIPT?

Checking for Typos and Doing Static Analysis of the Code

Since of this, the total number of faults in your code will decrease overall because TS will alert you whenever you make an incorrect usage of a particular type.

Runtime errors are also reduced, and since TypeScript does static code analysis, you will get warnings if any typos or other issues are found in your code. Therefore, there will be fewer mistakes, which might lead to testing being reduced in scope.

Annotations on Types May Serve in Place of Documentation for Code

Because of annotations on types, we are able to comprehend, for instance, what kinds of inputs a function anticipates receiving and what kinds of outcomes it will return. In addition, we are able to comprehend what kinds of outputs the function will deliver.

This makes the code easier to read, which in turn makes it simpler not just for ourselves but also for others to comprehend what the code is intended to do.

Users of integrated development environments (IDEs) are able to get more accurate and insightful IntelliSense feedback while using TypeScript, which is another benefit of utilizing this programming language. This is made feasible by the fact that IDEs are aware of the particular kind of data that the user is currently processing, which enables this functionality.

STARTING OUT WITH TYPESCRIPT: A CRASH COURSE

Installing the TypeScript package is where we should get started. In this situation, we have two choices: we can either install it globally so that we can use it on any project in the system, or we can install it locally so that we can use it just on the project that we are now working on.

By executing the following command, you will be able to install TypeScript globally:

```
npm install -g typescript
```

If you do not want to install anything worldwide, you need to perform this command:

```
npm install --save-dev typescript
```

Because we find it useful throughout the development process, TypeScript was included in the local installation as a development dependency. First, it has to be compiled to JavaScript before it can be used in production. The TypeScript language cannot be executed in the browser.

After TypeScript has been installed, the first step in getting started is to create a new project. You are able to do this by using the following command:

```
tsc --init
```

With the execution of this command, a brand-new tsconfig.json file will be created in the project's parent directory. This configuration file includes all the configuration settings available to us when we use TypeScript in a project.

You may provide all of the build settings for a given project in the tsconfig.json file under the compileOptions key. This file is located in the root directory of the project.

There are certain config settings already included in the file, but you have the ability to add additional options to the project if necessary. You may comment out or eliminate unneeded compiler options.

Establishing the Baselines for Your TypeScript Development Environment

Setting Up Your Development Environment

Code Editor   You need an integrated development environment (IDE) that supports TypeScript to use all the capabilities that TypeScript has to offer. Although we suggest Visual Studio Code (which is also designed in TypeScript), you may use any integrated development environment (IDE) that supports TypeScript.

Node.js and npm   Each of the projects described in this book calls on a functional Node.js development environment, in addition to using npm.

When you install Node.js, a JavaScript package management called npm is automatically installed on your computer. Open a new terminal window and put in the following command to determine whether or not npm is compatible with your development environment.

```
$ npm -v
```

If an error is shown or a version number is not written out, be sure you download a Node.js installation that contains npm.

Beginning the Process   Launch a terminal and go to the directory that will serve as the project's storage location for its files. Moving forward, we will be putting new files into the directory containing our project. In the following instances, the root folder of our project will be referred to as FinanceMe since we will be utilizing that name throughout.

Start with the package.json Initialization   Our project's package.json file includes essential information, such as the list of dependencies that must be installed, and is located in the corresponding directory.

Executing the following command will result in our package.json being initialized:

```
$ npm init --yes
```

Install the TypeScript# Language
Simply enter the following line into your terminal to install the most recent version of TypeScript:

```
$ npm install --save-dev typescript
```

The tsc (TypeScript compiler) version number will be shown in the output of the following command if the installation was completed successfully:

```
$ npx tsc -v
```

Install ts-node   ts-node is a tool that allows TypeScript applications to be executed straight from the terminal. This eliminates the need to compile. ts files to.js files and then execute the produced files, which is the procedure that would normally be required.

Execute the following command in order to install the most recent version of ts-node:

```
$ npm install --save-dev ts-node
```

The ts-node version number will be shown if the installation has completed successfully by using the following command:

```
$ npx ts-node -v
```

The ts-node command operates in a manner that is similar to that of the node command. If the command is given the name of a file, then that file will be executed, and the program will terminate after the file has completed its execution. We will be put in interactive mode if we do not provide the command with a file name. This mode allows us to import modules and perform TypeScript commands while they are being executed in real time. The interactive mode is very helpful for testing pieces of code that are just a few lines long.

Execute the following command in order to begin the interactive mode:

```
$ npx ts-node
```

Since we are now in the interactive mode, we will be able to execute code in real time. In the following example, we will do a straightforward computation, and the result will be printed:

```
$ 10 + 30 + 2
> 42
$ const today = new Date()
$ today.getFullYear()
> 2019
```

It is important to take note that we may define variables and utilize them throughout the session. Additionally, we do not need to report stuff directly by using the console.log() function since the result of the statement being run will be written automatically.

You may enter editor mode to copy and paste a block of code or to alter code that spans numerous lines. When you do so, execution will be paused until you simultaneously click the CTRL and D keys.

```
$ npx ts-node
$.editor
$ /*
* code can span multiple lines
* will run when you press CTRL+D
*/
```

You may quit interactive mode by using CTRL+C or by simply typing.exit followed by pressing enter on your keyboard.

Initialize tsconfig.json   Our integrated development environment (IDE) and the ts-node will use the key compiler information stored in the tsconfig.json file.

In the directory of the project, create a file called tsconfig.json and include the following settings in it:

```
{
"compilerOptions": {
"target": "es6",
"module": "commonjs",
"typeRoots": ["./node_modules/@types"],
"esModuleInterop": true,
"forceConsistentCasingInFileNames": true
}
}
```

Further discussion of each compiler option will be provided in the next chapter, titled "Compiler Options," but in the meanwhile, here is a quick description of what each of the aforementioned settings does:

- **target:** This option allows you to choose the version of ECMAScript the compiler will use when producing JavaScript files. We are able to use all of the capabilities that were added in ES6/ES2015 as a result of setting this to es6.

- **module:** This option allows you to specify the module system being used in the code being created. We have confirmed that our code is capable of running in Node.js by setting this to the commonjs value.

- **typeRoots** is an option that allows you to specify the directory in which TypeScript should look for global types. In order to avoid inadvertently inheriting types from parent directories, we configure it here to point to our own node modules/@types directory (which is the default behavior).

- **esModuleInterop**: This option guarantees that CommonJS and ES Modules are compatible with one another and is referred to as esModuleInterop.

- **forceConsistentCasingInFileNames**: We may use an option to guarantee that we do not bring defects into the system by inadvertently importing a module with the wrong case.

- Because VSCode and ts-node will automatically discover a tsconfig.json if it is there, there is no need to make any adjustments to any of these programs.

TYPESCRIPT FOR DEVELOPERS WORKING IN JAVASCRIPT

The connection between TypeScript and JavaScript is not what one may expect. TypeScript provides all of the functionality that JavaScript does, in addition to an extra layer on top of these features called the type system for TypeScript.

JavaScript, for instance, offers language primitives such as strings and numbers, but the programming language does not verify to ensure that you have consistently allocated them. TypeScript does.

This indicates that the JavaScript code you have already written that is functioning properly is also valid TypeScript code. The primary advantage of using TypeScript is that it reduces the likelihood of errors by pointing out areas of your code that exhibit unexpected behavior.

Types Deduced from Inference

TypeScript is familiar with the JavaScript programming language and can, in many instances, automatically create types for you. For instance, when a variable is created in TypeScript and a specific value is assigned to it, TypeScript will utilize the value as the variable's type.

```
let helloWorld = "Hello World";
let helloWorld: string
```

TypeScript can construct a type system compatible with JavaScript code but also has types since it understands how JavaScript works. This provides a type system without requiring you to add more characters to your code in order to make the types obvious. That is how TypeScript is able to determine that the helloWorld variable represents a string in the example that was just shown.

You could have used the editor auto-completion feature in Visual Studio Code while you were writing JavaScript. Under the hood, Visual Studio Code uses TypeScript, simplifying the process of working with JavaScript.

Defining Types

JavaScript gives you access to a vast library of different design patterns to choose from. Nevertheless, design patterns make it more challenging for types to be inferred automatically (for example, patterns that use dynamic programming). TypeScript is an extension of the JavaScript programming language that enables locations for you to tell TypeScript what the appropriate types are. This was done to accommodate the scenarios described above.

For instance, the following code may be written to construct an object with an inferred type that has the attributes name: string and id: number:

```
const user = {
name: "Hayes",
id: 0,
};
```

You may provide a detailed description of the form of this object by using an interface declaration:

```
interface User {
name: string;
id: number;
}
```

```
const user: User = {
username: "Hayes",
Type '{ username: string; id: number; }' is not
assignable to type 'User'.
Object literal may only specify known properties, and
'username' does not exist in type 'User'.Type '{
username: string; id: number; }' is not assignable to
type 'User'.
Object literal may only specify known properties, and
'username' does not exist in type 'User'.
id: 0,
};
```

TypeScript supports classes and object-oriented programming in the same way as JavaScript does because of this. A declaration of an interface may be used while working with classes:

```
interface User {
name: string;
id: number;
}

class UserAccount {
name: string;
id: number;

constructor(name: string, id: number) {
this.name = name;
this.id = id;
}
}

const user: User = new UserAccount("Murphy", 1);
```

You can use interfaces to annotate parameters and return values to functions:

```
function getAdminUser(): User {
//...
}

function deleteUser(user: User) {
//...
}
```

An interface may use the following basic types currently accessible in JavaScript: Boolean, bigint, null, number, string, symbol, and undefined. TypeScript adds a few more to this list, such as any (which means 'allow anything'), unknown (which means 'ensure that someone using this type announces what the type is'), never (which means 'it is not conceivable that this type might exist'), and void (which simply means 'nothing'). Additionally, you have the option to build your own kinds.

You are going to discover that there are two different syntaxes for constructing types: interfaces and types. You should give interface more weight. When you require characteristics that are quite particular, use the type.

Forms of Composition

You may construct more complicated types by mixing TypeScript's simpler ones using the language. There are two common approaches to accomplishing this goal: via the use of unions and generics.

Unions

You can define, when using a union, that a type may be any of a number of other types. You might, for instance, characterize a boolean type as having the property of either being true or false:

```
type MyBool = true | false;
```

Note: If you move your cursor over the word "MyBool" in the sentence above, you'll see that it has the boolean classification. That is one of the characteristics that the Structural Type System has. More about this may be found below.

One of the most common applications of union types is to express the set of string literals or integer literals that a value is permitted to be:

```
type WindowStates = "open" | "closed" | "minimized";
type LockStates = "locked" | "unlocked";
type PositiveOddNumbersUnderTen = 1 | 3 | 5 | 7 | 9;
```

Unions provide a solution to the problem of juggling several kinds. You may have a function that accepts either an array or a string, such as the following:

```
function getLength(obj: string | string[]) {
return obj.length;
}
```

USER AND EXPENSE ARE TWO OF TYPESCRIPT'S CLASSES

JavaScript that is object oriented is known as TypeScript. The object-oriented programming concepts like classes, interfaces, and other such things are supported by TypeScript. In object-oriented programming (OOP), a class functions as a template for the creation of objects. The data for the object is included inside the class. This idea, which is referred to as class, has built-in support provided by Typescript. Classes were not supported in JavaScript versions prior than ES5, though. This functionality is brought to Typescript by ES6.

Developing Classes

To define a class in TypeScript, you will need to use the class keyword. The syntax for the same may be found down below:

Syntax

```
class class_name {
//class scope
}
```

The name of the class comes immediately after the class keyword. When naming a class, it is necessary to take into consideration the rules that govern identifiers.

The following is an example of what may be included in a class definition:

- **Fields** that are defined inside a class might be referred to as fields. The data associated with objects is represented via fields.

- **Constructors** are in charge of allotting memory for the objects of that class.

- **Functions** are a representation of the many activities that an object is capable of doing. Methods is another term that is sometimes used to refer to them.

When taken as a whole, these components make up what are known as the data members of the class.

Consider the typescript version of the class Person.

```
class Person {
}
On compiling, it will generate following JavaScript
code.
//Generated by typescript 1.8.10
var Person = (function () {
function Person() {
}
return Person;
}());
```

A Class Declaration as an Example

```
class Car {
//field
engine:string;

//constructor
constructor(engine:string) {
this.engine = engine
}

//function
disp():void {
console.log("Engine is : "+this.engine)
}
}
```

An instance of the class Car is declared in the example. The name of the field in this class is engine. In the process of defining a field, the var keyword is never utilized. The function Object() { [native code] } for the class has been declared in the preceding example.

A class's function Object() { [native code] } is a specialized function that is responsible for initializing the variables that belong to the class. It is called a function Object() { [native code] }. The function Object() { [native code] } keyword in TypeScript is what really specifies the function Object() { [native code] }. Since a function Object() { [native code] } is a function, it is possible to provide parameters into it.

The "this" keyword refers to the instance of the class that is now being worked with. In this case, the name of the field in the class and the name of the argument are identical. As a result, in order to prevent confusion, the field of the class is prefixed with this keyword.

disp() is an example of a straightforward function definition. It is important to take note that the function keyword is not utilized in this context.

Following is an example of the code that will be generated when you compile it.

```
//Generated by typescript 1.8.10
var Car = (function () {
//constructor
function Car(engine) {
```

```
this.engine = engine;
}
//function
Car.prototype.disp = function () {
console.log("Engine is :  " + this.engine);
};
return Car;
}());
```

Creating Objects of Instance

Use the new keyword, then follow it up with the name of the class to create a new instance of the class. The syntax for the same may be found down below:

Syntax
var object_name = new class_name([arguments])

An Example of Instantiating a Class   var obj = new Car("Engine 1")

CLASS INHERITANCE

The idea of inheritance may be implemented using TypeScript. A computer program's capacity to derive new classes from pre-existing classes is referred to as inheritance. The class that serves as the basis for the creation of subsequent classes is referred to as the parent class or the super class. The classes that have just been produced are referred to as the kid or sub classes.

The 'extends' keyword allows one class to inherit properties and behaviors from another. Child classes take on all of the attributes and methods of their parent classes, with the exception of any private members and constructors.

The term "inherited" may also be used to refer to:

- **Single**—Each child class may only inherit from a single parent class at the most.

- **Multiple**—A class may take inheritance from more than one other class. There is currently no support for multiple inheritance in TypeScript.

- **Multi-level**—Inheritance on Several Levels The following example demonstrates how inheritance may occur on multiple levels.

Data Hiding

A class has the ability to govern how other classes' members see the data that is stored in its members. This functionality is sometimes referred to as data encapsulation or data hiding.

The idea of encapsulation is realized in Object Oriented Programming via the use of the concepts of access modifiers and access specifiers. Access specifiers and modifiers determine whether or not a class's data members are visible to classes other than the one that defines them.

public

Everyone may view the information contained in a public data member. The default access level for data members of a class is public.

private

Only other instances of the class that define a private data member's definition may access that member's data. An error is generated by the compiler whenever an external class member makes an attempt to access a private member.

protected

A protected data member is available not only to members of the same class as the member being protected, but also to members of any child classes that the parent class may have.

INTERFACES

An Outline of TypeScript Interfaces

Interfaces in TypeScript are what specify the agreements between different parts of your code. Furthermore, they provide granular names for use in type verification.

First, let's look at a straightforward illustration:

```
function getFullName(person: {
firstName: string;
lastName: string
```

```typescript
}) {
return '${person.firstName} ${person.lastName}';
}
let person = {
firstName: 'John',
lastName: 'Wick'
};
console.log(getFullName(person));
Code language: TypeScript (typescript)
```

Output

John Wick

Code language: TypeScript (typescript)

Here, the parameter to the getFullName() method is verified by the TypeScript compiler.

The TypeScript compiler will allow the argument to proceed if it contains two properties of type string. In such case, it will throw an error.

The code itself demonstrates how the type annotation of the function parameter complicates the code and makes it more difficult to comprehend.

TypeScript's idea of interfaces was designed with this problem in mind.

In the following, a Person interface with two string attributes is used:

```css
interface Person {
firstName: string;
lastName: string;
}
```

Format of code: CSS (css)

The standard for naming interfaces is to use camel case. In their names, just the first letter of each word is capitalized. Such as FullName, UserProfile, and Person.

The Person interface may be used as a type as soon as it is defined. The name of the interface may also be annotated on a function's argument.

```typescript
function getFullName(person: Person) {
return '${person.firstName} ${person.lastName}';
}

let john = {
firstName: 'John',
lastName: 'Doe'
```

```
};

console.log(getFullName(john));
Code language: TypeScript (typescript)
```

The code is much more readable now.

Function Types

Interfaces enable you to specify the sorts of functions as well as the characteristics of an object.

To specify a function type, you attach the interface to the function signature that includes the argument list with types and returned types. For instance:

```
interface StringFormat {
(str: string, isUpper: boolean): string
}
TypeScript, a programming language (typescript)

It is now possible to use this interface for functions
of a certain type.

Assigning a value of the same type to a variable
declared as a function is seen below.

let format: StringFormat;

format = function (str: string, isUpper: boolean) {
return isUpper? str.toLocaleUpperCase() : str.
toLocaleLowerCase();
};

console.log(format('hi', true));
Code language: TypeScript (typescript)
```

Output
HI

OBJECTS IN TYPESCRIPT

A collection of key-value pairs that make up an object is called an instance. The values might be anything from simple numbers to functions or arrays of other things. Here is the syntax:

```
var object_name = {
key1: "value1", //scalar value
key2: "value",
key3: function() {
//functions
},
key4:["content1", "content2"] //collection
};
```

As was just shown, objects may store not just scalar values and functions, but also arrays and tuples and other structures.

TYPE TEMPLATE FOR TYPESCRIPT

Suppose you wrote the following JavaScript object literal:

```
var person = {
firstname:"Tom",
lastname: "Hanks"
};
```

In the event that you need to alter an object's value, JavaScript provides the functionality you need. Let's say we find later on that the Person object needs an extra feature.

```
person.sayHello = function(){ return "hello";}
```

The Typescript compiler returns a compilation error if you try to utilize the same code. Concrete objects in Typescript must have a corresponding type template. In Typescript, all objects must represent concrete examples of predefined classes.

Duck-Typing

If two objects have the same set of characteristics, then they are said to be of the same type in duck-typing. Instead of checking the exact type of an object, duck-typing instead ensures that particular attributes are present [2–13].

TypeScript's compiler makes use of the duck-typing system, which permits dynamic object generation without compromising type safety. In the next example, we'll see how to send objects to a method that don't directly implement the interface but nevertheless have all the necessary members.

NAMESPACES IN TYPESCRIPT

Using a namespace allows you to organize your code in a meaningful manner. TypeScript was designed with this feature in mind, unlike JavaScript, where variable declarations are placed in a global scope and might be overwritten or misunderstood if various JavaScript files are used inside the same project.

Namespace Determination

In order to define a namespace, you must first use the term "namespace," followed by the actual namespace's name, like in

```
namespace SomeNameSpaceName {
export interface ISomeInterfaceName { }
export class SomeClassName { }
}
```

The term export must be used to indicate which classes or interfaces should be exposed outside of the namespace.

The syntax for using a class or interface that is defined in a different namespace is to use the form namespaceName.className.

SomeNameSpaceName.SomeClassName;

If the initial namespace is defined in a completely distinct TypeScript file, the triple slash reference syntax must be used to access it.

```
/// <reference path = "SomeFileName.ts" />
```

Nested Namespaces

An nested namespace definition looks like this:

```
namespace namespace_name1 {
export namespace namespace_name2 {
export class class_name { }
}
}
```

MODULES IN TYPESCRIPT

The goal of this TypeScript module is to provide a means of encapsulating and reusing similar pieces of code. It is possible to categorize modules as follows:

- Internal Modules

- External Modules

Internal Modules

Typescript's internal modules debuted in a previous version. This was done so that classes, interfaces, and functions could be logically grouped together into a single unit that could be exported to another module. In TypeScript's newest iteration, this logical classification is known as a namespace. As a result, namespace is superior than internal modules. While we currently allow internal modules, we strongly advise using namespaces instead.

Syntax of Internal Module (Veteran)
```
module TutorialPoint {
export function add(x, y) {
console.log(x+y);
}
}
```

External Module

The purpose of TypeScript's external modules is to allow developers to declare and load dependencies between numerous external js files. There is no need for external modules if just a single.js file is being utilized. Historically, browser script tags (script>/script>) were used for managing dependencies between JavaScript files. However, that can't grow with your needs since module loading is so slow. This implies that loading modules asynchronously is not an option and files must be loaded sequentially. Script tags don't even exist in server-side JS languages like NodeJs.

Dependent js files may be loaded in one of two ways, both of which involve a single primary JavaScript file.

- Server Side - NodeJs

- Client Side - RequireJs

FUNCTIONS IN TYPESCRIPT

Code that is understandable, easy to maintain, and versatile relies heavily on its functions as its fundamental building blocks. A collection of statements designed to carry out a certain activity is known as a function.

The functionality of the software is broken down into logical sections by the functions. When they have been defined, functions may be used to access code by calling them. This enables the code to be used in several places. In addition, functions simplify the process of reading and maintaining the code of a program.

A function declaration provides the compiler with information about a function's name, as well as its arguments and return type. The meat and potatoes of a function is its body, which is provided by the function specification.

- **Defining a Function:** A function description describes both the specifics of a job and the manner in which it should be completed.

- **Invoking a Function:** Before a function can be put into action, it must first be invoked.

- **Returning Functions:** Functions may return control and value back to the person who called them in a process known as "returning functions."

- **Parameterized Function:** Parameters are a means through which values may be sent to functions.

Parameters That Are Optional

It is possible to utilize optional parameters in situations in which it is not necessary to supply arguments to a function in order for it to be executed. Putting a question mark in front of the name of a parameter is one way to indicate that it is optional. When calling a function, the optional parameter should be sent in as the very last argument. The declaration syntax for a function that may or may not take an optional argument looks like this:

```
function function_name (param1[:type], param2[:type],
param3[:type])
```

Rest Parameters

Rest parameters are analogous to variable arguments in Java. The amount of different values that may be sent to a function is not limited in any way by rest parameters. However, all of the values that are handed in need to have the same type. To put it another way, rest parameters serve the purpose of being placeholders for many arguments of the same type.

The name of the parameter is given a prefix consisting of three periods when it is declared to be a rest parameter. Any parameter that is not involved in rest should appear before the rest parameter.

Default Parameters

It is also possible to set values by default to the arguments of a function. On the other hand, values for such parameters may also be provided in directly.

Syntax

```
function function_name(param1[:type], param2[:type] =
default_value) {
}
```

NUMBERS IN TYPESCRIPT

The Number class performs the function of a wrapper and makes it possible to manipulate numeric literals as if they were objects. Numeric values may be represented as Number objects in TypeScript, just way JavaScript does. A numeric literal may be converted into an instance of the number class by using a number object.

Syntax

```
var var_name = new Number(value)
```

In the event that the Number function Object() { [native code] } is given an argument that is not a number, it will return NaN. (Not–a–Number)

ARRAYS IN TYPESCRIPT

Making use of variables to store values provides a number of issues, some of which are as follows:

- Variables are scalar in nature. To put it another way, a variable declaration can never contain more than one thing at a time regardless of the circumstances. This suggests that in order for a program to be able to hold n values, there will need to be n variable declarations made before the program can be run. When one has to retain a larger collection of data, the use of variables is not an option since it is not realistic. This means that one cannot use variables.

- It may be difficult to retrieve or read the values in the order in which they were declared since the memory for the variables in a program is allocated in what seems to be an arbitrary sequence.

In order to address this issue, the programming language TypeScript has a component called as arrays in its toolkit. When we speak about arrays, we refer to collections of things that all have the same data type. An item collection known as an array has elements that are all of the same kind. It is a sort that the user chooses for themselves to have.

What Makes Up an Array

The following is a list that outlines, in more depth, the qualities of an array:

- Memory will be allotted in a sequential manner whenever a declaration of an array is made.

- There is never any variation in arrays. This signifies that once an array has been started, its size cannot be altered in any way after it has been started.

- Each memory block is a substitute for one of the array's items.

- The subscript or index of an array element is a single number that is used to identify that element inside the array specifically. This number may also be referred to as the array element's index.

- Just like variables, arrays need to have their definitions written down before they can be used in a program. This is a prerequisite for using arrays. Utilizing the var keyword is necessary before an array can be declared.

- The action of populating the elements of an array with data is referred to as "array initialization," and it is a part of many programming languages.

- While it is possible to update or edit the values of array items, it is not feasible to remove them. Array elements cannot be deleted.

Object Contained Inside an Array

An array may also be created from scratch with the help of the Array object if desired.

- A numeric value indicates either the array's dimensions or the array or the size of the array.

- A group of values that are delineated from one another using commas.

TUPLES FOR THE TYPESCRIPT LANGUAGE

It is possible that there may be circumstances in which it would be essential to keep a collection of values that belong to several categories. In this particular setting, the usage of arrays is not acceptable. TypeScript has made a data type known as tuple accessible to us, and it contributes to the success of such an endeavor by assisting in its completion.

Tuples are one more kind of data that may be sent into functions in the role of an argument. It is representative of a wide variety of distinct principles, ideals, and principles all at once. To state it another way, tuples make it feasible to hold many fields of differing types. This may be done in a number of ways.

Syntax

```
var tuple_name = [value1,value2,value3,…value n]

For Example:
var mytuple = [10," Hello"];
```

You also have the option in Typescript to declare an empty tuple and then decide at a later time whether or not to populate it.

```
var mytuple = [];
mytuple[0] = 120
mytuple[1] = 234
```

UNION IN TYPESCRIPT

Programs now have the capability to mix one or two different types thanks to TypeScript 1.4. Union types are an extremely useful approach to describe a value that may be any one of a number of different kinds. When referring to a Union Type, the pipe symbol (|) is used to indicate the combination of two or more data types. In a nutshell, the syntax for a union type looks like a string of several types with vertical bars in between each one.

Syntax

```
Type1 | Type2 | Type3
```

Example: Union Type Variable

```
var val:string|number
val = 12
console.log("numeric value of val "+val)
val = "This is a string"
console.log("string value of val "+val)
```

The type of the variable is shown to be union in the preceding illustration. This specifies that the value of the variable may be either a number or a string. Either one is acceptable.

AMBIENTS IN TYPESCRIPT

In TypeScript, ambient declarations are a method for alerting the TypeScript compiler that the actual source code is stored in another location. These declarations may be placed anywhere in a file. If it uses a variety of different third-party JS frameworks, such as jQuery, AngularJS, or NodeJS, you won't be able to rebuild it in TypeScript. This is because TypeScript is not compatible with these frameworks. A TypeScript programmer may encounter challenges while trying to utilize these packages while preserving typesafety and intellisense at the same time. TypeScript may be seamlessly connected to other JS libraries via the use of ambient declarations, which expand its functionality.

Definition of Ambients

By custom, declarations of ambients are stored in a type declaration file that has the following extension: (d.ts)

Sample.d.ts

The file that is being shown above will not be transcompiled to JavaScript. It is going to be used for both type safety and intellisense.

The following syntax will be used for defining ambient variables or modules:

```
declare module Module_Name {
}
```

The client TypeScript file ought to include a reference to the ambient files in the manner shown above.

```
/// <reference path = " Sample.d.ts" />
```
[1]

NOTES

1 A Brief History/A Static Type Checker/ (2022, October 19)/ www.type-scriptlang.org/docs/handbook/typescript-from-scratch.html
2 Main Pillars of Typescript/Features/How to Get Started/ (2022, October 19)/ www.freecodecamp.org/news/learn-typescript-basics/
3 Setting Up Your TypeScript Development Environment/ (2022, October 19)/ www.newline.co/books/beginners-guide-to-typescript/setting-up-your-typescript-development-environment
4 TypeScript for JavaScript Programmers
5 www.typescriptlang.org/docs/handbook/typescript-in-5-minutes.html
6 Classes in TypeScript: User and Expense
7 www.tutorialspoint.com/typescript/typescript_classes.htm
8 TypeScript - Objects
9 www.tutorialspoint.com/typescript/typescript_objects.htm
10 TypeScript - Namespaces
11 www.tutorialspoint.com/typescript/typescript_namespaces.htm
12 Modules
13 www.tutorialspoint.com/typescript/typescript_modules.htm

Appendix III

Handy JavaScript Tools

➢ *Gulp*

➢ *Grunt*

➢ *npm*

In the previous chapter, we covered a Brief Guide to TypeScript, and in this chapter, we will discuss the Handy JS Tools.

Because JavaScript is such a popular language and is used in some form by all front-end web apps, many excellent tools help us effortlessly develop high-quality JavaScript applications.

Every day, the tool ecosystem grows, and more tools for creating and debugging JavaScript applications are available.

OVERVIEW OF GULP

We will talk about Gulp with its installation and advantages and disadvantages.[1]

What Exactly Is Gulp?

Gulp is a task runner that runs on the Node.js platform. Gulp runs front-end tasks and large-scale web applications entirely in JavaScript code. It automates system tasks such as CSS and HTML minification, concatenating library files, and compiling SASS files. These tasks can be carried out via the command line using Shell or Bash scripts.

Why Should We Use Gulp?

It is shorter, simpler, and faster than other task runners. CSS preprocessors are SASS and LESS. After editing the source files, the page automatically refreshes.

Gulpfile.js is simple to understand and build because it uses pure JavaScript code to construct the task.

History

The CC0 license applies to all Gulp documentation. Gulp v1.0.0 was initially released on January 15, 2015, and the current version is v3.9.0.

Features

- Allows for minification and concatenation.
- Pure JavaScript code is used.
- Converts CSS compilation from LESS or SASS.
- The Node.js platform manages file manipulation in memory and increases speed.

Advantages

- Significant time advantage over any other task runner.
- Simple to code and comprehend.
- It is simple to test web applications.
- Plugins are simple to use and intended to do only one thing simultaneously.
- Repeatedly performs repetitive tasks such as minifying stylesheets, compressing images, etc.

Disadvantages

- It has more dependencies than Grunt and is a newcomer.
- We cannot perform multiple tasks with Gulp plugins.
- Grunt's configuration is not as clean.

INSTALLATION OF GULP

This session walks us through the installation of Gulp step by step.[2]

Gulp System Requirements

- Operating System Cross-platform

- IE (Internet Explorer 8+), Firefox, Google Chrome, Safari, and Opera are all supported browsers.

Installation of Gulp

Step 1: To run Gulp examples, we need Node.js.

To download Node.js, go to https://nodejs.org/en/, and we'll see the screen below.

download gulp

Download the zip file with the most recent features.

Step 2 Run the setup program to install NodeJs on your computer.

Step 3: Configure the environment variables.

User Variable Path

- Right-click My Computer and select Properties.

- Choose Properties.

- Select the Advanced tab and then click on 'Environment Variables.'

- Double-click on the PATH as indicated on the screen in the Environment Variables box.

- An Edit User Variable box will appear. In the Variable Value field, enter C:\Program Files\nodejs\node modules\npm as the path of the Node.js folder. If the path has already been established for other files, we must add the Node.js path after the semicolon (;).

- In the end, press the "Ok" button.

System Variable

- Double-click on Path under System variables.

- An Edit System Variable window will appear. In the Variable Value field, enter C:\Program Files\nodejs\ as the path of the Node.js folder, and then click "Ok."

Step 4: Open our system's command prompt and type the following command. The installed Node.js version will show.

Step 5: To show the version of npm (the Node.js package manager) that is used to install modules, type the following command into the command prompt. The installed Node.js version will display.

```
npm -v
```

Step 6: Type the following command to install Gulp at the command prompt. The "-g" parameter guarantees that Gulp is available for any project worldwide.

```
npm install gulp -g
```

Step 7: Type the following command to view the Gulp version to ensure it was installed correctly.

```
gulp -v
```

BASICS OF GULP

This section will introduce us to the fundamentals of Gulp.[3]

What Exactly Is a Build System?

A Build System is a collection of tasks (collectively known as task runners) that automate repetitive work.

Some of the jobs that the build system is capable of doing are listed below:

- Preprocess CSS and JavaScript compilation.

- File compression to reduce file size.

- Concatenation of multiple files into one.

- Activating the server's automatic reloading.

- Create deployment builds to keep the resulting files in one place.

- The build system in a modern front-end workflow consists of three components:

- Managers of packages.

- Preprocessors.

- Task managers and build tools.

Package Administrators

It automates installation upgrades, dependency removal, library cleaning, and package cleanup in the development environment.

Bower and npm are two examples of package managers.

Preprocessors

Preprocessors are particularly helpful for a productive modern workflow since they bring enhanced capabilities and optimized syntax that compile into the target language.

A few of the well-liked preprocessors include

- CSS – SASS, Stylus, and LESS.

- JS – LiveScript, CoffeeScript, TypeScript, etc.

- HTML – Markdown, Slim, HAML, Jade, etc.

Task Executors

Task runners automate various development activities, including minifying files, enhancing photos, and converting SASS to CSS. In the contemporary front-end work environment, Gulp is one of the task runners and runs on Node.

Setting Up Our Project

Create a folder on our computer called, for instance, "work" to save our project there. The work folder has the following files and subfolders:

- Src: Pre-processed HTML source files and directories are located in the Src directory.

    - Images: Uncompressed images are included.

    - Scripts: Contains several script files that have already been processed.

    - Styles: Consists of several pre-processed CSS files.

- Build: The production files are located in this automatically generated folder.

    - Images: Comprised of compressed pictures.

    - Scripts: A single script file containing code that has been compressed.

    - Styles: A single CSS file containing code that has been compressed.

- gulpfile.js: The configuration file used to specify our tasks is called gulpfile.js.

DEVELOPING AN APPLICATION USING GULP

We learned about Gulp installation and the fundamentals of Gulp in the previous section, which covered topics like the Gulp build system, package management, task runner, and Gulp structure.[4]

The following are some of the fundamentals for creating applications that we will examine in this session:

- Stating necessary dependencies

- Task creation for the dependencies

- Performing the task

- Observing the task

Declaration of Dependencies

We must indicate the plugins' dependencies when installing them for the application. Package managers like bower and npm take care of the dependencies.

Let's define dependencies for the gulp-imagemin plugin in the configuration file. The following command line may use to install this plugin, which can use to compress the image file:

```
npm install gulp-imagemin --save-dev
```

As seen in the following code, we may include dependencies in our configuration file.

```
var imagemin=require('gulp-imagemin');
```

Task Creation for Dependencies

Task makes it possible to configure Gulp in a modular fashion. Each dependent must have its task, which we must add to as we locate and set up additional plugins. The Gulp job will be organized as follows:

```
gulp.task('taskname', function() {
  //here, do stuff
});
```

Where "function()" carries out our task and "taskname" is a string name. Gulp.task defines the dependencies on other tasks and registers the function as a task with a name.

As illustrated in the following code, we may build the task for the previously created dependency.

```
gulp.task('imagemin', function() {
  var imgsrc = 'src/images/**/*', imgdest = 'build/
images';
  gulp.src(imgsrc)
  .pipe(changed(imgdest))
  .pipe(imagemin())
  .pipe(gulp.dest(imgdest));
});
```

The images are saved in the img srcobject and may be found in the directory src/images/**/*. The imagemin constructor pipes it to further functions. By invoking the dest method with an argument that stands in for the destination directory, it compresses the pictures that were transferred from the src folder to the build folder.

Running the Task

The Gulp file is configured and prepared to run. To execute the task, enter the following command in our project directory.

```
gulp imagemin
```

OVERVIEW OF GruntJS

We will talk about GruntJS with its installation and its advantages and disadvantages.

A JavaScript task manager is GruntJS. With no effort, it may use to automate various operations for our application, increasing developer productivity.[5]

GruntJS has plugins for many different tasks. One such instance is the nodemon plugin, which restarts the node server automatically anytime a JavaScript file changes in our application. Therefore, we don't need to manually stop and restart the node server each time we change the JavaScript. We may use the grunt-contrib-cssmin plugin to compress CSS files. We may format, search, or rewrite the JavaScript in our application with the grunt-jsfmt plugin.

Why Should We Use Grunt?

Grunt can easily do repetitive operations like compilation, unit testing, file minification, test execution, etc.[6] Grunt comes with built-in tasks that let our plugins and scripts do more. Grunt's ecosystem is vast; we can automate almost anything with minimal effort.

History

GruntJS's first lines of source code were added in 2011.

On February 18, 2013, Grunt v0.4 was released.

On May 12, 2014, Grunt v0.4.5 was released.

Grunt's current stable version is 1.0.0 rc1, published on February 11, 2016.

Advantages

- We may quickly execute file minification, compilation, and testing with Grunt.

- Grunt unifies web developers' workflows.

- Because it has the minimal infrastructure, Grunt makes it simple to work with a fresh codebase.

- It improves project performance by speeding up the development workflow.

Disadvantages

- We must wait till the creator of the Grunt changes it whenever npm packages are updated.

- Every job is intended to perform a specific function.

- If we wish to extend a particular assignment, we must employ some methods to complete the work.

- Grunt provides a plethora of configuration options for individual plugins.

- Grunt configuration files are often lengthier in length.

FEATURES IN GRUNT

Grunt is a JavaScript-based task runner that may use to automate repetitive operations in a workflow and as a command-line tool for JavaScript objects.[7]

The following are some of the most notable features of GruntJS:

- Grunt makes the workflow as simple as writing a configuration file.

- With no effort, we may automate repetitive operations.

- Grunt is a famous NodeJS task runner. It is adaptable and frequently used.

- It takes a fundamental approach, with tasks written in JS and configuration written in JSON.

- Grunt minifies JavaScript, CSS files, tests files, CSS preprocessor files (SASS, LESS), and other files.

- Grunt comes with built-in tasks that let your plugins and scripts do more.

- It improves project performance by speeding up the development workflow.

- Because it has the minimal infrastructure, Grunt makes it simple to work with a fresh codebase.

- Grunt's ecosystem is vast; we can automate almost anything with minimal effort.

- Grunt decreases the possibility of mistakes when doing repetitive activities.

- Grunt now has almost 4,000 plugins.

- It may be employed in large production facilities.

SETTING UP OF GRUNT

This section walks us through installing Grunt on our system step by step.[8]

Grunt's System Requirements

- Cross-platform operating system

- Support for Internet Explorer (version 8 and higher), Firefox, Google Chrome, Safari, and Opera

Installation of Grunt

Step 1: To execute Grunt, we require NodeJs. The screen below will show us when we click the link https://nodejs.org/en/ to download NodeJs.

download grunt

Download the zip file with the most recent features.
Step 2: Run the setup program to install NodeJs on our machine.
Step 3: The third step is to set environment variables.

User Variable for Path

- To right-click My Computer.

- Choosing Properties.

- Next, click Environment Variables under the Advanced tab.

- Double-click the PATH entry in the Environment Variables box when it appears on the screen.

- An Edit User Variable window will appear as displayed. C:\Program Files\nodejs\node_modules\npm should be added as the path of the NodeJs folder in the Variable Value box. If the path has already been established for other files, add the NodeJs path after the semicolon (;) in the format.

Click the OK button when we're done.

System Variable

- Double-click Path under System variables, as displayed on the screen.

- A window to edit system variables will appear, as displayed. As illustrated below, enter C:\Program Files\nodejs\ as the path to the NodeJs folder and click OK.

Step 4: To complete the installation of Grunt on your system, install its command-line interface (CLI) globally, as seen below.

```
npm install -g grunt-cli
```

By running the command above, the grunt command will be added to our system path and be available for use from any directory.

Grunt task runner is not installed when grunt-cli is installed. The grunt-function cli's is to execute the Grunt version installed next to a Gruntfile. It enables a system to install numerous Grunt versions at once.

Step 5: To use Grunt, we need to generate configuration files.

package.json

Alongside the Gruntfile, the package.json file is positioned in the project's root directory. When we execute the command npm install in the same folder as package.json, it uses package.json to run each dependent indicated appropriately.

We may generate the basic "package.json" file by using the following command at the command prompt:

```
npm init
```

The 'package.json' file's basic structure is seen below:

```
{
    "name": "tutorialsession",
    "version": "0.1.0",
    "devDependencies": {
      "grunt-contrib-jshint": "~0.10.0",
      "grunt-contrib-nodeunit": "~0.4.1",
      "grunt-contrib-uglify": "~0.5.0"
}
}
```

The below command may use to add Grunt and Gruntplugins to an already-existing package.json file.

```
npm install <module> --save-dev
```

The module to be installed locally is indicated by the word "module" in the command above. The preceding command will also automatically add the <module> to devDependencies.

For example, the following command will add the most recent version of Grunt to our devDependencies and install it.

```
npm install grunt --save-dev
```

Gruntfile.js

We define our Grunt setup in the Gruntfile.js file. It will be here that we write the settings. As illustrated below, the fundamental Gruntfile.js file

```
// (Required by Grunt and its plugins) our wrapper
function
// This function contains all configuration.
module.exports = function(grunt) {
  // CONFIGURE GRUNT
  grunt.initConfig({
    // get configuration info from package.json file
    // this way, we can use things such as name and
version (pkg.name)
    pkg: grunt.file.readJSON('package.json'),
    // here, all of our configuration goes
    uglify: {
      // uglify task configuration
      options: {},
      build: {}
    }
  });
  // log something
  grunt.log.write('Hello world! Welcome to
Tutorialspoint!!\n');
  // Load plugin that provides "uglify" task.
  grunt.loadNpmTasks('grunt-contrib-uglify');
  // Default task.
  grunt.registerTask('default', ['uglify']);
};
```

GETTING STARTED WITH GRUNT

We require Node.js to utilize Grunt, so ensure it is set up. Using the Node.js package manager, we may install Grunt and its plugins.[9]

We may update the Node package management using the command line before installing Grunt on the machine.

```
npm update -g npm
```

To provide administrator access on a Mac or Linux computer, use sudo word at the beginning of the command line, as seen below.

```
sudo npm update -g npm
```

Installation of CLI

The installed version of Grunt is launched using the CLI, or command-line interface. We must install Grunt's command-line interface (CLI) globally to begin using it.

```
npm install -g grunt-cli
```

By running the command above, the grunt command will be added to our system path and be available for use from any directory. By installing grunt-cli, we cannot install the Grunt task runner. It enables a system to install numerous Grunt versions at once.

Working of CLI

Every time Grunt is executed, the CLI uses the require() mechanism to check to see if Grunt is already installed on our system. We may launch Grunt from any directory in our project using grunt-cli. Grunt-cli utilizes the locally installed Grunt library and applies the configuration from the Grunt file if Grunt is being used locally.

Working on a New and Current Project

If we are working with a project that has already been configured and includes package.json and a Gruntfile, then follow the instructions listed below:

- Discover the directory's root path for the project.

- The npm install command may use to install dependencies.

- Use the grunt command to launch Grunt.

- Include the two files package.json and Gruntfile, in our project if we are starting a new one.

- package.json: When we execute the command npm install in the same folder, the package.json file, which is located in the project's root directory, is used to run each dependent that is indicated.

- Gruntfile.js: The project's configuration settings are written in the Gruntfile.js file.

package.json

When we execute the command npm install in the same folder, the package.json file is used to run each dependency mentioned and is located next to the Gruntfile in the project's root directory.

There are several ways to construct the "package.json," as noted below:

- To generate the 'package.json' file, use grunt-init.

- We may also use the npm-init command to build a "package.json" file.

As demonstrated below, we may write specifications.

```
{
    "name": "tutorialsession",
    "version": "0.1.0",
    "devDependencies": {
      "grunt-contrib-jshint": "~0.10.0",
      "grunt-contrib-nodeunit": "~0.4.1",
      "grunt-contrib-uglify": "~0.5.0"
}
}
```

The below command may use to add Grunt and gruntplugins to an existing "pacakge.json" file.

```
npm install <module> --save-dev
```

The local installation module is represented by <module> in this instance. The requested module will be installed and immediately added to the devDependencies section by using the preceding command.

For example, the command below will update Grunt to the most recent version and add it to our devDependencies.

```
npm install grunt --save-dev
```

Gruntfile
By default, our Grunt configuration settings will be stored in the Gruntfile.js file. The following components are present in the Grunt file:

- The function of wrapping

- Task and project setup

- Grunt jobs and plugins are loading

- Certain tasks

The 'Gruntfile.js' basic file is shown as follows:

```
// (Required by Grunt and its plugins) our wrapper
function
// This function contains all configuration.
module.exports = function(grunt) {
  // configure the grunt
  grunt.initConfig({
    // to obtain configuration information, see the
package.json file
    // We may utilize elements like name and version
in this way (pkg.name)
    pkg: grunt.file.readJSON('package.json'),
    // Everything we configure goes here
  });
  // Load the plugin that performs the "uglify" function
  grunt.loadNpmTasks('grunt-contrib-uglify');
  // Default task
  grunt.registerTask('default', ['uglify']);
};
```

Wrapper Function
In the code above, module.exports is a wrapper function that receives the complete configuration. It is a method of showing configuration to other program users.

```
module.exports = function(grunt) {
  //here do grunt-related things
}
```

Task and Project Configuration

Once our Grunt configuration is ready, we may configure Grunt tasks. The grunt.initConfig() section is where the project configuration may enter. Take the configuration data from package.json and store it in pkg inside grunt.initConfig(). We may use pkg.name and pkg.version to call our project's name and version, respectively.

Loading the Grunt Plugins and Task

Use the 'grunt.loadNpmTasks' function to load the tasks from a specific plugin.

The plugin may be installed locally using npm; it must be relative to the Gruntfile. The plugin may be loaded using the straightforward command described below.

```
grunt.task.loadNpmTasks(plugin_Name)
```

Custom Tasks

Grunt will search for the default task when executed through the command line. The task uglify, which may be executed using gruntcommand, is used in the code above. This is equivalent to manually using the grunt uglify command, and we may provide the array's job count.

```
grunt.registerTask('default', ['uglify']);
```

GULP VS GRUNT

Before delving into the Grunt versus Gulp debate, we may ask what both tools accomplish and why you would want to use either.

Both Grunt and Gulp, as previously noted, exist to assist automate operations and are popular tools among web developers and designers.[10]

A website designer's regular duties include debugging code, concatenating and minifying CSS and JavaScript files, compressing images, and making modifications to a server or server files.

Many of these chores are essential, but they can take a long time.

This is especially true if the website is vast or requires regular revisions and updates.

Someone may appoint to perform these activities, but because they are relatively simple, the person doing them could be doing more productive things.

This is when Grunt and Gulp come into play.

We can build up a process that automates tasks using a piece of really easy code, plugins, and either Gulp or Grunt.

Both of these programs enable you to check for new files or changes to files in specific folders and conduct operations that are relevant to them.

In other words, after we've configured the processes we want and applied them to existing files, any new or updated files can have processes applied to them automatically.

Assume we put up a procedure that compresses jpg files in the images directory.

When we perform the procedure, all photographs have their EXIF data removed and are compressed.

Once we've correctly installed and configured Gulp or Grunt, the image compression task code for each tool should look something like this:

Gulp

```
gulp.task('jpgs', function() {
  return gulp.src('src/documents/*.jpg')
    .pipe(imagemin({ progressive: true }))
    .pipe(gulp.dest('optimizedimages'));
});
```

Grunt

```
imagemin: {
  jpgs: {
    options: {
    progressive: true
  },
    files: [{
      expand: true,
      cwd: 'src/img',
      src: ['*.jpg'],
      dest: 'documents/'
    }]
  }
}
```

If we've also configured Gulp or Grunt to check for new or updated files, any altered or new files saved to the directory will compress, and the EXIF data will immediately erase.

Gulp or Grunt can conduct this job efficiently, and in the case of large amounts of files, they can do so in a fraction of the time it would take if it had been carried out manually.

Gulp vs Grunt: What's the Difference?

Now that we know what Gulp and Grunt can accomplish let's talk about how they do it. Both programs are task runners using Node.js, an open-source JavaScript runtime environment for developing tools and apps. Grunt and Gulp rely on plugins to do the tasks we want them to do for us.

To build tasks, both tools utilize.js files; for Grunt, you use a gruntfile. js, and for Gulp, we use a gulpfile.js. Instead of utilizing a function, we may define flows with grunt.task and gulp.task.

Some of the most frequent tasks that each tool can do and automate include the following:

- Image file compression

- Script debugger and console statements are removed

- CSS and JavaScript minification, concatenation, and cleanup

- Error-checking code

- Less file compilation

- Executing unit tests

- Sending updates to a live server

- Database updates

Gulp vs Grunt: Which Is Faster?

Regarding speed, Gulp has a significant edge, although the advantage may not be that significant, and changes to Grunt have done a lot to lessen the speed disparity.

Gulp's present speed advantage is because it uses streams and processes jobs in memory, resulting in only one file being written.

Furthermore, Gulp can handle several jobs simultaneously, whereas Grunt typically only handles one task at a time.

TMWtech did a speed test to compare the time it takes to do a Sass compilation using Gulp and Grunt. The findings reveal that Gulp was substantially quicker, consuming only 1.27 seconds compared to Grunt's 2.348 seconds. A temporary file is saved when a plugin executes a file in Grunt. A final destination file is written after a file has passed through all plugins.

Writing data to the disc can significantly increase the amount of time required to execute activities; however, significantly is a relative phrase. Unless we're working on a vast project, the output time for Gulp or Grunt will measure in seconds or milliseconds.

Even if Grunt takes 500 ms to perform a job that Gulp can complete in 50 ms, a tenfold difference, we're still talking about a half-second difference for the considerably longer Grunt time frame. When comparing Gulp versus Grunt, the scale of the project we're working on will decide whether performance is a concern. Even if speed is an issue for us, Grunt gained pipe support earlier this year (as of version 0.5), so the speed disparities are likely lower than when most comparisons were performed.

Gulp vs Grunt: Configuration vs Coding

The crucial distinctions between Gulp and Grunt in terms of configuration versus code have been heavily debated. Gulp is intended to help us achieve our goals using single-purpose plugins and scripts. In most circumstances, this makes writing plugins for Gulp considerably easier than developing them for Grunt. Furthermore, because Gulp is more focused on code and single-task plugins, setting plugins in Gulp is a lot more standardized procedure than it is for Grunt plugins.

However, the issue may be less about code and more about how comfortable we and, if applicable, our team are with node streams. Gulp largely relies on node streams, and unless we and everyone else who will be working with Gulp are familiar with them, as well as pipes, buffers, and asynchronous JavaScript, dealing with Gulp will be an uphill battle.

While configuring Grunt takes longer than setting Gulp, Grunt is far more user-friendly since it relies on configuration rather than code. Furthermore, while Gulp code is easier to read, many people believe that Grunt code is simpler to write. If we're working with a large group of individuals with diverse skill levels, Grunt could be a better option. To use it, read the manual, acquire and set up the necessary plugins, and produce some JavaScript code.

Gulp vs Grunt: Support, Community, and Plugins

Both programs have a huge and helpful community, as well as a significant number of plugins to pick from.

As previously stated, over 6,000 Grunt plugins are posted on the official site, and approximately 2,700 Gulp plugins are listed on the official site of Gulp.

Gulp is the new kid on the block, so it's not surprising that there are about twice as many plugins available for Grunt. In any case, both a program lacks plugins, and there is a Gulp plugin that, with principle, allows any Grunt plugin to operate in Gulp.

As of 2016, Grunt had over 70% of the market, compared to Gulp's 30% share. However, throughout the same period, the number of downloads for each tool was quite close. Grunt was downloaded approximately 1.85 million times a month, whereas Gulp was downloaded roughly 1.6 million times in the same time frame.

Which Should We Go With?

There is no right or wrong answer when deciding between Grunt and Gulp.

Both automation technologies have a lot to offer, and none has a significant flaw.

Our decision will be influenced by whether we prefer configuring (Grunt) or coding (Gulp) while setting up automation and our familiarity with node streams. There is a great deal of personal preference involved.

Speed, how plugins function and the number and types of plugins available may all factor into our selection. While some people find that they can efficiently utilize either method, others may not. If we're still undecided between Gulp and Grunt, we should experiment with both. Both programs are free and have active communities that may assist us in finding the right plugins and getting started with automation scripts. We can use both tools on separate tasks depending on how many projects we have.

OVERVIEW OF NPM

We will talk about npm with its installation and advantages and disadvantages.

What Exactly Is npm?

The npm is an abbreviation for Node Package Manager, the world's largest software registry.

It is used by open-source web project developers worldwide to share and borrow packages.[11]

The npm package manager also serves as a command-line utility for the Node.js project, allowing it to install packages, manage dependencies, and even manage versions.

Components of npm

The npm is made up of three distinct components, which are as follows:

- Website: The official npm website www.npmjs.com/ is used to find packages for our project and create and configure profiles for managing and accessing private and public packages.

- CLI (Command-Line Interface): The CLI interacts with npm packages and repositories from our computer's terminal.

- Registry: The registry is a large and open database of JavaScript projects and metadata. We can use any supported npm registry, including our own. We can even use someone else's registry if we follow their terms of service.

Setting Up npm (Node.js and npm)

We must install Node.js for it to be automatically installed on our machine because npm already includes Node.js. The installation of npm on a computer may be done in one of two ways.

- NVM use (Node Version Manager).

- Installing Node.js using.

It is strongly advised to install npm using Node Version Manager rather than the Node installer. When you attempt to execute npm packages globally, the Node installation process installs npm in the directory by granting local rights, producing an error message.

1. Setup Node.js and npm Using nvm

Using Node version management to install npm and Node.js on our device is strongly advised by npm developers. We may install many Node.js versions on our computer by utilizing the nvm installation method, and we can switch between them as needed to use any Node.js version for our project. They do not advise us to install npm and Node.js using the node installers.

Open https://github.com/nvm-sh/nvm to download and install npm using nvm on our Linux operating system.

- As we are utilizing a Windows OS device, we will download the nvm-setup.zip file for Windows from the Git link.

- Run the setup program after downloading it, then follow the installation instructions on the screen.

- Run the setup by either double-clicking it or selecting Run as administration from the context menu.

- Clicking the Yes option will permit installation.

- After carefully reading their licensing agreement, if we agree, click the Next option to accept it.

- Click the Next button after selecting the area where NVM should install. It remains the default place that has been chosen.

- Click the Next button after selecting the folder where the setup will build the symlink.

- Now that our setup is prepared for installation click the Install button to begin the procedure.

- The nvm setup has now begun to install on our computer, and we will need to wait a little while for it to finish.

- Our installation of the nvm setup is complete; choose Finish to leave the setup.

Verify the nvm Version

Verify whether we are installed and which nvm version is installed once the nvm setup has been completed. Run the following command on our terminal to accomplish this:

```
nvm -
v
```

Look through the List of Node.js That Can Install with nvm
Use the following command to discover the supported Node.js version for nvm installation. It will show a limited list of Node.js versions that are currently available.

```
npm list available
```

Installing npm and node.js
We may install any version of Node.js; on our system, we have LTS 14.15.4 installed. To install Node.js, just run the following command:

```
nvm install 14.15.4
```

Verify the Node.js and npm Versions
Use the command nvm use 14.15.4 to launch Node.js (make sure to replace 14.15.4 with our installed version).

```
nvm use 14.15.4
```

Then, use the commands node -v and npm -v to verify the Node.js and npm versions in our terminal.

```
node -v
npm -v
```

Verify the Installed Node.js Version List
Using the command below, we can see how many different Node.js versions are currently installed and active on our machine.

```
nvm list
```

On our system, Node.js version 14.15.4 is currently active. If necessary, we may also install other, distinct Node.js versions on a machine (while building another Node.js project based on a different version). Choose a different Node.js version from the list provided by nvm, then execute the command below to install it.

```
nvm install 12.20.2
```

Here, we've chosen to install Node version 12.20.2; it also downloads and sets up a suitable version of npm on our smartphone.

Node.js and npm now come in two separate versions. Run the following command to see how many Node.js versions are currently installed:

```
nvm list
```

2. Using the Node Installer, Install npm and Node.js

Consider a situation where we cannot install npm on our device or are having trouble doing so. The Node.js installer is the alternative method for installing npm and Node.js on our computers.

To install Node.js and npm simultaneously, go to the Node.js download area https://nodejs.org/en/download/ where we can locate Node.js installers for the various OS systems.

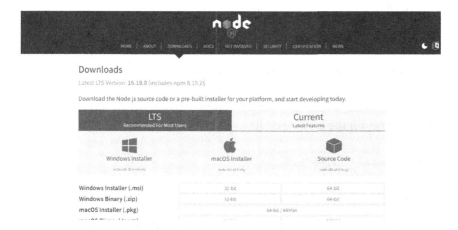

Download npm

Download any Node.js installation compatible with our operating system and its bits.

1. We are downloading a 64-bit Node.js installer for our device because we have Windows with the 64-bit operating system.

2. Run the setup program after downloading it, then follow the installation instructions on the screen.

3. To begin the installation procedure, click the Next button.

4. Click the Next button after reading and accepting the end-user licensing agreement.

5. Select a unique location for our Node.js installation and click Next to continue. It remains in its default position.

6. Click Next after selecting the Node.js functionality we want to install. We maintain it as a default functionality that is offered.

7. Check the box and select the Next option to install additional required tools (such as C/C++ and Chocolaty) together with our node.js and npm installation.

8. To install Node.js and npm on our device, click the Install button now.

9. To install Node.js, select Yes in the pop-up box.

10. To finish the installation, click the Finish button.

The extra tools are prepared for installation, as indicated by the checkbox above for automated installation of extra tools. Press any key to move forward.

To download the most recent version of npm, issue the command shown below on the command line.

```
npm install -g npm
```

Features of npm

- Package.json files, which are used to define all npm packages.

- The package.json file's content must write in JSON.

- The name and version fields must both be included in the definition file.

package.json

When we use npm init to launch a JavaScript/Node.js project, a "package.json" file will create with the essential metadata details supplied by developers:

- Name: This is the title of our JavaScript project or library.

- version: This is the project's version.

- description: Send details about the project's description.

- license: It is a license for a project.

When to Employ npm

- Use npm to modify code packages for our projects or use them exactly as-is.

- When we need to download standalone tools immediately, we can utilize npm.

- Utilize npx to run packages without downloading.

- If we need to share code with any other npm user, use npm.

- When you want to limit code to particular developers, we may use npm.

- Create teams using npm to organize developers, coding, and package maintenance.

- To handle various code versions and code dependencies, use npm.

- Npm may use to update apps when the underlying code is modified quickly.

- To locate additional developers working on related issues and projects, use npm.

Command-Line Client

The software package npm comes with a CLI (Command-Line Client) that may be used to obtain and install npm packages:

Example on Windows OS

```
C:\>npm install <package>
C:\>npm uninstall <package>
```

Example on Mac OS

```
>npm install <package>
>npm uninstall <package>
```

Publishing a Package

As long as a directory includes a "package.json," we can publish it from our PC.

Verify that npm is installed:

```
C:\>npm
```

Verify our logged-in status:

```
C:\>npm whoami
```

If not, login:

```
C:\>npm login
Username: <our username>
Password: <our password>
```

Go to our project's page and publish it:

```
C:\Users\my_user>cd my_project
C:\Users\my_user\my_project>npm publish
```

Global Mode Package Installation

We have the npm package loaded globally, which is all we have now. So let's alter it and install UglifyJS as a different package (a JavaScript minification tool). Although it may shorten to -g, we use the --global flag in this instance:

```
npm install uglify-js -global
C:\Users\JTP\AppData\Roaming\npm\uglifyjs -> C:\Users\
JTP\AppData\Roaming\npm\node_modules\uglify-js\bin\
uglifyjs
+ uglify-js@3.13.9
added 1 package from 1 contributor in the 12.32s
```

Packet Installation in Local Mode

A package.json file is typically used when installing any packages locally. Here is an illustration of how to make a project folder in our home directory:

```
mkdir project && cd project
npm init
package name: (project)
version: (1.0.0)
description: Instance of the package.json
entry point: (indexs.js)
test command:
git repository:
keywords:
author:
license: (ISC)
```

To generate "package.json" with default settings, press Enter. Then, type "yes" to confirm that the ".json" file is okay. By doing this, a "package.json" file will create in the project's root:

```
{
    "name": "project",
    "version": "1.0.0",
    "description": "Instance of the package.json",
    "main": "indexs.js",
    "scripts": {
      "test": "echo \"Error: no test is specified\" &&
exit 1"
  },
    "author": "",
    "license": "ISC"
}
```

Removing Local Packages

We can also uninstall a package because npm is package management that is always manipulable. Let's say there is a compatibility issue with the package packageName that is currently installed. Consequently, we'll uninstall this package and install an earlier version:

```
npm uninstall packageName
```

Installing a Particular Package Version

Now that we have the packageName package of the desired version, we may install it. The @ symbol can use to attach a version number.

```
npm install packageName@1.4.5
```

As we've seen, there are several approaches to executing npm instructions. The lists of some of the most popular npm commands are provided below (or aliases).

- npm i : Install the local package using npm i

- npm i -g : Install the global package using npmiI -g

- npm un : Uninstall a local package using npm un

- npm up: packages updated by npm

- npm t: run tests using npm

- npm ls: List installed modules using npm ls

- npm ll or npm la: Print more package details while listing modules using npm ll or npm la

We discussed the introduction, installation, and functionality of Gulp, Grunt, and npm in this chapter.

NOTES

1 Gulp – Overview: www.tutorialspoint.com/gulp/gulp_overview.htm Accessed on: 20 October 2022.

2 Gulp – Installation: www.tutorialspoint.com/gulp/gulp_installation.htm Accessed on: 20 October 2022.

3 Gulp – Basics: www.tutorialspoint.com/gulp/gulp_basics.htm Accessed on: 20 October 2022.

4 Gulp – Developing an Application: www.tutorialspoint.com/gulp/gulp_developing_application.htm Accessed on: 20 October 2022.

5 GruntJS: www.tutorialsteacher.com/nodejs/gruntjs Accessed on: 20 October 2022.

6 Grunt – Overview: www.tutorialspoint.com/grunt/grunt_overview.htm Accessed on: 20 October 2022.

7 Grunt – Features: www.tutorialspoint.com/grunt/grunt_features.htm Accessed on: 20 October 2022.

8 Grunt – Installing: www.tutorialspoint.com/grunt/grunt_installing.htm Accessed on: 20 October 2022.

9 Grunt – Getting Started: www.tutorialspoint.com/grunt/grunt_getting_started.htm Accessed on: 21 October 2022.

10 Gulp vs Grunt – Comparing both Automation Tools: www.keycdn.com/blog/gulp-vs-grunt#:~:text=Gulp%20vs%20Grunt%3A%20Speed&text=The%20reason%20for%20Gulp%27s%20current,one%20task%20at%20a%20time. Accessed on: 22 October 2022.

11 What Is npm: www.javatpoint.com/what-is-npm Accessed on: 22 October 2022.

Index

Printed in the United States
by Baker & Taylor Publisher Services